D1267379

"If You Were Only White"

Sports and American Culture Series   Bruce Clayton, Editor

University of Missouri Press   Columbia and London

"If You Were Only White"

The Life of
Leroy "Satchel" Paige

Donald Spivey

Copyright ©2012 by Donald Spivey
University of Missouri Press, Columbia, Missouri 65201
Printed and bound in the United States of America
All rights reserved
5 4 3 2 1   16 15 14 13 12

Cataloging-in-Publication data available from the Library of Congress.
ISBN 978-0-8262-1978-7

∞™ This paper meets the requirements of the
American National Standard for Permanence of Paper
for Printed Library Materials, Z39.48, 1984.

Design and composition: Jennifer Cropp
Printer and binder: Thomson-Shore, Inc.
Typefaces: Minion and Optima

In tribute to all who struggled
and soared in the Negro Leagues

Contents

Acknowledgments

When the research for this project began in earnest twelve years ago, I had no idea that it would take so long or that the debts owed to so many would be so great. I have been privileged to receive support everywhere I ventured in search of sources on the life of Leroy "Satchel" Paige. The sheer mention of his name still opened doors. I could not begin to thank every individual and institution that assisted in this project, and I hope that I can be forgiven for omitting a name or two that I may have forgotten or misplaced given the long duration of this project.

There are two names that I will never forget, for without them this study's richness would have been terribly diminished. They shared with me candid thoughts and recollections about the times, the places, the events, and the people. I will be forever grateful to Theodore Roosevelt "Double Duty" Radcliffe and John "Buck" O'Neil. They opened up to me and, as they said, as never before. Their insider knowledge of Satchel Paige and black baseball was and is unrivaled. I continue to smile every time I think about my conversations with them. These two legends of the Negro Leagues are gone now but never forgotten.

Other Negro Leaguers and associates were likewise generous with their time and kind enough to travel down memory lane to help bring the era to life for which I am beholden to: Hank Aaron, Samuel Allen, George Altman, Jimmy Armstead, Otha Bailey, Ernie Banks, William Barnes, Herbert Barnhill, William Bell, Joseph Black, William Blair, Robert Boyd, William Breda, Sherwood Brewer, Clifford Brown, Ernest Burke, William "Ready" Cash, Henry Clark, James Cohen, James Colzie, Charlie Davis, Ross Davis, Felix Delgado, Wesley Lewis Dennis, Eugene Doby, Larry Doby,

Joseph Douse, Mahlon Duckett, James Dudley, William Dumpson, Melvin Duncan, Henry Elmore, Lionel Evelyn, William Felder, Albertus Fennar, Wilmer Fields, John Gibbons, Louis Gillis, Harold Gordon, Harold Gould, Willie Grace, Acie Griggs, Arthur Hamilton, Charles Harmon, Isaiah Harris, Lonnie Harris, Willie Harris, Wilmer Harris, J. C. Hartman, John Head, Neil Henderson, Joe Henry, Francisco Herrera, Carl Holden, Ulysses Holliman, Gordon Hopkins, Cowan Hyde, Monte Irvin, James Ivory, Verdell Jackson, Clarence Jenkins, James "Pee Wee" Jenkins, Sam Jethroe, Clifford Johnson, Curtis Johnson, Donald Johnson, Ernest Johnson, Louis Johnson, Mamie Johnson, Ralph Johnson, Thomas Fairfax Johnson, Cecil Kaiser, Larry Kimbrough, Willie James Lee, Larry LeGrande, William Lindsay, William Little, Anthony Lloyd, Lester Lockett, Carl Long, Ernest Long, Lee Mabon, Raydell Maddix, Josef Marbury, Rendon Marbury, Frank Marsh, Edward Martin, Henry Mason, Willie Mays, Nathaniel McClinic, Clinton McCord, Walter McCoy, William McCrary, Ira McKnight, John Miles, Minnie Minoso, Jesse Mitchell, John Mitchell, James Moore, Robert Motley, Emilio Navarro, Don Newcombe, Orlando O'Farrill, Andrew Porter, Merle Porter, William Powell, Henry Prestwood, Marvin Price, Charlie Pride, Mack Pride, Henry Robinson, James Robinson, William Robinson, Jesse Rogers, Thomas Sampson, James Sanders, Ed Scott, Joseph Scott, Robert Scott, Pedro Sierra, Al Smith, Eugene Smith, George Smith, Quincy Smith, Alfred Surratt, Ron Teasley, Donald Troy, Thomas Turner, William "Cool Breeze" Van Buren, Ernest Westfield, Eugene White, Davey Whitney, Jimmy Wilkes, Clyde Henry Williams, Eli Williams, Eugene Williams, Willie Young, and Jim Zapp.

Talking with the great Bob Feller, Satchel Paige's leading barnstorming competitor from the white Majors after World War II, was an educational experience in itself for which I am truly appreciative.

Acquiring a grasp on Paige's family life to capture the full Satchel Paige would have been absolutely impossible without the help of the Paige family. Robert Leroy Paige and Pamela Paige O'Neal graciously allowed me into their homes and into their memories and their reflections on life with their famous father. To be the first researcher granted such exclusive access is, I must tell you, deeply satisfying personally, professionally, and intellectually. Satchel Paige was an icon of the African American community and countless others who saw him play. To be able to gain knowledge of the *other* Satchel Paige to share with the reader is both an honor and a privilege.

My sincere thanks to the staffs of research centers and libraries far and wide and especially to those of the A. Bartlett Giamatti Research Center, National Baseball Hall of Fame and Museum, Cooperstown, New York; Alabama Department of Youth Services, Mount Meigs Campus, Sandy Douglas especially; Alabama State Archives, Montgomery, Alabama, Norwood Kerr in particular; National African American Archives and Museum, Mobile, Alabama; Biblioteca José M. Lázaro, Universidad de Puerto Rico, San Juan; Black Archives, Miami, Florida; Chicago Historical Society; Lansdale Library, University of Baltimore; Library of Congress; National Archives II, Maryland; Negro Leagues Museum in Kansas City, Missouri; Newberry Library, Chicago; Richter Library Special Collections, University of Miami; Schomburg Collection on Black Culture, New York Public Library; Special Collections University of Virginia Library; University of Georgia Special Collections; Connecticut Historical Society; and the public libraries of Mobile, Alabama; Kansas City, Kansas; Kansas City, Missouri; Memphis, Tennessee; Birmingham, Alabama; Newark, New Jersey; Pittsburgh, Pennsylvania; and the City of Chicago; and to the university libraries of the University of Chicago, University of California at Los Angeles and at Berkeley, University of Memphis, University of Pennsylvania, Tulane University, and Williams College.

My debt is incalculable for the research assistance I have received over the years as this study commenced and when many sources were not digitized, which meant reading virtually every document that might prove valuable, some of them in foreign languages. I could have never completed this momentous journey without the extraordinarily capable and diligent aid of Aldo Regalado, Chanelle Rose, Cecile Houry, Douglas Kraft, and Ameenah Shakir. The longest-standing assistance and support have come—as it always does— from Diane Spivey, who took time away from her own research and writing to help with mine. All I can say to her is again, thank you.

I am beholden to my colleagues in the former Center for Research on Sport in Society at the University of Miami: Jomills Braddock, Robin Bachin, Marvin Dawkins, Jan Sokol-Katz, and Lorrie Fleishman. That was a marvelous group to work with, and our time spent in the pursuit of excellence in sport scholarship warms my heart just thinking about it.

For those who read and critiqued various chapters I offer once more a heartfelt thank-you, to David Wiggins, Elliott Gorn, Gerald Early, Guido Ruggiero, James Grossman, Jules Tygiel, Mark Naison, Michael Bernath, Richard Crepeau, Steven Riess, and Sydelle Kramer, and for either constructive advice or timely encouragement my indebtedness is warmly extended to Edmund Abaka, Gregory Bush, Harvey Schwartz, Henry Louis Gates, Hermann Beck, Howard Lindsey, Jeffrey Ogbar, Jeffrey Sammons, Joe Trotter, John Hope Franklin, Keith Wailoo, Lawrence Glasco, Monique Bedasse, Randy Roberts, Raymond Mohl, Roger Buckley, Thabiti Asukile, Vincent Thompson, and Whittington Johnson. A special Hall of Fame salute is owed to Larry Lester for lending his prodigious knowledge of the history of the Negro Leagues to the project. My never-ending gratitude to Frederic Jaher, professor emeritus of history at the University of Illinois at Urbana-Champaign, who read the entire manuscript and gave me sage advice, as he has done throughout my career. I have had the fortune to work with several superb copy editors over the years but none more capable and helpful than Annette Wenda. Thanks and praise are owed to the University of Missouri Press for its long-term commitment to the project.

Finally, I wish I could say to the many readers, fellow scholars, and countless fans of Satchel Paige that I have captured and been able to convey every crucial point of his remarkable historical journey. What I can say, without hesitation, is that I have given it my very best swing, and that I alone am responsible if I failed to touch each base and to make it all the way to home plate.

Warm-ups: A Prelude

Fans started streaming into the ballpark at nine in the morning for a game that would be played ten hours later. The attendance broke all previous records for a night game with a capacity crowd of 72,434. Concessionaires started running out of food and beverages before the game started. The home team was in a tight pennant race, but that was not the ultimate factor that had driven attendance to new heights. No. The big attraction that had the turnstiles spinning nonstop was the announcement days earlier that the man now standing on the mound would be the starting pitcher for the game.

There he stood for the Cleveland Indians against the Washington Nationals before a jam-packed stadium on the hot and humid evening of August 3, 1948. He cast an unmistakable silhouette from every angle in the ballpark with the white ball in his hand and his cap shading his eyes from the glare of the spotlights and the hundreds of camera flashes that popped like mini fireworks. The umpires bowed to the moment and gave extra time for the picture taking and for the ear-shattering cheering to die down. The cheering, however, remained steady and then exploded with even greater ferocity when Cleveland announcer Jack Graney, high-pitched voice and all, further punctuated the moment with the simple but pregnant phrase: "Pitching for Cleveland: Satchel Paige!"

It was a pinnacle moment in Paige's life. He was there—finally—in Major League Baseball after decades of beating the bushes barnstorming, playing scheduled and pickup games in every nook and cranny throughout the country, his travel averaging some years as many as fifty thousand miles. At age forty-two, when most players were long since retired, washed up, or considered over the hill, there he stood, taking on all the pressure of the world in his pathbreaking role for Cleveland as the first African American pitcher to start a game and the oldest rookie in the history of the Majors. The whole of Negro Leagues Baseball, past, present, and future, counted on him to come through, as did an entire race of people fighting against the stigma of inferiority.

Paige's childhood friend and former Negro Leagues teammate Ted "Double Duty" Radcliffe was in attendance at the historic game. He recalled the event and how he was bursting with pride, that tears rolled uncontrollably down his cheeks owing to the power of the moment. But there was also an incredible amount of anxiety. He, like other African Americans who were there, asked himself: could the elder player on the mound still deliver? Radcliffe knew that the man on the mound was forged of strong stuff, just as any black person, like himself, had to be who somehow climbed to the pinnacle of excellence and success over America's horrid color line. Radcliffe and others who knew Paige well found reassurance in what they knew to be an absolute certainty: that the ball was in the hands of the best pitcher to play the game and that he had no intention after traveling that long and hard road to now fail the biggest test in his life and to let his believers and the race down.[1]

The internal drive of Satchel Paige, given its deep roots, virtually ensured a stellar performance. First, he was a survivor. His steadfast determination drove him to be something more than what his circumstances of birth at the beginning of the twentieth century and the harsh impoverishment of his childhood in Mobile, Alabama, bestowed upon him. Paige, as part of the educational experiment at the Alabama Reform School for Juvenile Negro Law-Breakers, concluded that he wanted to become something more than just another throwaway colored boy. He did exactly that after his discharge from the reformatory, starting a steady climb to overcome the limitations placed on him in the Jim Crow South.

Within that same South that browbeat him at every turn there also existed a black South containing a wellspring of culture, sustenance, and renewal of spirit from which Paige drank deeply. African American culture and traditions imbued him with an inner peace and resilience compatible with his inner hunger. That culture also taught manners and empathy for others. His background, combined with his experiences, forged a tough-minded competitor and sage navigator of the American racial obstacle course and the business of baseball. He became a ballplayer whom, even with his star status, teammates genuinely liked and competitors universally respected. He never lost sight of his bearing and realized that no matter what mountain he climbed, he was no better than his fellow blacks and the equal to any whites, despite a society that defined him otherwise. Satchel Paige had his flaws; doubting in his own ability was not one of them. A noted psychologist once defined intelligence as the ability to decode one's environment and to overcome obstacles. On that basis, Paige was a genius.

Fans could not see his multidimensions as they watched him in his starting role for Cleveland that evening. For whites in the audience, they simply saw the remarkable spectacle of a black man pitching in Major League Baseball. African Americans saw something far more compelling and telling: one of their own who had prevailed and now stood in the spotlight with the opportunity to demonstrate that black folk could perform as well as—and even better than—whites. When Satchel Paige took the field that night to start the game for Cleveland, he was beyond bitter for having been denied his rightful opportunity for so long because of his color. The ban against blacks in Major League Baseball was finally rescinding. Paige was—typical for him—focused on the moment, supremely determined, and sure of himself.

Although his performance was momentous and the win put Cleveland back in the lead in the pennant race, Paige took it all in stride, with no hint of arrogance or the need for special accolades. In the finest tradition of the African American folkways of his heritage—long before the showboating of the modern era—he was cool. He strolled from the field with victory in hand as if it had been nothing more than just another day at the office. In many respects for him, it was exactly that, and he thought of it in no more or less than those terms. His start that night for Cleveland was for him only one of countless big games that he had pitched during his long, illustrious career in Negro Leagues ball against many hitters he would forever tout as just as good if not better than the best he faced in the white Major Leagues.

Paige's confidence came from the one undeniable fact that kept him going over the years and sustained him in the biggest of contests: he knew he could pitch. When asked years later by his eldest son, Robert Leroy Paige, "Dad, were you afraid, were you nervous in the big game with the record-breaking attendance and being the first black man to start on the mound in the Major Leagues?" his answer was short but pregnant: "I knew I could pitch." Paige was also the first African American to pitch in a World Series. When asked essentially the same question about that experience and other big games he pitched in, his answer was consistent: "I knew I could pitch."[2]

The elderly pitcher on the mound for Cleveland that evening was one of the most extraordinary athletes in the history of American sport, a trendsetter, record breaker, role model, and agent for change, and he was immensely popular to young and old of every race. In the estimate of this writer, and many others, he was the best pitcher who ever lived. Yes, he was faster than Dizzy Dean and Bob Feller, better under pressure than Whitey Ford, and more accurate than Catfish Hunter, and he had more strikeouts than Sandy Koufax, more career wins than Cy Young, more ability to dominate a game than Bob Gibson, and more durability on the mound than Greg Maddox. Of course, calling anyone the best of anything will always be controversial, but to say it of Satchel Paige one can make a compelling case.

Yet the public really does not know Paige at all. The biography presented here does not rely on anecdotal information. It rests on twelve years of meticulous research into documentary evidence from throughout the nation and the world and in-depth interviews with those who knew Satchel Paige best, including former players and friends, and especially family members who refused until now to share their most intimate and detailed knowledge of him. The result is a full account, faithful to the truth, and long overdue. His extraordinary American journey is explored and historically contextualized from his birth in 1906 to his death in 1982, from the black-bottom impoverishment of his youth through the tests and triumphs of Negro Leagues Baseball and the Major Leagues, from his induction into the National Baseball Hall of Fame to his family life during and after baseball. I am writing this biography to put Leroy "Satchel" Paige's important contribution on solid footing, front and center, where it belongs, in our understanding of the African American experience and community life, the history of sport, and popular culture. His remarkable journey also offers the reader the opportunity to relive a bit of the fascinating history of Negro Leagues Baseball and some of its greatest moments and players.

Paige's saga is that of a pioneer who helped to transform America through the nation's favorite pastime. His story educates us about the symbolic and substantive importance of race and sport in America. As he proved, baseball is the perfect vehicle to expose and challenge the contradiction of racial discrimination against America's lofty promise of freedom, equality, and justice for all. The game is premised on the ideals of fair play, athletic ability, competitive spirit, sportsmanship, honor, integrity, and purity, all wrapped up in the familiar slogan "May the best team win."

If, however, you ask today's baseball fan or, for that matter, most Major League Baseball players, who was the black player who integrated baseball, the answer you will likely hear is the name Jackie Robinson. You may not even hear the name Jackie Robinson, according to recent reports stating that most Americans and, incredibly, most Major League players, even those of color, have virtually no knowledge of Robinson. At any rate, if you received the name "Jackie Robinson" as an answer to the question, that answer would be misleading, incomplete, and lacking historical context. Paige was the most heralded player of the Negro Leagues. He paved the way to rescinding the color line long before Robinson took the field with the Brooklyn Dodgers in 1947. Hence, we need to rethink what we mean when we say "the integration of baseball" and also question whether Major League Baseball is the only baseball of importance.[3]

Neither was Jackie Robinson the first black to play in Major League Baseball. That honor belonged to Moses Fleetwood Walker in 1884 at the very beginning of professional baseball. After the encroaching color line drove Walker out of Major League ball, most do not realize that it was with the coming of Leroy "Satchel" Paige that integrated contests between blacks and whites gained widespread popularity. There had been some interracial ball games before Paige, but he turned it into a movement with his appeal and drawing power.

Giving recognition and voice to Paige's contribution in no way demeans Robinson's significance and tremendous sacrifice. Nor is it to suggest that without Satchel Paige there would have been no Jackie Robinson. If Paige were alive today, he would tell you much the same thing. He never publicly or privately belittled Robinson's achievement. What did give him, and other Negro Leagues stars, serious pause was the selection of Robinson over himself and the many other leagues' players who were, by all accounts, far better skilled. Paige was bitter about the racism of the Major Leagues that had kept him and others out when they were in their prime. Paige also knew that he could still outpitch most of his younger cohorts in the Majors despite his age. Moreover, he had been engaged in serious talks with several teams to bring him into the Majors before Robinson. He, however, made it clear that he was not willing to go into Major League ball for less money than he was making in Negro Leagues ball. It is often forgotten that Jackie Robinson signed with Brooklyn for a mere five-thousand-dollar salary. This was an amount totally unacceptable for the services of Satchel Paige, the highest-paid ballplayer in the Negro Leagues. Paige was earning six times the amount for which Robinson signed. Neither was this sour grapes on his part or a way of rationalizing that he was not the first black signed and second even behind Larry Doby at Cleveland. When Paige signed with Cleveland in 1948, it was for an excellent salary for a half season of work. "I was nobody's fool," he often quipped. "They had to pay me what I was worth."[4]

To explore Paige's legacy is to fill in the foundation and erect the shoulders upon which Robinson and all the Major League ballplayers of color who came after him have stood, whether they know it or not. It is to proclaim that Paige, indeed, helped make Robinson possible. Because of Paige's ability to draw fans of every race to the ballparks, the interracial matchups proved to be not only economic successes that put money in the pockets of players and management of both races, but also triumphant assaults against the absurdity of the color line. Paige relished his unique contribution to baseball and affront to racism. He and fellow Negro Leaguers competed against Major Leaguers in the West Coast Winter League before huge interracial audiences in the 1930s and beyond, very often defeating their white Major League rivals to the astonishment of whites, to the joy of blacks, and to the entertainment of all. During his illustrious career that began in the 1920s and spanned more than four decades, he entertained millions, filling stadiums to capacity with spectators of all races eager to witness what he almost always delivered—a dazzling combination of pitching and showmanship on the mound that made him a household name.

Paige knew exactly what he was doing as he bridged the racial divide with athletic performance packaged in slapstick humor. He entertained as he played to win and saw no contradiction in doing both. He performed for the crowds, and the crowds loved him for it. The master pitcher was a dapper and charismatic ballplayer, a perpetual showman who brought laughter and excitement to the game. Paige was a master at pushing the envelope, of fooling around minstrel-like just enough to satisfy both blacks and whites in the same audience. They could laugh along with his antics rather than laughing at him as a racial caricature, while, at the same time, he demonstrated his dominance over blacks and whites from the pitcher's mound. Paige was in many respects a one-man version of the original Harlem Globetrotters, the "Clown Princes of Basketball," who were able to entertain mixed audiences with their timeless buffoonery in the name of good, clean fun. When playing against a white team before a mixed audience Paige was like his good friend and Globetrotter star Goose Tatum, who mastered a delicate balance of gags and stunts without going too far. Satchel Paige sometimes did a "Stepin Fetchit," which was an exaggerated slow stroll to the mound that would have appalled today's sensibilities, but left whites and blacks of his era enjoying every moment of it. Double and triple windmills became his standard windups before letting the ball fly, as did playing a variety of warm-up antics that included fancy ball handling and imaginary throws to his catcher, which kept the crowds laughing and glued to his every move.

He constantly joked and talked trash to would-be hitters so loudly that fans were drawn into the exchange of competitive insults. "You might as well leave that bat where you got it from; it ain't nothing but wood" and "This one is coming so fast there ain't a thing you can do but watch" were two of his favorites. It was one thing in a baseball game for Paige to talk trash when playing against other black ball clubs; it was something else to talk trash when competing against Dizzy Dean or Bob Feller or other white all-stars. Paige did it to all of them but dished out such an accurate dose of good-natured trash that it was viewed as a normal and acceptable part of the game and within the boundaries of permissible competitive mouthing off.[5]

He played a role that was acceptable, while pushing the parameters to get more out of it than others intended. He was funny and always accommodating to the press. He wisely played to the media and used it to enhance his reputation and name recognition. No one could top him when it came to saying something worth quoting. His homespun philosophy of life both incorporated his personal and professional experiences and transcended race. His responses reflected a lifetime of thought about his world and how he deciphered it for himself rather than being merely the utterances of an unlettered black ballplayer. He had numerous sayings, many of which became fixtures of American popular vernacular and are still with us today. He delighted in offering up his long-lasting words of wisdom, which included such gems as "Don't look back. Something might be gaining on you," "Ain't no man can avoid being born average, but there ain't no man got to be common," the often-cited "Age is a matter of mind over matter. If you don't mind, it don't matter," and the one Paige often touted around the house to his children and to individuals he met in public who thought themselves superior to him in knowledge: "It's not what you don't know that hurts you. It's what you know that just ain't so."[6]

For years he intentionally played games with the media and the public about his real age. Some sportswriters claimed that Paige was already in his fifties when he entered the Majors. Others said that he was much older. Paige helped flame the stories, often claiming that he did not know for sure when he was born. He offered a reward to anyone who could come up with proof of his age and kept the debate going for the entire second half of his career as the ageless wonder of baseball. Paige made for great copy, a captivating human-interest story that kept readers following his every move and the media and the public in love with him.

That love affair was cultivated in the unique partnership he developed with three of the most influential white sport promoters of the era: Abe Saperstein, owner-manager of the famed Harlem Globetrotters basketball team who also promoted Negro Leagues Baseball; J. L. Wilkinson, owner of the Kansas City Monarchs, the most successful team in black baseball; and Bill Veeck, the maverick and arguably most innovative owner in the history of Major League Baseball. Their relationship with Paige was a world unto itself that helped set the modern course of sport promotions. There were mutual respect, mutual tensions, and profits. Creativity in presenting sporting events prevailed, such as using race as a promotional gimmick, having night baseball games, and installing special lighting to make those games possible. In short, the four together wrote in bold and bright ink for future generations the how-to book of promoting professional team sports and marquee athletes in one Leroy

"Satchel" Paige. In addition, Paige proved that blacks and whites could work together for mutual self-interests in professional athletics, with the black athlete not always coming away shortchanged. Superstar Paige would demand and command his share.

In a very real sense, his legacy was also a precursor of modern-day professional sports and the debates about athletic purity and sports entertainment. Should we allow pro football players to spike the ball and engage in end-zone dances? Does dunking the ball in basketball detract from the quality of play for the sake of adding excitement to the game? Have the changes adopted in baseball been for athletic or commercial reasons? The debates can be picayune or all-encompassing. The reality is that professional sport is now a multibillion-dollar entertainment business. Satchel Paige understood the monetary aspect of sport and therefore put his mark on it at the very beginning. He showed by example that sport flourished as a business when it was about both athletic performance and putting on a good show for the fans.

It was no accident that Satchel Paige became the first bona fide superstar African American athlete outside of boxing. He knew that he had the talent, as did those who promoted him. He did not save and invest his earnings wisely but, understanding his worth, negotiated hard and made owners and sponsors show him the money. More than once in the 1930s and early 1940s, he earned forty thousand dollars a year, making him one of the highest-paid players in baseball, black or white. Satchel Paige charted the course for the superstar black athlete long before Muhammad Ali, Michael Jordan, and Barry Bonds, or for that matter Sugar Ray Robinson, Jim Brown, and O. J. Simpson. Paige understood that by virtue of his fame he was an icon, a role model, a symbol of his race, whether he wanted to be or not.

African American superstar athletes of later generations would be faced with the dilemmas that Paige faced more than a half century earlier. Despite what Charles Barkley might say, he too is a role model, whether he likes it or not. It comes with the stardom. Paige understood this and managed to survive the trials and tribulations that came with the fame, from the scheduling madness owing to extraordinary demands for his services, the seemingly impossible expectations of fans and critics, and the idiotic questions of the press to those who wanted far more than he or any other mortal could possibly deliver. But he always gave it his best with the seemingly tireless professionalism and spirit of good cheer that the public relished and the racially skeptical found acceptable.

Only Joe Louis rivaled Satchel Paige as the African American athlete who was most beloved by both blacks and whites of that era. The world did, indeed, relish Joe Louis. Few other athletes could come close to him in overall public adulation and name recognition. This was especially true after he knocked out Max Schmeling—the Aryan-fashioned poster boy for German superiority—in their fight for the Heavyweight Championship of the World in 1938. Satchel Paige was one of very few sport idols mentioned in the same breath with Louis. Moreover, it was Paige who ruled supreme in America's most popular and important sport of the day—baseball—even though restricted to the shadows of the Majors until that evening in 1948. He was the most celebrated star in the history of Negro Leagues Baseball. He dominated black ball through the pre–and post–World War II era and was the darling of the black press long before the white press knew him. He was the star of stars of the Negro Leagues' East-West All-Star Game that routinely garnered record attendance of fifty thousand and more fans to the stands while the white Majors struggled at the gate.

No one, including Joe Louis, brought fans through the turnstiles in the thousands day in and day out over so many years as did Satchel Paige. While Louis might have twenty fights in one year, especially during his Bum-of-the-Month Club era at the end of the 1930s, Paige, as incredible as it may seem, often pitched in more than one hundred baseball games a year for more than thirty years. The math is overwhelming. This is not to suggest that Paige was more famous and more beloved than Joe Louis. It is to argue that Satchel Paige, too, was one of the all-time sport giants and recognized as such.

Catering to black audiences, integrated audiences, and himself, Paige knowingly put on a racial juggling act that was as complex as Joe Louis's. Both men were in so many ways the opposite of the first black heavyweight boxing champion, Jack Johnson, whom whites disliked with as much passion as blacks felt adoration. Booker T. Washington, the prominent race leader of the era, was a noted exception and labeled Johnson a disgrace to his people for his gallivanting, flamboyant lifestyle and brazen flaunting of his relationships with white women.

Joe Louis's public and private persona was premised on the notion of his being seen as humble, quiet, and respectful to whites, especially those he defeated in the ring. He was never to gloat or celebrate after knocking an opponent to the canvas, to show no emotion in or out of the ring, to be unassuming and polite at all times, to exude a wholesome and virtuous family life to the public, and, most important, to stay clear of any romantic entanglement with white women. His management did not want him to become another Jack Johnson.

Paige, on the other hand, offered a different public persona than that of either Jack Johnson or Joe Louis. He was neither the "Bad Nigger" that Jack Johnson personified nor the "House Negro" that some characterized Joe Louis as being. He was not the stoic, unemotional character that Louis played in and out of the ring. Paige was at times flashy and brash while at the same time treating his audience to virtual vaudeville humor that was right on the edge of racial stereotyping. He knew well to obey the number-one taboo and stay away from white women, at least in public, but was second to none as a lover of women of every race when on the road barnstorming. Neither did he bow to the inferiority complex that was internalized by many black Americans.

His pitching was his statement for civil rights, equal opportunity, and manhood. That arm of his was the equalizer that game after game directly refuted the lie that black baseball was inferior to white baseball and that black ballplayers did not possess the ability to play in the Major Leagues. Paige was a joker and showboater, but when that ball left his glove, it was all serious business. He mastered turning from joker to serious pitcher in an instant. Make no mistake about it: he always pitched to win. He mastered batters, black and white, with superior pitching, demonstrating how to play the game. The genius of Satchel Paige was his ability to perform all of these tasks while at the same time successfully navigating the seemingly inherent contradictions.

The hallmark of his repertoire was undeniably sensational pitching that earned the respect of the fans and any ballplayer who dared pick up a bat against him. He used his lanky six foot three and one-half inches and 140 pounds (180 in later years) to slingshot a baseball at a breakneck speed with pinpoint accuracy that left would-be hitters swinging at little more than thin air and spectators yelling for more. To everyone's delight he gave his favorite pitches special names such as his "bee ball," "trouble ball," "hesitation pitch," and "bat dodger." It was routine for him to, at some point in the game, yell out the name of the pitch that he was about to throw so that everyone knew what to look for, including the hitter, who nevertheless failed to benefit from knowing in advance what was coming. Always thinking of the fans, he more than once kept them on the edge of their seats when he called in his outfield and single-handedly struck out the remaining batters to retire the side. In one game he intentionally loaded the bases so he could pitch to Josh Gibson, the greatest slugger in the history of Negro Leagues ball, and struck him out to the roar of elated onlookers.

Let Paige tell it, and he did, he pitched in more than twenty-six hundred games and had three hundred shutouts and fifty-five no-hitters. A young Joe DiMaggio, who played against him in the California Winter League, declared his own readiness for the Majors when he finally got a hit off the great master. DiMaggio summed it up for many others when he said, "Satchel Paige was the best pitcher I ever faced." The great Dizzy Dean, who pitched against Paige in some legendary white-versus-black barnstorming battles, may have put it better than anyone when he told a listening audience on his radio broadcast, "If Satch and me was pitching on the same team, we'd clinch the pennant by July fourth and go fishing 'til World Series time."[7]

During his long, seemingly everlasting career on the mound, "Old Satch," as he became affectionately known, made an impact that transcended boundaries of every sort, and he enjoyed it. He took pleasure in his recognized role as the Johnny Appleseed of baseball. Playing anywhere and everywhere, both in the United States and abroad, his movement and actions, however, attracted the attention of domestic and international government agencies.

On the domestic front he early on attracted the interest of the Federal Bureau of Investigation because of the association of his name with the Communist Party of America. Not that Paige was a member of the Communist Party; he was not. But the CP in the sports column of its *Daily Worker* newspaper often cited his name in its propaganda blitz against Major League Baseball (and the United States of America) for its barring of players, like the great Satchel Paige, because of their race. Paige was an activist but not of the traditional sort involved in the civil rights movement. He believed in equality and was more an advocate of what later generations would term "Black Power." Had J. Edgar Hoover known that, he would have been even more suspicious of Paige's "questionable links" that he cited in justifying putting the baseball icon under FBI surveillance.[8]

Paige's links were international. He was a transnational icon who ushered in a new mandate and appreciation of the international importance of sport and the game of baseball that can best be described as *baseball diplomacy*. He constantly took his baseball skills across the borders into Canada, Latin America and the Caribbean, Cuba, Puerto Rico, Venezuela, Chile, Mexico, the Dominican Republic, and points in between. His jump from black ball in the States to the baseball team of dictator Rafael Trujillo in the Dominican Republic became a cause célèbre with the powerbrokers of Negro Leagues ball. They accused Paige of not only breach of contract but being an obstacle to the best interests of US foreign policy in Latin America as well. The US Department of State and Secretary of State Cordell Hull were drawn in to unravel the messy entanglement centered on one Leroy "Satchel" Paige.[9]

Yet writers at that time and since failed to grasp the complexity of the individual behind the blazing fastballs. We seem content to know him, if we claim to know him at all, as the oldest rookie in the Major Leagues who helped his team win a pennant and a World Series title; the man who pitched three innings for the Kansas City Athletics at age fifty-nine, making him the oldest man to play in a Major League game; and the man who in 1971 was the first player from Negro Leagues Baseball inducted into the National Baseball Hall of Fame.

But there was also the other Satchel Paige, who expanded his social, cultural, and political horizons beyond the limitations associated with his humble background and upbringing. The other Satchel Paige was determined to prove his worth off the playing field as well as on it. That other Paige was a Renaissance man of sorts, a gifted public speaker, talented musician and singer, superb dancer of international styles, appreciator of fine clothing and good food, excellent cook, passionate outdoorsman, and collector of guns, cars, and fine antiques, especially Chippendale furniture. The other Satchel Paige grew beyond chasing women and a bitter divorce to have a wonderful second marriage in which he succeeded in becoming a "homebody" and good family man to his wife and children. That other Satchel Paige ran unsuccessfully for political office in his adopted hometown of Kansas City, Missouri, adored Martin Luther King Jr., but questioned the goals of integration and whether integrating Major League Baseball made more sense than developing and supporting black-owned baseball.

To explore the life and times of Leroy "Satchel" Paige is to set off on a unique journey with a major figure in the African American struggle for equality who spoke in a different yet poignant voice. Paige was a contributor to the modern civil rights movement of the 1950s and 1960s. As the work for my biography of him entered its ninth year I contributed a chapter, "Satchel Paige's Struggle for Selfhood in the Era of Jim Crow," to a well-received anthology on the history of African American athletes that was published in 2006. What was a preliminary conclusion back then is my conviction today with the completion of the biography: "Leroy Paige would rise from the humblest beginnings imaginable to become one of the most famous and acclaimed athletes in the world, black or white, and he accomplished this feat in a period synonymous with Jim Crow, the color line, grandfather clauses, literacy tests, poll taxes, white citizens councils, nightriders, and lynchings. Baseball would become not only his ticket out of poverty but also a platform for self expression as he entertained throngs of thousands throughout the United States, Latin America, and the Caribbean."[10]

One wonders if black folk so loved Satchel Paige because he was brought in time after time when the big game was on the line and everything at stake. With all the pressure and watchful eyes, of blacks and whites, he had the opportunity to fall flat on his face or to rise to greatness. He chose greatness. Paige was a winner against the odds, just what the downtrodden African American population hoped for themselves. He reflected the aspirations of his race and in that was both symbol and substance. With little more than a fourth grade education and an incredible ability to throw a baseball, his is the story of the man who struck out Jim Crow.

I must admit to two regrets during this twelve-year-long yet rewarding journey into the life and times of one of African America's, and indeed America's and the world's, greatest sport icons. The first regret is that the book could not have been completed in time to commemorate the hundredth anniversary of Satchel Paige's birth back in 2006. Second, Theodore "Double Duty" Radcliffe and John "Buck" O'Neil passed away before they had a chance to read the work devoted to their friend and former teammate. I believe, however, that they would have forgiven me and said that it was more important to finish the job and get it right than to rush to publication. At any rate, I could have done no differently. The legacy of Leroy "Satchel" Paige is too important to me personally, to other African Americans and past generations who saw him pitch and experienced his magic firsthand, and to all of those of every race, ethnicity, nationality, and gender who enjoy the great game of baseball.

"If You Were Only White"

1

Without a Satchel

Leroy Robert Page (the change in spelling of the last name is a story in itself) was born on the wrong side of the tracks in a hostile South that had long ago defined him and his kind as just another "throwaway nigger." There was little or no real expectation that he could rise much above that, except for the faint hope and prayers of those who loved him. The challenges of his environment and childhood forged in him an inner toughness and resiliency. It was either succumb or survive. He chose the latter, which would characterize his life and career.

Being from the wrong side of the tracks was an ever-present reality for the Page family. For black folk in Alabama's oldest city, Mobile, and throughout America in 1900, "the other side of the tracks" was an apt metaphor of the all too real racial divide that plagued the nation and segregated Greater Mobile's rapidly growing population of 62,740, nearly half of whom were people of African descent. When you are from the wrong side, that side tainted as black, poor, lower class, unwanted, and unwelcome, your world is restricted, relegated, and in so many respects hopeless. The setting was becoming worse in Mobile with the passage of the new State Constitution of Alabama in 1901 that disfranchised the majority of African Americans and mandated the enforcement of the color line. The state capital in Montgomery was awash with Jim Crow legislation that made that city a bastion of segregation. Mobile, once considered more moderate in its race relations, passed new ordinances tightening the color line, as whites' fear of blacks intensified with the increase in the African American population.

This was the world of the Page family, the world that Leroy inherited. They were dirt-poor and, commensurate with their lowly status, lacked every conceivable amenity associated with a good life. The Page family lived at 754 South Franklin Street, down by Mobile Bay. They were on the so-called other side of Government Street, the well-known divide between North and South Mobile and white and black Mobilians. No signs were posted indicating that if your skin color was dark, you were restricted to live south of Government and near the railroad tracks down by Mobile Bay, but everyone knew it from long experience, and painful reminders, if you were caught where you did not belong.[1]

A new slavery of tenant farming, sharecropping, domestic service, convict lease, and common labor defined the role and place of black Mobilians like the Pages. John Page, the family patriarch, was born in 1877 in Albemarle, Virginia. He was the only son of Charles and Julia Page, two lifelong field hands who had both been born in slavery. As a young man John worked his way to Mobile on a tramp steamer, searching for a different and better way of life for himself. There he met Lula Coleman, a hardworking domestic. Lula was three years John's senior, born in 1874 in Choctaw, Alabama. She was the second of three children to Osena Coleman, who had been born into slavery in North Carolina and widowed only a few years after Lula's birth. Lula Coleman and John Page fell in love and were married. The actual date of their nuptials is uncertain. The results of their unison were not debatable. Their first child, Ellen, was born in 1896. They would have Ruth, John Jr., Julia, and Wilson, before their sixth child, Leroy, was born in 1906.

There would be considerable controversy and media speculation years later about the actual date of Leroy Page's birth. Census reports and family memory leave little doubt of the correctness of the year. The precise day and month of his birth remain open to speculation. Leroy was not born in a hospital, where the recording of birth would have been a routine matter. Mobile did have a small hospital facility, but it was a product of its times and the racial restrictions that whites mandated and blacks were obliged to obey. The hospital provided a modicum of service to those blacks so desperate and in need of care that they had no choice but to put up with the indignities of the Negro ward, which consisted of one room off the basement area. For something as "routine" as having babies, the black women of Mobile had them at home.[2]

Leroy, like his brothers and sisters and countless other African Americans in the South, came into this world at the hands of a midwife. Lula Page was a well-experienced hand at having children, as was the midwife who had delivered hundreds of babies previously. Afterward, the name and date of birth of her new arrival were, reportedly, dutifully recorded in the family Bible. Unfortunately, that Bible evidently vanished years later. Since it was fairly common for state authorities in the South to neglect to officially document black births, many went unrecorded or uncertified until employment or other demands necessitated it years after the fact. The document that would authenticate Leroy Page's date of birth was issued as the result of a formal request for proof of birth made in 1954. The Office of Vital Statistics in Mobile, upon receipt of the formal petition, followed its stated procedure in these matters and conducted an investigation, which consisted of asking questions and taking into consideration whatever evidence available, including hearing from surviving family members and other witnesses. The office then issued a certification of birth. It may well be that Leroy Page was born in some month other than July and on some day other than the seventh, perhaps days or months earlier or later, but the year was in all likelihood correct and the date of July 7 at least a close approximation if not the absolute date of his birth. Four more siblings would be added to the Page household after Leroy: Palestine, Clarence, Lula, and Inez, a total of six girls and four boys. There was also a set of twin boys, but they died prematurely.[3]

A family of twelve was large but not uncommon for the rural South or an emerging southern city such as Mobile. Neither would be the toil and sacrifice needed for the Page family to survive. They, like so many others, lived in a small shotgun house. One could have literally stood at the front door of the house and fired a shotgun from front to back without hitting much of anything. The four rooms were set two to each side in a simple A-frame box construction.

This, nevertheless, was home, and John and Lula tried their best to make it work. The place, as they say, kept the rain off their heads—for the most part—and, despite the sweltering heat in summer and cold in winter, the family was together and doing their best to eke out an existence.

Young Leroy and the rest of the children saw little of their father. Leroy later recounted that he never knew his father well and could "only remember pieces and snatches about him. He wasn't hardly a part of my life." It is not that John Page was a bad man. He would be defined as a poor father in large part because he was never around to share time and experiences with his children.[4]

John worked at least two jobs and picked up other work whenever and wherever he could find it. Work on the docks at the Mobile Shipyard was something that black men could often count on, as did John. Ships needed to be loaded and unloaded. A good, strong back and willingness to work for long stretches at a time were the only requirements.

The problem was that laboring on the docks kept you away from home for days on end, as was the case for James Radcliffe, the father of Mobile-born and future Negro Leagues legendary player Theodore "Double Duty"

Radcliffe, who worked long hours and days at the shipyard and did construction work to support a family, also of twelve. The requirements would be no different thirty years later when Herbert Aaron worked the same docks for long periods of time away from his wife, Estella, and their eight children, including a young son named Henry. Yet when Herbert Aaron was home he gave time and attention to his family and even taught his young son how to play baseball. When that young son later became the legendary Hank Aaron, the home run king of Major League Baseball, he credited his father for having taught him the game.

When John Page was home he was usually too tired to spend much time with Leroy and his siblings. There would be no family fishing expeditions or leisurely talks between a father and his children or backyard lessons from him on how to play baseball. Thus, young Leroy had no adult male role model to properly tutor and nurture him on becoming a man.[5]

Mother Lula was the pillar of the family. In Leroy's own words, his mother was "the real boss of our house, not dad." A part-time domestic and full-time washerwoman, she was often found at the side of the house laboring over a steaming cauldron full of white folks' dirty sheets, spreads, undergarments, dresses and trousers, shirts and blouses. But she was at home and available to the children.[6]

Leroy remembered how his mother ran the show like a military operation, with her primary attention on feeding the family. Food was always an issue and in short supply. To mother Lula's credit, diligence, and ability to stretch resources, the Page children always received something to eat. Some meals were extremely sparse, at times just biscuits and gravy, but at least it was there, and the children gobbled it down without complaints. Leroy and the family were fortunate that Lula Page was a superb cook. She could make the most meager of meals taste delightful.

Lula Page cooked the food, but everyone contributed, even Leroy when he was old enough. Mother Page's earnings and those of her husband were nowhere near enough to keep a family of twelve afloat. All of the Page children were expected to pitch in. "We all gave our money to mom so she could get food. She took real pains with what she bought," Leroy reminisced. "That was why I can't remember us ever missing a meal. We didn't always have a belly-busting dish full, but we had something. Mom made sure everybody got their share. She'd stand at the table and ladle out the food, looking real close at each spoonful."[7]

In Leroy's household and throughout the black South, if you were big enough to walk, you were big enough to do some kind of work and in short order to find a way to earn whatever you could on the outside to contribute to the family coffers. From the age of seven, Leroy Page had settled into a routine of hustling around town to make money—pennies and nickels and an occasional dime or two—venturing along roadsides to retrieve discarded bottles, hopefully Fosko or Dr. Pepper soda pop bottles that fetched a penny each, or less desirable beer bottles that took two or three or more to garner a penny. Fosko empties were preferred because the company was headquartered in Mobile, just across the divide from the Page family and the black community, at 9 North Franklin Street, in the low-rent commercial district. Some of the favorite fishing spots down by the Bay were always good for a few discarded moneymakers. The folks fishing relished an occasional soda pop or beer and might on chance or on purpose discard an empty bottle or two.

The daily toll of survival for Leroy and his brothers and sisters made play a rarity. The Page children never had many toys. The six girls shared two dolls. Other than that, there were no dollhouses, train sets, BB guns, cap pistols, or toy soldiers. Leroy would forever regret having missed out on a real childhood free of adult-size worries. When he did play, it was often nothing more than to run around outside in a game of tag or frolic in the dirt or explore the fields. The children often engaged in wrestling and games of marksmanship, throwing pebbles at tin cans and sometimes at one another, which Leroy loved to do and at which he was extremely good.

His typical clothing during the early years of childhood left him with many bitter memories. His wardrobe ranged from soiled diapers to raggedy shirts that came down to his knees. He, like most poor children in the South, black and white, went shoeless most of the time. Leroy received his first pair of shoes at age nine, hand-me-downs from John Jr., to Wilson, to him. Shoes were, if you were lucky enough to have any, saved for Sundays and church and other special occasions. As a middle child with two older brothers, Leroy's entire meager wardrobe consisted exclusively of hand-me-downs. When he grew taller than his older brothers, secondhand clothes were still the rule, and a source of great personal embarrassment for him. He often had on shirts and pants that were much too short for him. He was a funny-looking sight to the other children, tall and lanky with desperately undersized clothing that made him look even taller, a clothing dilemma that rapidly escalated because of the quick pace he grew. He never forgot how it hurt when his playmates teased him for looking like a scarecrow in his desperately too short pants and shirts.

Leroy was often the brunt of jokes owing to his clothing, but he quickly learned to give as well as he got. He excelled at the art of "playing the dozens," the old West African game of signifying and a fixture of African American cultural life, the art of the game being to top your opponent's verbal jousts with superior comebacks. That skill would remain with him all through his life, and he well applied it. The playmate who said, "You need to tell your folks to buy you some clothes!" was likely to hear from Leroy in reply something along the lines of "That's okay. You need to tell your folks to buy you a new face!" The whooping and laughter of the other playmates would designate the victor. The signifying might go on for several rounds or more. To say something about someone else's mother, however, was strictly taboo and could turn the verbal jousts from words to fisticuffs, with someone likely going home with a bloody nose.[8]

Name calling occurred all the time in Leroy's world. Playmates and friends routinely gave each other a pet name. In African American culture a nickname was virtually mandatory. If playmates and friends knew that one among their ranks had a particular love for eating pork chops or neck bones or chitlins, for example, that individual ran the risk of forever being known as Pork Chops or Neck Bone or Chitlins. A friend who had an addiction for cornbread found himself soon being called Cornbread. A playmate slow at becoming toilet trained might well find himself addressed among old friends for the rest of his life as Stinky. One of Leroy's playmates he dubbed "Two Fingers," although he had all of his fingers, "but he never could count past the second." To be given a nickname was also a badge of honor. It meant that you had endeared yourself to others or at least distinguished yourself as an individual. In a sense it was a right of passage, a childhood thing that might very well follow you into adulthood and to the grave.[9]

What Leroy loved to do as a child was to go fishing. A good cane pole or just some fishing line and a hook, a can of worms—preferably red worms but night crawlers would suffice—and Leroy and friends were set to catch fish. The entire black community of Mobile loved fishing, young and old, men and women, boys and girls alike. Next to fishing, Leroy enjoyed throwing at things. As he got older he became better and better at it. A discarded tin can was a favorite target, and he loved to set them up and knock them down. In a makeshift game of baseball, played at first with a stick and rock in lieu of a bat and a baseball, Leroy's playmates took turns trying their best to hit his pitched rock ball with rarely any success unless he slowed it down on purpose. After a while, none of the other kids wanted to engage Leroy in a rock contest and certainly not in a rock battle. He would literally spend hours each day just throwing at things. One of his childhood friends later swore that Leroy, at eight or nine years of age, "could hit a fly in flight with a rock."[10]

Pebbles and rocks came in very handy for Leroy on more than one occasion. The Pages had their own chicken coop out in back of the house. Mother Lula would send one of the boys to fetch her one or two of the birds for supper on special occasions. Young Leroy did not like the idea of hacking off the chicken's head and certainly not the common practice of taking the bird by the neck and popping it like a whip. He watched his older brothers inflict that lethal practice on many a chicken. John Jr. sometimes popped the chicken's neck and then dropped the bird on the ground to the entertainment of the other boys and to the horror of their sisters, as the chicken, with its head dangling, ran about for a few seconds before finally succumbing to the injury.

Leroy's rock marksmanship was put to use when the command came from mother Lula for him to go and fetch a chicken. With rock in hand, he would open the coop and then move off to a quiet distance of thirty feet or more to allow the unsuspecting birds to strut about freely. He then took aim with his rock at the plumpest of the fowl and let rip with precise and instantaneous results.

He engaged in rock hunts that contributed to the family table. Mother Lula accepted his offerings with gratitude and made squirrel and rabbit stews or fried them up just right. There were countless occasions in the Page household that the results of Leroy's hunt helped make the meal for that evening or at least added meat to the pot. Young Leroy varied his hunts. Some days he went out specifically after birds. He occasionally might spot a duck or two on the shore down by the Bay. They made easy targets for him and a very tasty main attraction at dinner.

The feathered targets most readily available to Leroy were sparrows. They seemed to be everywhere in Mobile. The tiny birds also made for a true test of Leroy's rock acumen. It was incredible enough to imagine an individual capable of hitting a sparrow with a rock, but Leroy often did it and when the birds were in flight. No rifle, BB gun, or slingshot, just a rock hurled with incredible speed and deadly accuracy was all that he needed to bring down game. He often returned home from bird hunting with a small sack of sparrows that he proudly contributed as a welcomed addition to the family's meal.

Survival was the name of the game for Leroy whether hunting, fishing, scrounging for bottles, or toting luggage at the Louisville & Nashville Depot. By the time he was nine years of age he had stepped up in his ability to contribute to the family's coffers by hustling down at the L&N train station, carrying bags of the passengers. Many a young boy in the black community knew of the work at the L&N and hustled there. They would gather around the front of the depot, waiting for departing or arriving passengers, and then run up to them and ask to carry their luggage. Sometimes a passenger might have eight or ten boys running up and pleading to carry the luggage. Whites were most likely to hire you and give you a nickel or dime for carrying their bags to the train. Elderly blacks were also good bets. Many of them would use your services but most often could afford to give you only a tip of a few pennies.

Leroy did not discriminate. He was a masterful little entrepreneur at the depot and outhustled his fellow competitors, including many of the older boys. His capacity to work and to hustle characterized his life. Leroy was clever and innovative when it came to earning money. He figured out an ingenious way of upping his rate of productivity by increasing the number of bags that he could tote at any one time. Acquiring a pole and some rope, he devised a contraption for himself that slung across his shoulders and from which he could hang three or four bags or more. This makeshift device enabled him to carry multiple pieces of luggage at the same time. When the other boys saw him toting all those satchels, they broke into laughter and poked fun at him. The signifying was nonstop at Leroy's expense, with epigrams such as: "Boy, you going to kill yourself," "You're that poor," "I'll give you a nickel," and "What good is an extra dime if you're dead?" The one-liner that his fellow train-station child workers used most was the one that came from his buddy Wilbur Hines: "You look like a walking satchel tree!"[11]

Leroy was a rather curious site with multiple pieces of luggage dangling from his pole as he navigated masterfully and swiftly like a ship's captain around obstacles and people to get to the train. He played to the ribbing of his friends, joshing back and forth with them, smiling and continuing to transport as often and as many satchels as he possibly could each time. Passengers applauded the youngster's tenacity. On many occasions, customers questioned whether he could carry all of those bags at once. They looked on as the skinny, tall kid strapped the satchels to his device, stooped into position under the pole, centered it across his shoulders, straightened up, and then successfully toted the entire load in a single trip. Leroy played, like he would the rest of his life, to the laughter of his friends and to the awe of his customers, and in the process made more money than the other boys while entertaining everyone. This adept hauling of so many satchels earned him the nickname that would be his unique moniker for the rest of his life: "Satchel." In short order, the name Leroy was forgotten forever except at home. "Nobody called me Leroy, nobody except my Mom and the government."[12]

To amount to something other than a throwaway would require more than a nickname. The only course to a better way of life for Leroy and his siblings, their mother reckoned, ran through the schoolhouse. Lula Page understood this and wanted her children to be educated. Schooling was available to African American children in Mobile, though it was severely circumscribed. Alabama and Mississippi consistently ranked at the bottom in terms of providing a basic education to its black citizens.

At age seven Leroy began attending the W. H. Council School, which had opened as a black neighborhood school only three years before he enrolled there in 1913. The school was part of *separate but equal* throughout Alabama and the South and the notion of providing racially segregated education. The Council School, like so many of its sister institutions, was understaffed, uninspiring, unattractive, unequipped, and underfunded, and its black teachers were underpaid in comparison to whites. The Council School teachers received salaries half that of their white counterparts. Industrial education was the major educational goal that those in charge deemed best for black students. The superintendent of schools issued a statement that made clear the mission of the colored schools in Mobile: "Furnishing common school education, together with manual training and domestic science, to the colored population, renders better citizens as well as more intelligent helpers and servants." Thus, the Council School was just like all other elementary schools for black children anywhere in the Jim Crow South. It subscribed to the principle of providing the students a basic grasp of the three R's of reading, 'riting, and 'rithmetic, and a firm grounding in manual labor and the big *B* of proper *Behavior.* Perhaps young Leroy had a natural rebellious streak or maybe he intuitively rejected the limited brand of education being offered him at the school. He certainly hated going, and it showed in his performance in class. It is not that he was unintelligent or uneducable. To the contrary, Leroy could be exceptionally quick in learning things. It is that the goals of the school, with the emphasis on manual work and rote memory exercises, he found exceedingly boring. Leroy hated the curriculum, with its emphasis on memorizing of passages from the Bible and epigrams from *McGuffey's Readers.* The educational environment he was in did not do a great deal along the lines of cultivating of inquisitive minds and pushing the students to engage in perspicacious thought and analysis of the world around them. The students did learn how to basically read, write, and count.[13]

The Council School could not satisfy or tame him. His appetite for adventure and his ability to get into trouble won out. Leroy's truancy escalated. During his first three years at the school, he gained a much-deserved reputation for being absent as much as he was present and getting into mischief when he did attend. Ironically, the teacher he knew best was the one who constantly expressed concern directly to him about his behavior, and on occasion to his family, especially his mother, about his many absences. Leroy so disliked the teacher that he erased her name from his memory. In his eyes she would be forever known only by the nickname he dubbed her of "Mrs. Meannie."[14]

She was neither mean nor married when she taught Leroy at W. H. Council. The teacher, Miss Aleitha Young, had a well-earned reputation as a caring educator and strict disciplinarian. She was born in Mobile in the 1880s and educated at two Alabama black colleges, Spellman and Talladega. Young returned to Mobile in 1907 and was one of the first appointed to the teaching staff at the W. H. Council School when it opened three years later. She actively engaged in community affairs and cultivated networks with other women educators of color throughout the state of Alabama. She was, despite Leroy's negative memory of her, a master teacher who, no doubt, wanted what she thought was best for young Page and felt honor bound to report his truancy to his mother.

There were painful consequences for his actions as a result of those reports. When Lula Page learned of her son's truancy, she did not spare the rod and spoil the child. In the black family, especially in the South in the early twentieth century, disobedience was intolerable. Leroy knew better than to cross that line, especially when it came to his mother's command that he not play hooky from school. When word reached mother Lula of his absenteeism, she took action. It was at great sacrifice to the family that any of the children were allowed to go to school, and to have Leroy throw that away was, to Lula Page's way of thinking, tantamount to blasphemy.

His actions were unacceptable, and she let him know it with strong words and even stronger emphasis to his backside. Mother Lula wielded a mighty switch—that infamous thin branch from a tree that she would have Leroy go and fetch himself—that punctuated the painful borders of unacceptable behavior. The switch method worked on most of the Page children but seemed unable to penetrate Leroy's defiance. It is difficult to understand why he could not or would not change his behavior. In the parlance of black folk, he was hardheaded. His backside paid a horrific price. After a couple of encounters with go-and-fetch-me-a-switch, the offender usually found obedience to mother Lula's orders, but not Leroy. His continuing ability to get into trouble defied logic, given mother Lula's stinging swings.

The children, including Leroy, preferred punishment from their father rather than their mother. John Page hit hard, but after three or four smacks with an open hand on the behind, it was over. Mother Lula was a completely different story, as Leroy experienced time and again. Once she got into rhythm with words and licks, she often stayed in the zone until exhausted or the switch broke. Bringing her a smaller switch in hopes of mitigating the punishment failed miserably. As Leroy learned for being a smart aleck, he was simply made to go and fetch another switch and, upon his return, received an extension of licks not easy to forget. In the length and ferocity of the "whup'in," mother Lula had no equal in the Page household. A devoutly Christian woman, she laid wood with righteous indignation. Leroy said of his mother's striking power: "She hit harder than I ever got hit in a fight."[15]

Lula Page's corporal punishment was likely doled out in part to correct bad behavior, in part out of frustration with her own life, and in part out of love and hope of keeping Leroy safe. He did not know that at the time, and when his mother tried to explain it to him, it fell on deaf ears. She punished him for disobedience yet more to drill into him the demands of conduct and appropriate behavior in a South where a black person's humanity and life could be taken by any white person on the slightest whim. In 1906, the year Leroy was born, a double lynching occurred in Mobile that same autumn. Later on,

Leroy too would come to realize that there was reasoning behind his mother's desperate attempt to get him to walk the straight and narrow:

> I used to think she hit me because she didn't know how I felt. She didn't know how it was when they told me I couldn't swim where the white folks did. Then I realized maybe she did. She must have been chased away from the white man's swimming places. She must have gotten run off from the white man's stores and stands for just looking hungry at a fish. She must have heard those men yelling, "Get out of here you no-good nigger." She must have heard it. I guess she learned to live with it.[16]

The racial divide of young Page's world dictated every aspect of black life, from swimming and fishing to where you could live, where you could eat, with whom you could play, where you went to school, where you went to church, and where you could be buried. For Leroy to step out of that prescription at any time and any place in Mobile or the rest of the Deep South was dangerous business. Leroy hated the restrictions forced upon him and how the society of his birth defined him: "I was no different from any other kid, only in Mobile I was a nigger kid."[17]

The major thing in his life that gave him a sense of purpose and feeling of pride and accomplishment was achieved in the simple game of sandlot baseball. It was in baseball that he found that something special, that place where he could express himself, show off his talent and ability, and be measured in the moment of how he performed.

It was his older brother Wilson who would give him his first lesson in baseball. Wilson early on was much more interested in baseball than his younger brother Leroy and somehow put together enough money to buy the first ball and bat that made their way into the Page household and the sandlot baseball games that he, Leroy, and their buddies played. It is difficult to understand why Leroy Page never credited his brother Wilson with giving him his first pointers in regulation baseball. He confirmed in later years that his brother Wilson was in many respects a better baseball prospect than himself, including having a faster fastball. Why he did not tell interviewers about his brother also giving him his first instruction in how to play the game of baseball may have been the result of stilted questioning, indifference or a lack of interest, or a media more bent on the stereotypical portrait of an absent black father, a black woman with too many children, and a family deficient in generosity of spirit and love and support for one another.

In the sandlot pickup games with other children of his age, and often older, Leroy began to establish a reputation for being able to strike out virtually anyone who tried to hit against him. Those sandlot years from 1915 to 1918 were unorganized and undisciplined forays of just plain having fun, playing as a kid, and more. Leroy needed a sense of order and structure in those childhood years. Perhaps that need led him to claim that he played on his school's baseball team. It may well have been an effort to reinvent his childhood to better match his success in baseball. In reality, W. H. Council had no baseball team during those years. Mobile was not about to devote funds to support recreation for African American children.[18]

Despite its lack of organization, it is within this child's play that Leroy's love of the game and ability to throw a ball continued to advance. In point of fact, the closest young Page came to playing organized baseball was in watching some of the games of the Mobile Tigers, a black semipro team, and seeing the Mobile Gulls—known later as the Mobile Bears—a white semipro baseball team, practice at Monroe Park.

The Park, like everything else in the Mobile of Leroy's youth, was a segregated facility. On certain Negro days, however, blacks were allowed to use the baseball field and the Mobile Tigers allowed to play their games there for a fee. Leroy was not permitted to be a spectator at the white Bears games. He could not have afforded the ticket at any rate. If he had the money, he in all likelihood would not have been permitted to attend the game because of his color. Semipro baseball in Mobile, like most of America, was segregated just like the Major Leagues. In those parks where blacks were permitted in as spectators, they were typically relegated to the far reaches of the segregated Negro section from which to watch the contest.

Young Leroy did get a peek at the white Bears team while he worked at Monroe Park, sweeping the stands and picking up trash in preparation for the game and cleaning up the area after the event. His work was more fulfilling when he worked the games of the black Tigers because he received the added benefit of being allowed to watch the complete game as part of his pay.

Baseball had already won a special place in his heart. He loved the excitement of the contest, the appreciation that a good play elicited from the fans, and the deafening roar of the crowd. Games captivated him, and he imagined himself standing out there on the mound as the most important player on the field—the pitcher. In his mind he could do all the things that he saw those semipro pitchers doing. Why not? No one could throw a rock harder and more accurately than he could, control it like magic, and bring down game with pebbles. His friends were unable to hit his pitches in the rock-and-stick versions of baseball. They had been equally unsuccessful at hitting the balls he pitched in their sandlot contests.

Leroy reasoned that he was as good as anyone in throwing a baseball straight over something as wide as home plate and fast enough that a batter would be unable to hit it. When his friend and running buddy Wilbur Hines asked him what position he wanted to play, everyone knew there was only one choice in his mind: the position he was made for and he knew he could do better than any other kid in the neighborhood. He told Wilbur, and he concurred, that he was a pitcher.[19]

Leroy's physique aided his pitching. He was tall for his age, well over five feet eight inches when eleven years old, and lean with long arms. He used his body naturally in an almost slingshot fashion to get great velocity behind his throws. Most impressive was his ability to throw hard and accurately. Youngsters on opposing teams in the sandlot did not stand a chance. Many a young batter broke down in tears as they stood helplessly when Leroy's lightning-fast pitch went whistling past for that third strike. Some actually wet their pants in fear of his powerful throws, as Leroy gleefully recounted. Childhood friend Ted Radcliffe gave an eyewitness account: "Satchel threw so hard even back then that kids cried for their mama. They were scared to death as fast as the ball whizzed by. They knew that if he hit you with that damn thing he might kill somebody. More than one pissed in his pants and wouldn't take his turn at bat. 'Forget it. I ain't getting killed for no damn baseball game is what they were thinking.' You couldn't blame 'em. He threw so damn hard!"[20]

The fun and success that Leroy gained playing baseball did nothing to improve his attendance at school or to keep him clear of trouble. If anything, his love of the game became another reason to skip school. He and his childhood chums Chester Arnold, Julius Andrews, Wilbur Hines, and Ted Roosevelt Radcliffe would often be spotted together choosing to play a game of baseball or go fishing rather than going to school. If baseball and fishing did not win out, toting satchels at the L&N station did. The need to earn money to help support the family held a much higher priority for Leroy than attendance at school, although his parents, mother Lulu in particular, did not require him to go to work and try earn some money on those days he was supposed to be in school.

Despite the constraints of work, baseball, fishing, and school (when he did attend), Leroy nevertheless found time to get into deeper trouble. It was tough being black and poor in the Jim Crow South of Mobile, Alabama. Leroy could not be expected to properly articulate this situation when twelve years of age, but he knew that he was angry about his situation and the circumstances. Understandably, he hated being called names and being constantly told that much of what life had to offer was off-limits or out of bounds for him and his kind.

Leroy knew from his baseball success that he could do some things well—indeed, better than virtually anyone else he had met when it came to throwing a baseball. No doubt he wondered silently and out loud why the white kids did not play against the black ones. He very much wanted the opportunity to show all of them that he was as good as they were, if baseball was used as a measure of ability. No such opportunity was possible in the Mobile of that era. Blacks played against blacks and whites played against whites, no matter what their ages. When the two races did meet in any sort of competition, it was by accident of design. That accident of design was one that Leroy and his buddies began to encounter on a frequent basis whenever they went past the white school on their way home, and the result was more trouble.

If it was in the late afternoon, like clockwork, groups of white boys would shout derogatory words at Leroy and his companions and give chase, throwing rocks at them, despite the respectable distance they kept from the white Oakdale School. Leroy and his buddies grew tired of the name-calling and of being chased and used as target practice whenever the white boys spotted them in the vicinity of the school. One day Leroy, Julius, Chester, and Wilbur replied to the rock barrage in kind. The racial rock wars ensued.

The white youngsters soon learned a very painful lesson—that the tall, skinny black kid with the long arms could rifle a rock with the accuracy of a marksman with a telescopic rifle. The racial rock fights were dangerous business, not just in the sense of someone possibly being seriously injured in the exchange but because of the greater consequences that might be exacted. Blacks fighting back against whites, whether adults or children, was absolutely forbidden behavior in the Jim Crow South. The consequences could be too grave.

Young Leroy was not a good listener. Although he promised his mother that he would avoid any more rock fights with the white boys, he never kept that promise. When word reached Lula that the rock fights were continuing, her scolding escalated to a steady stream of lickings. Young Leroy must have heard "go and fetch me a switch" so often that he thought it was his other nickname. Despite the constant doses of punishment, they failed to dissuade him from fighting back in the rock wars against the white boys. Nor did the punishment curb his growing feistiness and penchant for getting into additional trouble.

While his reputation as a good baseball player circulated around Mobile, so did his reputation as a bad boy. The chief of police of Mobile, Frank Crenshaw, began to take notice of him as a troublemaker and detained him on more than one occasion on charges of fighting. This was unfortunate for Leroy because Crenshaw believed that blacks who were old enough to walk were old enough to go to jail and should be put there for any misbehavior or misdemeanor. In short, Chief Crenshaw urged that any black boy, between the ages of seven and sixteen, should be put away in reform school for any act of delinquency or a single misdemeanor.[21]

Furthermore, he advocated that the reform school for black juveniles, located at Mount Meigs, just outside of Montgomery, should accept youngsters

from Mobile or that a reform school for that purpose should be established lo-
cally. Further still, he thought that the African American community should
want the same thing and wrote to race leader Booker T. Washington, suggesting that he should support the idea: "We have a great need for just such an
institution in Mobile. Judge Edington and myself have talked the matter over
and I see only one way out: institute a Detention School for the colored race,
and put the boys of that age there for all misdemeanors. It could also be used
for the purpose of reformation of some boys."[22]

Washington concurred in principle but reminded Chief Crenshaw that the
reform school at Mount Meigs had recently become the official state reform
school for blacks and should now accept youngsters from every region of
Alabama. "I have read with a great deal of interest your letter of January 6 and
am gratified to know that you desire to do something for the colored juvenile
delinquents," Washington wrote.

> This is a matter in which I am also deeply interested and will be pleased to
> cooperate with you in whatever way I can. I was under the impression that the
> State Reformatory for Colored Youths at Mount Meigs was designed to take
> care of just the kind of boys that you mention. If there is anything in the laws
> of the State of Alabama that prevents delinquent colored boys being sent there
> from all parts of the State, I think that at the next session of the Legislature ef-
> forts should be made to have these restrictions removed. I will take up the situa-
> tion in Mobile with Dr. A. F. Owens formerly pastor of a colored Baptist Church
> in your city and now connected with our Bible Training School. He did a great
> deal toward getting the State to take over the Reformatory at Mount Meigs and
> will be able to advise with you to what extent delinquent colored juveniles from
> Mobile might be sent there. We keep in close touch with this reformatory, and
> I know that it is doing good work for the boys that are there, who I understand,
> are of the ages and class that you describe in your letter.[23]

Young Leroy was exactly the kind of boy that Chief Crenshaw had in mind.
In addition, he found Leroy insufficiently humble. Nothing could be more
dangerous for a black male in the South than to be branded as an *uppity Negro*,
no matter what his age. Leroy Page was on extremely dangerous ground, and
mother Lula knew it, as did the W. H. Council School.[24]

Then came the eventful rock battle near the end of the school year in the
spring of 1918. In past confrontations, at least Leroy threw low to keep from
hitting anyone in the head. That would all change. Leroy, Julius, Chester, and
Wilbur were on their way home from school when they ventured too close to
the Oakdale School. Whether the four were looking for the challenge of another rock battle, or accidentally crossed the color line, or were convenient

targets of opportunity, a group of white boys saw them and immediately started throwing rocks at them.

Leroy and his friends fired back. Other young whites quickly came to the aid of their schoolmates. Outnumbered, Leroy and his buddies ran for home with the stone-wielding young whites in pursuit. One of the rocks, however, found its mark to the back of Chester's head, and he fell to the ground like he had been shot. He was bleeding and dazed. When Julius turned back to help him to his feet, the pursuers let loose with a rain of stones on the two of them.

Wilbur was gone, but Leroy stopped to help. He grabbed a handful of rocks and began firing as if laying down a suppressing barrage to protect his buddies. But this only slowed down the advancement. At that point Leroy began hurling rocks with full force and utterly bad intentions. The wisest of the pursuers took immediate flight upon witnessing the pinpoint accuracy of the throws. Others bravely stood their ground for a while and suffered the consequences of that wrong decision. In the exchange of rocks, some of the white boys would begin to duck as they saw Leroy about to throw. That did no good. His hesitation throws found their mark with intuitive precision. The pursuers fled, with many a young white boy going home crying that afternoon with a big knot on the head.

Luckily, the white youngsters did not seek the intervention of their parents, or the entire incident could have been blown into something far more insidious. It is likely that some level of complaint did reach the W. H. Council School. This, after all, was not the first rock fight between the two groups of boys. No official records were made of the incident, but unofficially everyone would have picked Leroy as a major instigator.

But before any action was taken or word reached mother Lula, Leroy managed to get into further trouble. Out playing and roaming about, he stopped in a little store in the adjoining white section of town and attempted to shoplift some trinkets. The colorful little toys, especially the red, green, and blue figurines, caught his attention. Not seeing anyone watching him, he stuffed his pocket with some of them and headed toward the door. He never made it. Unbeknownst to him, the white owner had been watching his every move and caught him before he could exit the store.

Leroy was taken into custody and brought to Chief Crenshaw's office. Word was sent to his mother, and she made her way to the station to see about her son. Arriving and seeing him under arrest, Lula Page broke into tears as Chief Crenshaw blasted away at Leroy with a loud and nonstop harangue of condemnation. Mother Lula stood crying through the ordeal and promising to severely punish her son.

Leroy was released in his mother's custody with the requirement that she take him to school the next day to meet with his teacher, who had been made aware of the arrest. Lula Page complied. No records or notes were made of the meeting she and Leroy had the following day at W. H. Council. It is reasonable to surmise that the meeting was with Aleitha Young, a.k.a. Mrs. Meannie. The conversation likely centered on his escalating bad behavior and the inability of Lula Page or anyone else to bring it under control. Whippings alone were clearly not effective.

Something different had to be done. Given the reputation of Miss Young, she would have devoted considerable attention to the matter before rendering a recommendation or a final decision. In the case of Leroy, she probably had been thinking about the appropriate course of action for some time. She saw him as a child at risk, a likely throwaway Negro, unless effective intervention could put him on the right path.

The stakes were high and the issues complex. Leroy was not a major problem while in school. The problem was to get him to attend school. Left to roam on his own, he managed to get into considerable trouble. The taking of a handful of trinkets from a store was only one part of the equation. The recent rock-throwing incident was most likely the deciding factor. That kind of behavior had the possibility of putting him and the entire black community at risk. It would not have been the first time that angry whites, propelled by a whim or misinformation, burned, killed, and laid waste to a black community. Considering all of these factors would have been logical, given the environment and the era.

It was some days later that Miss Young evidently concurred with the course of action that Chief Crenshaw championed. It was a decision that Leroy would never understand and one that exceeded his imagination in terms of anything approaching fair and just punishment for his actions. It was decided that he would be remitted to reform school.

The decision was devastating to the twelve-year-old. Leroy was the most frightened he had ever been in his young life. In his mind he was being sent to prison for an eternity for little or nothing. He begged not to be locked up, to please be given another chance, and promised to never do anything bad again. He pleaded again and again, but it all fell repeatedly on deaf ears. His knees weakened as he tearfully made one last futile plea to be allowed to stay with his family: "I was scared. Real scared. I cried. I couldn't stop shaking." Lula Page too was brokenhearted at the decision. At the same time, however, she may have been resigned to some degree that her methods had failed and that something more was needed. At any rate, it was out of her hands now. On July 24, 1918, just seventeen days after his twelfth birthday, Leroy Page was sentenced to six years—or until his eighteenth birthday, whichever came first—at the Alabama Reform School for Juvenile Negro Law-Breakers in Mount Meigs, Alabama.[25]

2

On the Mount

What terrified Leroy Page was the unknown that lay ahead. What actually awaited him was an educational experiment that would forever change his life. This period was pivotal in his transformation, and a rich interplay between sport, reform, and the ideologies of race leaders Booker T. Washington, W. E. B. Du Bois, and Cornelia Bowen, played out in an educational experiment in Mount Meigs, Alabama. These were years for Leroy that intertwined with the emergence of a little known but significant African American institution. On the Mount, as inmates referred to the Alabama Reform School for Juvenile Negro Law-Breakers in Mount Meigs, Leroy would receive an industrial schooling that brought structure and discipline to his life and that also by design gave him an education in the proper fundamentals of baseball.

Leroy woke to a bright and sunny day on July 26, 1918. The good weather outside and the sun's rays that poured through the cracks and crevices of the Page family's desperately overcrowded little shotgun house did nothing to brighten his day. This was the day of reckoning when he would board a train for Mount Meigs to begin his stint in reform school. Trepidation naturally ran wild in his young mind. He was leaving his family for the first time. In fact, this was the first time that he had ever been on a trip anywhere outside of Mobile.

His mother made him a special breakfast that morning. It was a meal fit for a king and an extremely rare one in the Page household. Leroy appreciated the food offering in his own way but lacked the appetite to take advantage of the loving gesture. His thoughts were on what awaited him. What would the place in Mount Meigs be like? How would he be treated? Would he be whipped and beaten? Where would he sleep? What would he eat? Would they make him toil in the fields like a slave? It was all guesswork now and the terror of an ordeal too great for a twelve-year-old to digest. He ate only a little of the scrumptious breakfast before allowing his siblings to finish the rest for him, which they readily accomplished.

With the final good-byes said, and a fifty-cent piece pressed into his palm, Leroy strolled slowly through the open homemade screen door and down the porch steps, where his brother Wilson was waiting to accompany him on the one-way walk to the train station. One can only imagine what the two brothers talked about, if they spoke at all, during their trek to the L&N station whose distance of a few miles from the house probably seemed much shorter than ever to young Leroy.

The inevitable came too soon in the form of the old familiar depot and the arrival of the northbound train that would take him to meet his fate. Leroy felt a little better when he realized that he would not be making the trip alone. There were four other boys at the station who were bound for Mount Meigs. One of them was his running buddy Julius Andrews, who had also been sentenced to reform school. Leroy did not think for a moment how unfortunate it was that Julius was going to reform school; he was too busy feeling a sigh of relief that he would at least have someone he knew along with him. Chaperoning the group was a local black minister charged with the responsibility of delivering the boys to Mount Meigs.

It took on average a solid seven hours for the steam-powered locomotive to make the 180-mile trip from Mobile to Montgomery, more than enough time for young Leroy's mind to run every conceivable gamut. The train ride gave the boys a great deal of time together to think about what was in store for them, to exchange ideas, or just to commiserate. Leroy's first train ride should have been something nice and full of positive wonderment. Under normal circumstances, a youngster would have delighted in the passing scenery and the new adventure of sight, sound, motion, and expectation. But not for Leroy. He focused exclusively on what might be in store for him. Who could blame him? One wonders if he found it a bit ironic that the same L&N he was riding on had been a source of revenue for him when he toted the satchels of passengers. He knew that his future was uncertain, if he had a future at all beyond what awaited him at the end of the train ride.

There was no way for Leroy to peer into a crystal ball and witness what lay ahead for him in a changing society or envision how he or the very L&N on which he rode would have a role in that futuristic battle for social change. Three decades beyond his train ride, the L&N would be center stage in the civil rights struggle, as crusading attorney Charles Hamilton Houston argued the discrimination case of William Steele, an African American who worked as a fireman on the Louisville & Nashville and had been summarily fired from his job and replaced by a white worker. The Alabama court ruled against Steele. The case was appealed to the United States Supreme Court, and the Supreme Court rendered its decision in favor of Steele, reversed the decision of the lower courts, and used some of the strongest language in the history of the Court in its condemnation. Justice Murphy in his concurring opinion gave a blistering indictment of Alabama's rule of law when it came to blacks. The case of *Steele v. The Louisville & Nashville and Brotherhood of Locomotive Firemen and Enginemen* (1944) became a pillar in the long list of precedents that attorney Houston put together and that his team, led by his former student Thurgood Marshall, would use to challenge and ultimately overturn *Plessy v. Ferguson* in the *Brown v. Board of Education* decision of 1954.[1]

The L&N's place in the history of the civil rights movement was yet to be written, and so was the story of Leroy Page, whose train ride was taking him to a rendezvous with destiny that he imagined would be a living hell for six long years. He was bitter and confused. Life, he felt, had dealt him the cruelest blow imaginable, and his self-esteem was arguably at rock bottom and dropping fast during that train ride. He thought of himself as a child largely in only negatives: "I was a no good kid."[2]

Leroy's imagination must have shifted into overdrive when the train began to slow and he heard the conductor's walk-through announcement of *Montgomery*. The thoughts that gave him nightmares and that had kept him awake so many nights, that stopped him from enjoying the good food that mother Lula prepared, and that gave him a constant sick feeling were about to become real, or so he reckoned. What would the people be like that met his train? Would they be prison guards with guns? Would he and the other boys be chained together like he had seen the road gangs of black convicts? Would he be made to wear a prison uniform for the entire world to know that he was a criminal?

Detraining under the watchful eye of their minister chaperone heightened his negative thoughts. Awaiting him, however, were neither guns, leg irons, prison guards, nor anything approaching the trappings of incarceration. Rather, he saw two black males, young but considerably older than himself, sitting aboard a wagon. The minister chaperone guided Leroy and the other boys over to the wagon, and the two young men climbed down to greet them. Neither one was dressed in a uniform or wearing chains or carrying any leg irons for the new arrivals. The two young men partially smiled and said hello. The minister had reached the end of his journey and gave a final good-bye along with a departing prayer.

Leroy and the others set off in the wagon. The wagon moved steadily under the power of the old mule pulling it. Both mule and wagon were the gifts of a white benefactor, Mr. P. W. Ross, to the school years earlier. The two boys at the helm were five or six years older than Leroy. It was customary on the Mount to make some of the model seniors "charge boys." Two of them were customarily entrusted with the additional privilege of taking the wagon into Montgomery to pick up the new arrivals at the station and escort them back to the school.

The ride to the reformatory gave Leroy and the rest of the boys plenty of opportunity to talk and to get acquainted. It was fifteen miles from Montgomery to Waugh, Alabama, the small black cotton-farming community where Mount Meigs was officially located. There must have been a thousand questions about what the place was like. The answers that the charge boys gave had to be surprising to Leroy and the other newcomers. All of the questions and answers, though, were confirmed upon arrival at the school. The Mount consisted of a two-story freshly painted white wooden main house and four other well-maintained large red wooden buildings centered on 20 acres with an adjacent 480 acres of cultivated farmland.[3]

The story of Leroy's new home began in 1887 when E. N. Pierce from Plainville, Connecticut, visited the plantation that he inherited, located fifteen miles east of Montgomery and known in the community as the old Carter place. He wanted to re-create it as a profitable yet humane venture. The sharecropper families were equally eager to better their condition. They pleaded with the new owner to make education available to their children and suggested that Booker T. Washington at the nearby Tuskegee Institute might know how it could be done. Pierce had heard of Washington and favored his ideas about education for rural blacks. Pierce was willing to advance the community two thousand dollars to build a school along the model of a "small Tuskegee" and subsidize the salary of one teacher, with the understanding that the loan would have to be repaid and that eventually the school should become self-sufficient and able to pay for its own teacher. The terms were agreeable. The old Carter place became the site for the Mount Meigs schoolhouse. Booker T. Washington enthusiastically recommended to Pierce a recent graduate of Tuskegee Institute to head the new school. Her name was Cornelia Bowen.[4]

Bowen would prove to be the perfect choice to make the experiment work for Leroy and the boys. She was dedicated to the task at hand. Bowen was admitted into the first class at Tuskegee in 1881. She had none other than Booker T. Washington, the most prominent race leader of the late nineteenth and early twentieth centuries, as one of her teachers. Bowen graduated from Tuskegee in 1885, a member of the first graduating class at the school.[5]

Leroy's new home, the Mount Meigs Colored Institute—the original name of the institution—opened in 1888 as a one-room schoolhouse until the spacious two-story main building was built and ready to be occupied four years later. The education he would receive there followed the industrial schooling model of Tuskegee Institute and its parent institution, Hampton Institute, in Hampton, Virginia, and emphasized education of the hands. In short, he and the others would be taught vocational skills in the hope of becoming productive workers and "learn practical farming, carpentering, wheelwrighting, blacksmithing, and some military training." It was hoped that the school would sustain itself by the planting and harvesting of its own crops and that the students would maintain the facilities and do work that benefited the white and black communities alike.[6]

A board of trustees was appointed to keep the school on track. Of the twelve-member board, six were white and six were black; all of those from out of state were white, and all of those who were local were black, including the board's most prominent member: Booker T. Washington. It meant, in point of fact, that the actual running of the school would be in African American hands.[7]

Despite the support of these northern friends of the school and the long hours of hard work the students were required to perform, the institution could not sustain itself or easily survive without additional support. Cornelia Bowen's role as principal, teacher, and fund-raiser gave the school viability and sustainability. She was a dynamo who worked the black communities throughout the state of Alabama for all they could possibly do to help the school survive. Her networking through the Alabama Federation of Colored Women's Clubs provided the contacts and the pocketbooks that opened to give additional support to Mount Meigs. The federation was composed of leading black women of the state and consisted of thirty clubs located throughout Alabama. The Alabama Federation of Colored Women's Clubs was a branch division of the National Association of Colored Women that Mary Church Terrell headed. Bowen served as an officer in the Alabama chapter for fourteen years.

It was these activist black women who purchased additional acres for the school to expand its mission and capacity to accommodate more youngsters like Leroy. The women were appalled by the increase in the number of black males who as young as ten and twelve years of age were being sentenced to serve terms in adult prisons in Alabama. If not for these women, Leroy and so many other black boys would have been sent to one of those dreaded facilities rather than to a reform school. The students ranged in age from eight to twenty-one, and their numbers continued to expand, largely owing to the support of the federation and Bowen's persistence. The six-member teaching staff consisted of Cornelia Bowen, her younger sister Kate Bowen, Phlacidia

Thigpen, Lottie Armstrong, Robert Edmondson, and John Johnson. Bowen and associates were also joined by Margaret Murray Washington, the wife of Booker T. Washington, in working to enhance the school.[8]

Bowen and Mount Meigs were lauded for teaching students to read, write, and cipher and that character counts, an instilling that would aid Leroy Page immensely. The daily Bible teaching fostered in Leroy and the other boys the idea that right living rather than emotion was the key to success. The Reverend E. E. Scott said of Bowen, the Alabama Federation of Colored Women's Clubs, and the work at Mount Meigs: "These women, 'God's Police Force,' as some one terms them, deserve the hearty support of every Negro in the State."[9]

Aleitha Young, Leroy's dreaded "Mrs. Meannie" back at the W. H. Council School in Mobile, was an active member in the federation and close associate of Cornelia Bowen. She too found the practice deplorable of sentencing black youngsters to adult prisons and wanted to save the future generation of black men. Young was intimately familiar with the work at Mount Meigs when she recommended that Leroy be sent there. She hated to think of what might be the alternative. Neither did she, Bowen, nor the federation forget the commitment to African American women, but its members considered the plight of black males to be at a critical juncture and more desperately in want of intervention.[10]

In 1911 the Alabama state legislature concurred with the women and made Mount Meigs the official state reform school for black males ages ten to eighteen, thus paving the way for Leroy's admission seven years later. The name of the school was changed to the Alabama Reform School for Juvenile Negro Law-Breakers. The governor, as mandated under the new legislation, appointed all the board of trustee members empowered to oversee the running of the institution. Bowen would continue to have a major oversight and teaching role at the facility for the next twelve years, although the state would now name the head of the school. The governor appointed men to the top post of principal of the reform school.[11]

When Leroy set foot on the Mount that early evening in July 1918, he and the other new arrivals would have been taken before the principal for orientation, which was standard procedure. One can only imagine the dread that must have run through Leroy's mind. He and the other boys did not know yet that they had a guardian angel to watch out for them in the form of Cornelia Bowen. Mr. A. Helms was principal of the Mount at the beginning of 1918 but replaced midyear by Principal Simms, who was in charge when Leroy got there. Three years later Walter Deck would head the Mount for the duration of Leroy's incarceration.[12]

The orientation speech that Leroy and the other new boys heard from Principal Simms was the same one that he and all the others gave to each group of new inmates: a reminder of the rules and regulations, the need to be attentive and punctual, to obey the orders of the teachers and guards, to always be respectful, and to be good workers. Failure to do so would result in instant and severe punishment. That punishment consisted of up to one hundred or more licks with a heavy oak switch the size of a club and soaked in turpentine to keep it from breaking.

Leroy disliked what he heard and immediately hated the Mount with passion. He deplored his surroundings and circumstances. A great deal of his hatred and frustration was also aimed at himself. He felt completely worthless. His inner battles were apparent in the 1920 US Census taken of Mount Meigs. Leroy Page's data had to be corrected at a later date because he gave wrong information about his name, date of birth, and where he was from. He was embarrassed about his situation and, in a sense, attempted clumsily to hide his true identity and to somehow reinvent himself—none of which worked.[13]

On a daily basis, however, he toed the mark on the Mount and obeyed the school's many rules and regulations and, in short, was a good inmate citizen. After orientation from Principal Simms, Leroy received his first meal on the Mount. It was stew, which was served four or five times a week at Mount Meigs. It was, to his thinking, of course, not as tasty as mother Lula's, but it was filling and full of fresh vegetables and little cubes of chicken, beef, and pork. Everything simmering in the four huge cauldrons in the mess hall came from the school's own farm. The cooks, two elderly black women, prepared the meals out of love as much as they did for the token salary they received, which Cornelia Bowen provided from the Colored Women's Clubs.

The Mount was a well-run operation. It had to be. Leroy joined 50 new boys at the reform school that year. Most of them came from Montgomery. The total inmate population at the reform school was 263, including Leroy. The boys lived military style in four large one-story wooden buildings that resembled massive barns. Sleeping arrangements consisted of bunk beds, cots, and single mattresses on the floor, evenly spaced bivouac style, filling both sides of the dorms. Whether in a double-decker bunk bed, a single bed, or one of the mattresses on the floor, two boys were assigned to share each.[14]

We do not know much about Leroy's bunk mates during those years. We do know that he would have had at least two different bedmates and that both would have been approximately the same age as he, since it was the policy of the school to bunk together those boys of the same age and to change bunk mates at some point. On rare occasions an older boy, usually a charge boy, might be awarded with assignment to a single bed. In general, the teachers on the Mount favored the doubling up of the boys because they thought it reinforced the idea of learning to live communally and to develop good interpersonal skills. The bottom line, though, was that money and facilities were always inadequate.

Most of the boys came from the humblest backgrounds like Leroy. Back home, young Leroy had always shared a bed with his other siblings, four or five to a bed until the boys and girls got older. The Page family never had more than three beds in their tiny shotgun house. The math was simple in figuring out occupancy per bed since John and Lulu Page shared a single bed after the youngest of the children were a bit too old to sleep with them. Banished to the children's quarters, with ten children for the two remaining beds, at least three or four would cramp first into the bed, with the others often opting of necessity to sleep on the floor. One or two usually bunked out on the tiny dilapidated couch in the front part of the house, or so-called living room, and one or two might choose to bed down on the floor in a favorite corner of the dilapidated dwelling that Leroy knew as home. Hence, he did not overspeak in the least when he said that sleeping two to a bed while at Mount Meigs was "nothing new for me."[15]

Like Leroy's mother did at home, every resource at Mount Meigs was carefully rationed, especially food. The rationing on the Mount also included clothing, work tools, hoes, picks, rakes, shovels, all the farming and gardening implements, and seeds. The lack of sufficient supplies and funding necessitated the scrupulous rationing even after the school became a state-run entity and began receiving state funds. That funding was pathetically meager. Without additional dollars from the Colored Women's Clubs and other friends of Mount Meigs, the institution could not have survived. Cornelia Bowen was always delighted to hear from her mentor, Booker T. Washington, especially when it was news of possible forthcoming financial assistance. Washington knew the answer when he wrote to Bowen asking if she could use four or five hundred dollars from the Rosenwald Fund to help "strengthen your industrial department and for repairs."[16]

Leroy and all the inmates at Mount Meigs were allocated two work shirts, underwear, socks, two pair of trousers, suspenders, and a pair of shoes. Some of the items were new and some were secondhand, but they were all clean. The shoes were usually secondhand. These pieces of clothing marked the first time in Leroy's life that he could remember receiving nice clothes. Albeit hand-me-downs, the shoes too were a grand gift for a boy who had gone barefoot for as many years as he had. More important, the shoes actually fitted Leroy's rather large feet, easily going on and coming off. For a youngster like him, whose standard attire at home had been ragged and tattered ill-fitting clothing, this was a pleasant new experience. Behind each bunk was a makeshift clothing rack consisting of a few nails and wooden pegs in the wall. Leroy finally possessed clothing worthy of being hung up to keep as neat as possible.[17]

The reformation process that he and the others underwent at Mount Meigs did not qualify as a scientifically conceived program of behavioral modification, but it put to use the latest educational models and programs to effect change. First and foremost in the arsenal to modify the behavior of Leroy and the other inmates was strict adherence to the black industrial schooling philosophy as taught by General Samuel Chapman Armstrong at Hampton Institute in Hampton, Virginia, after the Civil War and exemplified by Armstrong's most prominent pupil, the race accommodationist leader Booker T. Washington and founder of Tuskegee Institute in Tuskegee, Alabama. W. E. B. Du Bois, on the other hand, championed equal rights, liberal arts education, and unlimited educational opportunities for African Americans. While Washington and Du Bois battled it out on the public stage, Leroy was living the industrial schooling idea.

He, and each boy on the Mount, was given daily chores that had to be performed. Most of the chores were synonymous with the expectations of a farmer's life. Leroy started his day at sunrise. Chapel and the morning prayer were the first order of business, followed by breakfast. The breakfast was not one fit for a champion, but it did usually consist of milk, grits or hominy, a biscuit, and molasses. Given Leroy's impoverished background, he may well have thought of the breakfast as a feast. It certainly beat what he was accustomed to on a daily basis back home, except for that last breakfast before he left for Mount Meigs but was unable to enjoy. On the Mount he and the boys never started the day's work on an empty stomach. After fifteen minutes for breakfast, he and the boys divided into work details and proceeded to perform their chores of caring for the school's livestock of cows, pigs, the one mule; feeding the chickens; cleaning out the barn; and then going into the fields to make them ready for planting or to tend the crops or to harvest them, depending on the season.

Cornelia Bowen led the teachers and Leroy and the other boys in the tradition of her mentor, in the Booker T. Washington and Tuskegee industrial school model of attention to detail. Bowen and Mount Meigs followed the gospel of the toothbrush. Young Leroy along with his fellow inmates were schooled on personal hygiene: how to properly wash yourself and to brush your teeth. Time was taken to explain the importance of cleanliness. For some it was their first experience with the toothbrush on a regular basis. They had to be taught that it was not acceptable to share toothbrushes and that the toothbrushes were of little value without baking soda or toothpaste as the cleaning agent, the former being what was usually available to them. The boys were also taught that the brushes must be cleaned and rinsed after each use. Faces and ears were washed, hair combed, and each boy instructed in the art of taking a bath at least once each week—which was hardly sufficient given the amount of work in the fields done each day—but it was a positive first step for some.

Washing hands before meals was a lesson mother Lula well taught Leroy and his siblings at home, but it was practiced on the Mount with religious intensity and followed up by vigorous inspection. Leroy and the other boys meticulously cleaned the school each day, sweeping the floors, dusting every corner and object, straightening the chairs and other furniture, cleaning and otherwise preparing everything for the day's lessons. The dusting, sweeping, mopping, washing windows, washing clothes, washing body, and working the fields constituted the bedrock of the industrial schooling philosophy. We will never know how Leroy felt about these duties. He must have performed them satisfactorily because, as he later confirmed, he was never punished on the Mount.

Book learning, as Leroy experienced, was a distant second at best at Mount Meigs. He and the rest of the boys did receive instruction in reading, writing, and arithmetic. Schooling took place in the main house, where three large classrooms were always at the ready. Given the huge number of boys at Mount Meigs, classroom work was rotated, with eighty or more of the inmates receiving instruction on any given day. In short, each boy did classroom work two or perhaps three times per week. The emphasis was on working with the hands, Leroy found, and the bulk of the time, six days a week, spent in the fields, hoeing, weeding, planting, harvesting, tending to the livestock, cleaning away debris, chopping wood for the fireplaces, and performing an assortment of seemingly never-ending repairs and mending of the school's buildings.

Moses Davis, a member of the board of trustees and minister of a small Baptist church in Waugh, volunteered labor and time to the school and to Leroy and the other boys. Davis was a devoted patron. A cabinetmaker by trade, he joined with John Johnson to help lead the boys in making repairs, fixing leaky roofs, mending fences, and performing the variety of handyman tasks that seemed always to be needed. The presence of Johnson, Davis, and the few other black male trustees provided needed role models for Leroy and the other boys. Bowen welcomed the presence of the black men and encouraged it. On more than one occasion an adult male presence was also called for to discipline a boy or two the old-fashioned way, with a laying on of the dreaded oak wood to the offender's backside. On other more pleasant occasions, the black men, especially Davis, could be counted on to sit down with the boys and talk about issues and questions personal to young men, or to reward meritorious inmates with a day of fishing or leading them in a game of baseball, both of which were Leroy's favorites.

Every activity on the Mount that Leroy experienced was done with reforming of the behavior of the inmates in mind. He, along with twenty-nine other boys, sang in the Mount Meigs choir, an entity of great pride for the school

and one that Bowen believed built character and confidence. Bowen conducted the school's choir herself. She was an accomplished singer, grounded in the
gospel traditions of the African American church, the black Baptist church
specifically. During her student years at Tuskegee Institute, she stood out as
an excellent and talented vocalist. She worked to impart her appreciation of
the importance of music on the boys. It was she who instilled in Leroy the love
of music that would stay with him forever.[18]

Leroy stood out for his commitment to choir and his singing ability. He was
always on time for choir rehearsal and so distinguished himself that Bowen
appointed him youth leader of the choir. Leroy possessed a beautiful singing
voice, a splendid tenor. In later years his voice apparently deepened a bit to
become a baritone. The boys' choir primarily performed traditional "Negro
spirituals." When trustees held their annual meeting on the Mount or on the
other occasions when important visitors came to campus, the boys' choir, often featuring Leroy Page, performed a program of gospel standards, including two songs that he cited as his favorites for the rest of his life: "This Little
Light of Mine" and "I Just Come from the Fountain." The lyrics to "This Little
Light of Mine," with its repeated chorus of "I'm going to let it shine," were perhaps providential when viewed years later from hindsight. In those later years
Leroy would add "Precious Lord," among others, to the list of his all-time gospel favorites that held special meaning for him.[19]

Young Leroy also took up playing the drums in the reformatory's brass
band. His sense of timing, excellent dexterity, and eagerness to practice made
him a standout drummer in the band. His love for music showed in his grasp
of syncopated rhythms and the backbeats he loved to play on the drums. He
had a penchant for hearing what was missing and filling it in with his own
play. This enabled him to stand out individually and to showboat in the band
while having a great deal of fun. He showed a keen appetite for the spotlight
and fan adulation.

Leroy, in short, was an eager and talented participant in the school's activities. He demonstrated quite early on his versatility. In a nontraditional, and
peculiar, setting, to be sure, yet in a significant way, Leroy's openness to learning, to working with his hands, to music, and to sports signaled the emerging
qualities usually associated with the making of a Renaissance man. Granted,
Mount Meigs seemed an unlikely nurturing ground to cultivate a young man's
full cultural potential, but Leroy clearly showed signs of development and
change. The structured and supervised institutional setting of Mount Meigs
brought needed discipline to his life. He opened up to the idea of working on
task and bettering himself and absorbed much of what his educational environment had to offer. Yes, Leroy would also play and star in baseball at the
school, "but," as he reminisced about those days decades later, "it wasn't the

only thing I did on the Mount. I went out for the choir and soon I was the choir leader. And I made the drum and bugle corps, banging those drums."[20]

He and all the boys at Mount Meigs were required to engage in some form of athletics or sporting activity. This was done for reasons beyond that of a desire to maintain a degree of physical fitness. The inmates engaged in more than enough daily exercise gained from working the fields and maintaining the facilities and a sundry of multifarious chores. By the time Leroy Page entered Mount Meigs, sport was beginning to gain recognition and appreciation as a possible tool to reform young boys and men, owing to the success of the Carlisle Indian Industrial Institute, which also embraced the industrial schooling model and garnered national acclaim for its sports program under renowned coach "Pop" Warner and featuring the phenomenal Native American athlete Jim Thorpe.[21]

Two African American educators of particular note who began to embrace the importance of athletics to modify the behavior of boys and men were Booker T. Washington and Cornelia Bowen. Leroy Page never had any idea that he was part of an experiment in education and athletics that Bowen championed and her mentor helped to initiate. Washington was more than a casual observer when it came to sports. He was quite familiar with the great African American sportsmen and athletes: jockey Isaac Murphy, three-time winner of the Kentucky Derby; national cycling champion Major Taylor; heavyweight boxing champion Jack Johnson, whom Washington considered a disgrace to his race; college football All-Americans Fritz Pollard and especially William Henry Louis, with whom Washington maintained a lifelong association; and names such as Bud Fowler and Fleet Walker in professional baseball.

Washington was also both indirectly and directly tied to the establishment of what would become Negro Leagues Baseball. Even though the Negro Leagues were officially founded in 1920, five years after Washington's death, he had early on engaged directly in discussions regarding the future of blacks in baseball. F. C. Lane, editor of the magazine *Baseball*, initiated the dialogue when he wrote to the race leader in 1913:

> The colored man while he often has a great ability as a player is barred, as you know, from the professional ranks throughout the United States. In Cuba however some of the greatest players who ever trod a diamond are of Negro descent. Now it occurred to me that it would be perfectly possible to organize a colored league composed of negro players in this country which I believe would open to the negro here an opportunity which he does not at present enjoy, and which would also I believe be of benefit in a variety of ways to the negro population as a whole.

Washington did not disagree with Lane, but noted the activities already taking place that he believed served the same purpose. "There is already, if I remember right," Washington replied, "an amateur baseball colored league. In New York City and in Chicago, there is, I believe, also a city league made up of white and colored baseball clubs." Washington was aware of "an All Nations Baseball Club playing professional baseball through the West against local clubs, which was composed of a Japanese, an Indian, a woman first baseman, and a Negro pitcher." He wished Lane well in his endeavor and that he "should very much like to learn of the successful inauguration of a league in which superior Negro teams should be a part."[22]

Washington gave considerable thought to another of Lane's suggestions: that baseball could be used to educate and rehabilitate black males. "I have often wondered if baseball might not offer possibilities as a factor in education of our great negro population," Lane wrote. "As you probably know," he continued, "baseball has been used with remarkable effect by the wardens of several state penitentiaries as a humanizing influence on the convicts in their charge. It has been employed by the great city of Cleveland as the chief factor in her campaign of education among her own boys and young men, and I might cite other instances where it has exerted an enlightening influence far superior to its rank as a mere sport."[23]

Booker Washington's protégée, Cornelia Bowen, was also very interested in the interdiction possibilities that baseball might offer. Both she and Washington saw the potential usefulness of baseball for boys like Leroy Page. Washington and Bowen were both disciples of the nineteenth-century precept of "muscular Christianity." Bowen knew that in dealing with young males like Leroy, they had to be kept busy and at least some portion of the daily routine should be fun. She also appreciated the role that baseball might play in teaching boys like Leroy a sense of respect for rules and regulations, teamwork, the benefits of hard work and practice, cooperation, self-control, and obedience. These well-known benefits were attributed to participation in sports thanks to the pioneering work of Pop Warner and the Carlisle experiment.

Leroy was part of the reform movement in athletics that began in the twentieth century. On the Mount, Bowen innovatively incorporated games and athletics into the educational and work routine of Leroy and the other inmate-students, and Page enjoyed participating in the sport component. Bowen received encouragement and caution in her use of sports from the African American community. Mrs. L. F. Hadnot, treasurer of the Alabama Federation of Colored Women's Clubs, wrote from Birmingham: "It is my candid opinion that quite a few boys learn games and begin with bad boys to gamble largely because no games are allowed or encouraged in their homes." Hadnot believed, like Bowen, that properly supervised sport and recreation countered bad behavior and had an important role to play at Mount Meigs. Dr. Frank C. Caffey, a physician who also taught physical fitness and sparring, strongly advocated the use of sport at Mount Meigs and elsewhere. He trumpeted participation in athletics as a tool not only for reform but also for racial advancement. He urged, "Give the young Afro-American in the Southern Industrial Schools an Athletic chance." Caffey added a postscript to his message: "My advice to every boy who wants to excel in athletics is to refrain from cigarettes."[24]

Bowen made Leroy and the other boys adhere to this advice and much more, at least during their tenure on the Mount. There was no smoking at Mount Meigs, and only certain games would be allowed. Marble playing was, for example, not permitted because it was seen as too close to gambling. In reality, Leroy and the other inmates found a way to play marbles anyhow, and to smoke—a habit that Leroy embraced and would continue to engage in for the rest of his life.

Most of the boys greatly enjoyed the sport of fishing, especially Leroy, which called for very little physical exertion but a fair amount of patience and a bit of strategic thinking in trying to outsmart the fish. Bowen saw fishing as a healthy diversion and used it as part of a reward system on the Mount and under the supervision of Rev. Moses Davis. The fishing expeditions that Davis led the boys on were joyous occasions for them and Leroy to commune with nature and a privilege given to those boys whose behavior had been exemplary during the preceding weeks. With a can of worms for bait and a homemade cane pole, the good boys and Davis spent many an enjoyable early-Saturday morning at the old fishing hole. The crappies, bass, bluegills, perch, and ever-abundant catfish taken from the nearby pond or, on very special occasions, from an all-day twenty-mile outing to the Tallapoosa River supplemented in a most practical way the Saturday and Sunday dinners on the Mount for the lucky few.

But it was another sport that was by far the number-one pastime at the reform school. It offered no supplement to dinner, but it certainly fulfilled Leroy's soul as only the game of baseball could, and Bowen encouraged her boys to play it. Mount Meigs, with nearly three hundred boys eager to play, had no problem fielding good baseball teams. Moreover, baseball was an important outreach tool in building solidarity between the school and the greater community. When Leroy and the boys played baseball, the entire community was invited to enjoy the game.[25]

The boys' baseball team could also go out to the larger community as a positive example of the work at the school. The annual "Reformatory Boys Picnic at Mount Meigs" was a special occasion that the entire community enjoyed. There would be plenty of good food and entertaining musical selections by the school's brass band. The school choir, with Leroy, would sing as well on these public festive occasions to the delight of the visitors. "They showed their musical talent," the Reverend R. C. Justin reported in the *Colored Alabamian*, "as they sang those songs which were sung by our Slave Mothers and Fathers such as 'Going To See My Mother Sitting In The Kingdom,' 'Oh Lord, Keep Me From Sinking Down,' and 'When You Lose Your Mother You Have Lost Your Best Friend.' These songs pierced the hearts of many bystanders as they listened very attentively."[26]

There was no question, though, that at the annual reformatory picnics the highlight of the fun activities was the boys' baseball game. Leroy never spoke about this in later years, but it was a special event that he participated in since the tradition continued for many years. There is little doubt that he shined on the field and at Mount Meigs as an exceptionally talented pitcher and that he liked the notoriety. The contests were organized and disciplined and had a rich history of entertaining and pleasing the spectators, with the boys looking sharp in their Mount Meigs baseball uniforms. It was easy to understand why "every moment of our time was interestingly enjoyed" watching the boys play baseball. "Their uniforms attracted special attention as they played on a selected spot running bases and catching balls."[27]

Leroy was always a standout player and must have garnered many accolades. Such recognition surely boosted his sense of self-worth. Hearing praise from Bowen and the cheering and applause from the spectators when playing before the community had to console him and, no doubt, elevate the importance of the game of baseball in his life.

His ability to throw a baseball with blistering speed and accuracy were attributes that would have made any coach want to pay special attention to him. Bowen left the coaching of baseball to others. Teaching the fine points of the game was left in the capable hands of the school's most active trustee: the Reverend Moses Davis.[28]

Davis was known in the community and beyond for his excellence as a cabinetmaker and a dedicated minister. He was also well known as a lover of baseball. It was the Reverend Moses Davis who used his powers of persuasion to get J. A. Murray & Company, the leading sporting-goods store serving black Montgomery, to provide the baseball uniforms and equipment for the Mount Meigs team at a substantial discount. He solicited the community, including blacks in Montgomery, where most of the Mount Meigs boys were from, to support the baseball team. The Dexter Avenue Baptist Church demonstrated its community spirit and took up donations from its congregation to help outfit the team. J. A. Murray's, located at 316 Dexter Avenue, could hardly refuse being generous to a cause that its close and important neighbor supported.

Leroy and the Mount Meigs baseball players often benefited from the generosity of spirit of the Dexter Avenue Church, the oldest black church in Montgomery, established in 1877. That same church would demonstrate its pivotal community-leadership role many times, including in 1955 when a young assistant pastor there by the name of Martin Luther King Jr. built upon the work of Fred Shuttlesworth and joined with Rosa Parks, E. D. Nixon, and others in forming the Montgomery Improvement Association and in orchestrating the boycott of the city's bus service in what would be heralded as the beginning of the civil rights movement.

Besides his ability to rally community support for the Mount Meigs boys' baseball team, Davis took time with each player on the team, especially Leroy. It may be suggested that the man who proved to be the most important coach in teaching Leroy Page the basic fundamentals of the game of baseball was himself a former professional ballplayer. The suggestion that Davis may have played in his younger days in the International League on a team in either Chicago or New York cannot be confirmed. At the least, he was apparently quite knowledgeable of the game and its great African American players. Leroy and the boys on the Mount assuredly heard often from the reverend-coach Davis thrilling stories of the early black ballplayers, of the feats of the famed Frank Grant of the old Buffalo Bisons, and anecdotes about the play of Fleet Walker, Bub Fowler, Rube Foster, and others.

It is impossible to know what position Davis may have played, or if he ever played professionally, but he was likely a catcher or pitcher if his coaching emphasis was any indicator. Leroy could not have been more fortunate. Davis took an immediate interest in his ability to throw.

It is doubtful that any of the boys on the Mount would have been able as batters to counteract Leroy's pinpoint accuracy and speed as a pitcher. His fellow inmates loved to rib him about his height and lack of weight: "'Look there goes the crane,' some of the guys on the Mount yelled at me whenever I walked across the yard or went into a ball game." But it was he who got the last laugh when pitching. What Leroy possessed was an incredible throwing ability that went back to his earliest years of rock hunting in Mobile and now served him well as an unstoppable pitcher on the Mount. Mount Meigs boys only played a couple of games at most each year against boys from other schools. They played most of their formal and informal games against competing teams within the Mount. Leroy's natural pitching ability would have won him friends, but it would have also won him enemies. Whether a peer in age or an older boy, the likelihood of that individual being able to hit his pitches was slim to none unless he slowed them down a bit to allow the batter to connect, which was even more unlikely. The thing that Leroy cherished most and that won him acknowledgment was his throwing ability. He had no intention of allowing anyone to take that away from him or of giving it up. This may help to explain why he never developed any close associations while on the Mount, except with his hometown friend Julius Andrews. Julius, however, was older than Leroy and was released several years earlier than him, leaving Leroy with no bosom buddies on the Mount.[29]

Pitching was Leroy's closest companion, and fortunately for him Coach Davis took time to help him cultivate his talent. Davis not only showed him the proper mechanics of pitching but also taught him the philosophy of pitching and hitting. It was Davis who filled him without question with stories of George Stovey, the famed pitcher of the Newark team of the International League when the league was still open to blacks prior to the late 1890s, and whom Leroy liked to mention years later when talking baseball history. Leroy was speaking of the reverend Coach Moses Davis when he said, without attribution, that when he first went out for baseball and took to the mound on the Mount, and threw a few pitches, striking out several batters, the coach called him over and said, "That arm may do you some good someday. Take care of it. You concentrate on baseball and you might make something out of yourself."[30]

There has been credit given over the years to an Edward Byrd as the individual who coached Leroy Page at Mount Meigs. Research into the reformatory and its staff fails to find anyone associated with the school by the name of Edward Byrd. Indeed, US Census reports do not reveal anyone within thirty miles of the institute with the name Byrd. A careful examination of school reports and records—the few that survived the fire that destroyed the main administration building in the 1970s—and discussion with community elders point to the Reverend Moses Davis as coach of the Mount Meigs team when Leroy Page was in residence. It was Davis who struck the deal with the sporting-goods store in Montgomery to secure the team's uniforms and devoted long hours to teaching the boys his favorite pastime—baseball. Ironically, a movie version of the life of Satchel Paige went so far as to portray the baseball coach at Mount Meigs as a white man. Paige, who sat for some publicity photos at the start of the filming but was not a real consultant on the project, nevertheless did not bother to correct the rampant misinformation in the film. He saw it as just a movie and figured, according to lifelong friend Double Duty Radcliffe, "It was what white folks wanted to believe anyhow."[31]

The entire Mount Meigs teaching staff and volunteers were African Americans. Bowen's correspondence confirms that the white members of the board of trustees were all from out of state and usually visited the school only once a year at best. In addition, the claim that young Page's catcher at Mount Meigs was someone named John Knox is incorrect. Census records and the principal's reports of the school list no student at the Mount by the name of

John Knox during those years. Unfortunately, the aforementioned misinformation about who taught Page baseball on the Mount and played with him on the team continues to be recycled as fact.

The reverend and coach Moses Davis was Page's baseball mentor. Davis had to know, too, that realistically there was precious little opportunity for blacks in professional ball with the prevailing Jim Crowism of the era. Yet he would have also been made hopeful during the second year of Leroy's incarceration, for in that year, 1920, the Negro Leagues came into being at a meeting in Kansas City, Missouri. One can easily imagine that the reverend-coach prayed for a better future in which a black youngster with Leroy's talent might get an opportunity in the emerging new venue of black professional baseball. He also knew that all-black teams were barnstorming at present and that the best of those players could make a living playing ball. In short, there was hope, albeit small.

On the Mount, Leroy received the fundamentals of the game of baseball. Davis was the one who mentored him repeatedly of the most important rule for pitchers: warm up the arm properly before throwing. Pop Warner told the story of his own desire to become a professional baseball pitcher and how he ruined his chances when he permanently injured his pitching arm when he failed to warm up properly. Pop Warner's advice to all youngsters wanting to become pitchers was what he labeled as rule number 1: "1. Warm up gently and easily before you pour it on hard." Leroy heard that magical rule constantly, and he embraced it.[32]

Davis helped Leroy to fine-tune his throwing mechanics, to put to good use his six-foot frame (and still growing), and use his weight—what little there was of it at the time—to gain leverage and velocity behind his pitches. In addition, Leroy reminisced, "My coach showed me how to kick up my foot so it looked like I'd blacked out the sky. And he showed me how to swing my arm around so it looked like I let go of the ball when my hand was right in the batter's face." That early coaching helped him to perfect his delivery style, although it would be some years after leaving Mount Meigs before he began to add to his repertoire of pitches something other than a blistering fastball and a change of pace. For now his two-gun arsenal was enough to blow past batters and completely outclass any competition he faced while playing ball on the Mount. Having the proper pitching mechanics would make it relatively easy for him in the years to come to increase his arsenal, adding a good curveball and an array of other pitches—some unorthodox and spectacularly unique, requiring pet names.[33]

What Davis also gave Leroy were priceless pointers: a schooling in how to read batters; how to figure out their timing, strengths, and weaknesses; and where to keep the ball over and around the plate to confuse and defeat them. It was on the Mount that Leroy learned how to watch a batter's stance, his knee action and position of feet, and to begin to decipher his swinging motion in order to exploit his weaknesses to leave the poor soul swinging at nothing but air. He was taught to observe a batter the same way "a bullfighter watches a bull. You never look at a batter anywhere except at the knees, just like a bullfighter. The bullfighter can tell what a bull is going to do by watching his knees. I learned the same. When a batter swings and I see his knees move, I can tell just what his weaknesses are. Then I just put the ball where I know he can't hit it."[34]

Leroy's experience on the Mount during the Bowen years was similar to that of George Herman Ruth's experience at St. Mary's Industrial School for Boys, a reform school of sorts that housed eight hundred young males five miles outside of Baltimore. Ruth, like Leroy, was a difficult child, an at-risk boy from a family that could no longer function as a family and a father who could no longer or would no longer provide for his son. One of the teachers at St. Mary's, Brother Matthias, a hulk of a man, loved baseball and befriended Ruth and tutored him in the fine points of the game. Under his tutelage, young Ruth excelled and became an accomplished pitcher, signing on with Boston in 1912. Ruth also demonstrated early on the skill that would overshadow his superb pitching ability and make him into a larger-than-life gate attraction. With virtual ease he had an uncanny ability to knock the ball out of the park. Thus, Babe Ruth became the fiercest hitter in professional baseball, the legendary "Sultan of Swat" and "Homerun King." St. Mary's, which accepted non-Catholics, lauded two of its former residents who gained national acclaim: Babe Ruth and a Jewish youngster named Asa Yolson, who later changed his name to Al Jolson. Mount Meigs lauded two of its former residents who gained national acclaim: artist Lonnie Holly and Leroy Page.[35]

One can certainly question the goals of industrial schooling and the quality of academic education provided to the inmates at the Alabama Reform School for Juvenile Negro Law-Breakers. But when Leroy was released from Mount Meigs in December 1923, seven months short of his eighteenth birthday, he did take with him something that would prove invaluable and last a lifetime. He summed up his years of incarceration: "I traded five years of freedom to learn how to pitch. At least I started my real learning on the Mount." He learned more than that, as he would add to his statement in later years regarding his experience on the Mount: "They were not wasted years at all. It made a real man out of me."[36]

3

"If You Were Only White"

What awaited Leroy Page was the impenetrable color line of an unchanged Jim Crow South that he would either surrender to or find a way to circumnavigate. When he was discharged from Mount Meigs on December 23, 1923, two days before Christmas, his possessions consisted of a set of brand-new clothes—which was a tradition at the Mount—a couple of shirts, an extra pair of trousers, underwear, socks, a good pair of almost new shoes, two dollars, and a baseball and glove. He might say that he did not leave the Mount with very much after five and a half years, but it was far more than he had when he arrived in terms of not only physical possessions but also self-discipline, an emerging positive self-identity, and grounding in baseball fundamentals.

The same mode of transportation that brought him to the Mount would now take him back to Mobile. While the cloth satchel given him was only partially full with his belongings, his mind was fully occupied during the L&N train ride home with anxieties and uncertainties about what he would do next. He was only seventeen and a half years old yet fully an adult by the standards of the day. Leroy would later say that he did not remember how he traveled back home from the Mount. Perhaps the anxiety of coming home was in some ways reminiscent of the trepidation he experienced when traveling to the Mount from Mobile years earlier.

What would await him in Mobile? His father, John Page, had died a few months earlier, and Leroy was unable to gain release to attend the funeral. Unbeknownst to him, however, his father's death was the reason for his release from the Mount seven months before his eighteenth birthday. Lula Page needed the able hands of all of her children more than ever now for the family to survive. The State of Alabama often commuted a juvenile's sentence under such circumstances. Leroy was required at home. He felt good about being released from the Mount, but he was terribly worried about the future. Where would he find work? What would he do? There was no reason to expect the family's situation had improved during his absence. There was every reason to believe that the family's situation had deteriorated further, if that were possible.

After her husband's death, Lula Page changed the spelling of the family name from *Page* to *Paige*. That change in the spelling of the name, the adding of the *i,* may have been both symbolic and substantive. There could be no denying who the father was and the history of their past relationship and the ten children that documented that history together. The children were a likely reason that the now Lula "Paige" did not readopt her maiden name of Coleman. That small but powerfully symbolic change in the spelling of the name, she surely hoped, might give her some relief or distance, if not complete liberation, from her husband's debts and associations, as a later generation of the Paige family surmised was the case. There may also have been a desire on her part to help her son Leroy get a fresh start with a fresh new name that might somehow assist in distancing him from his delinquent past. Whatever the reason or reasons for the change in spelling of the family name, everyone needed to pitch in more than ever now with the passing of John Page.[1]

After being home for a few weeks and having a brief sabbatical of sorts, Leroy, who quickly embraced the name alteration of Page to Paige, began seeking work in earnest. The problem was what to do. There were precious few opportunities for a decent job for an African American male in Mobile or for that matter most of Alabama beyond the typical Negro work of common laborer, picker or sharecropper, domestic, handyman or gardener, or dockworker, loading and unloading ships or freight trains. He was not about to return to the L&N station and tote satchels or scrounge for discarded bottles around town. The little education he received on the Mount was not preparation for a serious skilled position in industry. That kind of work at any rate was deemed as a white man's job.

What he was finally able to find was, what he rightly called, a little piece of a job, back to working at Monroe Park, the white ballpark where the Mobile Bears played. This was demeaning work for him that surely reaffirmed old memories about the Negro's place in Mobile. Nevertheless, it was all he could find. He kept the stands in order, sweeping and cleaning the seating area, picking up trash from the field, and, doing one of the jobs his father did when he had been around, cutting the grass. There was not much money in ballpark custodial work. This was at best a part-time job, and it left Leroy with a considerable amount of free time. He quickly put that time to good use, as he had been taught on the Mount that idle hands were the devil's workshop. He had become a rather disciplined young man.

Leroy Paige turned to the one avenue and occupation that he was best prepared and capable of performing at an extraordinary level of competency—baseball. It was his older brother Wilson who led the way. He was the star pitcher and, when not hurling, a great catcher as well for the black Mobile Tigers. Wilson spoke to the team's manager about his younger brother's pitching ability and won him a tryout.

The young Paige did not disappoint. At the tryout he threw nine or ten pitches that blew by the team's best hitter, who was unable to do anything about the succession of strikes. The manager decided to see firsthand just how good the youngster was and took up the bat himself. He met a similar fate at the plate as the Leroy Paige kid struck him out with three blistering fastballs right down the middle. The manager was impressed, to say the least, and asked the youngster, "Do you throw that fast consistently?" "No sir," Paige replied. "I do it all the time." This was the first time young Leroy Paige said those words. In years to come, he would use that saying repeatedly.[2]

He felt good about himself as he made the team and soon earned the munificent sum of two dollars at the end of some games, or a keg of lemonade, depending upon attendance. Too often the pay was in lemonade rather than in dollars, but the young man was working at what he loved. As Paige's ability to win games increased, he became confident enough to ask for better compensation. The young hurler was becoming a standout pitcher.

The competing teams learned quickly to fear the tall, lanky, big-footed kid called Satchel. When Paige took the mound and let loose, you could hear the glove pop from every location and any seat in the ballpark. The velocity behind his throws was awesome. He seemed to get his entire body behind the pitch. Windup, release, pop. Sometimes a double or even triple windup, then release, and the immediate pop. This was no minor pop. The sound resonated like a rifle shot. As friends recalled, Paige did not throw balls; "he flung fire."[3]

Brother Wilson often caught him for the Tigers, and he knew to always have a sponge or two or a wad of cloth in the glove or be prepared not to use his hand for a week if catching his brother. Paige liked to call his fastball a "trouble ball" or "bee ball." Others often referred to his pitch as a "pea," since it came so fast that it seemed to shrink in size and was difficult to see. Catching Leroy Paige, however, was not that difficult because of his control. "Just hold your glove out there and the ball would come to you," Buck O'Neil attested. "Catching him was easy as long as you could stand the pain."[4]

The young Paige from the very beginning of his career was rarely wild with a pitch. Control and speed were his main weapons early on, and what weapons they were. Batters had little chance against the "bee ball." The pitch had such velocity behind it that, as some would-be hitters recounted, the ball made a buzzing sound as it blasted past you a fraction of a second before you heard that pop in the catcher's mitt. Often a batter did not swing at a Paige pitch at all. One, two, three, and you were out. Batters typically gave the same explanation for their lack of success against him: "You can't hit what you can't see." By the end of that first year with the Mobile Tigers, Leroy Paige was leading all pitchers, having won at least twenty-five games and many more than that if you included those he saved when he came on in relief.[5]

As his ability to win games increased, so did his desire to get paid. Paige was nobody's dummy. He could think on his own and was never hesitant when it came to standing up for himself and attempting to maneuver within the business of baseball. Since attendance at the games had increased and gate receipts were up, he made his case to the manager that he wanted to be paid more. Lemonade would no longer suffice. He soon received two dollars at the end of each and every game. In all likelihood he received his pay away from the other team members, since payment in lemonade was not curtailed for the rest of the players. It is impossible to know how this affected Paige. In all likelihood he did not lose much sleep over the exception being made for him. In fact, the lesson he was learning was that playing superior baseball could make for exceptions.

The young hurler was about to learn an early lesson of the market realities of black baseball known as *jumping*. The better players routinely freelanced. If another team needed a good hitter and you had a reputation for laying the wood, you were likely to get an occasional call to duty from another club and the opportunity to make a few extra dollars. A good pitcher was harder to come by and always in demand. Paige was a great young pitcher, and the demands for his talents on other teams would keep him constantly jumping throughout his career.

It was during his jump to the Mobile Bay Boys that he first displayed the antics that became one of his trademarks. In the game the Mobile Bay Boys proved repeatedly that they were a subpar team. The simplest one-base hopper turned into a double or triple, owing to the ineptitude of the team. Paige was on the mound and trying desperately to somehow hold on to a slim lead. As the fielding errors mounted and the lead dwindled to one run going into the bottom half of the ninth inning, he became fed up with the awful fielding and ordered the outfield to come in. Reluctant at first, they finally obeyed. He had them sit behind the pitcher's mound as he went to work. With the outfield called in and one man on base—and to the utter enjoyment of the crowd—Paige took on the next three batters. Had only one of the men been able to connect with a pitch, they would have had a home run and won the game.

He fired lethal fastballs that left the hapless batters motionless as the catcher's mitt popped, followed by the umpire's repeated calls of strike.

He struck out the side without anyone else getting on base, and the game ended with the Bay Boys victorious. The crowd went wild. His heroics brought the previously half-interested throng of spectators to absolute ecstasy. They yelled and hollered and broke into thunderous applause in appreciation of his bravado on the mound. He had won the hearts and absolute respect of the fans with his daring showmanship, pitching brilliance, and sheer audacity. Paige, probably picking up the stunt from the much-underappreciated elder black moundsman John Donaldson, turned it into an art form. The crowd of a little less than two hundred sounded like thousands as they continued pouring on the adulation as Leroy "Satchel" Paige strolled off the mound and onto the road to stardom.[6]

That had been a great moment, but a more gratifying event came late one afternoon in the midst of sweeping and picking up trash at Monroe Park when a quartet of white players from the Bears team called him over and made a challenge. They had heard about Paige. He had gained such notoriety in black baseball circles around Mobile that it spilled over into the white league. The Bears players thought it was all hype and were willing to make a wager to prove their point and superiority over the cocky black boy. Paige was also beginning to gain a reputation for brashness and confidence. For whites, this was absolutely taboo. This was precisely why the heavyweight boxing champion Jack Johnson had been so completely despised in white America, and especially south of the Mason-Dixon line. Johnson flaunted his prowess as he destroyed his white opponents in the ring. No sooner had he captured the Heavyweight Boxing Championship of the World in 1908 that an all-out effort began to find a Great White Hope to recapture the championship for white America and to put the uppity black back in his place.

Paige knew all the stories about the legendary pugilist and admired his boasting, trash talking to opponents, defiant attitude, and superiority in the ring. Paige believed, like Jack Johnson in the African American tradition, that when you were good, you had a right to flaunt it. And Paige certainly was good. He eagerly accepted the challenge of the Bears players.

The wager was one dollar. Whether Paige actually had a dollar in his pocket to cover the bet is doubtful. At any rate, he did not think much of the consequences if he lost. He was sure of his abilities with the ball. In his mind losing was not an option or a possibility. He had already gained that quality that he would maintain for the rest of his life: no doubt about his ability to pitch. He let the white boys know that he was confident that he was as good and better than the rumors claimed, and uppity to boot. "We went down on the field and one of them grabbed a bat and another a glove to catch me," Paige described the showdown. "I threw four of five real easy like, just to warm up. Then the batter headed for the plate. 'No néed for you to tote that wood up here,' I yelled. 'It's just weight. You ain't gonna need it 'cause I'm gonna throw you nothin' but my trouble ball.'"[7]

Three sizzling fastballs and the first batter was out. A second player took his turn at the plate and "just caught a breeze." The third would-be hitter saw nothing but peas go past the plate as he struck out. The white guys had to acknowledge what they had witnessed. They paid the dollar. For Paige that was "the easiest dollar I ever made." It was also a young man's personal statement of self-worth and racial pride. It all came together in the statement that one of the Bears players made regarding how Paige could help them on their team if circumstances were different. He spoke the words that Paige would always remember. "We sure could use you," the player acknowledged. "If you were only white."[8]

Paige was not. He was African American, a black man in white America, in Alabama, in the Deep South, in the heart of the Jim Crow era, and he knew it. Baseball for him was relegated to black ball, and he would try to make the most of any opportunity as his reputation as a pitcher spread in Mobile and outside of it.

Leroy Paige's pitching performances with the Mobile Tigers made him a household name in black Mobile. When the highly touted Gulfport team visited Mobile for a game against the Tigers, he treated the hometown crowd to a dazzling display of pitching supremacy. Paige was truly in the zone that day on the mound. His control was needle perfect. Although his entire repertoire consisted primarily of fastballs of varying speeds, and a change of pace that he dubbed his hesitation pitch, the accuracy of all his throws was something to behold. He brought smiles to the faces of spectators with his double and triple windups and a bit of trash talk, all of which humored the crowd. It also bespoke his growing confidence as a pitcher. The substantive quality of his performance spoke for itself by the end of the game in the two-pronged goal he had come to understand was the soul of the game: entertaining the fans with superior pitching. That day he struck out seventeen batters.

One of the spectators was Alex Herman, a fellow Mobilian who was spending a few days at home. Herman managed the Chattanooga Black Lookouts of the Negro Southern League. Enjoying a respite from his constant road trips, Herman decided to take in a local game. He had heard about the dynamic pitching of the youngster called Satchel and got the opportunity to see him in action for himself.

Herman was always on the lookout for new talent that he hoped might help his ball club. The Black Lookouts were one of the weakest teams in the Negro

Southern League. The other league teams, from Birmingham, Atlanta, New Orleans, Memphis, and Albany, Georgia, were stronger than Chattanooga, largely because of better pitching. Any baseball team is always on the lookout for another good pitcher, but the Chattanooga Black Lookouts were in desperate need of help on the mound to stave off finishing the year again at the bottom of the cellar. Paige's growing reputation, and dazzling confirmation in Herman's presence, left the Lookouts' manager drooling over his find and eager to sign him.

Paige was a youngster, only nineteen years of age, when Herman approached him in the spring of 1926 with an offer to play professional ball. Paige's first reaction was guarded when Herman spoke to him after the game about signing with him. Paige thought that Herman was talking about joining up with another semipro team like the Tigers. "I am talking about professional ball, not semi-pro!" Herman blasted. Now Leroy Paige took in the magnitude of what was being said. He was being offered the opportunity to start doing what he had longed to do: play professional baseball.[9]

He jumped at the opportunity without much attempt to negotiate salary or other particulars, except that Herman would have to seek mother Lula's permission. It was not that Paige needed his mother's consent at age nineteen. He wanted her to be a part of this important decision, which would mean that her young son was leaving home with a chance to make his mark in the world. Furthermore, Herman had no intention of signing a youngster of nineteen without the permission and blessing of his parent.

Mother Lula did not believe in Sunday sports or anything else on the Sabbath except church and prayer. Herman, in talking to her, simply neglected to mention that many of the games would be played on Sundays. Lula Paige gave her permission after lengthy discussion with Herman and Leroy. The firm financial arrangements were the final persuasive element. Young Paige would be earning fifty dollars per month, an amount that was almost unbelievable to mother Lula, Leroy, and the rest of the Paige family, and a portion of the wages would be sent home to her. Herman promised to take responsibility for watching over her son and for mailing home a part of his salary each month. Another hometown boy would be signing on with Herman as well, Julius Andrews, Leroy's old friend from the rock-throwing days and Mount Meigs and a great first baseman for the Tigers.[10]

Herman was also very interested in recruiting Paige's older brother Wilson, whom he considered as equally talented as Leroy and a bit more experienced. Wilson was an excellent pitcher and also a superb catcher and hitter. Leroy thought of him as a better baseball player than himself. It would seem an easy decision for any young black male in Jim Crow Alabama to take the offer. But it was not. Wilson eventually said no to Herman's overture.

The speculation as to why Paige's brother decided against turning pro has run the gamut from not wanting a career in professional baseball to being afraid of leaving home to wanting more money than the fifty dollars Herman was offering. None of these explanations alone fully explain Wilson's decision. Wilson was not afraid of travel outside of Mobile, though he did not do much of it because of the expense involved, nor was he averse to seeing more of the world, though Chattanooga and the teams they would play were not that far away. Neither was younger brother Leroy's explanation of why his brother did not accept the offer a convincing one. He later concluded of his bother's decision that he did not love baseball as much and want a career in it as badly.

The more plausible explanation of why Wilson decided to stay home is found in that realm that those too often espousing upon and analyzing the African American experience from afar overlook or dismiss. Wilson was a complex individual with strengths and flaws. The oldest brother, John Jr. was already married, out of the house, and helping to build a ministry. Wilson was next in line as "the man" of the house. He, no doubt, felt the awesome responsibility. On the other hand, Wilson was something of a maverick, with a temper that constantly got him in trouble. Often he found himself "on the lam," as one family member explained. He had all the traits of what the white South labeled as a "bad nigger." Herman likely sensed this and made only a halfhearted effort to recruit him. In addition, Wilson was also in and out of town during the crucial decisions and apparently "on the lam" again when his younger brother signed. Whatever the deciding factor or factors, Wilson stayed behind in Mobile. Leroy Paige was free to pursue his dream.[11]

From day one with Chattanooga it was clear that Leroy "Satchel" Paige was something special. His first day with the team foretold the future. He was introduced to his teammates as a new pitcher that Herman had found in Mobile. That was nice, but it hardly brought any fanfare from his teammates, who included, among others, Ralf Cleage, Anthony Cooper, James Gurley, Bill Love, and Leonard Miller.

That all changed when Herman told Paige to warm up and throw a few to the catcher. They were not on the field and had no base. The catcher stepped off the distance between home plate and the mound, and Paige offered him a small piece of cloth to serve as a makeshift home plate. The catcher warned him that the piece of cloth was too small. Paige assured him that the small target was all that he needed. He warmed up and threw. The catcher's glove popped with the rifle shot of Paige's deadly accurate pitch. The catcher's glove barely moved an inch from the target as Paige let loose with one daily rifle shot after another. The speed and accuracy occupied the complete attention of his teammates. They saw that manager Herman had brought them something very special in the young kid from his own hometown. One of Paige's new teammates standing near the catcher to get a close-up view shouted out that the ball was coming so fast that it "hummed like a bee." Paige shouted back that it sounded like a bee because it was his "bee ball." Indeed, his fastball would have many a player confirm over the years that the ball blew past with such velocity that it made a humming sound like a bumblebee.[12]

In working with Paige, Herman impressed upon him the importance of the two *p*'s: practice and preparation. The two talked baseball nonstop. The young hurler had a good ear and a burning desire to be the best. It is often overlooked or discounted that Paige was an excellent student of the game, paying special attention to Herman's advice on warming up properly, improving control of his throws, and setting up batters for the next pitch, which reinforced the sage lessons that the reverend Coach Moses Davis had taught him during those five years on the Mount.

In the accounts and assessments of Paige's baseball prowess, little is ever said about his penchant for the two *p*'s. Indeed, Paige himself in numerous interviews in later years rarely mentioned how hard he practiced over the years to develop his skills. He knowingly played to the stereotypes of the white media and its sports journalists, joking with them about how he hated practicing and had made it his mission, including when he first started playing, to avoid it no matter what. One of Satchel Paige's supposed cardinal rules that he, indeed, later said he subscribed to was to avoid running at all costs. The truth was something quite different. In his formative years he ran with the best of them and outworked most. But Paige knew that the image of the lazy Negro possessing natural-born talent comforted his white audience. The black audience of the times was little different in consciousness and laughed along with the role playing.

Herman set up a regimen of control drills for the young hurler, consisting of throwing repeatedly through a hole in a fence and knocking over a line of pop bottles. "I was putting in plenty of hours on the baseball field before the other players got up in the mornings and after they went home at night. I'm still trying to rest up from all that practice." Even before his first start for the Lookouts, the practice paid dividends. One afternoon a spectator watching Paige go through his paces bet him that he could not knock over the entire line of bottles that Herman had set up for him. The bet was on. Paige methodically picked off each of the bottles without missing a single one. That wager paid for his and Herman's dinner that evening. "It got so that I could nip frosting off the cake with my fastball. Because of that control, I got clear to the top in baseball. If you know where the ball is going, you can do a lot no one else can and you can stay around long after the real good stuff you throw has gone." It all paid off in the quality of his play. Paige got his first start against a visiting New Orleans team, and he brought home a 1–0 victory.[13]

He, Herman, and teammates assuredly also discussed another crucial component for success in black baseball: the ability to entertain the crowd. Black ball was played with more zip, more base stealing, and more flamboyant fielding. A little bit of stunting was always welcomed and expected. The two were never mutually exclusive in black ball. Add dynamic pitching and hitting to the mix, and you had the setting for a great Sunday afternoon of fun for the entire family. Paige absorbed the wisdom around him and the long-standing culture of African American sporting tradition. Putting it all into play, especially his pitching, and his game value continued to rise. After his fourth week with Chattanooga, Paige's salary had been increased to eighty-five dollars a month.

Leroy Paige's introduction to life on the road in the Negro Southern League was a rude awakening. His larger education came on his first road trip against the Memphis Red Sox on May 16, 1926. In later years, Paige did not recall much of the details of that particular game. He vividly, however, remembered the trip to Memphis.

The Chattanooga Black Lookouts were a second-tier team in the league. Like many of the squads, they did not own their own bus. Given that they were also not among the major draws in the league, salaries and travel accommodations for the team were second class even by Jim Crow standards. The bus that the team hired for transport to away games would never have met the safety and minimal comfort standards of any accrediting body. To call the bus rickety, as most players did, was a kind description. In addition to the noise, the bus burned fuel with a vengeance. Various oil leaks and holes in the exhaust system made for a sickening and dangerous mixture for passengers, exposing everyone to possible carbon monoxide poisoning. Several of the bus's windows were missing, which was ironically positive in that some amount of constant ventilation helped compensate for other windows that were permanently stuck shut.

The team's star players, which Paige was not yet, were easily identifiable because they commanded seats with working windows. That ranking particularly had its benefits in times of inclement weather, although a good seat with a working window did not guarantee that you were sitting under a nonporous portion of the bus's roof and thus possibly secure from getting drenched if it rained.

On that first road trip, Paige was instantly awakened from any illusion and expectation of a special status being conferred to pro ballplayers. If the bus ride itself had not done it, the accommodations afforded the team when it arrived that night in Memphis most certainly did. There were none. The bus went straight through town to the ballpark. It was approaching nine o'clock and pitch-black at the park. Herman announced the arrival, and players began filing off the bus, all except Paige. Tired from a long, bumpy ride and anxious to get into bed, he told Herman that he wanted to go straight to the hotel and get some sleep. The awakening came with Herman's response: What hotel? This was it. Paige reluctantly stepped off the bus into the pitch-black night and joined his teammates sleeping on their suitcases in the open skies of the ballpark. The next morning he awoke sore and stiff from an uncomfortable night of rustic semisleep. For breakfast he and his teammates dined alfresco. A hot dog and an orange constituted the breakfast menu for each member of the team.

Nevertheless, there was humor and jovial jousting among the teammates. These were African American men and forged of stern stuff, as was a quickly maturing Leroy Paige. Players recounted the uncomfortable night and the chill that had gripped them in the early morning just before the sun mercifully brought warm relief. Some joked about the experience and offered comparisons with previous adventurous outings on the road. There was nothing new about sleeping in the ballpark the night before the game. Experienced team members had done it many times before.

Paige was still not in the best of humor after his restless night sleeping under the stars. He would learn later from experience that even spending the night sleeping on your suitcase in a ballpark could be imminently better than a night in some of the hotels that accepted blacks. There were a few good, clean hotels or rooming houses owned by African Americans, but the Chattanooga Black Lookouts could not afford those. When the team did have the resources to stay at an available hotel, it was typically one of the fleabags with the inevitable "hot bed."[14]

The beds were known as such because they often supported a living menagerie of tiny bloodsucking bedbugs known throughout the black South and North as chinches. Many of the so-called hotels available to blacks in the Jim Crow South were poorly kept and infested with the opportunistic chinches that made that night miserable for the guests, who awakened the next day to a string of blistering bumps that were the uncomfortable, telltale signs that they had been dined upon while they slept. Paige experienced his first "hot bed" a month later and lamented tongue-in-cheek that "the chinches sucked me so dry that I need a transfusion."[15]

Despite having spent the night in Memphis sleeping in the ballpark, the stiff and aching muscles, and a breakfast that left stomachs growling, Paige and his teammates rose to the occasion at game time. Black ballplayers long knew that their fellow countrymen and -women were not interested in hearing of their hardships; they had enough of their own. It was all about the baseball game and the escapism that a well-played contest could provide for several hours. The fans got their money's worth, as both squads began their warm-ups with a few gags of fancy ball handing and trick catches. It was all followed by a lively game of first-rate ball featuring daring base stealing, solid fielding, and fine pitching, with Paige making his mark. Though their hometown Red Sox lost to the Lookouts, the ultimate goal was attained of a good time had by all at the ballpark.[16]

Back in Chattanooga, the Lookouts were a Sunday happening for the entire black community. The Sunday game meant everything. It brought the entire community together. It was the place to be to see and to be seen, and the young Paige enjoyed himself and came of age. Anyone who was anyone or had any pretense of being someone of importance was sure to come to the game. Singles, couples, and entire families came out to the ballpark. It was not an accident that many of the contests were scheduled to be held immediately after church services. Indeed, pastors made sure that the services would be over in time for worshipers to make it to the ballpark in time for the game. Black Chattanoogans came to the event in their best finery. The stands looked like a fashion gallery, with the patrons "dressed to the nines," as folks liked to say.[17]

The actual game was a festive affair, with many bringing their own baskets of food, others purchasing from vendors, some sporting hidden liquor flasks, and all having a great time. One might argue that the actual baseball game itself was an afterthought. It was not. Black Chattanoogans were baseball connoisseurs and followed the Lookouts religiously. The perennial doormat of the Negro Southern League, the Lookouts started looking like pennant contenders after adding a young fireballer named Leroy Paige. He was putting on a real show for the Chattanooga fans and causing nothing but trouble for opposing teams. Attendance was up at the ballpark, and he was a major reason, and he knew it.

Paige filled his days and nights away from baseball with what the town could offer a young black man on his own. It did not matter much to him that he lived in a flophouse at two dollars per week. In Chattanooga for the first time in his life he had his own room. Sometimes Paige went out in the company of Alex Herman, who had become both mentor and friend. They would "grab a bottle and go looking for dolls."[18]

Chattanooga was not the cultural center of the universe, but it possessed some venues for young Paige to explore. Chattanooga, Tennessee, a town in the shadow of Lookout Mountain, from which the baseball team took its name, made its mark as an important trade juncture for manufacturing and for coal and iron, with active Tennessee River traffic and a conveyance of railroad lines connecting it with Atlanta, Birmingham, Nashville, and Knoxville, all of which were within a circumference of 150 miles from Chattanooga. The larger circumference was linked via railroad traffic and trade-feeder routes to and from Chicago, Memphis, St. Louis, Cincinnati, Philadelphia, Charleston, Washington, New York, Jacksonville, and New Orleans. After the Civil War, many former Union troopers in addition to former Confederates settled in the area. The town continued to attract settlers from South and North. Chattanooga in 1926 and 1927 numbered approximately fifty-nine thousand individuals, of whom twenty thousand were African American.

There were places to go and people to meet for young Paige, and he relished seeing the sights. During the afternoons and early evenings, he frequented the pool halls. He was not that good at the stick game, and a couple of hustlers took advantage of his naïveté. They let him win a few games, including a few for nickels and dimes. After Paige had his confidence boosted, the hustlers suggested upping the ante. He obliged, and the sharpies then played him for real, quickly relieving him of five dollars.

He was being educated in the unkind realities of the world around him, better known as city life. Paige perfected his pool skills over the following months and gained sweet revenge over the two who had taken advantage of him earlier, winning back five dollars and a few more in the triumph. Pool had become one of his favorite pastimes. Sometimes he spent an entire day playing nothing but pool and repeated the process for a countless number of days and nights over many years. It became well known in and out of the circles of black ball that Paige was as deadly with a pool cue as he was with a baseball.

His time off the field in Chattanooga was not totally occupied with pool. He engaged in favorite activities of black Chattanoogans such as roller skating at the Stoops Rink on "colored days," promenading early-Sunday evenings on Ninth Street and on Eleventh Street just south of the Market, partaking of the Spring Festival, and going to minstrel shows and other performances at the Ivory Theatre, where he watched them from the colored section. Most of all he liked hanging out at night spots, dancing and enjoying the booze and the music. Blues was plentiful in Chattanooga's black bottom, with visits from Ma Rainey and hometown girl Bessie Smith.

The nightlife, coupled with his rising-star status on the Black Lookouts, soon brought Paige in contact with many women. A young man away from home and free of parental supervision, he made good of every opportunity to sow his wild oats. Despite the time and energy extended chasing women, late nights on the town dancing and drinking, and the endless hours playing pool, he never lost sight of his true love and commitment to his bread and butter:

baseball. The Chattanooga Black Lookouts finished the first half of the 1926 season at the top of the league for the first time in their history. A large part of that success was owed to their talented young hurler.[19]

Success bred other opportunities. With slightly more than a month left in the 1926 season, Paige jumped out of Chattanooga for the more promising, greener pastures of New Orleans and the New Orleans Black Pelicans baseball team. The Pelicans went over the top, at least in Paige's mind, when they added an old Model T to the offer. It may have been little more than a jalopy, but it was Paige's first automobile. The car meant for him something he eagerly wanted to do more of: travel on his own terms. That jalopy afforded him the freedom of the road and the opportunity to explore, a sense of real independence, a symbol of prestige, and the powerful seduction that a nineteen-year-old adventurous young man could not refuse.

Living in New Orleans, although only for the brief period of a month, opened him to an entire new world of sights and sounds that he would keep coming back to for years and the good life that he was beginning to experience with ever-increasing frequency, thanks to his improving financial status. New Orleans was the heart of the most sophisticated black cultural life in the South. The penchant for parties, celebrations, parades, Mardi Gras, great music, and great food was enough to keep the most avaricious appetite satisfied. The nightlife in the Crescent City was never-ending. From the dancing, singing, music, and bartering outdoors in Congo Square to the indoor late-night play of house bands in cabarets, barrelhouses, and bistros, the good times were everywhere in New Orleans, and young Paige absorbed them every possible moment.

The great Charles "Buddy" Bolden, Sidney Bechet, and Joe Oliver were gone from the New Orleans jazz scene when Paige arrived, but their musical legacies were everywhere. Joe Oliver's protégé, Louis Armstrong, was in his prime and wailing in the French Quarter on South Basin Street and Bourbon Street. Paige had plenty of opportunities to laugh, drink, and dance to the music of the fabulous Satchmo and his hot trumpet sounds before the musical giant pulled up stakes full-time for Chicago.

Paige took special note of Armstrong's stunting onstage. In the African American tradition of good showmanship, Armstrong kept his fans entertained, using daring trumpet solos and a bit of slapstick to spice up the performance. These were lessons quite transferable to Paige's profession as an entertainer of a different sort, but definitely an entertainer. He and Armstrong became friends, buddies, as Paige liked to say, and he often reminisced too how Armstrong loved red beans and rice and loved baseball too. Louis Armstrong sponsored his own baseball team.

Paige also became friends with the one and only Jelly Roll Morton. He enjoyed many a night listening and dancing to the music of Morton and his group, the "Red Hot Peppers." It was Jelly Roll Morton who advised him about the importance of wardrobe and invited Paige to his hotel room to tour his personal collection of fine garments. Paige was a little apprehensive. "OK, so now I'm saying to myself, I'm saying, Satch, this guy's a straight up fairy and he's going to get you up in his room and there's no telling what kind of tricks he's going to try and pull. Hell, he might even have a gun." He had nothing to worry about. Morton was completely devoted to the opposite sex and used his celebrity status to take full advantage of those desires. "So we went up to his rooms, I think he was living on Rampart Street or someplace pretty close." What he saw had him awestruck. "Lord," Paige reflected on Morton's wardrobe, "I thought I had some clothes and some shoes but when he started laying out suits and shirts and shoes on his bed, I like to fell out. I've never seen stuff like that before or since, it was like a rainbow had come in that room. He had him an orange suit and a purple suit and a damn yellow one. I mean it, yellow. Yellow as a lemon with yellow shoes and socks and suspenders to go with it."[20]

Master piano showman that he was, Jelly Roll Morton never liked to dress in the same outfit twice, particularly in a town in which he was performing. Paige and Morton often hung out together, chasing women. "And that crazy fool had women lined up four deep that wanted to go out with him just so they could be seen with him. They'd do anything he wanted them to do as long as he let them hang around."[21]

Leroy Paige was being tutored in the ancient art of man and woman. No one actually needed to tutor Paige in clothes. Ever since he joined the Lookouts, the young hurler began to dress with considerable style. After the second month with the team, and money in his pockets, he bought himself a suit and then more suits and an ample supply of brand-new shoes. While there is no record of how often Paige frequented South Basin and Bourbon Street nightspots or the Garden District, it is only reasonable to surmise that a young man in his prime, with nice clothes and money in his pocket, his own car, and in the cultural mecca of the South, would take advantage of the rich gumbo of offerings.

Paige bathed himself in African American culture and good times. He enjoyed stepping it in the "second line," a New Orleans tradition, and if that line of musicians and singers came by him on the street, he was sure to start strutting and singing along. Dancing was part and parcel of a good time anywhere and everywhere in the Crescent City. Audiences did not simply listen. In the streets or in a club, they got their dates up and on the dance floor or found them a willing partner for the moment. Paige loved to dance and took advantage of every opportunity to show off any new step or two that he had picked up or created. He mastered dance forms easily and, perhaps tongue-in-cheek, claimed that dancing kept his legs in shape for baseball. Although it is doubtful that he pursued the quick step, hully gully, black bottom, buck dances, and blues bump and grinds to keep his legs in shape, as he claimed, modern science confirms the cardiovascular benefits of dancing.

But Paige did everything in excess in New Orleans, and not just the dancing. He spent considerable time in pursuit of the opposite sex. With a population of more than three hundred thousand, New Orleans offered a great many opportunities for a young man to ravel among the fairer sex. It is likely that he spent, like many in the sporting crowd, a fair amount of his nighttime activity north of the French Quarter in the remnants of the once decadently popular Storyville, the most famous or infamous red-light district in America. Paige's extracurricular activities were exhausting.[22]

Despite his late-night follies and time spent driving and tinkering with his jalopy, he somehow managed to play brilliant baseball in New Orleans. He was the talk of the league, and Alex Herman and his former Chattanooga teammates never gave up hope of luring him back from the glitter and glamour of the Big Easy. Herman's persistence paid off as the regular season drew to a close. Paige jumped back to Chattanooga, leaving the Black Pelicans without his services in the final week of the regular season. "Those guys still probably are waiting for me to pitch that last week of ball."[23]

He rejoined the Chattanooga Black Lookouts in time to hit the road barnstorming. Despite the crummy living conditions on the road, Paige was ready to endure it. Two factors made it bearable: having his own means of transportation and a much higher salary. The Black Lookouts raised the ante to two hundred dollars per month for his services, enough for Paige to live better and to buy himself a shiny new roadster during his second year with the team.[24]

Paige was getting used to barnstorming now, and that transition was made easier by Herman's intervention. Having coaxed the rising young star back to Chattanooga from New Orleans, Herman did his best to ensure Paige's comfort on the road trips. When they were barnstorming in a town where Herman had friends or connections, he arranged for Paige to stay at the home of someone he knew.

It was a black tradition in the South to stay at the home of others when traveling. It did not have to be a relative or personal friend who opened their home to you. In an era before a wide assortment of racially accessible good hotels and motels, some enterprising black families took in overnight or weekly borders. This was usually preferable to some of the dilapidated Negro hotels that did exist in the South. It was common, though, for complete strangers to give you a place to stay. Many folks did not have much, but the generosity of the African American spirit never died, even under Jim Crow.

Paige, with the new salary, could stay at one of the better Negro hotels or rooming houses when one was available. For a rising star, some fan was always willing to offer a place to sleep and a home-cooked meal. But most of the time he stayed with his best friend of all, his automobile. Paige succumbed to the lure of the automobile like most Americans and perhaps all people. If, as some psychologists claim, the automobile is often an extension of one's personality, then Leroy Paige liked being independent and worshiped speed. His car enabled him to travel either by himself or with a teammate or friend to the next barnstorming gig and at speeds that brought him so many traffic citations that he quickly lost count.

His penchant for speeding would follow him for the rest of his life. He sped religiously and could never be counted on to back off the accelerator. On one of those occasions of blasting through a small town, he was pulled over for speeding and brought before the magistrate. He was levied a hefty fine of forty dollars. Paige reached into his pocket and presented the magistrate with eighty dollars. He was informed again that the fine was forty dollars, not eighty, to which Paige replied while handing the magistrate the eighty dollars: "I'll be coming back this way." A similar driving story was credited to Jackson Johnson, but Paige experienced it too and told the story much better. It was pure Paige who, when pulled over by police for traveling the wrong way on a one-way street, told the officer, as Buck O'Neil, who was traveling with him, confirmed, "I was only going one way." He earned another ticket, among many.[25]

The automobile enabled Paige to navigate around Jim Crow. Leroy Paige loved driving and the freedom he felt on the road with his car. Avoiding those horrid bus rides was heaven sent. His automobile was transport and motel all rolled into one. Arriving at the town for the next game, he loved to park along a lake or stream and do a little fishing. He had started keeping a rod and reel in the trunk of his car. When night fell, he stretched out in the backseat with his blanket and slept in the relative comfort and security of his beloved automobile.

Most long-distance travelers on the road during the early era of the automobile in the 1920s, and the improved roads in subsequent years, often used the car as overnight travel accommodations. You kept a blanket, packed a basket of food, and brought a jug (later a thermos) with water or something more interesting to drink, which Paige did. The great outdoors served as your bathroom facilities, and a nearby lake or pond offered the means for bathing or just freshening up. It was rustic by most contemporary standards, but it was considerably better than spending the night in a hot bed or other appalling accommodations. You were almost self-contained with your automobile, a packed lunch and drink, and nature at your beck and call. Only stopping to get gas cut into your independence. In addition, the automobile quickly established itself in the 1920s as a favorite place for sexual liaisons among young people. There were those who faulted the automobile for being a rolling bedroom and contributor to the increase in the lost of virginity by teenage girls. The car proved itself to be of infinite value to Paige in all of those capacities. It became one of his primary tools, he proudly admitted, for "picking up dolls." The car, a bottle, and a couple of ladies, and he and Herman were set for a night of good times in the Chattanooga black bottom.[26]

There was also for Paige the occasional catcall that inevitably came from some whites jealous of seeing a black man behind the wheel of his own automobile. It could be dangerous business for a black man to be caught driving a fine-looking automobile in Dixie. The road could contain man-made hazards. That possibility was one of the central reasons that Paige, like Fleetwood Walker, virtually always carried a weapon; for Paige it was usually a pistol or a rifle in the trunk of his car.

The reaction of the African American community to Paige's fancy cars was most positive. He was well aware of the symbolic importance, as his automobile attracted smiles and admiration from blacks. Seeing an automobile, especially a nice one that a black person owned, was not that common in some of the smaller towns of the South in the 1920s. Fans gathered around before and after the game to take a closer look at Paige's car, which he always parked right at the field where the game was being played. Children goggle-eyed it, and men were intrigued by the machine.

When the Black Lookouts made their road trips to Memphis, Paige was sure to avoid the team bus and go by car. Sometimes he arrived the day before the team. Other times he made it just in time for the game. Whatever the occasion, he spent extra time in Memphis, enjoying the city's special offering of good food and good music. Everyone who was anyone in the black South eventually came to or through Memphis. It was a happening place. In spite of its ongoing racial divide, the city had another side to it that black folk looking for a good time were able to tap into.

The slave trade and the trade in cotton were the foundation upon which Memphis was built. After the Civil War ended, the city's reputation as a center of antiblack sentiment and its continued exploitation of African American labor were paramount. Former Confederate general Nathan B. Forrest, who amassed his fortune as the most successful slave trader in Memphis, continued the fight for white supremacy as the founding father of the Ku Klux Klan after the Civil War. The headquarters of Forrest and the Klan was located on

Manassas Street, just across from Beale Street, which by the 1920s was the recognized Main Street of black America in the middle South.

Paige, along with countless others, enjoyed the good times on Beale Street, with its twenty-four-hour clubs, cafés, and merrymaking. There was the Palace Theatre, where he heard W. C. Handy, more of Ma Rainey and Bessie Smith, the vaudeville comedy hysterics of Butterbeans and Susie, and Memphis locals Charlie Payton, Son House, "Bukka" White, Willie Brown, Rubin Lacey, Sleepy John Estes, and the young Alberta Hunter. There was Church Park for nice strolls in the late afternoon or evening, and Dixie Amusement Park for rides, and other attractions, especially the well-known Spring Jubilee Ceremony. Both Church Park and Dixie Amusement Park catered to blacks and were the creation of arguably the South's wealthiest black man, Robert Church, who had worked on the steamboats and after the Civil War became the first black saloon owner in Memphis. He later invested in real estate and owned a considerable amount of property. He built a public park and an amusement park for blacks. The Palace Theatre was originally an auditorium that Church constructed for black performances and patrons, facts that had not escaped Paige.

What would in the 1960s be renamed Handy Park to honor the great jazz musician and Memphis resident W. C. Handy was the former Church Park where black Memphians and those just visiting, like Paige, enjoyed the facilities that Church built. The park and the auditorium were family venues. Single black men and women enjoyed them, to be sure. Those seeking more lively adventure in the after hours partook, as Paige did, of the black saloons and cafés that dotted Beale Street and earned it the reputation of the "hottest spot" between New Orleans and Chicago.[27]

The blues was great, but what dominated the Memphis scene that Paige and other more "sophisticated" folks sought out in greater numbers were the places featuring the city sounds of barrelhouse piano music. The blues had its audience, but among the well-dressed city slickers, as Paige was now seeing himself, the move was more toward the robust urban fun music that had derived from ragtime decades earlier. The piano players were the rage, and Paige adored them. He spent many a late night listening and dancing to Willie Bloom, Hooks Hatchett, and the notorious but fabulous piano player Benny Frenchy, who, it was claimed, had bested Jelly Roll Morton in more than one late-night piano burn session when the great Jelly Roll came through Memphis. Paige enjoyed the music, whether it was piano sounds, down-home blues, or a local jug band.[28]

Beyond the music scene, there is only hearsay about what Paige may have also enjoyed during his many stays in Memphis. Beale Street featured some of the best black entertainment in the world. The street also had more than its share of crime. Gambling was everywhere. Alcohol was plentiful. Cocaine was very popular and legally sold in tiny boxes for five and ten cents at local drugstores. The drug was also used in small doses in a popular soft drink out of Atlanta, Georgia, called Coca-Cola. Prostitution, a service Paige did not need, was big business, especially with white men coming into the Beale Street area, looking for the "high yella gals" of the night.[29]

Violence, which Paige luckily avoided, was also a trademark of nightlife on Beale Street. Memphis and New Orleans led the South as the two cities with the most prostitution and the largest number of homicides. Memphis had won the title of murder capital of the South by the late 1920s, averaging more than one hundred homicides per year, with most of those occurring in the black community, which was 50 percent of the Memphis population and numbered nearly seventy-five thousand in 1927. W. C. Handy lamented that on Beale Street, business never closed until somebody got killed.[30]

Alex Herman urged Paige to be careful in Memphis and in life. Their relationship, however, had soured after Paige jumped to New Orleans. Ever since his return, Herman was giving him greater space and little supervision, except for the occasional warning. Herman probably had little sway over Paige because earlier he had joined him in nights out on the town. A companion in a debauchery one night is hardly a father figure the next day.

Paige received blistering words of advice from Herman, some likely containing four letters, involving an incident with the white Chattanooga Lookouts. The incident so angered Herman that he lashed out at Paige nonstop for his naïveté. Stran Niglin, who was with the white Chattanooga Lookouts, made the young hurler an offer for him to come and pitch a game for them against the Atlanta Crackers. The only stipulation was that Paige would have to do so in whiteface. The offer was real. Niglin had seen him pitch and thought him superb. His reasoning for wanting his services, however, was twofold. He could use Paige's skill on the mound, and with him in whiteface it would surely entertain the white audience. Niglin offered Paige five hundred dollars for the game. He reasoned that the advance publicity would ensure a huge turnout and be well worth the cash outlay. When Paige innocently broached Herman for permission to pitch the game for Niglin and the white Lookouts, he was dumfounded when Herman became outraged. Paige never candidly addressed the incident and his culpability. Rather, he tended to make light of what happened. "I sure hated to pass up that five hundred dollars. And I think I'd have looked good in white-face." Herman was furious because of the racism and stereotyping behind Niglin's offer. Paige either was unaware of the embedded racial insult or chose to ignore it. To him it was just a coach's strategy to get into the game the most talented pitcher, who happened to be black. It remained a mystery to him why Herman "got as mad as anybody I've ever seen."[31]

While Leroy Paige's worldly sophistication and consciousness may have been advancing slowly, his maturation on the mound was occurring at a phenomenal pace. In less than two years with the Chattanooga Black Lookouts, he had already outgrown the team. Everyone in the Negro Southern League knew of and coveted the Lookouts' ace pitcher. It was simply a matter of time before some greater opportunity came his way.

4

Turning the Paige

It was of little surprise that the premier African American team in the South, the Birmingham Black Barons, came calling for Paige. Although the Barons had an excellent pitching staff with aces Sam Streeter and Harry Salmon, they needed a fresh arm now more than ever because of their reentry in 1927 into the more prestigious and competitive Negro National League (NNL). Paige would bolster their bullpen. This was his ultimate dream come true. The Negro National League was the "Major League" of black ball.

The new pitcher they had signed was a youngster who first impressed them in May 1926 when he held the Barons to a 5–4 defeat with blazing fastballs that kept them "on their heels the entire game." They labeled him back then "one more pain. He fanned 17 Cubans in a game last week and came back two days later to hurl in another set-to and fanned seven more." Now they sang a different tune because the Barons signed him to pitch for them. His name was Leroy Paige, but everyone was starting to call him "Satchel."[1]

At a salary offer of $275 per month, Paige was in heaven with Chattanooga. That salary would reach $450 per month with Birmingham, a sum that his former team could not think of matching. Alex Herman and his old Chattanooga squad had no choice but to let him go. To make the departure a little easier, the Black Barons paid Chattanooga a small sum as a token of compensation. That was not often done in black ball, as players routinely jumped from one team to another. Birmingham was trying to follow the wishes of former league president Rube Foster to compensate teams for signing away one of their players. Foster had hoped too to slow down the trend of jumping that left teams embittered and hostile toward one another beyond normal rivalry. The deal went through, and Paige signed into the black Majors, becoming a Birmingham Black Baron of the Negro National League. His career was on a steady upward trajectory.

Paige joined a rich tradition of black ball in Birmingham. Birmingham was a baseball town, and baseball was the major public pastime as early as the beginning of the twentieth century. Indeed, blacks began playing the sport at the first "Juneteenth" celebration commemorating Emancipation. By the Roaring Twenties the region's population topped more than three hundred thousand, with no end in sight. Birmingham sported rich deposits of coal and dolomite. Steel mills dotted Jefferson County, boasting such names as American Cast Iron Pipe Company, Stockham Valve Company, Tennessee Coal Iron and Railroad, Debardeleben, and US Steel. African Americans accounted for at least 50 percent of Birmingham's population. They were 65 percent of the workers in the mills and only slightly less abundant in the coal mines. Nicknamed the "Magic City," Birmingham was the leading industrial site of the New South, with African American labor contributing mightily to its continued growth and development.[2]

Despite the large throngs of hardworking industrial laborers, Birmingham did not support a large number of social outlets, such as cafés, saloons, and restaurants, as Paige would quickly learn. It had some, but compared to New Orleans and Memphis, it was a quiet place for him and the other ballplayers for its size and makeup. Moonshine and bootleg liquor were to be had. But much of Birmingham's social life revolved around the family and the church. This especially held true in the African American community. This may explain why single men like Paige were best members of the church if they ever hoped to meet single women. The young Paige was not a churchgoer. Those, like himself, wanting more worldly entertainment would need to seek it in Memphis or New Orleans.

Other than that there was baseball, a passion of Birminghamians of every race. Virtually every foundry, plant, and mill put together a baseball team. The industrial leagues abounded as early as 1885 with aspiring ballplayers and the many hundreds of fans who came out routinely to cheer them on at each game.

The Black Barons began in 1904, born out of their own industrial league with players from the American Cast Iron Pipe Company and Stockham such as George "Mule" Suttles, the six-foot-six, 230-pound coal miner, who became the first legendary player on the Black Barons. Whites had their industrial league and teams, and blacks had their industrial league and teams. Whites had the Birmingham Barons, and African Americans had their own professional baseball team that they dubbed the Black Barons. The two races did not play each other in baseball, given the traditions of the Jim Crow South. They did, however, attend one another's games at Rickwood Park, the oldest ballpark in America. Both the park and the white Barons were owned by coal and iron magnate Richard Woodward. Blacks attended the white Barons games in Rickwood Park in substantial numbers, often filling the designated "nigger" bleachers. Between one and two hundred whites attended games of the Birmingham Black Barons.[3]

Beyond that bit of incidental mingling at the same ball games, Birmingham, as Paige experienced, was one of the most segregated cities in the entire nation. Martin Luther King Jr. would later speak of the deepness of the racial divide in Birmingham. In addition to working in the coal and iron mills, black folk worked in white people's homes, preparing their meals, taking care of their children, and in other employment that called for interaction between the races. Nevertheless, the color line held firm on all things social, at least in public. White fear of the large black population of the city also showed itself in violence against blacks and the numerous lynchings that occurred. Always just beneath the surface was the possibility of racial violence of all sorts.

The Black Barons team and Paige navigated these racially treacherous waters in and outside of Alabama. Before the first pitch of a game the Barons were playing in Texas as part of a Juneteenth Celebration, the white owner of the other team, who was also the local sheriff and likely had a few dollars bet on the contest, spoke to Paige and the Barons in no uncertain terms about the necessary outcome of the game: "If you niggers beat my niggers, all you niggers going to jail!" Paige and his teammates refused to throw the game and won, and then quickly fled town.[4]

The most Paige or any person of African descent could hope for in the South was often no more than being left alone. Black Barons hoped for that at least at Rickwood Park. Going out to a Black Barons game could not provide escapism from the daily reality of being a person of color in the heart of Dixie. Concession stands were owned and controlled by whites, as was every other feature of Rickwood Park. White vendors typically charged more for anything that blacks purchased. Consequently, most blacks when they went to the game packed a picnic basket with refreshments from home. Bathrooms were strictly segregated, with the worst-of-the-worst facility designated for coloreds only.

Use of the stadium was exclusively on white terms. It was required that the white announcer for the white Birmingham Barons' games be used and paid to call the games for the Black Barons. "Perhaps it was feared that a black announcer might contaminate the microphone," one Black Baron surmised. At any rate, the announcement system was rather primitive at best, and the announcer spent much of his time yelling the results of the play through the ineffective amplification system. Since 1922 the announcer for the games of the white Birmingham Barons was an individual named Eugene "Bull" Connor, a racist whom Paige and his Black Barons teammates would have to endure. Connor got his nickname "Bull"—long before his brutality against civil rights demonstrators in the 1960s that earned him the reputation of arch villain of the civil rights movement—as a sports announcer known for his ability to ramble on between baseball plays and to have the bellicose power required to be heard. With Bull Connor on the mike at Black Barons games, derogatory phrases, slanderous name-calling of players comparing them to monkeys and apes and speedy baboons, and the general use of racial epithets abounded. "Today's game features two nigger teams. On this nigger team at first base you have, and so forth, was the kind of thing you heard," a former Black Barron reminisced. Paige heard "nigger pitcher" so many times that he lost count.[5]

Despite the racial slights, blacks somehow navigated around them. They lived in two worlds and, as Paige did, found solace within themselves. He as well as his teammates and the fans managed to block out the inconveniences at Rickwood Park and concentrate on the positives and beauty of the game. Not even the ramblings of a racist announcer could destroy that. The Black Barons regularly outdrew the white Barons. The black community took great pride in the team, even though it was owned by a white man, Joe Rush, and played at a white-owned park. Nevertheless, the team managers were always black, and, of course, so were the players.

Paige would find that whenever the Black Barons were playing, it was a major social occasion. A Sunday game was something to behold. The game would be scheduled for the late Sunday afternoon to coincide with the end of church services. Blacks were extra meticulous about what they wore to church on a baseball Sunday because they knew they were going directly to the ball game after the services. It was a fashionable outing, to say the least. African Americans took great pride in dressing up in whatever finery they had for the Sunday matches. One wanted to look the perfect gentleman and lady for such an important social occasion.

Paige became part of the largest single gathering of black Birminghamians—a Barons baseball game. When the Black Barons began their 1927 season, everyone who was anyone or ever hoped to be anyone was at the event. Since the opening game was on a Monday, some mills actually allowed workers to leave early. The superintendent of the city's schools, C. B. Glenn, issued Bulletin Number 43 on April 24, 1927, to "Principals of the colored schools: Permission is granted for pupils bringing requests from their parents to be excused at 2:00 o'clock on Monday, April 25, to attend the opening game of the National Negro Baseball League at Rickwood Park."[6]

Paige's first start for the Black Barons on June 27, 1927, was, however, less than auspicious. It was a baptism by fire. It was the team's first major road trip of the second half: a four-game series against the St. Louis Stars. Unlike the transition period that Paige received under Herman's tutelage with the Chattanooga Black Lookouts, manager Ruben Jones of the Barons treated him like an old pro and started him right away.

The road trip to St. Louis, Missouri, to play the St. Louis Stars proved to be an unmitigated disaster for Paige. Game 3 featured him on the mound. While he was being treated like an old pro, the reality was something quite different. Ten days short of twenty-one years of age and still green behind the ears, it was a bit daunting to be in the black Major Leagues and playing rival St. Louis in their home park. Fans did their usual booing and nagging efforts to distract the visiting team. It was in all likelihood a combination of all those factors that negatively impacted the young hurler's performance.

Whatever the causes, Paige's debut as a starter for the Barons in St. Louis was one of the worst experiences in his young career. The Barons had lost the first two games of the series, and everyone knew that they needed the third. The pressure was doubly on the young starter to deliver. Paige would in the course of his career earn the reputation of being unflappable, cool as they come, the ice man. But on this day the pressures got to him. He was wild, all over the place with his throws.

Early on in the first inning, St. Louis players were ducking and dodging for their lives as his fastballs went off course. He nailed the St. Louis starting catcher with a wild pitch that took him out of the game. Later on in the contest, with the score tied 1–1 and relief catcher Murray Mitchell up to bat, Paige had two outs and two strikes on Mitchell when an errant fastball caused Mitchell to duck but still struck him hard on the hand. The crowd had been yelling foul for some time.

Mitchell was convinced that Paige deliberately threw a beanball and went after him full throttle, with bat in hand. A woman spectator in the crowd yelled out, "Murder, murder, you don't have a weapon, you better run!" Paige took her advice and took off running toward his team's dugout. He proved in an instance that he not only possessed one of the fastest fastballs in the league, but was equally fast afoot. The pursuer, unable to gain ground on Paige and losing distance rapidly as the youngster shifted into full gear in flight for his life, flung the bat and struck him in the back.[7]

Accounts after that vary. Some claim that Paige picked up the bat and then gave chase. Others say that no such thing occurred, that Paige flew into the dugout and never came back out. What is known for sure is that the game had to be halted and calm restored. Police took the field, as both benches began to empty and it looked possible that "all hell might break out." There were shouts from the stands to "put them [the Barons] in jail" and "Black Jack them." One spectator approached a player for the Barons with a knife as the situation worsened.[8]

The umpire ruled that Paige could not finish the game as pitcher. For a moment it looked like the contest would be forfeited until manager Jones and umpire Donaldson talked things out. Jones agreed to have his team finish the game under protest. The contest continued, with St. Louis victorious, taking the fourth game as well to sweep the Black Barons. It was a disastrous road trip and a painful welcome to the black Majors for Paige.[9]

The young hurler gained headlines as a result of the embarrassment in St. Louis. It had to hurt. Paige was unused to being a laughingstock when it came to baseball. He used the hurt for motivation. Exhibiting the heart of a champion, he bounced back stronger and more determined than ever. Paige gave solid performances in all the remaining games he pitched. In a series against the Detroit Stars in early July, Barons ace pitcher Harry Salmon allowed only four hits, but those four hits were good for four runs and the Barons lost the game. The only bright spot of that road trip was in the fourth game and the performance of Paige, who in relief of the starter shut down the Detroit team for the rest of the way to take home the only win in the four-game series.

It was an up-and-down few months, but the Barons continued to win more than they lost and their young hurler, Paige, was steadily advancing as a pitcher. When the Black Barons faced off against the Kansas City Monarchs in mid-August 1927, the Barons were in first place in the National League. That game against the Monarchs may well have been the contest that separated Paige from mere good pitchers. In the first game of the doubleheader, the seasoned veteran pitcher of the Barons, Sam Streeter, was hit freely, and the team fell to defeat, 6–1. In the second contest, starting pitcher Poindexter was blasted for five runs in the first inning. With hope quickly dissipating for the Barons in the second game, Paige was summoned in relief.

The Barons and the Monarchs knew that Paige was an excellent pitcher, but this was that moment of truth that he needed to prove it against one of the finest teams in the NNL. The young hurler did not disappoint. He immediately went to work with surgical precision. Monarch players, one after another, left the plate shaking their heads in disgust and disappointment as Paige brought the fans to their feet, striking out eleven men and completely shutting down the Monarchs for the rest of the way. The Black Barons won the contest 7–5, and Leroy "Satchel" Paige won the hearts and admiration of his teammates and every lover of black ball in Birmingham. The victory gave him the boost he needed to his ego. He was not one for gloating, and he certainly did not. But he felt mighty good, especially as teammates complimented him on his performance.[10]

Back in St. Louis to face the Stars in a four-game series beginning August 20, 1927, all eyes were on both teams and remembering what happened in their last meeting. Extra police were on duty in case old wounds had not healed. The Black Barons took the opener 5–4 behind solid pitching from their old ace Harry Salmon. After that the wheels fell off the wagon. In the third game of the series on August 22, starting pitcher Poindexter gave up eight hits and five runs in the first three innings. It meant that the manager would have to go to the bullpen, and Paige was his likely choice to close.

Performing well in St. Louis after his earlier embarrassment meant something special to the young pitcher. The question was, could he do it? Paige was as determined mentally as he was physically to stay within himself and maintain his poise and concentration. The crowd booed continuously as he strolled to the mound and kept up the booing through his warm-up tosses. The St. Louis fans remembered him all too well from last time. The question was what was going on in Paige's own mind. Could he rise to the occasion? Would he be able to focus? Could he deliver pinpoint accuracy with his team trailing by five runs in the fourth inning? Was he capable of being a bona fide closer? The ball was in his hand, and so was the game.

Paige barreled down and completely halted the onslaught. He held the Stars to only one hit and struck out seven. His teammates were unable to score any more runs. The Barons fell to St. Louis that day by a score of 5–4. Although his team lost, Paige had put on a splendid performance. Thanks in no small part to his continued excellent pitching the rest of the season, the Black Barons remained in contention for the league championship.

The pitching of Salmon, Streeter, and Paige strengthened going into the home stretch. The Barons swept a solid Cubans team for three games at Rickwood Park. Salmon, in superb form that Monday afternoon, made sure the Cubans "never had a chance," with his fastball and other pitches working as well as they did. The Barons took the contest 5–1. In the second game, Paige mesmerized the fans with a sterling mound exhibition. "Paige allowed the Cubans only four widely scattered hits Tuesday and had little trouble in shutting them out. Besides letting them down with four hits, Paige struck out twelve men," the *Birmingham Reporter* served notice. Streeter brought the third game home with a 3–1 performance.[11]

Behind excellent pitching, the Birmingham Black Barons finished the 1927 season at the top of the standings and having earned the right to face the mighty Chicago American Giants for the pennant. The Chicago Giants were repeat champions and difficult to defeat. They had superb hitting with catcher Larry Brown on board. They were the odds-on favorite.

Nevertheless, black Birmingham had faith in their Barons and touted it to the heights in the press, the churches, on the streets, in barbershops, in beauty parlors, and everywhere people gathered and could chat. Whether it was over the dinner table or over a beer at one of the few saloons in Birmingham, the Black Barons and Paige were the topic of conversation and attention. The team was lauded and spoken of in reverential terms. The black press urged the community to come out for the first three games that were going to be played in Rickwood Park and to buy tickets now for what they hoped would be the fourth and final game of the seven-game series in Chicago. If luck was with the Barons, it was advised to get your tickets now and plan on spending a little bit more time in Chicago while the Barons took care of business and brought back the championship.

What was inescapable to all Birminghamians who followed baseball, and that was just about everyone, was that this team was one of the best in the history of the Black Barons. They had never been this far before in the Negro National League and the high-caliber competition synonymous with it. The Barons won the second half, and that alone was a milestone in the team's record books. Blacks were urged to come out and support this wonderful team because it represented them and "the honor of the South." The Black Barons had "come more nearly reaching their goal than any unit from this section in the history of baseball." The dynamic new pitcher Leroy "Satchel" Paige received a great deal of credit for the newfound success.[12]

Reality set in quickly for Paige and his teammates after the arrival of the Chicago American Giants in Birmingham. Chicago took the first game easily that Monday at Rickwood Park. On Tuesday the Giants won again, but Birmingham was able to take the third game. With Chicago leading two games to one, the series moved to the Giants' hometown.

Hundreds of faithful followers of the Black Barons took the special excursion cars made available and traveled to the Windy City to cheer on their team. Game 4 on Saturday, however, witnessed a similar fate, as Chicago overpowered Birmingham to move within one game of the pennant. The Black Barons played their hearts out in the fifth game that Sunday in Chicago. The Giants blasted away at Streeter, who gave up a quick four singles and a triple by Larry Brown. The rest of the rotation, including Paige, could do little to stop the Chicago juggernaut.

Paige received mention for his hitting; at least he got on base. All efforts were for not, and Chicago took the fifth and final game, 6–2, to retain the pennant and claim the right to meet the winner of the Eastern Colored League in the Negro World Series. Birmingham was still proud of its Black Barons. People praised the team in the streets of Birmingham and wrote notes of thanks to the players. To the entire team went "our thanks and the thanks of thousands of fans for the wonderful showing made during the second half." There was a feeling, however, that the Barons were afraid of the Giants and were never convinced mentally that they could defeat them. The season was over, the strengths and weaknesses of the team duly noted, with supporters urging, "Start building now and next season give to the fans of this city a winning baseball team, a team that will not shut up and quit when certain teams are met. We can have one but the time to start is now, not next spring." The team, despite the final defeat, gave Birmingham one of the best seasons on record, and a fair amount of the credit went to the additional strength in the bullpen owing to the acquisition of Paige. It was not a one-man show, but his presence made a significant difference. He won eight games during his first year with the Barons, struck out eighty, and threw three shutouts against only three loses.[13]

The celebrated young pitcher was maturing with the Barons and coming into his own. Birmingham fans looked forward to the 1928 season with great expectations. Spring training for the Barons indicated that there were problems that required attention. Paige, for one, wanted more money, as did their other ace, Harry Salmon. Paige may have been just a country boy, but he was no shrinking violet. He could add, and that addition told him that his record and the attendance at the games meant that his salary should be increased. He let the manager know he wanted the raise and wanted it now. Paige almost left the training facility because of the disagreement. The intervention of the owner of the Black Barons settled the matter to Paige's satisfaction. He received a higher salary, although the amount was kept confidential. Salmon received his increase as well.

Both Paige and Salmon were in good spirits, and it showed in their performances during the season. Although the fortunes of the Black Barons overall slid considerably from the previous year, Paige's trajectory continued upward. He and Harry Salmon were a one-two duo that left most hitters perplexed. Game after game, Salmon and Paige logged brilliant performances on the mound. Early in the season, on June 9, 1928, the Barons took a doubleheader from their nemesis, the Chicago American Giants. In the second game, Paige was on the mound and brought home the 5–3 victory.

His star rose above that of Salmon as the season progressed. The game in Detroit, Michigan, against the Detroit Stars in the heart of the season on September 15 yielded a typical Paige output. The Barons lost the first outing 4–2 to the Stars. The second game, with Paige starting, proved a different story. He completely outgunned Detroit. They could do nothing with his pitching: "Satchel Paige chucked the second game and was invincible, yielding four blows and whiffing ten of the Detroit sluggers, who proved to be lambs in the hands of the Dixie hurler. The withering fire of Paige mowed the Stars down like wheat."[14]

He finished the season with a 12-4 record, 112 strikeouts, and 3 shutouts. "Perhaps the most impressive statistic on Paige's ledger is his base on balls total," a researcher of the Black Barons recorded, "issuing only 19 free passes the entire season. It signifies terrific control, as well as maturity beyond his 22 years."[15]

The 1929 season featured much of the same. Paige captivated fans at Rickwood in the first game of the season when he struck out seven of the Cuban Stars to win the game 6–2. The Detroit Stars suffered the same fate as the previous year with Paige defeating them, this time by a score of 5–1. In that contest, Paige was in typical form, setting 17 of them down via strikeout.

Indeed, Paige established an incredible strikeout ratio of 184 strikeouts in 196 innings. He was now on most everyone's list of the finest pitchers in black baseball. His reputation preceded him to ballparks to the lament of opposing teams. In archrival St. Louis, hometown sports pundits conceded, "Birmingham is enjoying some good pitching on the part of Satchel Paige. Paige is winning quite a few games for the Slagtown nine and probably will continue his winning ways here." For a final encore at the end of the season before admiring Birmingham fans, he pitched and won both ends of a doubleheader against the Memphis Red Sox.[16]

The 1929 season had been a relatively good one financially for Paige, the Birmingham Black Barons, and the Negro National League. The league actually finished the season intact with the same teams with which it began the year. This was the first in the history of the Negro National League. NNL president Judge W. E. Hueston proudly reported that the league enjoyed its most profitable season of the past four years.

Paige's success and statue in black ball continued to grow. Other teams saw him as a hot commodity. William "Dizzy" Dismukes, the veteran pitcher of the Indianapolis ABC's, pinned several columns in the black press giving his assessment of Negro Leagues Baseball and the best players in it. In a 1929 issue of the *Pittsburgh Courier*, Dismukes published his selection for an All-Star Negro National League Team. He chose twelve players for his All-Star squad including, "Page (Satchell) [*sic*], pitcher, Birmingham." He misspelled *Paige* and *Satchel*, as did some other writers early on, but they would all soon get it right, as the young hurler from Mobile continued to dazzle audiences from the mound.[17]

Many teams began sending out subtle feelers for the young fireballer. A nice offer for Paige came from Cuba to play for the Santa Clara team. He and fellow teammate Harry Salmon ventured to the Caribbean island to play Winter League baseball there following the 1929 regular season. This began a long extended-season relationship between Paige, Latin America, and the Caribbean that endured for the rest of his career.

He played in eleven games in and outside of Havana that season with mixed performances but good paydays. The Cubans took their baseball seriously and were not pushovers. It was true too that Paige and his fellow Negro Leaguers were not necessarily going all out for each game. There were very often eating and drinking a bit too much and "chasing dolls," as Paige liked to call it. What impressed him most was how nicely he and the other black ballplayers were treated in Cuba as compared to the United States.[18]

Paige stayed in what he described as the best hotel of his young life while in Cuba. This was the Hotel Boston in Old Havana. It was not of the caliber of Cuba's finest lodging, the Hotel Nacional, but it was very nice, a midsize hotel, clean and with a courteous staff that treated Paige and the other ball-players as celebrities and catered to their every need. The food was good, too. The peas, rice, and pork were spiced just right, which truly made Paige feel at home. Jackie Robinson would stay at the same hotel in 1947 for his spring training prior to opening the season with the Dodgers. The Hotel Boston had lost much of its luster by then. Robinson's white teammates were booked into the Hotel Nacional. However, the slights that Robinson experienced in Cuba paled in comparison to the treatment he could expect in the Dodgers' traditional spring-training facility in Florida. Make no mistake about it that there were class and race lines in Cuba during Paige's era, too, the point being that Paige and company were treated well and responded to that kindness and respect. He, like most of the Negro Leaguers, felt an instant affinity for the Cuban people.[19]

What became abundantly clear to Paige while soaking in the hospitality of the island was that his skill was a commodity for which teams both in the United States and abroad were willing to pay him top dollar. When he returned to the States after winter ball, he was well rested, relaxed, and possessing a new attitude of greater self-confidence and business acumen.

The downturn in the American economy with the stock market crash of October 1929 gave him pause and a wake-up call to the need of earning every dollar his skill and reputation might fetch. In black America there had been strong signs of the coming economic collapse as early as 1927. The downward trend accelerated in 1928 and became visible in every quarter one year later. Black America fell victim to an unemployment rate twice that of white America and suffered living conditions where hand-to-mouth existence became routine. "Last hired, first fired" aptly characterized the devastating blow the Great Depression unleashed on African Americans.

The rarefied world of black professional baseball gave Paige an economic lifeline that the average black person did not have. Paige realized this and felt fortunate. At the same time, he knew that it was up to him alone to make his star status count. Those who wanted his services would have to pay as much as the market would bear. After his return to the States, Paige immediately jumped from the Black Barons to the gray pinstripes of the Baltimore Black Sox at the beginning of the 1930 season.[20]

The twenty-three-year-old seasoned hurler arrived on the East Coast with much fanfare. "Cannon Ball Redding and others of days gone by had plenty of speed," the black press announced, "but Frank Wickware, speed ball artist from Coffeyville, Kansas, was recognized as the king until Leroy (Satchel) Paige arrived on the scene with his fastball." Paige proved to be an important drawing card, as attendance at Baltimore Black Sox games increased at least 25 percent, despite the steadily worsening Great Depression.[21]

He did not disappoint, mowing down East Coast teams with the same relative ease that he did back home. The press sang his praises: "Satchel has been breezing his fastball past batters in the Negro National League for five years. This spring the elongated Alabamian tried his speed against the eastern swatters and compiled a nice winning average." Paige amassed an official record of 3-1 as a starter, but he contributed to many more victories to the team coming off the bench in relief.[22]

His stay in Baltimore lasted a mere three months before he jumped back to Birmingham with the promise of better pay. Hope sprang eternal in Baltimore that Paige would jump back that season to help them in their upcoming series against the formidable Homestead Grays. "Satchel [sic] Paige, ace hurler, who jumped the club several weeks ago, has signified his intentions of returning," it was announced. The added strength of him to the lineup made it easy to think that the "prospects of the Black Sox for the remainder of the season are unusually bright."[23]

The Pittsburgh press too thought that Baltimore's chances were extremely good, since the team was coming into town with "the finest array of twirlers" that the Grays would be meeting all year, especially with the announcement of Black Sox management that Paige would be throwing for Baltimore. "Satchel's work does not need any comment," the *Courier* concluded. The claim of Baltimore's management that Paige would be pitching for them proved to be premature. The hurler's understanding of the business of pro ball, and how to take advantage of it, was growing. The final contractual relations could not be agreed upon, and Paige declined the offer to jump again. He felt something for Baltimore's needs, but he had needs too and this was business. The Grays topped the Paige-less Black Sox later that week in both ends of a doubleheader.[24]

Jumping back to the Birmingham Black Barons in 1930, Paige's final year with the Barons was a respectable eleven, or possibly twelve, wins against four defeats. The number of innings he pitched, however, was far higher. Fans were, in increasing numbers, coming to the games just to get a glimpse of him in action. In order not to disappoint, the Barons began using Paige for a few innings on almost every occasion to satisfy the crowds. He entertained the spectators with great pitching and the drama he often provided by coming through in the clutch. Game after game, it was Paige to the rescue. His star status was taking off in Birmingham, and countless others were getting on the Satchel Paige bandwagon. An ever-increasing list of teams throughout the Negro Leagues coveted the sensational fireballer, and Paige knew it. The question was, how long could even the well-respected Birmingham Black Barons hold on to their ace before he jumped again and perhaps permanently?

5

Blackballing the Great Depression

How to survive the worst economic catastrophe in the history of the United States of America, and much of the world, occupied the thoughts and actions of most Americans during the 1930s. This, however, was a period of steady advancement for Satchel Paige. Even the Great Depression could not curtail the new Negro movement and the vestiges of the black Renaissance and the spirited African American cultural life to which Paige contributed. He put it this way: "Like most people, I won't forget 1929. 'Course most will remember it because that's the year the stock market crashed, but for me 1929 was the year Ol' Satch's stock just started going up and up. It got so I'd pitch so many games every year I couldn't count them. Tell the truth, I pitched more than twenty-five hundred games, I guess. I even threw 153 in one year. And I guess I've had more than a hundred no-hitters, but I just tell people it's a hundred." Paige rode his stardom through the mouth of the Great Depression, feeding his hungry fans the soothing elixir of baseball on some of the greatest stages imaginable. He offered a service that on any day of the week provided relief, joy, and excitement.[1]

The stresses and strains of economic disaster were everywhere. The coal, iron, and steel mills of Birmingham drastically scaled back their output. Thousands of workers were laid off. Some mines closed. Others reduced their workforce by as much as 60 percent. Already at the bottom of the economic ladder, fewer and fewer African Americans in Birmingham could afford the price of the ticket to attend a baseball game. Reducing the price of admission to a Black Barons game to as little as twenty-five cents could not stop the slide in attendance owing to the Great Depression.

Paige could read the handwriting on the wall. Every player was taking a cut in salary. The next question would be whether the team could actually meet its payroll. Paige decided not to stay for the final act. On April 29, 1931, he jumped to Tom Wilson's Cleveland Cubs.

Paige did not disappoint Cleveland. Even when he lost a game, it was usually highly entertaining. Take the case in point of the doubleheader between Cleveland and the Detroit Stars on June 28, 1931. Paige pitched the second game of a road-trip doubleheader in which he was the primary reason that the four thousand spectators came to rented Tiger Stadium. He put on a marvelous pitching performance, as did Willie Powell for hometown Detroit. The only score came in the fourth inning, when the heralded Norman "Turkey" Stearnes, playing for the Stars, broke up the pitching duel between Paige and Powell with a solid blast for a home run off of a Paige pitch.

The Detroit faithful went wild. Paige stayed cool and did not give up another score for the rest of the day. Neither could his teammates score. The contest ended 1–0, with Powell getting the win and those in attendance treated to an excellent game of baseball. Paige hated defeat, but he and the other players were working and earning a living, a reality becoming more difficult for an increasing number of Americans, especially blacks.[2]

The escapism that a good game of baseball provided, however, was temporary. Wilson spoke openly about the problems facing the team and the season. Paige heard every word, as did his teammates. He kept his thoughts to himself, but he was thinking hard about what the alternatives might be. Only a few months into the first season, Wilson and his Cubs organization were wondering how long they could last. Thirty-five percent of black Clevelanders were unemployed, another 18 percent underemployed, and the numbers were getting worse as the summer of 1931 approached. Attendance at Cubs ball games began dropping despite Paige's presence.

Paige's survival instincts led him to make the best out of every opportunity. He took temporary jumps from the Cubs to the Homestead Grays for a game or two, to the Nashville Elite Giants, to the Baltimore Black Sox, and hosts of semipro teams for a game or more or just a few innings. He hustled nonstop to make ends meet during these steadily worsening times as "fastballer for hire" to the highest bidder. Only halfway through his first season in Cleveland, the Pittsburgh Crawfords, one of the few teams that could possibly hope to pay Satchel Paige's tab in a distressed national economy and struggling Negro Leagues Baseball circuit, bought his contract from the fading Cubs for a mere $250. There were those who criticized Paige for his decision to leave the Cubs and accused him of having no team loyalty. Bill Gibson of the *Baltimore Afro-American* wrote, "Paige has deserted about every team he has ever played with, packing his grip and leaving without notice." Notice had been given, and no matter what anyone thought or said, Paige bailed out of Cleveland for Pittsburgh just in time. He was not going to linger on the vine with what was clear to him was a dying enterprise. As he saw it, it was about business and survival. The following year the Cubs succumbed to the Great Depression, and Wilson's Elite Giants moved back to Nashville, with intermittent shifts of the franchise between there and the Washington, DC, area.[3]

Pittsburgh suffered under the yoke of the Great Depression like everywhere else. The Steel City's black population numbered slightly more than fifty thousand in 1931, one-third of whom were unemployed. Although its black population was smaller than that of Cleveland's, they were rabid baseball enthusiasts. The community came out for baseball, especially in support of their perennial champions: Cum Posey's Homestead Grays.

Others sought the spotlight too and the influence that came with it. The chief challenger to direct the spotlight away from Posey and the Grays and onto himself was William "Gus" Greenlee, also known as "Big Red," owner of the Crawford Grill and the leading bootlegger and numbers runner in black Pittsburgh.

Several times members of a sandlot baseball squad known as the Crawfords beckoned him to assume sponsorship of the team. He did more than that. Greenlee took ownership of the team in 1930 and immediately set out to make it the best black ball club in town. While the team had improved its hitting capacity, everyone in and out of baseball understood that to be a championship-caliber team, you had to have superior pitching to reverse the first two season losses to the Grays.

Greenlee concurred with the *Courier*'s admonition that to be successful against the Grays called for significant strengthening of the bullpen. He concluded that he had to find a closer, a pitcher good enough to halt the onslaught of the talented sluggers for the Grays. "Superior pitching," Greenlee preached at the Crawford Grill to listening patrons, "wins every time over superior hitting." He sent word for a new pitcher to pack his satchel and come to Pittsburgh. He sent for Satchel Paige.[4]

The Cleveland Cubs' loss was the Pittsburgh Crawfords' ultimate gain. Paige gassed up his reliable Packard and filled the trunk and passenger interior to capacity with his belongings for the permanent move to Pittsburgh. The fastballer for hire hit the road and drove the 135 miles to Pittsburgh nonstop, which did not take him that long, given his penchant for driving at speeds that may have equaled his hundred-mile-an-hour fastball.

He reduced it to cruise speed as he arrived at his destination, riding into town like a scene from a Tom Mix western and parked right in front of the

Crawford Grill, where he dismounted and went inside looking for the owner. He and Greenlee met and immediately hit it off. They chatted, ate, and drank for hours while a Greenlee assistant toted Paige's belongings to the Grill's third floor, where temporary accommodations had been made ready for him. Every person who came into the restaurant that day was introduced to the new star pitcher for the Crawfords.

On Saturday afternoon, August 1, 1931, the Crawfords met the Grays for their third showdown. The ballpark was not the best facility in the world, to put it mildly. The grounds were unkempt, the base lines were faded and hard to judge, and dips and ridges punctuated the playing field. The seating capacity was inadequate, and many spectators brought their own lawn chairs with them to ensure a degree of comfort.

Despite the inconveniences, this was a game that everyone in black Pittsburgh wanted to see. The Grays were ready to go, and Ted "Double Duty" Radcliffe seemed as confident as ever that his team would reign supreme over the new pitcher for the Crawfords. Radcliffe knew his old friend's ability on the mound but also knew that winning the game was a team effort. He and the Grays believed, as did most spectators, that the Crawfords had a ways to go before reaching the point where they could take the full measure of the Grays with or without the heralded new addition to the bullpen.

The Crawfords, however, came to play. The team was pumped up and trash-talking before the contest began. It was easy to see that there was new life in the Crawfords and that they were not afraid of their much-touted opponents. Sure enough, the first two innings were all Crawfords, and the team jumped out to a 7–2 lead over the stunned Grays.

It was after that point that the wheels fell off the wagon, and the starting pitcher for the Crawfords, Harry Kincannon, quickly began to fade against the heavy hitters of the Grays. By the end of the third inning, the score was tied 7–7, with the momentum overwhelmingly on the side of the Grays. It was time to do something.

Paige was given the nod to warm up and that he would start the fourth inning with the mighty task of stopping the hemorrhage or at least slowing it down. Some of the spectators had already begun to shout: "Satchel! Satchel! Satchel!" They could see that he was getting ready and in all likelihood would come out at the start of the fourth. Paige, for his part, seemed relaxed and at peace within himself as he took easy throws to get the muscles limbered up to answer the call.

When the Crawfords took the field for the start of the fourth, Paige began his slow, relaxed stride to the mound. You could hear some of the fans laughing at his effortless gate and seemingly slow-motion stride. Some thought that

Paige was making a mockery of the situation. He was not. Neither was he playing Stepin Fetchit.

He took his time on most occasions to get to the mound, taking deliberate slow and easy strides as if in no hurry to meet his opponent. Those who knew Paige said that he did it on purpose to save his energy, while others said that the slow, methodical walk helped to throw off the batters' timing. Still others said he did it to entertain the crowd with a little light vaudeville. At any rate, hitters seemed almost hypnotized by his slow pace and perhaps expected the ball to come across the plate in similar slow motion.

Paige also knew that the game could not start until the pitcher was there to make things happen. He was a student of psychology in that regard, playing both the fans and, most important, the hitters. Relaxed, seemingly impervious to the cheers and jeers, he began his incessant trash talk, telling the next hitter up that he would soon be going back after three fastballs struck him out. Those fans who heard the exchange of words enjoyed the signifying.[5]

In reality, this was Paige's moment of truth. He was facing the championship Homestead Grays with the game on the line. There was no room for error as he worked against the talented Grays' batters. This was what a later generation of sports fans would call the Michael Jordan moment. With the game on the line and all eyes focused on the star, the question was whether he could deliver, if he could make the miracle happen.

Paige stopped the Grays dead in their tracks. Not one of them could squeeze out a hit from that point forward. His Crawfords teammates came through with three additional runs off of his old friend Ted Radcliffe, retiring him from the game. "Mr. Paige was masterful," a Grays believer grudgingly admitted. The Crawfords jumped with joy as they beat the mighty Grays for the first time. Fans lauded the game as "a 10 to 7 thriller." The *Pittsburgh Courier* gave this as its headline: "Paige Stops Grays as Crawfords Cop, 10 to 7."[6]

The Crawfords' defeat of the Grays was the topic of nonstop conversation throughout black Pittsburgh for the coming weeks. In those discussions one name was repeated over and again, that of Leroy "Satchel" Paige. He was branded as the man who finally stopped the mighty Grays and made Gus Greenlee's dream come true. Paige did what a true star does. He delivered the great performance when called upon. Harold Tinker, manager for the Crawfords, recounted Paige's exploits that day: "He was mowing those guys down like mad. He was throwing nothing but aspirin tablets—fastballs." Double Duty Radcliffe said:

> there was nothing you could do with those fireballs he was throwing up there. We all experienced the same thing. You can't hit what you can't see. At

least I didn't make a fool of myself. When it was my turn at bat, I had already made up my mind that I was not going to swing. Satchel wasn't going to make me look like a damn fool swinging at nothing but air. I stood there with the bat on my shoulder and took it like a man. One, two, three, and I was out. It was over quick and I set my ass down.[7]

When Paige arrived later that night at the Crawford Grill, he reportedly strolled nonchalantly through the door, commanding everyone's attention as he made his entrance. Spontaneous applause broke out as he attempted to make his way to the table that awaited him. He did not make it there for an hour or more. One grateful patron after another greeted him with handshakes and pats on the back. They wanted to touch him and offer their individual salutations to the man of the hour. The adulation continued, and everyone knew who it was for. If you somehow did not know, the person next to you was bound to tell you that was Satchel. There were offers to buy him a drink, but that was not necessary. Drinks were on the house, courtesy of a beaming Gus Greenlee. It was likely that more than one round (legal or otherwise) was consumed courtesy of the Crawfords' proud owner. Paige was the center of attention for the rest of the evening.

Paige was twenty-five years of age and riding high in 1931 despite the economic uncertainty throughout the nation. Cum Posey saluted his talents and named the rival ace to his "Posey's All-America Ball Club" at the conclusion of the season. The year also ushered in another conquest for Paige, one that he had his eye on from the moment that he first arrived in Pittsburgh and set foot in the Crawford Grill.[8]

Her name was Janet Howard, a walnut-brown-colored petite beauty who worked behind the counter at the Grill. Paige began sweet-talking her the moment he laid eyes on her, which was often, since he took most of his meals at the Grill. Howard usually served him his food and drink, and he incessantly joked with her, always leaving a generous tip.

Janet Howard was in no way flirtatious. Born in Pittsburgh on January 18, 1913, the eighteen-year-old was reared conservatively in a black middle-class family. Her father, George Howard, was the son of a Baptist minister, and her mother, Luella Howard, stayed at home and focused on rearing her three daughters properly. That mother Luella did not work outside of the home was made possible because of George Howard's job as a postal clerk, a much-sought-after position, relatively speaking, in the black community. Janet was the eldest of the siblings. Her sister Bernice was one year her junior, and youngest sister Amy trailed by five years. Education was stressed in the Howard household. All three girls attended high school, and it was hoped that they would go on to college.

The Great Depression abruptly ended the family's dream of higher education for the children. Moreover, when George Howard lost his job at the post office a year before the stock market crash of 1929, the family's fortune and the relationship between husband and wife became stressed and soured. Luella and George divorced in 1930, and he left for New York City, where he found work as a Pullman porter. He continued to send money back to the family in Pittsburgh when he could.

To make ends meet, Luella took in borders at the family's home on Chestnut Avenue. When Janet graduated from high school, she immediately sought employment rather than college, and it was Gus Greenlee who, impressed with her tenacity, manners, intelligence, and good looks, hired her onto the staff at the Crawford Grill. She had been working there less than a year when Paige walked into the Grill and into her life. The two were soon inseparable.

Paige now had a good woman constantly at his side, perhaps too constantly. Wherever he went in Pittsburgh, Janet tended to be with him. "I was out on the streets whenever I could," Paige confessed, "but Janet kept pretty close watch on me. A gal who got her eye on a man got ways of keeping him so busy he never gets out enough for another gal to get him. But I was a tough one to hold." He could "cut loose" when on the road, but back in Pittsburgh, it was him and Janet.[9]

Satchel Paige gained such instant celebrity status in black Pittsburgh that he often drew crowds when walking down the street. He heard constantly, "Good afternoon Mr. Paige," "How are you Satchel?" "My man Paige!" and "How are we going to do against such-and-such team this Sunday?" In Paige's words, "The whole town was glad to see me. I'd walk down the streets in Pittsburgh and everybody tried to talk to me." When he went in every two weeks for his haircut at the Crystal Barbershop, on Wylie Avenue, across the street from the Crawford Grill, he quickly drew all eyes and was the center of attention and conversation. He patiently waited his turn like everyone else, but the establishment's owner, Woogie Harris, cut Paige's hair himself with his prominent patron seated in chair number one, closest to the window. Paige easily spent from three to five hours at the Crystal for his haircut, fielding questions, entertaining everyone with stories, joking, lying, and having a good time talking baseball with the guys. He was becoming a master storyteller. He was always careful to know his audience, though, and whenever there was a sprinkling of young boys there to get their haircuts along with their fathers, he kept the stories clean, as did most everyone else. It was not uncommon for Harris to send someone over to the Grill to bring back soda pop and cracklings or some pickled pigs feet to treat the customers and keep the conversation going.[10]

Those conversations inevitably turned to the crowning glory that Greenlee promised with the start of the 1932 season and the grand opening of Greenlee

Park on Friday, May 6, 1932. Greenlee paid one hundred thousand dollars for land and construction of the new stadium, an especially tidy sum in the midst of the Depression, and the first black-owned venue of its kind in the North. Greenlee built the park to ensure a proper facility to showcase his team, host games and other major events, and also, as he liked to say, demonstrate racial pride and the ability of his people to own and operate business ventures of their own.

There was no doubt, when the starting lineup was announced, whom the Crawfords would have on the mound against the New York Black Yankees on that all-important opening day in the new facility. Paige drew the assignment to face Yankees ace Jesse Hubbard in the big game. No expense was spared in promoting the big event. The *Pittsburgh Courier* carried ads in every issue for two months prior to the opening. Black Pittsburgh could not wait to see the new facility and the new incarnation of the Crawfords.[11]

It was a splendid turnout, with four thousand fans in attendance. They bristled with excitement as the two teams filed in behind a twenty-five-piece marching band and took their position at the flagpole in deep center field, where Old Glory was raised to the tune of the national anthem. Robert Vann, editor of the *Pittsburgh Courier,* gave a short address and then asked Gus Greenlee to stand and be recognized for his civic pride, leadership, and contribution to the community.

After the thunderous applause died down, it quickly rose up again as each Crawfords player was introduced. Insiders questioned whether Janet was at the game. She was there, of course, and catching the attention of many, as she was dressed to the nines and stood out among the well-dressed fans with her new white chiffon dress, accented by matching white-satin high heels, wide-brimmed flowing silk-laced white hat, and arm's-length white gloves. The game, many thought, was in the bag because Paige was always better with Janet in attendance.

The only question was whether the game could live up to all of the hype. The visiting Black Yankees led off. The Crawfords faithful broke into wild applause again when their home team took the field. The ovation grew only louder as Satchel Paige strolled out last to take his position on the mound. The stadium was filled with laughter and giddiness as he finally arrived at his destination. Fans yelled out, "Satchel is the man!"[12]

The first three batters for the Yankees confirmed that he was going to be at his best, as he struck them out in order to the deafening roar of the crowd as he leisurely strolled back from the mound with the first half of the first inning in his pocket. Jesse Hubbard took the mound for the Black Yankees and responded in kind, striking the first three Crawfords out in order.

The two aces kept on repeating this with only a slight break in the routine with a rare pop-up or even rarer hit. The game went on this way until the ninth inning. In the top of the ninth the Yankees put a dent in Paige's superb performance when, with the bases loaded, a hit scored Ted Page. Paige reached down deep, regained his composure, and retired the side. It was now up to his teammates in the bottom of the ninth to get that run back and to bring home a victory. Hubbard had other things in mind, as he bored down against the Crawfords in their desperate effort to regain momentum and to score. Oscar Charleston hit a mighty blow that sent the right fielder scrambling to make the play for the out.

It was Josh Gibson's turn at bat. Many of the Crawfords fans stood up, yelling now for Gibson to "do something!" When Gibson smashed a solid shot deep to center field, it looked like their wishes would be answered, only to have the ball fall a tiny bit short of a home run and caught to retire Gibson, end the game, and save the victory for Hubbard.[13]

Fans pulling for the Crawfords were instantly deflated. They were terribly disappointed at the 1–0 outcome, of course, but no one felt that they had not witnessed a great game of baseball. No one seemed to blame Paige for the defeat. He gave up only six hits and one run in the contest. Jesse Hubbard, however, bested him that day, giving up only three hits and no runs. "And while the New York hurler got the better of the argument with Satchel Paige," the *Courier* reported, "the local rifleman had nothing to be ashamed of the manner in which he retired the Gotham hitters. The breaks of the game were in favor of the visitors and that just about tells the story of the brilliant game."[14]

Nevertheless, Paige did not like losing. "Satchel was something else when he lost," Buck O'Neil recalled. "If you were on his team, you knew to stay a long, long way away from him. He did not take to losing. You did not want to be around him if he got beat. No sir." Paige did not sulk or shout or curse. His pain was deeper than that. He was not a good loser. Although it is true that he did not explode and throw his glove, kick over chairs, or let loose with other shenanigans, it burned at him internally. He took defeat personally.[15]

Paige experienced many sweet victories that invigorated his heart that season. Winning made him feel complete. The one thing that continued to gnaw away at him was the defeat he suffered opening day at the hands of the New York Black Yankees. He pitched well despite that earlier setback, but that loss made him a man with a mission that could be settled only when the two teams met again.

That opportunity presented itself eight days after his twenty-sixth birthday, on July 15, 1932. It was a scheduled doubleheader Friday afternoon at Greenlee Park against the Black Yankees. Fans flocked to the stadium to see the eventful showdown and whether Paige would be able to exact his revenge against his nemesis from New York. Double Duty Radcliffe, now teamed up with his hometown friend, pitched for the Crawfords in the first game of the doubleheader, which the Black Yankees took 9–7. In many respects everyone knew that game was a prelude for the second half of the doubleheader.

The second game was what the energized crowd came to see. All of the talk during the previous weeks had been about Satchel Paige getting his chance for retribution against the Yankees. Despite the defeat the Yankees had given them in the first outing, when the Crawfords took the field at the beginning of the second game, they were greeted with reinvigorated applause.

The applause rose to new heights as Paige deliberately lumbered last to take his place center stage. Everyone knew who was pitching for the Crawfords, but when the public announcement system blasted the obvious that Satchel Paige was now pitching for the Pittsburgh Crawfords, the stadium rocked again with applause, cheers, laughter, and shouts in tribute to their man on the mound. He performed his usual animated warm-ups to catcher Ted Radcliffe, who showed again why journalist Damon Runyon called him "Double Duty." After pitching in the first game, Radcliffe was now catching for Paige in the second. The Crawford faithful laughed as Paige performed, getting ready for the eventual showdown against Yankee hitters.

When the first batter took his stance, Paige cut out all showboating and got down to the business of serious pitching. "I knew the Yanks were in big trouble from that first that Satchel threw me," Double Duty Radcliffe reminisced about the game. "His delivery was so smooth and the ball came with such speed on the money that I knew right away he had it. And that the hitter knew it too 'cause all he caught was air and strikes." Double Duty Radcliffe was a master trash-talker in his own right and loved telling each Yankee hitter who came up to bat: "Now why you want to insult Satchel like that by bringing a bat to the plate!"[16]

Perhaps fans sensed this too, because there was no question about it that Paige was in the zone. He was relaxed, confident, fluent in his movements, and deadly accurate. It was at the start of the seventh inning that people were starting to talk about the possibility of the near impossible, a pitcher's dream—a no-hitter—because no one at that point had gotten a hit off him.

There was dead silence at Greenlee Park during his last windup and final toss of the final inning. When the umpire bellowed out those anxiously awaited words of "Strike three, you're out," Greenlee Park erupted with such jubilance that those unfortunate enough not to be at the game reportedly heard the crowd's blast a half mile from the stadium. Teammates rushed Paige on the field; exuberant fans had to be held back from rushing him and joining the celebration at the mound. Headlines in the black press told the story all over the nation during the days that followed. In a full-body photo of Leroy Satchel Paige that took more than half the length of the sports page of the *Courier,* the headline boldly proclaimed: "NO-HIT, NO-RUN HERO."[17]

Paige's career in black ball continued to skyrocket. "By 1933 I'd hit my full stride," he said, "which is a pretty long step when you figure the size of my legs." But he was not quite at the epitome of excellence and recognition in black ball. Negro Leagues Baseball was rich with talented players in every position and whose illustrious careers spanned many years and ballparks throughout the nation. Paige was still an up-and-coming star among stars. This point was driven home to him when the balloting for the first East-West All-Star Game at the end of the 1933 season was tallied.[18]

The new East-West All-Star Game was the brilliant brainchild of three leading race men of Negro Leagues Baseball: Gus Greenlee, Robert Cole of the Chicago American Giants, and Tom Wilson of the Nashville Elite Giants. Greenlee played the leading role and put up the lion's share of the initial financing. The three men envisioned the best players from the West against those from the East in a major public showdown each year in Chicago's Comiskey Park. Starting with the first year of the contest, it was a tremendous success, with the East-West All-Star Game easily outdrawing the white Major Leaguers. The makeup of the teams would be dependent solely upon public balloting through African American newspapers.

Many, including sport pundits, assumed that the talented and flamboyant Satchel Paige was a shoo-in for the first All-Star contest. In fact, there were those who gave the East All-Stars a chance only if Satchel Paige pitched for them. Paige was one of the few pitchers who those in the know believed had a reasonable possibility of defeating the great pitching in the West, especially that of the legendary Willie Foster of the Chicago Giants. Articles were written comparing Paige to Foster and to other greats in the West such as the Kansas City Monarchs' Wilber "Bullet Joe" Rogan. The betting on the big game was reported as even odds if Foster and Paige started.

Indeed, Paige's performance for the year was extraordinary. He pitched in thirty-five starts that year and amassed the amazing record of thirty-one wins with only four defeats. Nevertheless, the public decided who would constitute the All-Star teams, and there were many names of long-standing contributors to the game with whom Paige would have to contend and overtake to be selected. Once the final ballots were tallied, Willie Foster headed the list of pitchers for the West, with a total of 40,637 votes. Satchel Paige led the balloting early on for the top spot as pitcher for the East, with slightly more than 1,500 votes. But by the time of the final count just days before the start of the All-Star Game, he was third in balloting for the East's selection of pitchers. Sam Streeter of the Crawfords pulled in the most votes, with 28,989. George

Britt of the Homestead Grays came in second, with 26,716 votes. Paige tallied 23,089 ballots in his favor.

Although he did not lead the vote getters, he was technically voted on the All-Star team. There is little doubt that Streeter at this point and time had a larger following than Paige. He had been around many more years and was a better-known quantity in the Midwest and to readers of the *Chicago Defender*. Paige was quickly gaining national stature, but was not quite there yet.

He likely saw his vote total as a slight. It was untrue when he later claimed that he had been passed over for the first All-Star Game: "I'd given up on that All-Star game by the time the regular 1933 season ended. The Negro Leagues had their first All-Star game in 1933, just like the Major Leaguers. But I hadn't been in that first game. I was new around the league then and I guess that's why they didn't name me, even if I was one of the top hands around."[19]

That first East-West All-Star Game went on without him on September 10, 1933, in Chicago's Comiskey Park. An enthusiastic crowd of 19,568 braved an early downpour and defied the Great Depression to see the pick of the East's baseball players battle the pick of the West in the much-publicized game of games. The outcome of the contest was settled early on behind the splendid pitching of Willie Foster. Sam Streeter for the East was unable to tame the bats of Mule Suttles, Double Duty Radcliffe, and Larry Brown for the West. The final score of 11–7 told the story.

Supporters of the West contended that they could have completely shut out the East if all the best players who were selected to the West All-Star squad had accepted the offer and played. Supporters of the East made similar arguments, especially lamenting that Satchel Paige did not play. "They say Pitcher Page [*sic*], string bean twirler, would have held the West after Streeter went out," reported the *Defender*. Even if he had received first place in the balloting for the East, he was not around to participate in the All-Star Game. Paige had jumped in late August to a semipro team in Bismarck, North Dakota, following the lure of higher pay for his services.[20]

It was money that lured him away from the Crawfords before the end of the 1933 regular season, and it was money that would lure him back to Pittsburgh the following year. It was a year that would prove to be his best season ever, a year to be remembered in baseball annals whether of the Negro Leagues or the Majors.

Indicative of the year to come, Paige began the training season on fire. He and Josh Gibson led the Crawfords to victory in the opening of the training season down in Louisiana against the Monroe Monarchs on April 5 by a score of 6–4. Paige was unbeatable during spring training and continued his winning ways right into the regular season.

The Crawfords' ace was on a roll. Whether supporters or foes, spectators flocked to witness Paige's magic on the mound. He seemed invincible. When there was even a hint of faltering, his great teammates came to the rescue on cue. Paige's pitching was solid in the four-game series at Greenlee Park against the Bacharach Giants of Atlantic City. He won the first game of the series 8–2, giving the Crawfords confidence and momentum. It was the fantastic play of his teammates, however, especially that of Cool Papa Bell, Vic Harris, Judy Johnson, Oscar Charleston, and Josh Gibson, that carried the day. The Crawfords took the first three games of the series behind spectacular hitting and fielding. In the fourth and final game on Monday night, they trailed the Bacharach 2–1, with two outs in the last of the ninth inning, when Josh Gibson came to bat. With one on base and the game on the line, the incredible Gibson delivered with a thunderous blast into the stands, scoring two runs and giving the Crawfords the dramatic last-minute victory, and clean sweep of the visitors, to the deafening cheers of Pittsburgh's satiated supporters. Black Pittsburgh could not ask for much more than what Josh Gibson gave them that day in June.[21]

However, Satchel Paige gave them one better on the Fourth of July. The city embraced the national holiday of independence despite the continuing challenges of the Great Depression and cascading numbers of unemployed, especially in the African American community. In search of relief, if only momentary, a record-breaking throng of ten thousand spectators filed into Greenlee Park on that holiday Wednesday to see the Crawfords play host to their cross-town rival Homestead Grays in a doubleheader. Massive fireworks were promised between games.

Those in attendance would be treated to fireworks of a different sort in the form of one Satchel Paige in a display of pitching brilliance that kept everyone glued to his every move on the mound. The earlier announcement that Paige would pitch the first game accounted for, in large part, the record-setting audience. Excitement had been building for weeks and was in full blossom the day of the contest. Paige was ready to pitch a great game, and with such an enthusiastic crowd behind him, he was motivated to deliver. During warm-ups he entertained fans with his familiar windmill windups and exaggerated high-kick pitches that spectators seemed to never tire of. He was in his element, and confidence exuded from the very first pitch. Except for an occasional curveball that he used as a "waste ball," those in attendance swore that Paige threw every pitch more than one hundred miles per hour. The Grays fell like wheat as he mowed down seventeen of them on his way to a no-hit performance. The Grays had never suffered a no-hitter. Paige put himself in elite company with his stellar performance that afternoon in Pittsburgh.[22]

Had the 1934 season ended for him that Fourth of July, it would have been a storybook conclusion. A greater test awaited Paige as the season's end drew near. The East-West All-Star Game promised to provide a national spotlight for him and all the other greats of the game. This time he vowed to participate if voted in. "I went to sleep on last year's game," Paige said, "but if the public votes me in the Eastern All-Star lineup this year, I'll be there, on time, and ready to work. I believe the East-West Game is the best idea ever tried out to improve Negro baseball."[23]

The second East-West classic was set for Sunday, August 26, 1934, in Chicago's Comiskey Park. The East-West game was by far the best financial hope for the always-struggling Negro Leagues Baseball during the hard times of the era. The many supporters of black ball around the nation were most interested in the showcase event because it brought together all of the best players in the sport at one time, in one place. It promised to be a monster afternoon of first-rate baseball entertainment.

Finally, game day arrived. It was a perfect day for baseball, with not a cloud in the sky. The first All-Star Game in 1933 had to compete against a deluge that cut into attendance. The weather this time was on the side of the classic, and the fans showed their appreciation. The crowd kept coming, and when the final tally was taken, more than thirty thousand had shown up to witness the battle. This was the largest number in history at that point to witness a black sporting event.

The lineup excited everyone, offering the opportunity to see the very best against the very best in America's national pastime—baseball. Two names, however, were bandied about more than any others: Willie Foster and Satchel Paige. Everyone knew, or thought they did, that Foster was to start for the West and Paige for the East. That was the thinking right up until the time to play ball. Instead, both managers, Lundy and Malarcher, decided to keep their super aces in reserve for the final stretch. The strategy was to get two or perhaps three superb innings out of each pitcher before going to a fresh arm. The strategy made sense, given the quality of the competition and availability of talented hurlers for both sides beyond just Foster and Paige.

The East was the visiting team and first at bat. Superb pitching and equally fine fielding retired the East All-Stars with no hits and no runs. The West's turn at bat produced much the same, with fine pitching and fielding on the part of the East's All-Stars, retiring the westerners with no runs and no hits. The second inning was a repeat of the first, as was the third.

In the fourth inning, manager Malarcher decided to go with a fresh arm against the eastern sluggers and sent in Chet Brewer to replaced Ted Trent on the mound. Gibson singled in the inning, and Double Duty Radcliffe made a fine pickup and threw Harris out. Those were the highlights of the inning that ended with no runs and one hit for the East.

Lundy's thinking was similar to that of Malarcher, and he replaced Slim Jones on the mound with Harry Kincannon to start the fourth. The highlight of the inning saw Mule Suttles hit a tall fly ball into short center; the ball sailed between the two defensive players for a triple. Throughout the fifth inning the ball game stood at 0–0, with only a few scattered hits. The pitching and fielding thus far were things of beauty to behold.

But in the West's half of the sixth inning, Kincannon showed signs of tiring. Wells got a solid two-base hit off him. With no outs, Lundy was worried that momentum was swinging to the side of the West All-Stars. He made a decision then and there to snatch the pitcher and to go with his closer. He walked to the mound and graciously accepted the ball from Kincannon, who received sincere acknowledgment from the crowd for his fine two innings of pitching. Lundy sent the signal for his ultimate ace to take the mound. He called for Paige.

The setting was perfect for a hero or an absolute flop. The game was on the line, with the most dangerous entourage of West hitters coming up next. With Wells on second and nobody out, Lundy figured he needed his very best out there. Paige had been biding his time, occasionally warming up between signing programs and autographing balls for admirers, while keeping one eye on what was happening on the field. Now his number had been called to put a halt to the West's drive for victory.

The game stood at 0–0 as he began his slow, methodical stride to the mound. More than one West supporter let loose with the thinking of the moment: "It's Paige. There goes the ballgame!" The East's supporters were hopeful that the sentiment was correct. Although largely outnumbered that day at Comiskey Park, the eastern faithful cheered and applauded with the enthusiasm and vigor that made their numbers seem far larger than they were. It was a thunderous ovation filled with hope that Satchel Paige could take them the rest of the way to victory.[24]

They were yelling and screaming as Paige circled the mound one time as if to claim the territory. He positioned himself in perfect silhouette at the top of the mound, his cap pulled low to shade his eyes, his glove resting on his left knee, which was perched forward. His right arm hung limp at his side and the ball motionless at the tip of the fingers.

After a few warm-up pitches, he was ready to go. The crowd continued to roar as he began his patented double-windmill windup for the first pitch against the first West All-Star at bat, his old childhood friend and former teammate Double Duty Radcliffe. Paige was a notorious trash-talker, and he did not make the All-Star Game an exception. He talked stuff continuously to his old buddy Radcliffe, telling him, "Duty, it's my time and I'm going to have to stop you. You know me when I've made up my mind. That's the way it's going to have to be. You might be an old friend, and we will still be friends when it's over. I hope you won't be angry 'cause I'm going have to strike you out."[25]

Radcliffe talked trash too. He told his old chum on the mound, "I am sorry for what I have to do to you today. I am not going to go down to your little fastball or anything else. I will be knocking it down the line, and you can talk to me when I am on base." There was tension in Radcliffe's words. As he recalled, "The problem was I had never gotten more than one or two hits off of Satchel in my whole life. It wasn't that I was afraid of his fastball. Problem was you couldn't see it. You can't time it. But I was determined this time I was going down swinging, and I felt I had as good a chance of laying something on the ball as anybody. I wanted to win as bad as Satchel."[26]

Paige did his patented double-windmill windup and let loose with, of all things, a wide curveball that Radcliffe swung at and missed for strike one. "I said, I be damn! Where the hell did you get a curveball from?" Radcliffe shouted out, "Throw me another one!" Paige replied that he had all kinds of other pitches as well. "You know, through most of his early years Satchel only had a fastball. It was a hell of a fastball, but that was the only pitch he really had. But I guess he started to put some other ones together. He fooled me with that first pitch," Radcliffe said.[27]

Perhaps Double Duty Radcliffe began to believe that Paige had an arsenal of different pitches that he was about to see for the first time. The second throw was an all too familiar one. It was a fastball so blistering that one reporter claimed, "It cut through the ozone." It was strike two, and he had Radcliffe on his heels. Paige was talking trash about how he would "have to get you now, Homey. Have to get you." "And he got me too," Radcliffe lamented. "It was another fastball. This one down the middle. At least I went out swinging. But I was behind it [the ball] for strike three. My friend Satch."[28]

Next up was the ever-dangerous Turkey Stearnes. Paige went at him with a combination of pitches, keeping them low and to the outside, until finally forcing Stearnes to foul out to Crutchfield in right field. Next up was none other than the great Mule Suttles. Paige continued to talk trash; Suttles replied in kind. Then Paige let loose with a blistering fastball that nipped the inside corner for the first strike. He was telling Suttles, in no uncertain terms, that he was master of the mound and would take him down. Suttles was not one to back off. Paige finally forced him to hit a pop-up to Crutchfield to retire the side. The crowd went wild. Satchel Paige had stepped into the mouth of the tiger and pulled three of his biggest teeth. He had just stopped one of the toughest trios in the history of Negro Leagues Baseball.

The drama heightened in the seventh inning as the West's manager, Malarcher, went to his bench to bring in his ultimate ace to put a halt to any new momentum that the East might have behind what Paige had just done in the bottom of the sixth. Malarcher called upon none other than Willie Foster to start the seventh inning.

The fans, West and East, now had what they had always wanted. There had been much speculation about whether it would happen. It had. The show was on. It was now Foster versus Paige like everyone wanted. The best two aces were going head-to-head in the primo stage of fiercely fought black ball that stood at 0–0 going into the last three innings. Everyone was on the edge of their seats. The excitement was so thick that it made it hard for spectators to take their eyes off the field for even a moment for fear of missing the one play that could bring victory or defeat.

Foster lived up to the billing in the seventh inning and mowed down the East All-Stars for no runs and no hits. Paige gave a repeat performance in the bottom of the seventh, striking out the feared Larry Brown and closing down the West with no runs and no hits. At the start of the eighth inning, Foster seemed to be working on all cylinders until he momentarily lost control and sent Cool Papa Bell to base on balls. In that one slip, he had allowed the fastest man in baseball to get on base. That was always a red flag to Bell to try to steal, which he did. Bell stole second as Perkins hit for Crutchfield and struck out.

When Oscar Charleston popped up deep to Mule Suttles, Bell tagged up and then turned on the afterburners to blast his way home. A hard throw was made to home plate, but Bell was already across it for the score when the ball arrived behind him. The East now led the dogfight 1–0 as they headed into the West's half of the eighth.

Paige did not let up and was able to halt them for another inning in the bank. Foster started the ninth inning on the mound for the West and was able to close the East down for no further damage. The West had one last chance going into their half of the bottom of the ninth against Paige on the mound. No one in the stadium dared blink. All eyes were on Satchel Paige.

First up was the always dangerous Turkey Stearnes. Paige showed him nothing but blistering fastballs and struck him out. Mule Suttles came next and was able to get a hit to first. The next batter, however, hit into a double play to end the inning and the game. It was all over.

The East All-Star team cleared the bench and rushed the mound, surrounding, patting, and hugging the hero of the game, Satchel Paige. The press dubbed him immediately after his performance "Sir Satchel." Paige could barely walk back to the dugout, with teammates slapping his hands, arms, and back, grabbing and tugging at him in salutation all the way. Comiskey Park rocked with a standing ovation for Paige, the roaring melody of cheers and whistles seemingly unending. Even diehard West supporters gave the great one their salute. This had been a fabulous ball game. Both teams played with splendid ability and daring, but no one exceeded the play of the hero on the mound.[29]

In most minds the question had once and for all been answered as to who was the very best pitcher in all of black baseball. His name was Leroy "Satchel" Paige. The headlines recounted the compelling story, proclaiming the heroics of Paige in the East's victory over the West in what was dubbed one of the most dramatic games of baseball in the history of the sport.

It was a tremendously well-played contest that in the end witnessed the two most heralded pitchers in the game go at each other for the right to claim the supremacy of the mound. In the end, the young man from Mobile, Alabama, had succeeded to the throne as the very best hurler in the land.

The press echoed the sentiment: "Speedballer Satchel Paige Ambled into East-West Game and Simply Stole the Show," "Paige Bests Foster in Great Mound Duel," "We Saw a Baseball Epic Unfold Itself on This Historic Field This Afternoon," "One of the Greatest Mound Exhibitions Modern Baseball Has Ever Seen," "Satch Stops Big Bad Men of West Team," "Satchel to the Rescue," "Satchel Lived Up to His Reputation," "Paige's Pitching Saves Day," "Satchel Was Out There Today," "The Zero Hour in This Battle of Pitchers Came Early in the Sixth," "Satchel Paige Had 'Em Striking Out Like a Labor Union Leader," "It's Satchel Paige and Goodbye Ball Game," "You Saw Pitching Like You Have Never Seen It," "East Beats West in 1–0 Thriller," "Willie Foster Loses Contest with S. Paige," and "Sir Satchel Was the Master of the Situation."[30]

The impact of the East-West All-Star Game of 1934 punctuated the resiliency of black baseball in an era of hard times and infused new life and euphoria into everyone associated with the sport. Chicago itself was in a state of ecstasy and held several other huge events earlier in the week that fed nicely into the All-Star Game weekend. Coming off of the World's Fair just one year prior, the city's black population was back to a fever pitch because of the miraculous All-Star Game and everything surrounding it. Entertainment overflowed in the Windy City around the game. After the final out, fans and players took to the streets in celebration.

Paige celebrated with the best of them. He and the East All-Star team hit virtually every club and nightspot Chicago had to offer, and the City of Broad Shoulders had a never-ending list of possibilities. They strutted down the mecca streets of black Chicago, which were, according to music impresario William Samuels, Thirty-Fifth, Thirty-Ninth, Forty-Second, and Forty-Seventh Streets.[31]

The Grand Terrace Café was first on the list for a sumptuous meal for Paige with some of his All-Star teammates and in the accompaniment of his girlfriend, Janet Howard, who made the trip to be with him. They danced at the Grand Terrace Café to the joyous music of Earl Hines and his orchestra. Ever since he opened there in 1928, Hines had been headlining the club whenever back in Chicago.

Satchel Paige was a superb dancer of all styles, and he cut a rug with the best of them on the dance floor with his lady love. The West All-Stars may have lost the big game, but they, too, were at the Grand Terrace Café, enjoying themselves despite the defeat. Other stars of the African American entertainment world could be found there as well.

Paige's good friend, famed tap dancer, and star of stage and screen Bill "Bojangles" Robinson was in town with his wife, and the two couples were seen at several of Chicago's famed black nightspots having a good time. Robinson arrived in Chicago that Saturday to support the "O, Sing a New Song" pageant, a national audition to showcase African American talent from all over the country in the aftermath of the World's Fair. The auditions culminated with a mega performance in Soldier Field, with Satchel Paige and Janet Howard among the sixty thousand in attendance.[32]

Robinson was also there to see the East-West All-Star Game. He was a great lover of baseball and always enjoyed watching Paige pitch, even when it was against his own team. Robinson and Paige had become buddies two years earlier when the Crawfords ventured to New York to play against the Black Yankees, a team of which Robinson was part owner. The two were connoisseurs of the Harlem Renaissance and frequently made the rounds together when Paige was in New York. They often got together at the Crawford Grill whenever the Yankees played in Pittsburgh or when Robinson was traveling that way.

The Paige and Robinson couples were spotted on the Windy City's South Side at the Rendezvous Club, at 5039 Indiana Avenue, drinking, dancing, and enjoying themselves. Paige took the floor with his lady love, showing off tasteful new dance steps. The rage was the Lindy Hop, and Satchel Paige was a master of the sensuous Harlem original jazz dance that combined swing with a variation of Charleston and a little bit of tap to up-tempo polyrhythms and syncopated big-band sounds. He loved that dance and was taking center stage on the floor, with Janet doing her best to keep up with him. Folks knew it was Satchel Paige, and he took the spotlight, so to speak, in a room full of African Americans who were able dancers in their own right. He would have stolen the show except for one factor: he was on the dance floor at the same time as Bill "Bojangles" Robinson. If there was anyone who had a higher profile than Satchel Paige, it was Mr. Bojangles, whom everyone recognized from coast to coast and everywhere in between. He had just made another new movie with child star Shirley Temple, whose warmhearted films were megahits throughout the depression era.

Bojangles Robinson started dancing, and everyone knew to surrender the dance floor. He cut loose with his version of the Lindy Hop. Indeed, there were those who thought that the King of Harlem may well have originated the dance himself. If he had not, he certainly took ownership of it and the dance floor. Everyone stepped aside as Robinson did his thing. Satchel Paige was no fool. He relinquished center floor and joined in the circle of spectators, with all attention miles removed from any hard times and every eye on Robinson as he put on an impromptu dancing clinic for black Chicago. Even the band, which was great to begin with, played with new vigor with Bojangles Robinson dancing to their music. Paige and Janet, like everyone else, were all smiles and giggles and clapping to the beat as they concentrated on the Bill "Bojangles" Robinson show. When their friend concluded with a touch of fancy soft-shoe, the room broke into thunderous applause. Yes, Satchel Paige was a fantastic dancer. But everyone, including him, was second best when Mr. Bojangles danced.[33]

The Paige and Robinson couples also caught Duke Ellington and his big band, fresh back from a European tour, in concert at Chicago's Washington Park at the conclusion of the Bud Billiken Parade. They followed that evening with a brief stop for some more dancing to the music of Don Redman and his group and finished the night off in laugher to the comedy routine of Red and Struggle; the next night both stars and their companions evidently buzzed past the famed Pekin Theater, deciding, instead, on some dancing at the Savoy Ballroom on Forty-Seventh Street and South Parkway to the foot-stomping, syncopated rhythms of Cab Calloway and his orchestra. For their final night in the Windy City, Satchel Paige, Bojangles Robinson, and their entourage took in a performance of Jack Ellis and his Wildcats Orchestra along with Johnnie Long's Roaming Troubadours and the famous Tramp Band before heading back to the East Coast. The Paige and Robinson entourage had a glorious time imbibing the post-East-West All-Star Game cultural milieu of black Chicago.[34]

Janet Howard, for one, had fallen in love with Chicago's black Renaissance and New Negro attitude and what the Windy City offered people of color. All had a joyous culmination to a spectacular All-Star week of activities, thanks, in no small part, to Paige's heroics on the mound in the game of games.

Paige had the world in a jug and the cork in his hand. Everything seemed perfect. He received a hero's welcome back in Pittsburgh wherever he went. When he walked into the Crawford Grill, the whole place reverberated with the name Satchel. Pats on the back and the many other glad-handing accolades and toasts signaled his triumphant return.

On the home front, his girlfriend, Janet, congratulated him in her own special way. But she was now asking more of their relationship. Janet knew only too well of her man's "wandering" ways and had no doubt witnessed signs of it even when they were together in Chicago. Paige loved women and women loved him. He reaped all the perks of a star athlete, especially when on the road. What Janet wanted most now was permanency and commitment, and she made it plainly clear that it was about time that he settled down. She wanted to get married.[35]

Paige was not keen on the idea and had previously eluded the question many times. This time Janet was set on getting an affirmative answer. They discussed it in some depth, with Paige expressing doubts about her ability to live with a man who would be traveling constantly. Janet, thinking that marriage would end his wandering, argued passionately in her belief that wedlock could solve all things.

There is little doubt that Paige was riding high from his great victory at the All-Star Game. The postgame euphoria may not have been the only reason he decided to go forward with the idea of marriage. He was at the apex of his game and Janet more beautiful to him than ever. The timing, circumstances, caring for one another, and many other unknown intangibles drove them to embrace and pledge themselves to each other.

The date for the nuptials was set for October 26 of that year, with Janet handling all the details. Gus Greenlee was extremely glad when he heard news that his number-one ace was about to settle down permanently. This could also mean for Greenlee that he might have more control over Paige. Perhaps he would be less likely to jump to another team once committed to a wife and family.

Just prior to the date of the wedding, Greenlee and Paige agreed upon a new contract, and the Alabama ace signed his name on the dotted line for an undisclosed amount. Many in the know believe it was the highest amount paid to any player in Negro Leagues Baseball. Whether it was actually one thousand dollars a month or less, it put Satchel Paige in rarefied company. No other player earned as much as the young man from Mobile, including Josh Gibson, Oscar Charleston, Judy Johnson, or Willie Foster in Chicago.

Greenlee felt that Paige was worth every cent because he was a winner. "With Satchel on the mound, they always figured that the game was in the bag," Greenlee boasted. He likened Paige to the fighter he owned, John Henry Lewis, who he believed would be the next light heavyweight boxing champion of the world, and to a rising star in the heavyweight division whom he wished he had a piece of and believed would soon be heavyweight boxing champion of the world, a fighter named Joe Louis. Greenlee was correct on both predictions.[36]

The Great Depression seemed to fade in Satchel Paige's mind. Indeed, he would later say that he had barely noticed the Depression. After all, he was making a salary far above that garnered by professional blacks and most whites during this period of hard times. He was, to be sure, basically a one-man franchise: king of the All-Star Game, prince of the gate, the magnet man of the turnstiles in attracting ticket-buying spectators to the ballpark. He was Sir Satchel.

On Friday, October 26, 1934, the Crawford Grill was all decked out in honor of the wedding of Leroy Paige and Janet Howard. Gus Greenlee reportedly spent a considerable amount of money in hosting the event. The Grill was closed to the public for the wedding. The invitation-only guest list dined on shrimp, oysters, ham and chicken, fancy breads, luscious cakes, and an endless supply of legal booze since the repeal of the Volstead Act a year earlier. A band provided live music. The wedding was beautifully done, and everyone had a great time.

They were married, with Bill "Bojangles" Robinson serving as Satchel Paige's best man. Janet's mother was in attendance, but neither Lula Paige nor any of the Paige family relatives attended the wedding. Leroy Paige continued to send his mother money each month and would do so and fully support her for the rest of her life. Nevertheless, his trips to Mobile to visit the family became less frequent over time, and the distance between him and most other family members expanded beyond miles. After the wedding, the two newlyweds slipped away for a few days to themselves before returning to Pittsburgh to begin their new lives as Mr. and Mrs.

Upon their return, the couple was in for a rude awakening, a reality check that confirmed that both had miscalculated one of the major necessities of wedlock. "After that honeymoon," Paige recounted in his memoirs, "I started noticing a powerful lightness in my hip pocket. Married life was a mighty expensive thing and those paychecks of mine just weren't going as far as they used to." As a single man, Paige lived from gig to gig with little thought of recurring expenses or the cost of maintaining a household. He had somehow remained insulated from some of the worst aspects of the Great Depression in that he always had a relatively substantial amount of money in his pockets thanks to black baseball and his pitching talent.[37]

Now he was really beginning to understand and appreciate that these were tough times. After all, the nation was in the grips of massive unemployment. The drain of his new economic responsibilities drove the point home to him. Moreover, African Americans continued to suffer under the double yoke of Jim Crow that barred Paige and other blacks from equality of opportunity such as playing in the Major Leagues and failed to provide them with equal protection under the law.

In Paige's home state of Alabama raged one of the most blatant miscarriages of justice and due process in the twentieth century, the Scottsboro case, in which nine black boys were falsely accused of the rape of two young white women in Scottsboro, Alabama, and the black youths sentenced to death. Fund drives took place on the East Coast and in the Midwest to support the retrials of the young boys. Blacks and sympathetic whites in the North rallied to support the nine. During the entire week of the All-Star Game, black social and political groups in the Windy City conducted fund drives to aid in the defense of the Scottsboro Boys.

Paige's good friend Bill "Bojangles" Robinson was a firm supporter of the boys and gave money and time to their cause. Robinson was well known for taking an active role in local and national civil rights cases, especially when it involved youngsters.

Understandably, given his own youthful experiences, Paige had a warm spot in his heart for any miscarriage of justice against young people as well. He and the other black ballplayers deplored the violation of human and civil rights and contributed money in support of the Scottsboro Boys. According to Double Duty Radcliffe and John "Buck" O'Neil, all the black ballplayers contributed something to help the fight in Scottsboro, especially since most of the players were originally from the South and understood the problems in Dixie only too well.[38]

On October 27, 1934, the day after Leroy Paige and Janet Howard were wed, one of the vilest lynchings in recorded history took place. It occurred in Buck O'Neil's home state of Florida, in the town of Greenwood, where a mob tortured, murdered, mutilated, and dismembered a black man named Claude Neal and then led a massive public celebration afterward. The NAACP's Walter White condemned the Neal lynching as "one of the most brutal crimes ever committed by a mob."[39]

The dilemma of being black in America, East, West, South, or North, was exacerbated during the era of the Great Depression. In Chicago, where Paige ruled supreme in his great East-West triumph and enjoyed the city's vast amenities before and after the game, black folk were in a fierce tug-of-war for diminishing resources and dwindling jobs. Unemployment of blacks in the Windy City topped 40 percent. Spontaneous racial clashes broke out. Carter G. Woodson, W. E. B. Du Bois, A. Philip Randolph, Mary McLeod Bethune, and Robert Abbott, among others, wrote and spoke of the national economic struggle that was being played out in every section of the country, including the richest city in the Midwest.[40]

Paige was not alone in his newfound financial woes. Neither was his boss, Gus Greenlee, immune. When Paige approached him for a raise, he found that Greenlee too was suffering and turned him down flat. Indeed, it is likely that the Crawfords, despite the team's success on the baseball diamond, was not a profitable enterprise.

Gus Greenlee may well have been carrying the squad from the resources of his other business enterprises. There were political advantages for Greenlee as owner of the popular team and other positive intangibles hard to equate financially, including his evident love of the game of baseball. The baseball team fed his public persona, his ego, and his soul. It was his numbers racket and the Crawford Grill, however, that turned the major profits for him, but these too were straining as the Depression deepened.

He told his heralded hurler no to his request for an advance and a higher salary, reminding him that only a few days earlier, he had signed a new two-year contract that he expected him to honor. Greenlee's emphatic no angered his ace pitcher, who either failed to understand or did not believe that financial constraints and worries gnawed away at his employer. The pitching sensation was learning the hard way that his celebrity status did have limitations, given the times.

Paige made the decision that his personal economic well-being and that of his family must be his top priority. Team loyalty was important to him, or so he proclaimed. Loyalty to Gus Greenlee was important to him, too, he said— but! Since Negro League contracts were generally considered not worth the paper they were written on, Paige ignored his for the open market as fastballer for hire. The best offer came from the West. He was not in the same situation as the tens of thousands of displaced farmers and laborers who were going out West in search of employment as a result of falling produce prices, droughts, foreclosures, and plant closings, but the promise of better opportunities in the West called him back to that region of the country again and again.[41]

6

How the West Was Won

Paige took his baseball pitching talent and high-riding celebrity status on the road, selling his services to the highest bidders. He moved from place to place and team to team, wherever they showed him the money. Playing out West in interracial contests against whites, browns, and various ethnic and religious groups, Paige became much more than just a baseball player. He became a baseball ambassador for improved race relations. It was not his life's work to break down the barriers of Jim Crow as much as it was his drive and determination to be the best at what he did. Through his prowess on the mound he attracted huge audiences of baseball fans of every race and ethnicity who awed at his ability. Paige was becoming the flash point at which the lie of black inferiority and white superiority collided for all to see. He was symbol and substance all rolled into one, and they loved him out West.

He donned the uniform of Tom Wilson's Philadelphia Giants, a team composed of all-stars from throughout black baseball. The team played primarily in the California Winter League. The California Winter League dated back to 1899 and consisted primarily of teams in San Francisco and Los Angeles. The Southern California area soon won out and became the host arena for league play. What made the California Winter League so unique was that it permitted interracial baseball competition, something strictly forbidden in the South and many other regions of the United States. The league boasted various ethnic teams: white, black, Hispanic, Native American, and Japanese. This is not to suggest that the teams themselves were integrated.

On numerous occasions you found a black or Hispanic player on one of the other ethnic groups' teams. Blacks and whites on the same team, however, was strictly taboo.

Despite the interdiction of Kenesaw Mountain Landis, commissioner of Major League Baseball, whom Paige and other Negro Leaguers never liked, in an effort to thwart the interracial baseball games in 1927, coupled with the challenges of the Great Depression, the California Winter League survived. The Joe Pirrone (white) all-stars versus Tom Wilson's (black) all-stars was the hottest ticket in town whenever the two teams met.

In 1931 Tom Wilson added a new pitcher to the illustrious roster of his Philadelphia Giants Negro All-Star Team: Satchel Paige, a promising hot pitcher who was already gaining a reputation for attracting fans to the ballpark. The Philadelphia Giants rolled through the Winter League that season with Paige leading the way on the mound. They were undefeated November 6 when they took on the White King Soapsters in a doubleheader at White Sox Park. The White King Soapsters became victim number six and seven, with Paige leading the way in the first game, striking out ten of them. These victories were making Paige feel very good about himself; better still, he was making money.

He topped that performance on December 2 in what many called "the greatest game ever played at White Sox Park." The Philadelphia Giants led the league with fourteen wins against one loss when Paige took on Lefty Nielsen and the Planters of San Diego in what became a fantastic pitching duel that kept the spectators on the edge of their seats, with neither pitcher giving up a base on balls. Nielsen struck out five of the Philadelphia Giants. Paige answered the call and struck out thirteen of the Planters. The Giants scored the only run of the game in an early inning when the catcher for the Planters, with lightning-fast Cool Papa Bell at bat, missed the ball. In the brief time that it took him to retrieve it, Bell sprinted safely to first base. Bell then proceeded to steal second. When Vic Harris singled to right, the fleet-footed Bell scored from second base. At the end of the contest, the racially mixed crowd of several thousand cheered its appreciation of a well-played game of thrilling baseball that featured the clutch hitting of Harris, the incredible base running of Cool Papa Bell, and the one-hit scoreless mound work of Paige.[1]

The first season for Paige in the California Winter League could not have gone much better. He enjoyed the competition, the racial climate, and the pay. Despite his first-year success in the league, Paige kept his celebrity status well in check. There is no question that there were players who were envious of his spotlight role. Nevertheless, any animosity was put aside in the name of making a living and the good common sense of not antagonizing your key drawing card, which Paige was and he knew it. Amazingly, you could not find one person who said that the talented hurler had let success go to his head. He maintained the self-control that they had taught him at Mount Meigs. He was just one of the guys and always eager to have a good time with his teammates. That attitude kept him in good stead with his fellow ballplayers. The fact too that he often reached into his own pocket to pay for drinks helped him come across as more down-to-earth and made him even more likable. Only he knew if he was doing it out of good cheer or to win favors. It certainly worked. He was immensely popular.

Before the season was over, others were vying for his services. Abe Saperstein, owner and manager of basketball's Harlem Globetrotters and a major investor in and promoter of black ball, announced in February 1932 a proposed baseball tour of the South in March with his newly acquired Rube Foster Memorial Giants, under the management of Jim Brown, the famous catcher for the late Rube Foster. Saperstein confirmed rumors that overtures were being made to the top players of Negro Leagues Baseball to join the tour, which included Satchel Paige.

At the end of the 1932 regular season, Page was back in uniform in Los Angeles on November 4, pitching a two-hit, eleven-strikeout victory over Joe Pirrone's white all-stars for Tom Wilson's black All-Star Nashville Elite Giants. Wilson frequently changed the name of his touring all-star team that he entered in the California Winter League. His lineup of all-stars varied as well, depending upon who was available and most likely to draw fans, which meant that he always wanted Satchel Paige on the roster.

Paige was a perennial all-star selection, as were his winning ways. He amassed an incredible record each year, rarely losing more than two games during the entire Winter League season. On Sunday, December 22, 1932, in White Sox Park, Paige pitched the first game of what was listed as an iron-man doubleheader.

He was a crowd pleaser taking his deliberate walk to the mound, with his exaggerated windups and incessant trash-talking. In what proved to be a tug-of-war game that day with the Pirrone all-star team made up of some Major Leaguers and Triple-A white ballplayers, Paige created a sensation by striking out his lucky number of thirteen hitters. His team took the opening showdown, 5–3.

The second game was an African American versus Mexican American contest, with Paige and team pitted against the El Paso Mexicans, which attracted a large contingent of the Chicano population. The Chicano team was not really from El Paso, but they chose the name nevertheless. It was a team composed primarily of Mexican ballplayers from the Los Angeles area.

Baseball was very popular among Mexican Americans in Southern California during the 1930s and 1940s. There were also teams composed of native Mexicans that came up from Mexico City to play in the league. Sometimes the games between African American and Mexican and Mexican American teams were full of racial tension and animosity. Most of the time the two groups got along famously, with Paige leading the way as goodwill ambassador.[2]

There were those Mexican players who played on teams with blacks. Jess Guerrero suited up frequently for the Los Angeles Colored Giants and took great pride in having played in the California Winter League. He also played against the Los Angeles Nippons, a Japanese American team, and against the German Institute team, which was a team actually composed of Native Americans, and, on several occasions, Guerrero competed against Paige and his all-star compatriots. The black all-stars coasted to easy victories over their brown opponents due to the gap in baseball experience and quality of play. In years to come that discrepancy would be overcome.

Paige enjoyed nothing more than the contests against Mexican and Mexican American teams, not because they were easy opponents but because of the rich ethnic ambience. He relished the opportunity to mingle. Paige spent much of the game against El Paso, for example, on the sidelines, chatting with admirers, signing autographs, and overindulging in Mexican food from some of the ethnic street vendors working the crowd selling spicy tamales, tacos, and other goodies that he proclaimed to onlookers as among his favorite dishes.[3]

The Mexican community, like so many other groups on the West Coast, quickly fell in love with Paige. He possessed a special combination: he was a great ballplayer, a showman on the field, a master storyteller off the field, easily approachable, and not self-possessed of his own importance, with a personality and sense of humor that made anyone of any race or background warm up to him. Whether Paige's star status translated into romantic involvements is a matter of speculation. It seems highly unlikely that he went celibate during those long temperate months in friendly Los Angeles and the San Francisco Bay Area. There is no doubt that he appreciated the ethnic beauty surrounding him and would in later years be involved with a Hispanic woman.

Opposing teams and their supporters found it very difficult to dislike the ace from the Negro Leagues, because both sides made more money with Paige headlining. He was a favorite of blacks, whites, and browns as he barnstormed with his teammates throughout California, playing games against the local nines in virtually every part of the state. When Paige and his all-star teammates took on the celebrated Reds in Modesto, California, at Roosevelt Field, he promised to strike out the first twelve batters, and did so to the astonishment of the spectators, winning their respect for his great moundsmanship. The locals complimented him for being a great hurler and a first-rate guy.[4]

Pirrone did not make it easy for Paige and the Wilson All-Stars to loom supreme whenever they met in competition. A fiercely fought contest was promised and usually delivered. Pirrone did everything in his power to put together an all-star group of white players that could stop the Negro Leagues stars, especially after he saw again and again what Paige could do. That sort of challenge seemed not to bother Paige. Indeed, he relished it.

Pirrone recruited Major League pitcher Louis Norman Newsom of the St. Louis Browns to turn the tide. Buck Newsom was a venerable force, a show-man in his own right, a braggart, trash-talker, and seasoned Major League starting pitcher. Newsom would anchor the Pirrone All-Stars against Paige and the Wilson All-Stars in a showdown scheduled for the early evening of Thursday, November 9, 1933.

Paige knew full well that whenever he went up against a white opponent, most folks were making comparisons. For him it was an opportunity each time to prove that he was just as good as any white man. That kind of talk was frequent among Negro Leagues ballplayers off the field and among African Americans who saw the color line in baseball as one of the most visible sym-bols of their badge of second-class citizenship and alleged racial inferiority. When Paige won against the Major Leaguers, he not only triumphed at base-ball but also struck a blow in support of the African American cry for equal opportunity.

No one was disappointed in the game that evening. Buck Newsom and Satchel Paige put on a spirited pitching battle. In the end, however, it was all Paige, who struck out thirteen to lead his team to an 11–3 triumph. White Sox Park glowed with excitement and a thunderous approval of the mound magic that Paige displayed. He could hardly get out of the park. The adulation expressed was overwhelming. Some spectators talked about putting his name forward for mayor, while others suggested he could run the entire state. On a more realistic level, there was overwhelming sentiment that something spe-cial needed to be done to recognize this one-of-a-kind player.[5]

Wilson and Pirrone seized the opportunity as good businessmen. The fol-lowing morning it was announced that plans were under way for a "Satchel Paige Day" at White Sox Park later in November, at which time the beloved ace would be presented with gifts from the management and from the pub-lic. Paige, to the community's way of thinking and that of baseball enthusiasts throughout much of the Golden State, deserved the special recognition. The *Los Angeles Times* paid tribute to him for having won the heart of Southern California baseball. In North Dakota, the *Bismarck Tribune* reported in its November 22, 1933, edition: "Los Angeles Wild over Satchel Paige; Smoke-Baller Throws Spell over City."[6]

One can only imagine Paige's reaction when he was informed of the plans to honor him with his own special day. He had to be thrilled beyond belief. There was no doubt that "Satchel Paige Day" was also a marketing tool being used to sell tickets. Nevertheless, it was a positive gesture for all concerned and a fine tribute to the anointed superstar of California Winter League baseball.[7]

When Satchel Paige Day came in Los Angeles on Sunday, November 12, 1933, it was memorable for two compelling reasons: this was the first time for Paige being honored with his own special day of recognition, and he and his teammates would have to prove themselves against one of the best pitchers from Major League Baseball. If there were any thoughts that Joe Pirrone figured on making Satchel Paige Day a cakewalk for Paige, nothing could have been further from the truth. Taking the mound for the Pirrone All-Stars was southpaw Larry French of the Pittsburgh Pirates. On his own very special day Paige was being called upon to once more prove his greatness in an ultimate test against the best of the white Major Leaguers.[8]

There is little doubt that blacks attending these interracial contests saw them as conclusive demonstrations that African Americans were capable of playing Major League Baseball if only given the opportunity. Not only that, there were those who came away convinced more than ever that many of the black ballplayers were actually superior to many of the white Major Leaguers. Others contended that the white Major Leaguers were mostly interested in the payday and often gave a halfhearted effort to avoid possible injury and to save themselves for the Major League season. It was difficult, however, to imagine athletes wanting to coast with so much hype injected into the contests.

Paige stood as a shining example of black prowess to many. If there were any doubts about his ability and white players putting out their best effort, they should have been dispelled on Satchel Paige Day. French and Paige put up a great pitching duel before an estimated twelve thousand paying fans, the largest crowd of the Winter League season. The game seemed far from being settled when two of the Negro Leagues stars, Sam Bankhead and Mule Suttles, homered off of French. Three more runs scored in the eighth inning. Pirrone was ordered out of his own ballpark for attempting to strangle the umpire. Meanwhile, Paige was virtually flawless in pitching his second successive shutout, striking out fourteen on the way to the 5–0 drubbing of Pirrone's All-Stars.

A less action-filled highlight of the day but one filled with special emotion came later when Paige was called center stage and showered with a wide array of gifts from team owners and his adoring public. He graciously gave most of the credit to his teammates and thanked the huge crowd for its support and for giving him the greatest day of his life. Neither did it escape him that he was being honored by whites, blacks, Hispanics, and others. California was no racial haven, but it was more progressive on the race question than many other segments of the country as far as Paige and the rest of the Negro Leagues ballplayers were concerned.[9]

This inspired him to the pinnacle of performance. He promised to do his best to help the team bring home the league championship, and he kept that promise, continuing his winning ways right through the five-game series in February when Tom Wilson's Colored All-Stars were crowned California Winter League champions. Paige finished the 1933 winter season with a record of sixteen wins in eighteen starts, striking out 229 to take the crown as strikeout king, with more great Winter League seasons to come and many more miles to travel.[10]

The fastest gun alive and for hire, figuratively, could have been Satchel Paige's calling card. Literally, rather than a gun he offered the services of the pitcher with the fastest fastball and was available for hire to anyone ready to pay the price. It seemed perfectly fitting that his services were called for in the Great Plains of the former Indian Territory.

The Indian Wars ended in the 1890s, but a battle of a different sort raged on in the plains, one in which Paige would play a significant role. It was the less lethal war of baseball. The roots of baseball in the Great Plains harked back to the aftermath of the American Civil War. Soldiers found reprieve in playing baseball. The day before the Battle of the Little Bighorn, some members of General George Armstrong Custer's Seventh Cavalry passed time in a game of baseball while others cheered them on. The soldiers often played baseball when not on duty. Miners, prospectors, and frontier towns were known to enjoy an occasional game of competitive baseball.

The sport flowered in popularity as settlers swelled the plains. The Bureau of Indian Affairs and the American government encouraged baseball on the reservations and in the emerging Indian industrial schools as a tool to help reform and Americanize the so-called Indians and their children. The sport gained in popularity among Native Americans, and some of them excelled at it to an outstanding level, such as Charles Albert Bender and Jim Thorpe, who both became successful Major League ballplayers.

Whites and Native Americans of the Great Plains formed their own teams and baseball associations. They competed against one another and sometimes played on the same teams. The racial animus between whites and Indians was usually not far away but held in check enough for integrated baseball to be rather commonplace in the plains by the turn of the twentieth century.

Part of the tolerance for Native Americans on the part of whites stemmed from the doctrinaire position that they could possibly be civilized and at least partially assimilated into some corners of American society. There was far less feeling of magnanimity where blacks were concerned. But by 1931 baseball had become a religion of sorts in the plains. The competition grew steeper, and the desire to win, especially when big bets were made on the outcome, pushed teams and their managers to seek out the best talent available. The result was that teams in the hotly contested baseball territory of North Dakota began bringing in paid Negro Leagues ringers who obviously stood out for what they were. The objective was simple: to help the squad be victorious.

The baseball battles between Jamestown and Bismarck, North Dakota, two towns separated by about a hundred miles, were legendary. Year after year they engaged in an intense rivalry for baseball supremacy, with heavy wagers being made on the outcome of the game. Beyond the money, it was a matter of local pride. Virtually all of Bismarck and all of Jamestown put stock in the games and came out in full force in support of their teams.

It was victory at any and all costs. Jamestown was the first to use black talent to bolster their chances for victory when they stepped over the color line and brought in Barney Brown, a left-handed pitcher from the Negro Leagues, to help them best Bismarck. It worked. In successive games Bismarck went down in defeat, as it was unable to overcome the boost that Brown gave to the Jamestown team.

After several years of frustrating losses, Bismarck decided to make a change and in 1933 placed the team in the hands of Neil Churchill, a local businessman who owned a Chrysler automotive dealership. Churchill played on the Bismarck team a decade earlier and was a rabid team supporter. He constantly talked about the need of the team to up its talent level. He had personally witnessed and played against touring black ball clubs and understood very well the need to tap the talent that was available. Since he too placed heavy bets on the games, arguably having put up one thousand dollars on one contest, which he lost, he was anxious for revenge and victory.

Churchill's desire to win was more powerful than the racial taboo, and he contacted Abe Saperstein in Chicago to solicit his help in getting an ace black player to help neutralize Barney Brown's advantage for the Jamestown team. Churchill ended up bringing in three Negro Leagues players to fortify his roster that year. The recruitment also included Roosevelt Davis, a respected Negro Leagues pitcher. The wagering was heavy on the next Jamestown-versus-Bismarck game. The final results were not to Churchill's liking and certainly not to those of the town of Bismarck, as the team failed again under a brilliant performance on the mound from Barney Brown.

Churchill went back to Saperstein, asking specifically if he could recommend a pitcher who could beat Barney Brown. Saperstein recommended Satchel Paige, while posing the question: "If you can afford him?" In early August 1933 word went out that Leroy Satchel Paige was on his way to pitch for Bismarck.[11]

Paige's arrival on Saturday, one day prior to the big game with Jamestown, was heralded in the *Bismarck Tribune* like the heroic arrival of a hired gun whose reputation preceded him as the fastest gun alive and able to conquer any foe for his employers. All was not well in Dodge, however, or in this case Bismarck, as Paige and his companion, Janet Howard, would quickly learn.

The racism was visible in the otherwise positive news coverage of the arrival of the "dusky hurler" and "Ethiopian" who was portrayed in the *Tribune* with apelike features. Despite the racist images in the paper, Bismarck was actually glad to have the Paiges, if he were as good a pitcher as proclaimed.[12]

Bismarck had its nicer side, but it most certainly had its limitations. Despite Neil Churchill's connections, no one in the town was willing to rent Paige and his companion a room because of their color. Try as they might, there was no place for them to stay. Likely having already counted on the worst, Churchill escorted his visitors to a railroad freight car that was no longer in use in its original capacity and had been refashioned into living quarters of sorts.

Old freight cars were sometimes used to accommodate railroad work gangs and other laborers when the accommodations of the town were not available. In this case, they were certainly not available to the two black visitors to Bismarck. Having nowhere else to stay, Paige reluctantly accepted. Janet's reluctance was far greater than his. The accommodations outraged her, and she complained bitterly that this all could have been avoided if he did not travel as much and put real roots down in Pittsburgh. Paige's response to her was brief and to the point. He simply told her that this was what they had to do if she wanted to eat. Janet did not say much after that exchange.

Paige actually felt no better than she did. It was a tremendous letdown to him to see that all the hoopla about his coming did not earn him and his lady love housing befitting his celebrity status. On a personal level he felt that he had failed Janet, and he most certainly did not want to look small in her eyes. The reality, however, was that the situation was what it was. They were in a "take it or leave it" dilemma. He was not handling their problem well with the terse reply to Janet of "You want to eat, don't you?" He felt pushed into a corner with no alternatives. It was he, however, who made the business "deal" that brought them to Bismarck. Hence, he was the one responsible for their predicament. Black men were having similar feelings of inadequacy all during this period of the Great Depression, as the decisions that most impacted on their lives were basically out of their control, just like they were for many other Americans. The Paiges were better off than most. He and Janet settled into their boxcar home and attempted to make the best that they could of their primitive accommodations.[13]

When Paige was introduced to his new Bismarck teammates the following day, he claimed that he was surprised to find that they were white. It is difficult to believe that Saperstein and Churchill would have left out that little detail in any earlier discussions with him. For the first time in his life he was playing on an integrated baseball team with white teammates. Paige had stepped across the color line in baseball. It was not the recognized Major Leagues, but it was the Majors as far as the people of Bismarck and the Great Plains were concerned. Paige struck his own singularly important blow against segregation or, as he modestly put it, "I'd cracked another little chink in Jim Crow."[14]

His teammates quickly accepted his presence, especially after they saw him pitch a few balls. They had little time to do otherwise. Less than twenty-four hours after his arrival, the big Sunday showdown of Bismarck versus Jamestown would take place. Churchill had wisely put in additional seating to accommodate the overflow crowd expected to attend the event. At least one thousand Jamestown fans came to Bismarck for the game. Some estimated that far more than that actually attended. The additional seats were not nearly enough to accommodate the crush of humanity who came there to see the big contest between the two North Dakota rivals, with the two black aces facing off against each other. Nearly four thousand fans packed the ballpark.

Barney Brown was brilliant throughout the contest, striking out thirteen of the Bismarck team while allowing only five hits. Paige put on a performance that was nothing short of miraculous. At one point, to the amusement of the crowd, with a ball hit directly to him, he bent over and wiped his hands on the rosin bag before making a bullet throw to first base to beat the runner by inches. On a more serious note, he struck out eighteen of the Jamestown hitters.

It was late in the sixth inning before either team scored, with first blood being drawn off Paige for two runs. He became angry at that point and told his team as they went back on the field, "They get no more runs." Paige seemed to have that incredible ability that goes with superstardom of being able to reach down deep and perform at a higher level when called upon. Whether it was racial pride, a champion's heart, or just plain dogged determination, he had that something special, as he demonstrated that afternoon. He then proceeded with only ten pitches to retire the side. His Bismarck teammates came through with hits and runs, all off of Barney Brown. As the last base runner dove to beat a close call at home plate, he was ruled safe, and Bismarck won in the final inning. The crowd went absolutely mad and rushed Paige, hoisting him, pulling and tugging on him, and tearing parts of his jersey off. The Bismarck media gleefully proclaimed: "North Dakota baseball has officially arrived."[15]

Paige had done his job. He had delivered. His thinking at that moment was to gather up his belongings, load up his beloved Packard, and wave good-bye to his boxcar accommodations as he and Janet sped off in search of the next barnstorming gig. Neil Churchill had other thoughts. Bismarck's and Jamestown's appetites for baseball had not been quenched. Management of both teams felt that the matter remained unsettled, especially with the thoughts of doing it again and drawing another huge audience of ticket buyers to the ball game. Churchill and the management of the Jamestown team both agreed to extend the matter to the best two out of three, with two additional games in Jamestown.

Paige's thoughts about leaving quickly vanished when Churchill offered him more money. He would start the big game on Sunday, but his opposing pitcher for the Jamestown team had yet to be announced. This did not upset him. He was used to facing any and all comers. As fastballer for hire, Paige was there to take on all challengers. All of North Dakota was excited about the showdown. Work immediately began in Jamestown to expand the ballpark to accommodate the record-breaking crowd expected at the games.

Unbeknown to Bismarck, Jamestown made other investments to up its chances of being successful against Satchel Paige and his teammates. They sent word to Abe Saperstein to find them a pitcher who could possibly go head-to-head against Paige and win the game for them. Saperstein recommended the Chicago Giants' Willie Foster as the only person likely to have a reasonable chance against fireballer Paige.

The deal was struck, and a few days prior to the showdown, it was announced that Willie Foster would be facing Satchel Paige. This announcement sent fans into a frenzy, as they realized that they would be treated to a game featuring arguably the two best pitchers in Negro Leagues Baseball if not all of baseball, white or black. The sponsors of the game were now rightly worried more than ever about their ability to control the crowd.

The enthusiasm was at a fever pitch on game day, September 2. At least two thousand made the trek from Bismarck to Jamestown to support their team. The best estimate put attendance at well over four thousand. Spectators filled every seat and lined up five to six deep or more in the aisles to see each game. An hour or more was lost starting and stopping things to tell fans to stay off the field.

The Saturday contest featured Paul Schaefer and Barney Brown going at each other in a match that ended in a 7–7 tie. The game was finally called on account of darkness. That left all eyes focused on what everyone was waiting for: the big game on Sunday that would pit Satchel Paige against Willie Foster to settle the whole matter. If they had a bigger baseball stadium at Jamestown, it too would have been filled to capacity. Everyone who was anyone wanted to see Paige versus Foster.

At game time the ballpark overflowed with spectators crammed into the facility, standing rows deep and circling the playing field. No one was disappointed. The game lived up to the hype, with the two best pitchers in Negro Leagues Baseball fighting to the death. It was a rip-roaring great game that went down to the very last inning before it was settled. Paige struck out seventeen would-be hitters in an incredible display of pitching finesse. Willie Foster was superb as well, with a smaller number of strikeouts but with a game that stood at 2–2 going into the bottom of the ninth inning. It remained that way, and the game went into extra innings. In the bottom of the tenth, with Paige up to bat against Foster, and with a man on third and two strikes, Paige let loose with a single blast for a base hit that drove in the game-winning run.

Paige not only pitched the winning game but also won the game with his bat. The crowd went berserk and rushed the field. They mobbed Paige and hoisted him into the air several times before he was able to get back on his feet and walk under his own power. Naturally, he felt good about his treatment on the field. Off the field had its limitations, but it was still better than the Jim Crow South, all things considered. He was the hero of the moment and living the dual existence that historian and social activist W. E. B. Du Bois wrote about. In that dual world, Satchel Paige existed as a sport hero on the baseball diamond and a boxcar dweller off of it. He imbibed the adulation that came his way but knew only too well that it was given only because of his service in the winning cause. Paige possessed that double consciousness that Du Bois articulated. He was being touted as the best thing ever to have come through Bismarck. The Bismarck team was now the North Dakota semiprofessional baseball state champions of 1933 and Satchel Paige considered a near god of the plains.

The showdown between the two teams was not only good for baseball in the region, but a major moneymaker for both sides of the diamond. Bursting with pride and joy, Churchill virtually promised Paige a job for life. He could pitch for Bismarck anytime he wanted, and, indeed, they wanted him to stay and continue hurling for them for the rest of the season.

There was, however, a little matter of the forthcoming first East-West All-Star Game, scheduled to begin shortly in Chicago. Willie Foster left almost immediately for the train ride back to be in time to suit up for the West in the 1933 first All-Star classic. All the talk was that Paige would be right behind him. Supporters of Bismarck lamented: Bismarck probably would be without the services of Satchel Paige this week, though it was possible he would return there for the winter and next season.

Paige was planning tentatively to accept an offer and pitch for the East in the East-West All-Star showdown the next Sunday in Chicago against Willie Foster. The prediction was that Paige was on his way back East and nothing could change that. Things changed in a matter of a day or so when Neil Churchill made him an offer he found impossible to refuse, virtually promising him double what he was likely to make in the East-West All-Star Game—the real reason Paige was a no-show at the first East-West All-Star match. Paige went with the money, and Bismarck had his fastball services for the conclusion of its season. The East-West All-Star Game, the showdown with Willie Foster, Chicago, and the fans back East, would have to wait until next year.[16]

The Bismarck team, with Paige on the mound, started barnstorming throughout the Dakotas, Montana, Oklahoma, Kansas, and Minnesota. Despite the victory over Jamestown and the championship, the Bismarck team was nowhere near the level of play that Paige was used to in the company of great ballplayers on the Crawfords and throughout the Negro Leagues. In one of the games, Paige's Bismarck outfielders kept missing easy fly balls. Paige gave them a tongue-lashing on the bench, criticizing their lack of hustle, and pointing out that they would never make it in the Negro Leagues. His frustration with them caused him to break his own cardinal rule of never letting others know what you really think.

For his white teammates, they felt insulted in the worse sense of the word since an uppity black, of all people, had the audacity to criticize the level of their performance on the field. One of the players called Paige a "dirty nigger." The situation was so tense and acrimonious that when the next inning began, Paige looked around and found himself on the mound by himself with no outfield and no men on base, only him and the catcher and the opposing batter. Ironically, the fans, believing that it was all a gag, cheered and laughed.[17]

It was no gag. Neil Churchill was busy talking frantically to the players, trying to defuse the situation and persuade them to go back onto the field. They were steadfastly refusing. Paige took the whole matter in hand and commenced to pitch despite the absence of his teammates. He struck out the next three batters and retired the side without any assistance. The crowd loved it. They applauded his bravado on the mound and never knew that it was not an entertainment stunt.

The mistake was Paige's. There was no call for him to have lashed out at his teammates. While he was frustrated with their playing errors, he needed to realize that they were not the caliber ballplayers he was used to having out in the field in the Negro Leagues. Churchill talked to both sides to help soothe egos and restore teamwork. Once back in the dugout, Paige apologized for what he had said. Unhappy about the living accommodations and Janet's uncomfortableness with their entire situation there, he had perhaps allowed the combined negatives to get to him and to vent his frustrations on his teammates. His apology was accepted. His teammates apologized to him as well. The matter was settled, and the next inning all the players took their positions on the field. Paige made a promise after that episode to always keep bad

thoughts and criticisms about any of his teammates to himself, whether playing with Bismarck, the Negro Leagues, or anyone else.

From that point forward, he and his squad did well together. With Paige
on the mound, Bismarck seemed impossible to beat. That was exactly what
Churchill hoped for and the reason for his expenditure in bringing to town
the fastest fastballer for hire. At the end of his first season in Bismarck, Paige
promised to return the following year.

Churchill wasted no time in beginning the renovations of the Bismarck
ballpark for what he knew would be another banner year. Putting up his
own money and obtaining federal relief dollars for emergency labor assistance through the Works Progress Administration of the New Deal, he followed President Franklin Roosevelt's edict that baseball needed to survive
the Great Depression and was important to the renewal of the health and
spirit of the American people. Churchill expanded the ballpark's seating capacity by an additional three thousand seats and added a new grandstand,
a bleacher area for children, and parking to accommodate five hundred automobiles.

After all of that, Satchel Paige did not show. Churchill was disappointed but
refrained from chastising Paige in the media, remembering that there was always the possibility of a change of heart or a chance of getting him the following year, and he did not want to close that opportunity. Paige for his part was
soft-spoken but tough-minded when it came to making deals. He had never
been shy to ask for a raise. Once he became the undisputed leading draw in
Negro Leagues Baseball, and all of baseball, he did not hesitate to ask for and
to expect more money. He knew this was professional sports and it was all
about selling tickets. He left it to others to draw their own conclusions about
his behavior. Paige was determined, long before free agency and mega salaries for star athletes, to negotiate hard and get as much for his services as the
market would bear. Churchill was the momentary loser. Paige spent the entire
1934 regular season largely focused on his play with the Pittsburgh Crawfords
and turned in the best performance up to that point in his career in the Negro
Leagues. Part of the reason he stayed home was that Gus Greenlee upped
his salary substantially, knowing only too well that the Crawfords' ace was
the major drawing card in baseball, the best pitcher in the business, and that
someone else would meet his price. As for Neil Churchill, Greenlee reportedly promised to "cut him from ear to ear" with his straight razor, if he ever
met up with him.[18]

Greenlee paid Paige what he demanded. In addition, he agreed to lease his
ace to other clubs in need of superior pitching. Paige was in constant demand,
and the flow of bids for his services benefited him and Greenlee too, as he
took a percentage for each of Paige's lend-lease pitching offers.

A substantial offer came from the House of David Baseball Team, part of the Israelite House of David, a midwestern religious colony, which desperately needed the fastballer for hire to boost their chances in the Denver Post Tournament in Colorado. The House of David saw Paige as the missing ingredient that could help bring them the tournament championship. The team came close on several occasions to winning the Western Championship but failed due to inadequate pitching. The addition of Paige to the bullpen gave them more than a fighting chance to win it all for the first time. Greenlee agreed to terms, and Paige was leased to the House of David team for their run at the championship for two weeks in August 1934, with the understanding that he would make it back in time for the second classic East-West All Star Game in Chicago on August 26, which he did.

Abe Saperstein was much involved in negotiating the deal between the House of David and Gus Greenlee. Both parties were satisfied with the final terms, and that included Paige, who was to receive at least half of the fee paid to Greenlee. Paige proved to be worth every cent of the investment. Thanks to his fine pitching, the House of David team dominated the tournament during its two weeks of play. There were rumors that he would wear a fake beard to blend in with his bearded teammates. Paige confirmed that the story was true and that he was willing to wear a beard or anything else if that would help the team win. Whether this was team spirit on Paige's part was debatable. He was the consummate professional, and although there were reports that he donned a false beard while playing on the House of David team, those reports were false. He never did. Even if he had, there was little doubt that the beard could not have camouflaged his identity.

Paige started for the House of David in the three stretch-round final games to the championship on August 6, 8, and 10. The first of the three games he and his teammates faced a tough squad from Enoch, Oklahoma. Paige held the Oklahoma team in check, with the victory going to the House of David 6–1. In the next major game two days later, he humbled a strong Humble Oilers team from Texas, completely shutting them out to lead his squad to a 4–0 victory.

The game for the championship pitted the House of David against the famed Kansas City Monarchs of the Negro Leagues, who planned on taking the tournament. What they had not planned on was taking on Satchel Paige, who held them scoreless while his House of David teammates came through with solid hitting for two scores and the 2–0 triumph and the championship of the Denver Post Tournament.

Everyone at the contest readily admitted that the House of David was a good team, and with the addition of Satchel Paige they were an unbeatable one. All thanks went to the fireball thrower for hire. "Paige was a great flinger throughout the tournament" and without question "easily stole the play from all other competitors." The Denver Post Tournament provided more than just a nice trophy, too. It also provided a sizable purse to the victors. The media reported accurately: "Paige's arm wins $5,000" for the House of David.[19]

Paige likely received a bonus that Greenlee knew nothing about, as the House of David made every effort to get him to continue barnstorming with them. For now, Paige's fastball was required in the East-West All-Star Game, and he caught the next train out of Denver to make it to the Windy City in time to lead the East to its first victory over the West All-Stars in the 1934 second annual showdown.

After his wedding to Janet Howard in October of that same year and the refusal of Gus Greenlee to up his salary yet further, many insiders predicted that Paige might not wear a Crawfords uniform for the next year's season in the Negro Leagues. Gus Greenlee attempted to put the best personal face possible on an otherwise fait accompli when he announced on April 26, 1935, that Paige had been "assigned to Ray L. Dean, western promoter for one year."[20]

He gave the strongest implication that his pitching ace was being disciplined and suspended from the league during this period of time. Greenlee further intimated that other Negro Leagues teams would honor this suspension and not hire Paige or participate in games in which he was involved. Greenlee said that "a clause prohibiting his [Paige's] appearance or service in games against league clubs has been inserted" in the decree.[21]

The truth of the matter was that Paige had already jumped from the Crawfords to Neil Churchill's Bismarck Baseball Team for the 1935 season. Paige found Churchill's latest offer virtually impossible for him to turn down. He would be paid the munificent sum of $1,000 per month in Great Depression–era dollars. In short, it was a small fortune and far more than the $500 or possibly $650 per month that Greenlee was willing to pay him for his services on the Crawfords. Compared to the rest of the society, even the lesser amount was formidable, considering that a monthly wage of $200 put you in very good stead in the 1930s.

Moreover, there were other assurances that added to the offer's attractiveness to Paige. He was still upset about the living accommodations he and Janet suffered through in 1933 in Bismarck, and that was one of the principal reasons he did not return in 1934. Janet never forgave Bismarck for the indignity and blamed Paige for not providing better. She was constantly put second in Bismarck to baseball, which received the vast majority of Paige's attention. He promised to devote more attention to her this time. Moreover, Churchill purchased the Prince Hotel, the city's major hotel, and promised Paige and his wife the best accommodations. There would be no more sleeping in refurbished railroad boxcars for them.

The guarantee of first-rate accommodations and the best of food coupled with a princely salary was irresistible. Gus Greenlee could make any decision he wanted to make, but the reality was that his ace hurler was set to go West. But no promise in the world was going to persuade Janet that she should accompany her new husband back to what she considered a living hell. The earlier experience in Bismarck left her with nothing other than sour memories of the entire region, and no amount of money could erase the discomfort and indignities she suffered through during their first stay. She was a student of the old adage of "Fool me once, shame on you; fool me twice, shame on me." Janet Paige informed her husband that if he went, it would be without her. She was staying put in Pittsburgh. After considerable discussion that assuredly ran the gamut from heated to tepid, from intense to tenuous, from steadfastness to uneasy resolve, it was decided that Satchel Paige would venture forth on his own back to the Great Plains to take advantage of the lucrative offer.[22]

He would not be alone in the adventure. Accompanying him was the potent auxiliary support in the form of his childhood chum and former teammate Double Duty Radcliffe, whose versatility on the diamond as pitcher, catcher, and third baseman provided awesome backup to Paige and fortification to the Bismarck lineup.

Churchill recruited some others to round out his arsenal. Paige and Radcliffe were joined by Red Haley, Barney Morris, Quincy Trouppe, and highly talented southpaw pitcher Hilton Smith to strengthen the Bismarck team. The six blacks combined with the five whites, Vernon "Moose" Johnson, Joe Desiderato, Axel Leary, Danny Oberholzer, and Ed Hendee, for the total eleven who would carry the banner of North Dakota's capital city on a first of its kind racially integrated team that completely outclassed every opponent. Double Duty Radcliffe fondly recalled the 1935 season with Bismarck as one of the highlights of his career, second only to his tagging of a home run in the 1944 East-West game.

He and Paige hung out together constantly in Bismarck. They roomed together, ate together, played together, and shared confidences unique to lifelong friends. The setting in Bismarck was not exactly the best in the world. North Dakota, like South Dakota, Oklahoma, Montana, and much of the Great Plains, was not free of racial blight. The Ku Klux Klan, for example, had strongholds all through that part of the country. No sooner had Paige and Radcliffe and the other black players arrived than the Klan began to clamor about the presence of so many blacks in the capital city. The KKK occasionally paraded in Bismarck dressed in their hooded outfits in broad daylight to the accompaniment of a marching band, followed by long-winded racist speeches, topped off with a family picnic for members and their guests. Neil Churchill, however, was a force with whom to be reckoned. He eventually became mayor of Bismarck. He intervened with the Ku Klux Klan and anyone else who dared to interfere with his ball club and his black auxiliary.

Paige, Radcliffe, and the rest of the black players lived in peace for most of the period of time they were there. Their fellow players accompanying them from the Negro Leagues were warehoused in the old boxcars that Paige and Janet experienced during their earlier stay in Bismarck. The superstars Paige and Radcliffe were "treated like kings," according to Radcliffe, and accommodated in the Prince Hotel, with all the amenities that went along with it.[23]

Some of the amenities they received were way off the menu. Radcliffe led the charge in securing female companionship for the two roommates. The two stars apparently proved to be irresistible to a wide range of local white females. On more than one occasion, white visitors of the opposite sex were seen entering and exiting the Paige-Radcliffe room in the Prince Hotel. Such unwelcome attention unfortunately drew the wrath of the Ku Klux Klan and discussion about what might be going on at the hotel. The ultimate taboo of black men with white women made for a highly combustible situation for the two roommates. The well-being of the other black ballplayers was also in jeopardy, though they were innocent of any hint of interracial mingling with the town's fairer sex.

Radcliffe long before that embraced the pro-gun attitude of his adopted hometown of Chicago and carried a .32 Colt revolver in his pocket at all times, except when on the baseball field. "I always carried a pistol in my pocket and nobody better had fuck with me," he said. "Satchel carried too. He loved guns of all kinds and had a couple of them in Bismarck, a .22 and, I think, a .38 too. We weren't scared of the K-boys or nobody else. We wanted to be left alone like men. I know I would have shot any son of a bitch messing with me."[24]

Rather than halting his and Paige's dangerous liaisons, Radcliffe informed Churchill in private conversation that he would be unable to stay in Bismarck for four long months without the benefit of female companionship and came up with a novel solution to how the suspicions could be allayed. He requested that Churchill give him some wood panels and provide the services of a carpenter. With that Radcliffe was able to fashion an apartment in the basement of the Prince Hotel. The new dwelling allowed the female visitors to rendezvous with the stars in the privacy of relative seclusion. Radcliffe recalled his solution:

> Here's what we'll do. We'll build me and Satchel a four-bedroom apartment in the basement. There will be two ways to bring girls down. They can come by the regular elevator or by the freight elevator. Nobody will know who they're going to see. Satchel said, "Homey, I'm going to call President Roosevelt." I said, "What for?" He said, "I'm going to tell him to put you in his cabinet 'cause you

got brains!" The first night we got some girls, Satchel turned to me and said, "Duty, you a lucky son of a gun 'cause you one of God's children." We had a lot of fun, and we never had no problems after that, and we got all the girls we wanted. Them were good days.

He elaborated further: "Me and Satch did our part for integration right there in that Prince Hotel. You could call us kind of baseball goodwill doers for some real better understanding of the races. We made them women believers, I tell you. Yes, sir, we did our thing for the cause!"[25]

Perhaps Radcliffe's bedroom adventures could be excused on the grounds that he was unmarried at the time and the women were of age and eager participants. Paige, however, had no such fallback position. He was legally married to Janet and brazenly breaking his marriage vows. He evidently was unwilling to curb his sexual appetite in Bismarck. His extramarital activity suggested that there were already serious problems in his one-year marriage.

Paige found solace of a different sort in the relationship he developed with Native Americans in the area. The West had Indians and they fascinated him. Whenever he saw any of the area Native Americans, he greeted them, and they responded politely in kind. Paige served as an African American emissary of sorts who bridged the chasm between the blacks and the reds with an enduring friendship.

Conversations begun between him and one of the Sioux elders blossomed into a mutual admiration. Paige was invited to supper with the Sioux and there for the first time had the pleasure of trying buffalo meat, which, according to Radcliffe, was roasted, lean, and mighty tasty. Paige and his Native friends spoke of many things over food and drink, including baseball, as he confided to them about the aches and pains he endured from so much pitching.

It was in this context that he found that the Sioux elder was also an important medicine man. This proved to be extremely beneficial. Paige heard tales about secret potions, powerful elixirs, and miracle poultices known only to the Native healers. During one of his visits to the reservation, Paige's medicine-man benefactor, and baseball fan, allowed him to sample the powerful poultice. It was rumored that two of the secret ingredients in the ointment were gunpowder and rattlesnake venom. Paige was justifiably reluctant to try it at first, but given that it had been around in use by the Sioux for hundreds of years, if not longer, he reasoned that it might well be safe and possibly effective.

No sooner had the ointment been rubbed into his right shoulder and arm did he experience an intense tingling sensation. After the burst of heat, and beyond the pungent smell, the ornament brought a soothing numbness that relieved all pain and made his arm feel relaxed and resilient. Paige was given a huge jar of the ointment, which he used on a regular basis. Whenever he was back in the Bismarck area, he made contact with his old friend and when possible obtained a refill of the secret solution that he credited for extending his years as a pitcher. "So I tried it on my arm," Paige said, "even though those Indians said it would burn me up. It didn't. It was just fine and I started using it after every game. Since then I always keep some of it in a jar and it kept my arm nice and young. It's real fine oil, the best. The formula is a secret. I promised those Indians I wouldn't tell it, but I guess I'll put it in my will so folks will have it when I got no more need for it."[26]

Radcliffe remembered the ointment. Although he pitched too and suffered many nicks, strained muscles, and soreness somewhere virtually all the time, he decided against trying the poultice after he heard that one of the ingredients was rattlesnake venom. Other than that, he, like Paige, enjoyed the camaraderie with the Sioux and other Native Americans they encountered.[27]

The Bismarck baseball team respected each other and the different teams and people with which they came in contact. In doing so, they struck a powerful blow for interracial understanding and coexistence, if not downright integration, throughout the plains. The racially integrated team of six black and five white ballplayers, plus manager Churchill, cut a striking image as they traveled through North Dakota, South Dakota, Montana, Kansas, Minnesota, Colorado, and more, playing such teams as the Jamestown Nine, Davis Lake, Mexican LaJunta Charros, Fort Worth Cats, San Antonio Missions, Twin City Colored Giants, Monroe Monarchs, San Angelo Colored Shepherds, and Denver White Elephants, among others.

The team's experiences on the road together and their ways of handling Jim Crow were informative and refreshing. The attitude on the Bismarck team was basically "one for all and all for one." Paige could hardly believe the openness and good nature of his teammates. They traveled together to most game sites in two of Neil Churchill's biggest four-door Chrysler automobiles. When the team stopped for gas or refreshments, everyone used the same facilities or no one did. Joe Desiderato, one of the whites on the team, recalled how great it was on the Bismarck team for all the players: "It was fun playing on Bismarck. Very good. Of course it was a little rough at times because we were mixed," Desiderato recounted. "In some places we were even barred from going into restaurants. We paid no mind. I remember two places we came into at night, after the game, and we were refused rooms because we had blacks on the team. We packed up and left together. We always stayed as a family."[28]

When not on the ball field, the players hung out together, very often playing poker or pinochle in a player's room, where, according to Radcliffe, he "used to take their money—they didn't know what was happening. We were always together. It wasn't like in Chicago and different places where whites and blacks were separate. 'Course I had all the girls. They'd all hang around with me to get a girl. We had a lot of fun together!"[29]

The team played together, ate together, and when on the road touring was spotted walking around the town centers as a group, taking it easy, chatting, and enjoying each other's company. Most of the time they talked baseball. Desiderato remembered well how much Paige and Radcliffe loved to tell stories. Those two would go on and on with fantastic yarns about their experiences in the Negro Leagues and life in general. "We had a lot of fun together," Desiderato reflected. "Let me tell you, the two best talkers you ever want to hear are Double Duty and Satchel. Both of them fellas could really carry on. They'd hold a whole room full of people and you'd be in awe at the way they would come out with their conversation. They were really street-wise. They were above the rest of us. It was wonderful to be with them guys. They were very well educated even though they didn't have the chance to go to school like we did. They were very smart in all respects and gentlemen, too. Couldn't beat 'em."[30]

The white members of the team were also struck with the "down-to-earth" ways of Paige and Radcliffe. "You never forget them kind of people," Desiderato reminisced. "'Cause Satchel sticks out with everybody, I imagine. The man was so outstanding and it never fazed him one iota. He never got the big head or anything like that. He was always amiable with all us guys. We were very close. As a matter of fact, I roomed with Satchel for a while on the road. He was terrific."[31]

Indeed, there were several occasions on the road when the hotel the team stayed at could provide only a limited number of rooms, which necessitated that blacks and whites sleep in the same room. Desiderato's recollection confirms that Paige and he, along with other teammates, were in all likelihood the first integrated sport team on which blacks and whites also roomed together.[32]

Imagine Paige's surprise when it became clear to him that his white Bismarck teammates had no objection to rooming with blacks. It was one thing for blacks and whites to play together on the same team, which was a bold and progressive step that went far beyond the norm, but it was an incredible leap forward to think of a team so egalitarian and advanced in its thinking that there were no objections by the white ballplayers to sharing rooms with their black teammates. It would be easy to argue that the team was just so tired and in need of rooms that they did not care about the rules of the color line. That might suffice as an answer if the white and black players roomed together only once; they did so on several occasions. The players of the Bismarck team treated each other with respect and refused to succumb to the color line. Paige and Radcliffe had gone all the way to the Great Plains to get a glimpse of what baseball could look like once the sport and the nation could move beyond the racial divide.

There were for Paige many fond memories associated with the 1935 Bismarck team, such as the day his passion for fishing nearly cost him dearly. The touring schedule relaxed a bit one week, and he and Radcliffe decided to take a few days in upstate Minnesota to relax and do a little fishing, and they took two lady friends along with them. While Radcliffe stayed in the cabin with his female companion, Paige and his companion were down at the lake, supposedly fishing. Whether they were actually fishing or engaged in more amorous behavior is a matter of speculation. Paige dearly loved to fish, and loved women too. Whatever they were doing, they were interrupted. A foraging black bear startled them, and they took off running for the cabin.

They ran for their lives for the safety of the cabin, where they found the door securely locked. Paige banged away, yelling for his buddy to let them in, that there was a bear after them. Radcliffe was otherwise engaged inside and, thinking Paige was joking, refused to open the door and shouted back to "go away." Luckily, the bear changed its mind and diverted elsewhere. Radcliffe eventually opened the door to find a breathless, heart-pounding Paige "angry as hell with me for not opening the door."[33]

Whenever the two later reminisced, they would always talk about the Minnesota fishing trip and invariably break into laughter about how funny the whole thing was, with Paige fleeing for his life with a bear in hot pursuit and Radcliffe refusing to open the cabin door. The incident was one of countless memories the two stars shared together.[34]

For Paige, nothing topped the 1935 Bismarck team, their camaraderie, and their pursuit of the championship. He often spoke of the team spirit, the unselfishness, the hustle, and blacks and whites playing together in harmony for the same purpose and all getting along fabulously as they achieved their goal of their first national championship, the All-Nations Baseball Championship of 1935.[35]

They loved Satchel Paige throughout the western plains. He skipped the Negro Leagues East-West All-Star Game of 1935, though fans voted him on the team. He kept playing out West, making money and building an expanded base of supporters and admirers. Ironically, the East lost to the West in the 1935 game. Many thought that if Paige had been there, the outcome would have been different. He was in demand everywhere. His reputation spread far and wide. The traveling man of Negro Leagues Baseball became the sport's greatest goodwill ambassador throughout the plains and most visible challenger by example to the unfairness of the color line in Major League Baseball.

Nowhere was this better demonstrated than in his barnstorming games against the hero of the plains, the most popular player in Major League Baseball after Babe Ruth, and arguably the best pitcher in the Majors in the 1930s: Jay Hana "Dizzy" Dean. In 1933 Dean achieved stardom with the St. Louis Cardinals, becoming one of the first twenty-game winners and setting the Major League record for the most strikeouts in a single game at that time—seventeen. His 1934 season was, like that of Paige, his best year in league play. Dean won thirty games that year, led the Cardinals to victory in the World Series, and was on virtually every scorecard the best pitcher in Major League Baseball.

Yet Dean was woefully underpaid in the Majors and, like many of his league colleagues, took to barnstorming in Winter League ball out West or where and when he and some of his fellow Major League all-stars could team up and take on aspiring locals or a competing traveling squad that promised to draw fans and provide a good payday. It was in this setting that the best pitcher in Major League Baseball met the best pitcher in Negro Leagues Baseball to settle the matter of who was the best pitcher in all of baseball. The two kings of the mound first clashed at the end of their heretofore best year in their respective leagues. They squared off against each other on Sunday, October 21, 1934, in the heart of the Midwest—Cleveland, Ohio, with Dean pitching the first three innings for the Rosenblooms against Satchel Paige and the Crawfords before a crowd of twelve thousand.

A good barometer of the popularity of these two aces was their joint ability to bring folks to the stadium despite the economic woes of the times. In Dizzy Dean's first three innings of pitching, he gave up one run and four hits before retiring. In comparison, Paige gave up no hits and struck out thirteen batters during the first six innings. The Crawfords took the contest 4–1. To the amazement of the many Dean fans attending the contest, it was Satchel Paige who proved himself the superior pitcher and the "hero of the battle even though the fans had turned out to cheer the Dean brothers." Paige followers were likely not surprised with the outcome, as he "gave local baseball fans an idea of just how good he is here Sunday by beating the famed Dizzy Dean."[36]

Meetings between the two were repeated many times further west, in Nebraska, Kansas, North and South Dakotas, and Oklahoma. Paige versus Dean and Dean versus Paige packed stadiums with audiences of all races to witness the two titans square off. The combination of Dean versus Paige drew six thousand fans to Oxford, Nebraska, in a field so small it was likened to a shoe box for someone with small feet. Again, Paige was victorious. He did not win every meeting against Dean. They traded victories. But everyone with open eyes could see that Paige and the other best players of the Negro Leagues could compete favorably against the best players of the Major Leagues and may well have been superior to them.

The absurdity of the color line based on any criteria of competency and ability was an insult to the national pastime and to anyone who believed in fair and open competitive sports. Thousands scraped together the cost of a ticket to watch Dean and Paige go at it. The spectacle, the entertainment, the excitement and joy of the game brought relief and exhilaration to lovers of baseball throughout the plains. Their contests seemed to momentarily overcome the particular hardships of that section of the nation, including the ravages of the Dust Bowl. Folks came from hundreds of miles by train and by automobile for that moment of escapism that these two magical players provided. They swept westward like the dust storms, but they brought joy and fun that families and communities imbibed and relished.

After the Major League All-Star Game of 1934, sportswriter Al Monroe of the *Chicago Defender* concluded that the National League won because of the superior pitching of Dizzy Dean, Carl Hubbell, and Lon Warneke. It made him ponder what the outcome would have been with Paige on the mound for the American League:

> With this in mind we just wonder what would have resulted had Satchel Paige started the game instead of Lefty Grove who gave up two runs or Schoolboy Rowe who permitted the final two tallies? Certainly Paige has faced the bulk of the star hitters in both leagues and the records will show that few hits have been recorded off his delivery in the pinches or out. Really, it is hard to figure why discrimination can remain so powerful and keep Race players out of the majors in these days of poor gate receipts. At present, only three or four teams are keeping out of the red and those doing so by keeping on top of the pack. Imagine, if you can, the turnout that would be on hand for a game between the St. Louis Cardinals and the Chicago Cubs with Dizzy Dean twirling against "Satchel" Paige.[37]

Paige relished hearing these compliments and comparisons being made between him and the Major Leaguers. All he could really do, however, was to do what he did best—pitch. It was a bitter pill to swallow that despite the performances he delivered against the best professional ball players, black and white, that Major League Baseball was out of the reach of him and his kind because of the color of their skin.

When Paige met the great Major League pitcher Bob Feller for the first of what would be many meetings between the two stars, they drew five thousand spectators who packed the tiny stadium. Feller pitched three innings that game, struck out eight, and gave up only one hit. Paige also pitched three innings, struck out seven, and gave up no hits. He and his Negro Leagues All-Star squad won 4–2.[38]

In another contest out West, Paige faced a young player named Joe DiMaggio. DiMaggio had made contact with the ball on several previous occasions but had not gained a single hit off of Paige. He grounded out on two previous trips, popped out to center field on the other, and got on base only when Paige nicked him with a pitch in the third inning. Other than that, DiMaggio was hitless to that point in the contest. With a man on third, he had DiMaggio down by two strikes in the tenth inning when the youngster connected with a short hopper for a base hit that brought in the winning score. It was over, with the Major Leaguers squeaking out a one-run victory. On Paige's long walk to the dugout and passing the Major League rivals, he heard DiMaggio say what DiMaggio would repeat many times later, "Now I know I can make it with the Yankees. I finally got a hit off of Satchel Paige."[39]

Paige had only a baseball in his hand, but with it he was conducting public workshops on race in America that were attended, in total, by hundreds of thousands each year who may or may not have been initially aware of the real topic of the forums. To California repeatedly and through the Rocky Mountains and Black Hills of the Great Plains, he challenged there and throughout the world the absurdity of the color line while bringing joy and entertainment to throngs of grateful fans, of every race and ethnicity, who loved baseball.

7

Baseball Diplomacy

Satchel Paige was baseball's foremost globetrotter, the national and international Johnny Appleseed of the game, whose pitching talents and economic importance ignited passions across the borders, north and south. He rarely traveled fewer than forty thousand miles a year, throughout the United States and to foreign shores, wherever duty called and the price was right, from the cooler yet inviting corners of North America to the warm embrace of the Caribbean basin and Latin America. His jump to the baseball team of Dominican Republic dictator Rafael Trujillo in 1937 had serious international implications. Who Paige would be allowed to pitch for was fought out in the courts and in international politics. The matter eventually worked its way to the US secretary of state as Negro Leagues owners plied political pressure, legal maneuvering, and pleas for national sovereignty and racial uplift in an effort to obtain an injunction against what they considered to be an unfair encroachment on black baseball emanating from south of the border.

Paige's play across the northern border into Canada, however, had the positive impact and goodwill between nations that he exemplified as America's leading baseball ambassador, without portfolio. The master hurler triumphed in Maple Leaf country, where he was, for example, the featured attraction in the kickoff of the 1934 baseball season. "Great Colored Hurler Coming Here Next Week" was the talk throughout Winnipeg, Canada's first baseball capital. The *Winnipeg Free Press* called Paige the gent, regarded as the greatest pitcher in the world, white or black, and urged the sporting community to take the opportunity to see for themselves, since he would be on view for the critical and observant eyes of the Winnipeg public the next week. Harvey Cann, who managed the Wesley Park baseball facility in Winnipeg that would host the series, gleefully announced that he had secured the services of the Bismarck nine and their great pitcher Satchel Paige to take on the Union Giants in a five-game series to kick off the new season. He reminded the public that many believed Paige to be the best pitcher in all of baseball because he had defeated the best, black or white, including Dizzy Dean and Larry French.

You have to see Paige to believe him, Cann challenged any doubters. To help them do exactly that, he and the other promoters wisely scheduled the series to begin on Victoria Day, Thursday, May 24, 1934. Canadians celebrated the birthday of Queen Victoria, a date also known as Empire Day, and saw it as the official beginning of summer and the leisure activity associated with the months of warmth. There would be two games on Victoria Day, one game the following Friday, and the concluding two games on Saturday. Paige featured prominently in the advertisement and with the full house that came out to see the contests.[1]

Paige attracted legions of fans wherever and whenever he played in Canada. The name Satchel Paige proved magical for promoters who vied for his appearance to ensure a good game of baseball and good gate receipts. The Winnipeg promoters were so enthralled with the ability of Paige to put fans in the seats that it became almost a ritual to feature him in the first game of the season.

In 1935 Paige and his Bismarck teammates took on Chet Brewer and the Kansas City Monarchs to open the new season and to christen the remodeled Osborne Stadium in Winnipeg. Cann and other Canadian promoters invested a small fortune in renovating and expanding Osborne Stadium. They could ill-afford to take any chances that the venture would not bear fruit. Hence, they contracted with Paige for the first series to be played at the newly renovated facility. The gamble proved successful despite inclement weather.

Lingering frigid temperature and frost characterized the entire week leading up to opening day in Winnipeg that early June. Miraculously, seven hundred people showed for the opener despite the blustery weather. Fans wanted to see Satchel Paige. They did and he did not disappoint. The setting that Thursday night at the remodeled Osborne Stadium might have been chilly in terms of weather, but it was warm in terms of the intense competition generated on the playing field and the enthusiastic engagement of the audience. Paige no doubt felt good about doing his part, and he got paid.

He and Brewer put on a marvelous display of pitching brilliance. Brewer struck out thirteen batters and kept Bismarck scoreless. Paige, however, was even more brilliant. He struck out seventeen of the Monarchs and allowed no score. The audience was enthralled with the quality game they witnessed and the incredible pitching performances. They cheered through the whole affair and paused only when they took time to eat roasted peanuts, which may have provided a little additional warmth.

No fan went away disgruntled or complaining about the weather when the game was finally called late in the ninth inning on account of darkness. Throughout the contest, "Cann marched around feeling very proud about everything (except not having the press box complete); and Satchel Paige, often called the world's greatest baseball pitcher, really appeared in person."[2]

In the second game of the series the following day, the Monarchs took the contests 2-1 to lead the series by one game. Everyone focused on the remaining two games scheduled to be played Saturday. In particular, all eyes were on the scheduled rematch of Paige versus Brewer for the 2:30 p.m. matinee game. After only one day of rest, spectators were hopeful to see Paige and Brewer go at it again and provide another sterling pitching exhibition of scoreless baseball. Paige's pitching schedule was merciless. What pitcher could pitch again after going a full game a day earlier?

The pitching turned out to be lackluster for both Paige and Brewer. Who in their right mind could have expected anything else? The fans were disappointed in the performances. The game was described as a drab affair in terms of pitching. Brewer was quickly knocked out of the game on a series of hits. Paige was branded as playing without any zip in his pitches, although his team won 11–4 and he contributed to the victory more with his bat than with his arm. This did not sit well with him on a personal and professional level, but he did hit for two doubles and two singles in five trips to the plate and pitched well enough for his team to be victorious.

Paige remained the darling of Winnipeg's baseball lovers, despite their criticism of his most recent pitching performance. Whenever he played at Osborne Stadium or anywhere else in Winnipeg or throughout the Maple Leaf region, attendance substantially increased. He did much to establish baseball in Canada with the luring of new patrons to the parks and stadia to watch him and his teammates in action. Year in and year out throughout the 1930s and beyond, Satchel Paige was the calling card and biggest single draw in Canadian baseball, an accomplishment that gave him deep satisfaction.

Word came in short order of a team in Puerto Rico needing the services of the fastballer for hire, and willing to pay good money. Paige consented to the intermediate jump with no consultation with his wife. When he finally did inform her that he had signed on to go play in Puerto Rico, she thought they could turn that into some sort of trip for the two of them until her husband informed her that the management was not allowing the players to bring their wives. Janet, to say the least, was furious.

From that moment on, their marriage was on the skids. When Paige returned from spending the rest of the winter season in Puerto Rico, he knew it was all over. "As happy as the fans and ballplayers were to see me, that was just about how unhappy Janet seemed," Paige explained it. "It was all over, that feeling we once had. She'd boiled all winter at my being gone and when I got back she couldn't wait to start nibbling at me about it. One thing led to another and soon we were just waiting to fall apart."[3]

Paige's explanation for the breakup was stilted in his own favor. He was honest and correct that he had warned Janet that their marriage would be a difficult one to sustain because of the demands of Negro Leagues ball that he be away from home in a moving schedule of games and barnstorming. He was, however disingenuous in not mentioning another factor that also did not sit well with Janet. He alluded to it in only a small way when he said that Janet greeted him with the remark, "Did you have a good time without me?" Paige had been a wandering man in more than just being away playing baseball. There was the documented indiscretion while playing in Bismarck and on the fishing trip to Minnesota. In probability, there may have been others, although this is impossible to document. What was clear was that Janet's hope of changing Paige's "wandering ways" had failed.[4]

Greenlee thought he had conquered Paige's baseball wandering ways and had his guaranteed services with the Crawfords for the 1937 season. However, Paige was being hotly pursued by representatives of the Dominican Republic, whose leader, dictator Rafael Trujillo, was determined to have his baseball team, Ciudad Trujillo also known as the Dragones, victorious in the national championship against his political rival.

The news as late as April 19, 1937, reported that team Ciudad Trujillo was advancing but was having trouble. The Dominican sports page raised the specter of possible defeat of team Ciudad Trujillo. There was a general consensus that Trujillo's team was not quite strong enough. One of the opposing teams had recruited the heralded Martin Dihigo. The Trujillo team needed strengthening if they hoped to have a chance to outclass their rivals and make it to the finals and win the best-of-seven series for the championship.[5]

Dedicated to put together a winning team for President Trujillo, Dr. José Aybar traveled to America in search of Satchel Paige, who was in spring training with the Crawfords in New Orleans. He followed Paige around for several days, observing his pitching firsthand. Trujillo's emissary had already made an offer to one player, whom he successfully recruited for $750, and was looking to recruit others, but had to have Satchel Paige. He knew Paige's reputation as the greatest pitcher in Negro Leagues Baseball, if not all of baseball, and he saw demonstrations of it during the spring.[6]

Greenlee became so upset with the interest of the Dominicans in his star hurler that he launched a complaint with the US State Department. He had good cause. Although it is likely that Paige felt some pains about abandoning Greenlee, these were just as likely quickly alleviated when Aybar upped the ante. He offered $30,000 for the master hurler's services, and that of seven other players of his choosing, in the Dominican Republic for the 1937 season. The money proved to be irresistible to Paige, who approached his catcher, William Perkins, to go with him, and then enticed Cool Papa Bell, Josh Gibson, and others to join with them. Able to offer them several thousand dollars each, and pocketing something extra for his putting together the team, it was an extraordinary payday for Paige and his Negro Leagues supporting cast.

Greenlee was outraged and furious when he realized that he had lost Paige and several others of his top Crawfords. He filed suit and pressed the US State Department to take action against the Dominicans for violating American sovereignty and hampering American business. Paige and the others were in breach of contract, thanks to the Dominicans, or so Greenlee and other owners argued.

Paige justified his actions in his mind by saying that Negro Leagues contracts, and indeed the contract with Greenlee, were flimsy documents that no one took too seriously. Be that as it may, he had given his word, and now he broke it. Paige explained: "Now some of the papers said I'd paid back all Gus done for me by busting up his club, but like I said I wasn't the only one heading down to the islands like that. Anyway, I didn't have any real contact with Gus then and I had to look out for number one. Gus was feeling the money pains, too, and the checks from him weren't what they used to be."[7]

That was an explanation, but it was hardly one that satisfied Greenlee or the fan base back in Pittsburgh. The press was decidedly anti–Satchel Paige this time. They felt they were being cheated of his services, too. If he was playing in the Dominican Republic or elsewhere in the islands for the regular season, it meant that he would not be gracing ballparks in the United States for all to witness and partake of his magic.

The $30,000 won out and Greenlee lost. Greenlee and the other Negro Leagues owners could not match up against the resources and, in the end, the reciprocal foreign policy understanding between the US government and the government of the Dominican Republic.

It was clear from correspondence and other documents of the US State Department and other agencies that the United States was receptive behind the scenes to President Rafael Trujillo's desire to have a winning baseball team to bolster his administration. Trujillo understood the importance of sport, especially baseball, and its political power. He recognized early on that organized sport could help his regime.[8]

There was no question that baseball was being used as symbol and diversion by Rafael Trujillo. As historian Rob Ruck notes, Trujillo was intense in his use of baseball to bolster his regime. Making his bid for "reelection" in 1937, Trujillo considered it imperative that he demonstrate his machismo by fielding a winning baseball squad. His team had lost in the championships the previous year, and another loss was simply unfathomable. His political rival was making headway with symbolic shows of power via his stronger baseball team. No one was more conscious of image than Trujillo, who would set the Guinness Book of World Records for having more statues made of himself than any other person in history.[9]

The Dominican population itself, the majority of whom were people of African descent, identified with the exploits of successful people of color as reported in the newspapers. They touted the story of Joe Louis's victory in Chicago that year and celebrated his success, just like black Americans and the black world did, in knocking out the "gringo." The Dominicans long ago embraced Negro Leagues ballplayers and welcomed them to the island.[10]

The news that Paige and his supporting cast of star players were coming drew excitement galore. When Paige landed in the Dominican Republic, he was mobbed by reporters and photographers wanting to capture the moment. He was greeted with *mucho entusiasmo para los juegos proximos*. Paige was treated like an arriving head of state. He and the other black ballplayers were made honorary Dominicans and hailed as goodwill ambassadors, which Paige relished. All eyes were on him. He brought in William Perkins, Cool Papa Bell, Josh Gibson, Sam Bankhead, Leroy Matlock, and Robert "Schoolboy" Griffith, to help round out the team and provide the manpower necessary to guarantee victory. Victory, however, would not be easy.[11]

There was some controversy surrounding the arrival of Paige and his teammates. A great deal of money had been spent to bring the man, or so the public had heard, and now some questioned why this was being done while there was so much poverty in their country that needed to be addressed. The number-one export, sugar, was down 70 percent because of the Great Depression. Coffee sales were down, as were those for bananas. Most Dominicans could not afford milk for their children. These were some hard-hitting truths. Aybar immediately intervened and assured the press and any other questioners that all the funds for the Paige team were coming through private sources. Those private funds most likely came from Trujillo's private coffers. He could easily afford it, since he had already stashed away nearly a billion dollars.

Paige and the other ballplayers loved playing south of the border because of the way they were treated. He enjoyed the accommodations in the Dominican Republic. They were housed at one of the best hotels and took full advantage of the services and pampering. In fact, they were out every night until the wee hours of the morning, drinking, enjoying music, and having a great time fraternizing. Paige high-stepped the nights away, having a ball with President Trujillo's favorite dance, the merengue, which originated in the Dominican Republic and was sweeping the nation. The nightly overindulgence in good times soon became evident in Paige's and the other black ballplayers' performances on the field. They lost several games. They had tough teams to play against, to get past a highly talented Santiago team and to make it to the championships. The Trujillo regime had not paid prime cash to Paige and company to come in to lose. It was at that point that the master hurler and his teammates were sequestered on a nightly basis. They were given a curfew and made to stick to it so that they would have enough rest before each game. Army personnel were placed outside the hotel entrance.[12]

Immediately, Paige and company started winning and advanced to play for the championship in July. In the final game, Paige came in for the last three innings to shut down the other team. One can only image how fast his fastballs were, but, as he said, he never threw harder in his life. He shut down the Estrellas Orientales. Team Ciudad Trujillo took the game 8–6 and the Dominican Republic National Championship in Baseball.

Paige would later say that they had to win because armed soldiers had ringed the stadium. He gives the impression that they were going to shoot him and his teammates if they were not victorious. As he described the situation: "If we didn't win we would've been gone over Jordan." He exaggerated a bit. There were also those who claimed that the game was fixed in that Trujillo controlled the umpires. If that were the case, Trujillo could have saved thirty thousand dollars and just simply fixed the game. Who knows all the intricacies of what went on, but it was clearly an educational experience for Paige and the other ballplayers, an event that was multidimensional as well for what was transpiring behind the scenes in international relations.[13]

No matter how the game was won, and most think it was won fairly, the victory benefited Trujillo and his image as strongman. It is doubtful that Paige realized the impact of his participation in assisting the Trujillo regime, although later he would quip about the article that appeared in the *Pittsburgh Courier* that recounted how "Satch saved our president [Trujillo]." Even if made aware of the serious implications of his role, Paige would likely have simply shrugged it off and said that he was only a ballplayer, not a politician or diplomat. Actually, he was all three, whether he wanted to be or not.[14]

The fight to stop Paige from going down to the Dominican Republic in the first place and, failing that, the attempt to force him back to the United States and to halt any future jumping of Negro Leagues ballplayers to the tropics was played out in the courts and the US State Department. The issue became a cause célèbre, a virtual Negro Leagues Baseball versus President Rafael Trujillo and the Dominican Republic.

It was apparent as early as May 29, 1937, that the State Department was taking seriously—or at least giving the impression that it was—this issue of Negro Leagues ballplayers and the whole question of their being enticed to break their contracts to go play in the Dominican Republic. In the State Department documents file, one finds: "Practice of inducing Negro baseball players to break contracts in the United States: request for negotiation of agreement with Dominican Republic to the aim that the latter will stop." Gus Greenlee and Abe Manley voiced their outrage about the Negro Leagues players being stolen by the Dominicans.[15]

Ferdinand Morton wrote to Senator Robert Wagner on behalf of the Negro National League. Morton was the civil service commissioner for New York City and had been solicited by the Negro National League to assist them in this matter. They wanted to make their case through Senator Wagner because they knew that he was a fan of Negro Leagues Baseball and of course of Satchel Paige. He was also senator from nearby New York State, and, even more important, he was the architect of the Wagner Act of 1935 and one who had a long history of being intimately involved with issues of labor, contractual relationships, free trade, and ethical business practices. In short, they knew his reputation for fairness. But if they had read between the lines, they would have also known that Wagner tended to be prolabor, and they were, after all, management and owners. It was Wagner's reputation that they were counting on. They thought he was the perfect person to help in this matter. When Wagner received a letter from Morton, he gave the issue his full consideration.[16]

The Negro National League was hopeful that the senator would see the encroachment of Trujillo and the Dominican Republic as a violation of the sacred ground of contractual relationships between labor and management and help them. The Negro National League was also concerned that "American sugar interests," as they put it, seemed to be involved in this whole matter from both sides of the border and had undertaken "the promotion of baseball in the Republic of San Domingo and . . . induced and procured 10 of our players in violation of their contracts to desert their clubs and go to San Domingo for the purpose of playing there. The Pittsburgh Crawfords, champions of last year, have been hardest hit; all of their star players having been induced to go to San Domingo."[17]

Of course, the Negro National League's and the Crawfords' biggest concern was that of Satchel Paige, who left and took key players with him to the Dominican Republic. They suspected that attendance at Negro National

League games would be hurt. In short, the owners placed the onus of the success of the raids on Paige and blamed him later on for diminished ticket sales. The master hurler was an international concern.

Senator Wagner felt that this was a serious issue but one that should be taken up with the appropriate body, which he advised was the State Department. He wrote on June 4, 1937, to Ruth B. Shipley of the Department of State and requested that her office look into the matter. Senator Wagner, in his letter to Shipley, made note of the following: "The enclosed letter from Ferdinand Morton, Commissioner of the Municipal Civil Service Commission of New York City, concerning certain Negro baseball players who have left the United States to enter into a contract to join baseball players in San Domingo, is respectfully referred to the State Department for such consideration as the matter may in your judgment merit. I shall appreciate your advice together with the return of the enclosure."[18]

Wagner had written himself out of a hot potato in one sense, but, in another, the matter was now in front of the appropriate authority—the State Department—with a request that it look into the complaint. Satchel Paige was now going to be discussed within the highest echelons of the US government.

This matter had delicate implications, given American fruit and sugar concerns. The United Fruit Company was being accused of being in collusion with the Trujillo government. This was not a small matter. Delicate relationships may well have lay in the balance. Did the State Department think that Negro Leagues Baseball and concern over one Leroy "Satchel" Paige was worth upsetting far more powerful economic interests and international relationships? The Negro Leagues team owners were making their case but were likely in well over their heads.

Morton's letter that was passed on to the State Department told of a desperate situation for Negro National League baseball. He said that the "outrageous acts on the part of our players are legally unanswerable to us in damages." He advanced the argument that if this jumping of Paige and other ballplayers to the islands persisted that it would likely destroy the Negro Leagues: "Our problem is a great one for the very existence of our league is threatened. All the work which we have done to secure for the colored ball player a decent wage will go for not unless we are able to prevent further inroads."[19]

Morton listed other violations under which Senator Wagner or other US government officials or the State Department might act. He said that he had it on good authority that Paige and the other players had flown from the United States to the Dominican Republic and, most important, exited without obtaining passports.

He was at least correct about the mode of transportation. The Trujillo operatives contracted with Pan-American Airlines to provide a charted Clipper plane to transport the master hurler and other Negro Leagues stars. They were priority travelers, with convertible sleeping berths and all, aboard the new Sikorsky S-42 that brought Paige and company in style for a water landing in the Caribbean Sea at the doorstep of picturesque Ciudad Trujillo.[20]

Morton ended his plea on behalf of the Negro Leagues owners with the strong suggestion that international treaties were being violated and that the State Department should take action to get Satchel Paige and the other players back. "In view of the foregoing, it occurs to me that the treaty that prevails between nations would require the government of San Domingo, upon friendlier representations made to it by our Department of State, to direct the immediate return of these players to the United States so that they may fulfill their lawful obligations here." If this did not happen, Morton reiterated, Negro Leagues Baseball would not be able to survive; the economic damage was too great. He argued passionately that what was happening was unconscionable and irreversible if not stopped immediately. "Actions at law for damage are not adequate by reason of the fact that irreparable loss will be sustained by us unless these unlawful acts are terminated and actions at equity are impracticable for the reasons mentioned. I am certain that if the course of action proposed by me is feasible, you will exert every effort to induce the State Department to adopt it."[21]

Senator Wagner seconded the owners' appeal to the State Department, which ensured that the international jump of Paige and the others to the Dominican Republic would get the very fullest attention of the State Department. It indeed did. Secretary of State Cordell Hull responded to Senator Wagner, informing him that "certain Negro baseball players have been induced to break their contracts with the National Association of Negro baseball leagues and to leave the country for the Dominican Republic to play professional baseball," a matter that his department had already been apprised of and was investigating. Secretary Hull continued on in his response:

The department already had been advised of this complaint by Ira Hurwick, Esquire, who states that he is the attorney for the association, and who requested an appointment with the appropriate division of the Department of State in order that he might fully set forth the case. Mr. Hurwick was advised in a letter of June 8, 1937, that he might call at any time during office hours at the Division of the American Republics of the Department of State where he would have ample opportunity to state his problem. He was told further that if he cared to fix a definitive date and hour for his call, arrangements would be made for the assistance of one of the legal advisors to be present in order that the legal aspects of the case could be examined. As yet, Mr. Hurwick has not called, nor has he arranged for an appointment.

The letter was signed "Sincerely yours, Cordell Hull." Wagner apprised Morton of the results of his personal inquiry and the response from Secretary Hull. The effort of the owners against the Trujillo government over Paige and the other "jumpers" was gaining momentum.[22]

The Satchel Paige matter was in play in Congress. Secretary Hull began receiving a large array of correspondence from members of the United States House of Representatives and Senate, inquiring into the Satchel Paige matter, all of which were the result of Negro Leagues owners and their repeated pleas for help. A resolution was pushed forward by the Negro Leagues owners, through their attorney and finally through their congressional representatives. "I have enclosed a copy of the letter and the Resolution which was sent to me by attorney Ira Hurwick of Pittsburgh, Pennsylvania, concerning the National Association of Negro baseball leagues" and the Satchel Paige problem.[23]

The owners continued their strategy of soliciting help from friends in Congress. Representative Henry Ellenbogen of Pittsburgh, who was a co-sponsor of the national legislation that proposed establishing public housing, was also a big fan of Negro Leagues Baseball and the Crawfords. Hurwick and the Negro National League solicited and got his support.[24]

Representative Matthew Dunn of Pennsylvania also received a copy of the resolution from attorney Ira Hurwick in a communiqué dated June 12, 1937. The Satchel Paige jump to the Dominican Republic, Hurwick added, was detrimental to the well-being of the entire population of people of color in the United States. He wrote, "The enclosed resolution involves a matter of great importance not only to us as club owners but also to the American Negroes generally." Dunn requested that Secretary Hull investigate the matter.[25]

The owners attempted to up the ante. All political friends of the colored race in America were being asked to join in support of the efforts to stop Satchel Paige and the other stars of Negro Leagues Baseball from any further international intrigue. The owners wrote in soliciting support from congressional representatives: "We believe that if you and our other friends in Congress who are interested in our problems, would intercede for us before the Department of State, the difficulty resided in the resolution would be removed and a friendly arrangement be made which would be satisfactory and beneficial both to Organized Negro Baseball in the United States and baseball in the Dominican Republic."[26]

The Negro Leagues owners were also conveying a strong feeling of helplessness. This was an international crisis as they saw it, yet all they could do was to keep pressing home the urgency of the problem, continue soliciting letters from congressional supporters, and hope for the intervention of the

State Department. Attorney Hurwick pleaded further: "Since we have no other means of protecting the interests of organized Negro baseball we respectfully seek your aid and urgently request your cooperation."[27]

Satchel Paige was just that important. Although the owners attempted to make the issue a broader one, and not just focus on Paige, everyone knew that Paige was the key to all of this, since he was by far the superstar of Negro Leagues Baseball and without him the league would suffer dire economic consequences that might indeed be irreversible.[28]

The owners played upon the theme of patriotism and national loyalty in pushing their case. In the resolution made by them, every effort was made to present themselves as American businessmen who believed in the principles and practices of capitalism, free enterprise, and fairness. They were, they wrote, a patriotic and law-abiding American business that was being done wrong by international forces beyond their control.

The ownership pointed out in the resolution how they operated under a constitution and bylaws, with rules and regulations that were in complete accord with the fairness doctrine, and abiding by business ethics and the goodwill of labor relations in the sanctity of written contracts subject to set rules and regulations, which they reiterated that Paige and the other jumpers were violating. Theirs was the cry that the State Department and every other American government agency should back the owners in their struggle. The owners beseeched the State Department to help them in preserving "this good-faith effort with the intervention of foreign governments working against the best interests of an American business enterprise—Negro National League baseball."[29]

As far as the league was concerned, Satchel Paige and his jumping buddies were destroying a fair-minded and productive business enterprise at a time of American and global economic crisis. To let this continue, the owners argued, was bad for the United States. As stated in the resolution, "Said association by hard work, effort and large sums of money spent in the organizing, developing and training of its personnel, management and players since 1933, has made organized Negro baseball a substantial business with assets of over $500,000, an annual payroll of approximately $150,000, employing hundreds of persons and enjoying the good will and respect of organized baseball and the public which it serves." They urged support of their organization. They believed that Trujillo and the others would stop it if the US government intervened on their behalf in this crucial moment.[30]

The owners also took a substantive jab at Major League Baseball and its prevailing color line. "Whereas Negro baseball players are unable to become members of any of the teams in either the Major or Minor leagues in the

United States and that this league therefore has given opportunity and employment to hundreds of Negro baseball players, has given the American Negro youth a chance to display and develop his talents in the National sport and has provided entertainment for millions of Negro baseball fans." In sum, Negro Leagues Baseball, the owners pleaded, served the special needs of the African American community. It was an all-American game that was being pirated by external forces. They passionately pleaded that the practice must be stopped.[31]

As far as the owners were concerned, and as the rhetoric ratcheted upward, the Trujillo government's pirating of Paige and others was a form of foreign invasion, a violation of American sovereignty and Manifest Destiny, an affront to the sanctity of American business enterprise operated by and for black Americans, and detrimental to fans, and players, in every sport.[32]

The owners expressed their condemnation of Paige and his belief that he was free to sell his baseball skills and abilities to the highest bidder. There were those owners who also questioned Paige's patriotism. Paige was prone toward taking care of himself. The owners, while painting him as coldhearted and cold-blooded, avoided the reality that Negro Leagues Baseball, like most businesses, was premised on making profits on the backs of its workers. Paige was virtually a preview of baseball free agency. He recognized his own value as a marquee athlete and was determined not to be shortchanged in that regard.[33]

There was no question, however, that Paige could have communicated better with Crawfords owner Gus Greenlee rather than jumping ship during spring training. There is no indication anywhere that Greenlee received a letter or any other communication from the star hurler indicating his dissatisfaction and possible readiness to accept the Trujillo offer. In that regard, Greenlee could argue that Paige blindsided him. Paige, on the other hand, would argue, as he later did, that it was strictly business and making the dollar came first for owners and for him.

There was a stated groundswell of support for the notion of no longer allowing the gifted hurler to control Negro Leagues Baseball, as the owners stated, but for them to take back that control by giving him the opportunity to come back home and honor his contract or forever be banned from Negro Leagues Baseball. The owners issued the following statement aimed at Trujillo and Paige:

> Whereas this practice, still continuing, has disrupted the morale and conduct of the players, injured the investment and assets of the teams of this league and has caused and is causing an irreparable loss to the club owners, Negro baseball players, and the Negro public; and Whereas there has been no effort

made by the Dominican promoters to lure away baseball players of the other leagues in organized baseball, concentrating solely on the Negro baseball players; and Whereas appeals to the Dominican Republic and Trujillo City and to her Minister in Washington have been made to stop this practice, but from communications received the Dominican government has denied both help and cooperation; and Whereas although this practice could be stopped if said players were used by baseball promoters in the United States it cannot be stopped when said players leave the United States and hence and in this manner this league has suffered and continues to suffer irreparable damages; and Whereas negotiations for friendly working arrangement between this League and the Dominican promoters has failed.

The owners made it clear what they wanted: "NOW, THEREFORE, be it resolved that these actions on the part of the Dominican baseball promoters and permitted by the officials of the Dominican Republic BE AND ARE HEREBY CONDEMNED. Be it further resolved that steps be taken to have these practices STOPPED."[34]

The owners requested a Washington hearing to make their case directly before Secretary of State Cordell Hull and the US State Department. They saw this matter as one of national and international importance, and they wanted to personally place the matter "in the hands of the proper officials for action." That audience was not granted.[35]

The final resolution of the owners, which was signed by Greenlee in his capacity as president of the Negro National League, directed that their official appeal be delivered to the Honorable Matthew A. Dunn, representative from the Thirty-Fourth Congressional District of Pennsylvania, who would then, they hoped, place it before the secretary of state. They wanted Dunn's help in "requesting urgent support on behalf of organized baseball and the use of his good offices to stop the practices set forth in the premises which endanger the existence of organized Negro baseball." The owners unanimously adopted the resolution at a special meeting held in Philadelphia on May 27, 1937, at which all of the teams of the Negro National League were present, including the Newark Eagles, Homestead Grays, Washington Elite Giants, Pittsburgh Crawfords, Philadelphia Stars, and New York Black Yankees. Dunn did forward these demands to the secretary of state.[36]

The owners were desperate to stop Trujillo and the other nations south of the border from their infringement. They had no problem with their players being engaged in "winter league ball" in those countries, but the taking of Paige and the other jumpers at the start of the regular season was a devastating blow. The list of countries they accused of being the main perpetrators of the "pirating" of Satchel Paige, Josh Gibson, Cool Papa Bell, and fourteen other star Negro Leagues ballplayers included the Dominican Republic, Puerto Rico, Cuba, Venezuela, and Mexico.[37]

The persistence of the Negro Leagues Baseball owners and their barrage of supportive letters from elected officials paid off by the end of June, when Secretary of State Cordell Hull's office made an official inquiry into the jumping of Paige and others to the baseball team in the Dominican Republic. Sumner Welles, writing on behalf of the secretary of state, on June 24, 1937, communicated to Franklin B. Atwood, the American chargé d'affaires ad interim in Ciudad Trujillo, to investigate the complaint from the National Association of Negro Baseball Leagues "alleging that certain Dominican promoters had enticed star Negro Leagues players to break their contracts and leave the United States to play baseball in the Dominican Republic."[38]

The letter on behalf of the secretary of state also included a copy of the resolution submitted by the Negro Leagues owners. The secretary shared with the American representative in the Dominican Republic the formidable list of seventeen players identified as having jumped to the Dominican Republic. That list of players included ten players from the Pittsburgh Crawfords, and heading the list was Leroy "Satchel" Paige, along with "Christopher, Williams, Patterson, Carter, Matlock, Bell, Bankhead, Perkins, and Brewer." The Philadelphia Stars were missing three players who had gone to the Dominican Republic: "Parnell, Thomas, and Hunter." The Black Yankees were missing two players: "Thompson and Seals." The Washington Elite Giants were "missing Griffin, and the Homestead Grays were missing Josh Gibson."[39]

Secretary Hull did receive a report from the American attaché, but it was not what the owners had hoped for. Secretary Hull's office communicated the following: "There seems to be very little that the Department of State could do in the way of action on behalf of the Association, either official or unofficial; that, of course, we were glad to offer suggestions, but that the case did not appear to contravene the general principles of international law or our treaty rights with the Dominican Republic." The lawyers for the owners replied that they could appreciate this, but they "hoped that it might be possible for the Secretary of State or one of his assistants to intimate to the Dominican authorities that the present practice was not a very friendly one to this country."[40]

A subsequent meeting between the Negro Leagues owners and a representative of the Dominican Republic was held. The two sides met in New York City to discuss the concerns. We may never know the details of that meeting, but following it, Negro Leagues owners met with the director of the Department of State division of Latin American affairs in Washington, DC, on June 29, 1937. Present at the meeting were Gus Greenlee, president of the National Association of Negro Baseball Leagues and the Pittsburgh Crawfords; Vernon

Green of the Washington Elite Giants; Ed Bolden of the Pittsburgh Stars; Effa Manley of the Newark Eagles (who was listed simply as Mrs. Abraham Manley); Major R. Jackson, president of the American Association of Negro Baseball Leagues and other Chicago baseball clubs; and attorney Ira Hurwick. The Negro Leagues owners explained that they had made several serious efforts to negotiate with the Dominicans that proved fruitless. The owners were disheartened. There was no escaping the wider-ranging psychological impact of the jumping of Paige and the other black baseball stars. The owners lamented, "In this manner organized Negro baseball has become demoralized."[41]

The owners complained that once the "raiding" became clear to them, they made formal appeals to the Dominican government both in Trujillo City and to the Dominican minister in Washington. They noted that for several weeks these appeals remained unanswered and that when they finally did receive a reply, the Dominican government claimed that the acquiring of Satchel Paige was "a private matter" over which the government had no control, meaning that private citizens contracted with Paige and the other ballplayers. Frederico Nina, an assistant and attorney to the Dominican minister to the United States, said that President Trujillo and the Dominican government had nothing to do with contracting with the American ballplayers: "These teams were organized as civic propositions and were nonprofit organizations, supported by subscriptions and small admission prices." The owners knew better. There was no debate in their minds, and they reiterated their contention that Paige and the others had been lured south with "at least the approval and sanction of the national Dominican government."[42]

Effa Manley suggested that some sort of arrangement had to be reached between the owners and the Dominicans because a prolonged legal battle would prove harmful to all sides. In short, she wondered out loud if a more "amicable solution" could not be found. It was suggested that the Latin American Office make the case to the Dominicans. The Latin American Office rejected that idea. Satchel Paige was one thing, but the State Department was now getting to the point where it felt that the Negro Leagues owners either did not understand diplomatic relations or wanted the US government to be involved where it should not be. The owners and their attorney were told, "This does not seem to be proper for the State Department to do this if you ask me."[43]

The owners, however, did not easily take no for an answer, and they continued their laborious campaign for injunctive relief. In a lengthy, rambling, and intentionally redundant letter to the State Department, they demanded that the Dominicans be told to "keep their hands off of our baseball players."[44]

The fiery approach to the Satchel Paige issue worked to a degree. Another meeting was called between the attorneys of the Negro Leagues owners and the Dominican minister to the United States, Andres Pastoriza. They were at least talking, although with little result. After all of the discussions, secret talks, and polite and heated exchanges ended, the Negro Leagues owners made their final plea to the State Department: "Organized Negro baseball has provided to the Negro ballplayer and Negro youth the only opportunity he has for the development of his talent, and should be fostered and helped by our government."[45]

The State Department in its "off the record" investigations of the case concluded earlier on—which it kept from the Negro Leagues owners—that President Trujillo was, indeed, behind the pirating of Satchel Paige and the other star Negro Leagues ballplayers but apparently concluded that if the "borrowing" of Paige and the other Negro Leagues ballplayers made Trujillo content, that was good for the greater interests of the United States. On the other hand, perhaps the repetitive pleading of the Negro Leagues owners, and the show of support by their congressional sympathizers, worked to some extent, and the State Department intervened behind the scenes in support of the owners. We may never know.[46]

What we do know for sure is that after 1937, baseball in the Dominican Republic, at least so far as professional and semipro ball were concerned, ceased to exist for nearly twenty years. It may have been an internal economic and political backlash to the championship run, or there may have been other factors involved. The world economic downturn impacting the Dominican Republic and Trujillo's spending habits made matters only worse. The Trujillo pursuit with Satchel Paige of the 1937 championship most likely had something to do with it. US State Department documents may help us in the quest for a definitive answer. Those files, however, remain classified.

Despite the international squabbling, national economic woes, and politics embedded in the quest for the National Baseball Championship of the Dominican Republic in 1937, the people of the Dominican Republic were treated to some superb baseball. Great baseball throughout the world was becoming synonymous with the name Satchel Paige. In his book *Baseball's Other All-Stars,* William McNeil rightly concludes that Paige and the star Negro Leaguers "were the ambassadors of the sport around the world." These baseball globetrotters of color were revered in Latin America, the Caribbean, and other parts of the planet. Paige's legendary exploits on the diamond were well known throughout the world, including in Japan, although he never played there. Thanks in no small part to these baseball ambassadors of color, the game grew in popularity throughout the 1930s, and leagues were established. One of the most exceptional and controversial leagues in the world was the Dominican Republic Summer League of 1937, due in large part to Satchel Paige.[47]

8

The Fugitive

The uppity-Negro complex was the proverbial line in the sand of black-white race relations throughout much of the history of the United States and a guiding principle during Paige's lifetime. Blacks, like Satchel Paige, who defied conventional norms could find themselves at the mercy of white authority. In Paige's case, however, the difference was that the authority he defied was black rather than white. After all of the furor from the Negro Leagues owners, according to Paige, when he and his teammates returned to the United States in July 1937, it was like they had never left. The Negro Leagues owners were previously talking about what they would do to him, how he was banned forever from Negro Leagues ball, and that he would never play another game in the United States. The so-called ban against him was, at best, short-lived. Paige found that the threatening owners quickly "smiled real pretty at me." "They wanted me so bad they developed the shortest memories you ever saw anywhere around about me jumping the Crawfords. Through that summer there were all the jobs I wanted and more, so many I couldn't get anywhere close to taking care of them."[1]

He was back again as the star of stars. Actually, he had never vacated the throne; he just left the States for a short while. He was proving repeatedly that he was Negro Leagues Baseball and that it needed him just as much or more than he needed it. He was getting offers to play everywhere. In his hurry to make gigs, Satchel Paige many times showed up late. It was also true that he missed more than one game because he overbooked himself, changed his mind, or just plain forgot.[2]

In some respects he was becoming, in the old adage, bigheaded. An incident occurred that punctuated the notion that his uppityness, while he kept his attitude in check among his fellow players, was beginning to carry over to his public life. The incident became a touchstone for Paige, a reminder that defying baseball owners was one thing, but disrespecting his public admirers was intolerable. Paige was eating at a restaurant when he was told by one of the waiters that some old friends of his from Mobile, Alabama, were in the lobby and inquiring whether he was there. They wanted to see him and to say hello. Paige told the waiter to tell them that he had already left. Later, leaving the establishment, he ran into the folks from Mobile, who questioned him on whether he had tried to avoid them and was too important to give a few minutes to those from his old stomping grounds. He told them that the waiter had made a mistake and that he had been there all the time and that of course he had time for his folks from Mobile, but at that particular moment he had a meeting downtown and was in a hurry. He gave his fellow Mobilians the short end of the stick and continued his quick exit. He told them, "You get a hold of me later, hear?" Paige ducked out and never thought anymore about it. It was some years later that he rethought his behavior that day and vowed to never act that way again. "It took me a lot of years before I found out it was a mighty little man who did things that way." He was indeed capable of making mistakes. He was also capable of learning from them.[3]

The joyous reality for Negro Leagues Baseball fans was that Paige was back in the country. He was barnstorming with his Trujillo All-Stars team, also commonly known as Satchel Paige's All-Stars. They won the Denver Post Tournament and then were scheduled to come to Chicago in August 1937. Paige told people a lavish story about how he and his teammates fled dictator Trujillo and the Dominican Republic, yet he and his team were known as the Trujillo All-Stars, with the name Trujillo actually on their team uniforms. In fact, the *Chicago Defender* ran an article stating that "Satchel Paige's All-Stars, representing the Dominican Republic, after winning the Denver Post Tournament last week and annexing the $3000 prize that goes with the triumph, invaded Chicago this week." The team did not represent the Trujillo government. It was a marketing ploy that Paige and Abe Saperstein concocted.[4]

Paige and his Trujillo All-Stars, or Satchel Paige All-Stars, were certainly making the rounds all through the remainder of the summer and fall of 1937. On September 10, "Paige and his Santo Domingo champions [another name used for Paige and his band of ballplayers], who also won the Denver Post League tournament, will meet an All-Star team from the Negro National League in the first game of a doubleheader, and in the nightcap. Winners of this game will meet a team of the International League All-Stars featuring players of Newark and other clubs." Paige was in high demand and doing well outside of the regular channels of Negro Leagues organized baseball. The press went on to note that he headed the most sensational team "in the history of race baseball." The publicity surrounding Paige played up his winning of the Dominican National Baseball Championship for Trujillo and how he and his team had successfully overpowered a superb Cuban team led by the great Martin Dihigo.[5]

Paige had become bigger than Negro Leagues Baseball. He was a one-man show, and he assuredly enjoyed the attention and the pay that came with it. The ads for games in which he would appear typically touted his name above all others, such as the announcement of his next game: "Satchel Paige to appear in big game at the Polo grounds." There was much talk about this one being a "gala celebration." Harlem was making ready for a good game of entertaining baseball with Satchel Paige on the mound.[6]

His public was interested in every aspect of his life. Al Monroe, sportswriter for the *Chicago Defender*, noted how well Paige dressed and focused on that for one of his columns

> Satchel Paige, sensational speedballer who came here to strut his stuff at the Polo Grounds Sunday, has undergone a change. Not in his pitching delivery but in his dress. Today Satchel is perhaps the best dressed man in baseball, owner or otherwise. Yesteryear Satchel Paige was just another ballplayer wearing clothes to either keep him warm or to hide his frame. Satchel, one of the quietest men in baseball, lives in the room next to your columnist while here in New York. That is they tell me he does. I have yet to hear or see him in his room. For several days I thought Satchel lived in the lobby of the hotel—that was the only time I saw him or ever heard his voice. A quiet man is Satchel Paige. Perhaps that isn't strange to you but it truly is to your correspondent. With the exception of old Smokey Joe Williams, of speedball lore, all good pitchers are generally just as adept with the lung power.

Paige also knew he was a superstar, and that was another factor in his commitment to always dress well in public. His whole demeanor suggested someone who was soaring above the fracas. He was Sir Satchel. He received further anointment when Joe DiMaggio of the New York Yankees made the statement that "Satchel Paige is the best pitcher he ever faced."[7]

Paige was not always victorious, to be sure. His high riding in September 1937 had its downside as well. He met his Waterloo on Sunday, September 24, against pitcher Johnny Taylor, who bested Paige in a 2–0 victory. The press triumphantly noted that Taylor "white washed" Paige and his team. Witnesses of the contest confirmed that Taylor was superior that day but that Paige "was not exactly a slouch." He allowed a total of only seven hits that were scattered throughout the early going of the game. Paige pitched extremely well until the eighth inning. That inning opened with the other team putting together successive hits off Paige. One of the homers continued to rise as the fifteen thousand fans screamed. They knew the ball would clear the fence the moment he connected. It was a sterling climax to what all seemed to agree was "one of the most thrilling games ever to be witnessed anywhere." Even when Satchel Paige lost, the game was definitely entertaining.[8]

The master hurler met Johnny Taylor again on October 1, 1937, and it was Paige who rose to victory. Paige beat the young Connecticut ace by a score of 9–5. It was the return match that everyone had waited for, including Paige. He never liked losing and made it a point in their rematch to show, in fact, who was still the master. A crowd of more than twenty-five thousand witnessed the contest, the fifth in the series.[9]

To those questioning Paige on occasion as to whether he thought that Gus Greenlee and some of the other owners might still be carrying a grudge and want him banned or at least heavily penalized, he replied that "he had heard nothing like that from Gus. He ain't said nothing about baseball to me all winter." Paige went on to say, "The league's all right. All the owners are all right with me. Some of the players make it hard for me because of the publicity I get because of my salary." Paige also claimed that he preferred playing on a Negro Leagues team rather than barnstorming with his all-star squad. He emphatically stated, "I would rather play in the leagues if they want me. If they don't I got to look out for myself. Nothing wrong in that."[10]

They wanted him. It seemed clear that Paige was going to play again for the Pittsburgh Crawfords for the coming season and that all sins had been forgiven between him and Greenlee. All of this proved that Satchel Paige was bigger than Negro Leagues Baseball. His magic at the gate was too much to walk away from. Paige showed his business acumen and his earning powers. Teams met his demands or would have to do without his services. He may well have been not only the first free agent in baseball but the first successful one.[11]

When April 1938 came, Paige was in the news because he was holding out for more money before reporting to the Crawfords. "I'm holding out because Joe DiMaggio advised me to," Paige told his inquiring fans. He may well have received a pep talk from DiMaggio and been advised to hold out, since DiMaggio himself was contemplating similar action. Paige spent the downtime effectively, from his own point of view, taking dancing lessons in New York and trying to decide whether to accept the salary offer of Greenlee and the Crawfords or succumb to the princely offers that Latin interests were making him, reportedly at three times the salary he could command in the United States.[12]

Friends and family knew that the dynamic Paige expected to go first-class all the way, especially when it came to baseball and his salary. He was not happy with what Greenlee was offering him: "Before I will do what Gus Greenlee wants me to do I will quit and give up baseball." From other sources it was learned that Greenlee was offering Paige only $350 a month that year. Paige wanted much more. Paige thought that part of the factor behind Greenlee's "low" salary offer was that "Gus was made to accept a penalty because I left the US last year for Santo Domingo which caused a group of players to leave also. He says I caused the whole thing. The Negro National League penalized the Santo Domingo rebels one fourth of a month's salary before they became members of the league this season." Paige was not interested in paying any fine, either outwardly or through a lower monthly salary. He asked the media, "What would you do? Say you are getting $600 a month and someone comes along and offers you three times that amount. Would you take it?" Asked what was his mission in New York, Paige hinted that there was plenty going on in terms of interest from the Argentines who had been seeking star players for the season and trying to raid the leagues. The Argentine story was, of course, a fabrication on Paige's part, as he shined the media on. "I came here only to bring Anthony Cooper from Pittsburgh and see him off. He is going with the Argentine team," Paige claimed. He thought Cooper a splendid utility man who could play all positions on the team. Asked if he too planned to make a deal with Argentina, Paige answered, "It is not definite. I'm waiting on the results of another meeting with Greenlee and Pittsburgh. After I leave New York I'll return to Pittsburgh before making any decision."[13]

Asked about a possible offer from the Newark Eagles, he said that he was going over to Mrs. Manley's in Newark on Sunday afternoon. He missed Abe Manley by one day, the latter having left for Jacksonville early Saturday. Effa Manley, when asked about Newark's interest in Paige, said that they were not authorized to pursue him, that he was, to her way of thinking, still the property of Greenlee and the Crawfords, "We do not have permission of Mr. Greenlee to talk business to Paige. However, if he comes over in time I will talk to him on general matters. Because of the etiquette observed by team owners one owner cannot talk directly to a player he wishes to get from another team. All such discussion must be made with the players and owners. Therefore the Newark visit of Paige will not include discussion of his purchase." Paige did not believe in this procedure. He considered himself independent and free to speak to anyone he chose.[14]

Greenlee tried to disguise his mixed feelings about Paige's continued success. He was still angry about 1937, but with the promise that Paige was going to report to the Crawfords for the 1938 season, Greenlee displayed a positive public face. That public face quickly turned to outrage when Paige failed to show up in Pittsburgh to play for the Crawfords as promised. Word had it that he had jumped, or would shortly, south of the border for the promise of bigger paychecks. Greenlee had enough. He immediately entered into talks with Abe Manley and his wife, Effa Manley, owners of the Newark Eagles, to buy Paige's contract.

Unfortunately for the Manleys, Paige was a no-show at Newark as well. "There is no question but that Satchel is a great pitcher and would help our club," Abe Manley acknowledged, "but we cannot let even a twirler so good as Paige run our leagues. This is not Satchel's first offense, you know. He did the same thing last season."[15]

There was widespread speculation that Paige was jumping to the islands. Others thought he would be headed for one of the Latin countries. There were those who predicted that none of that would happen because of a restraining order issued in New York to keep Paige from breaking his contract and fleeing the country. The Manleys and Greenlee, along with the Negro National League, succeeded in getting a restraining order issued by the New York Supreme Court to keep the much-sought-after pitcher from leaving the country. They sought the order once rumors began to intensify that Paige was thinking seriously about prospective offers from somewhere in Latin America. Justice Ferdinand Cora mandated in the order that if Paige failed to show up in court, he would be a wanted man. League attorney R. F. Kerry said that he was pleased with the ruling and reiterated that if Paige fled the country, he would be an outlaw.[16]

Then came the news on May 21, 1938, that "Satchel Paige has disappeared!" The headline story went on to suggest that it might be necessary to call in Sherlock Holmes because this was a strange mystery, so baffling that Scotland Yard was perhaps the only organization qualified to handle it at the present time. Satchel Paige was gone. He evidently left the country before the restraining order was issued. Supposedly, law enforcement was "anxious to find the great one and settle a few matters with him."[17]

Under "fugitive," the *Pittsburgh Courier* reported that "Satchel is now classified as a fugitive from justice, a contract breaker and under a number of other technical terms." Paige was being ordered to present himself and to answer charges of "fraudulent conversion" and violation of the court-issued order not to leave the country. But he had vanished. In the meantime, Abe Manley, it was reported, waited "for Satchel to return from his hideout and join up with his baseball team, which is now in the midst of a fight for the leadership of the Negro National League. As yet, no one seems to know of the colorful pitcher's whereabouts. Two weeks ago he left Pittsburgh via the airways and evidently disappeared in the clouds."[18]

Paige had defied Negro Leagues ownership once again. An outraged Greenlee had him banned effective as of the end of May 1938. Already, Negro Leagues ball was touting the name of a new pitcher that many thought might eventually surpass Paige. People were taking good notice of the twenty-two-year-old sensational thrower, Johnny "Schoolboy" Taylor, to replace the gap left by Paige on the pitching staff of the Crawfords. The headline went on to say that Schoolboy Taylor was "making them forget Satchel." The article made note that Paige was great, eccentric, and colorful, but he had "been barred from playing in the Negro National League for the rest of his life." The Negro National League owners gave an official press conference and announced that they voted to "strike the name of Paige from the records of the league and refused him permission to ever play again in organized Negro baseball." They went on to say that Paige's constant refusal to comply with the rules of the league for the past two years brought about the drastic action on the part of the officials. The claim was made that Satchel Paige had become known as "the bad-boy of Negro baseball."[19]

None of this really bothered Paige. He had constantly broken contracts and jumped from one team to another. The owners went on to report that this year, he again joined the holdout ranks when he refused to sign the contract that Greenlee offered him. Paige evidently broke his word but had not signed a contract with Greenlee, giving him only the promise that he would do it. On the other hand, Greenlee was not offering Paige the amount of money he demanded. The press, especially the *Pittsburgh Courier,* was pro-Greenlee and readily condemned Paige's behavior.

Paige indeed jumped ship and played ball in Venezuela and from there went, in his words, up north to Mexico. Also going across the border to play ball were Chet Brewer, Cool Papa Bell, and other stars who could command much better pay on the other side of the border. Journalist Wendell Smith lashed out at Paige. It was, likely, in part because of Paige's actions, which did not sit well with Smith. One might also deduce that the heralded sportswriter was beholden to Greenlee or perhaps just bitter that the key sport attraction in Pittsburgh and much of the nation was not going to be available for him to write about. Smith reported that rumors had it that Paige was being well paid south of the border and "drawing down 100 coconuts a week" in Mexico. His advice to the talented hurler, who was now a fugitive from justice, was to stay where he was, because if he did return, "soon as he comes back here they're going to throw him in the clinker!"[20]

No matter the onslaught, Paige's reputation as the greatest pitcher in all of baseball stood firm: "Diz Says Paige Is Best Pitcher in Baseball." Dean lamented the absence of star colored players from the big leagues. He recalled an incident at his favorite barbershop in which an argument ensued over who was the best pitcher people had ever seen. Some said it was Lefty Grove; others contended it was Walter Johnson, Pete Alexander, Dizzy Vance, Karl Hubble, or Johnny Carden. Dean pontificated that he had seen all of these great pitchers:

> I know who the best pitcher I ever seen and it's old Satchel Paige, that lanky colored boy. Say, old Dean was pretty fast back in 1931 and 1933, and you know my fastball looked like a change-of-pace alongside that little pistol bullet old Satchel shoots up to the plate. And I really know something about it, because for 4 or 5 years, I toured around at the end of the season with All-Star teams and I see plenty of old Satch. He sure is a pistol. It's too bad these colored boys don't play in the big Leagues, because they sure got some great players.[21]

Paige's new absence from Negro Leagues Baseball made for a void that no one could fill, despite the rhetoric to the contrary. The impact in black Pittsburgh was particularly hard. Greenlee Park, which had been the dream of Gus Greenlee, was by 1938 clearly failing. Greenlee had wanted to give black fans a modern ballpark of their own and was able to make that dream come true back in 1932 when Greenlee Park, on Bedford Avenue, in the heart of black Pittsburgh, was opened as the crowning glory of Negro Leagues Baseball.

The structure, built of concrete and steel, cost more than one hundred thousand dollars and seated seven thousand people. Greenlee Park was within a ten-minute walk of more than ten thousand African Americans. The facility was a welcomed answer to a long prayer of black baseball fans in the tristate area for their own baseball stadium and a way for Negro Leagues team owners to avoid the high rental fees they had to pay to white-owned stadiums. Now the once-grand idea was on its way to being demolished. Bricks were destroyed, lumber and floodlights removed. The Pittsburgh Housing Authority, using all of its vested power, selected the site, along with others along Bedford Avenue, for the erection of housing projects, or what some were calling the colored colony. The Housing Authority bought the land and what was on it. The initial offer of sixty thousand dollars for Greenlee Park was gradually reduced to thirty-eight thousand, and the stockholders had reluctantly accepted, having to because of eminent domain. Reports made it clear that no definitive answer was available to explain how the property's value rapidly declined to only twenty-two thousand dollars—the final price for which the Housing Authority purchased the stadium and its land.

Greenlee took the demise hard and personally. He did not outright blame the demise of the field and the Crawfords on Satchel Paige, certainly not on him alone. His anger was broader than that. He blamed the African American community. The race, it would seem, let the venture fail. Regardless of what mistakes were made, or who made them, the field belonged to the race, and it was disappointing, as the *Pittsburgh Courier* editorialized, that the race had let the stadium die: "Pittsburgh is no place to attempt big things for Negroes."[22]

It, of course, did not help that Greenlee had lost Satchel Paige. Paige, on the other hand, felt no responsibility for the closing of Greenlee Park, although commenting that he wished it could have stayed open as a symbol of racial pride. One can only suggest that it was a project from the beginning that was at risk, coming to fruition in the heart of the 1930s and the ongoing Great Depression.[23]

There were those who blamed the demise of Greenlee Park and the other problems of the Negro Leagues on the big cash from Latin America and the Caribbean that pulled Paige and other players away: "Like rabbits they jumped at it, and left his highness holding the well known empty shotgun." Greenlee, for all practical purposes, seemed to be moving away from baseball and devoting more of his attention to his championship fighter, John Henry Lewis. Paige eventually became agitated with the negative publicity and blame for the financial woes of Negro Leagues Baseball. He said that he could share some of the responsibility but that the Great Depression was the real culprit. It was hard all over. The Major Leagues were having hard times as well.[24]

Those faulting the recalcitrant Paige for what was wrong in Negro Leagues Baseball may have gotten their revenge when they learned of his suffering in Mexico in the spring of 1938. He was pitching for the Mexico City team and doing his usual of playing in game after game without any rest. He was paid to play, and fans came out to see him pitch. Even if that pitching was only for a couple of innings, Paige needed to perform.

Doing so much pitching in Mexico, Paige also attempted to add to his pitching repertoire. Particularly, he started working on upgrading his curveball so that he would not have to rely as much on his blistering fastball and the wear and tear that meant on his arm. But what he did not understand was that a curveball meant a slightly different use of muscles, tendons, and the rotator cuff. Pitching every day, and now adding his new curveball, it was in a game in Mexico City that he first began to notice a tightening in his arm. Paige would later joke that "if you are hankering to be a pitcher don't start your curveball in Mexico." It was not so much the difference in altitude, as Paige thought, although that may have been a factor as well. The end result was Paige hurt his arm. The pain was excruciating, so great that "I couldn't scratch my head."[25]

After the first inkling that his arm was failing him, Paige tried to work it off, thinking that it was a momentary thing and once he had his usual boiling-hot shower and rubdown, the arm would be as good as new. As he told his manager, "I'll shake it, you can tell my fastballs' just as quick as always. It just hurts some when I throw it." His manager thought his throwing looked fine but told him "to take this afternoon off. Maybe you just need a little rest." That was what Paige tried to do, and after getting a hot rubdown with boiling water as hot as he could stand it, he went to bed, hoping that the rest would put an end to his arm problem. He found himself tossing and turning through the night because of the pain in his throwing arm. That morning he rose with an incredible feeling of stiffness in his arm and the greatest shock in his life when he tried to lift his arm and realized that "I couldn't lift it." This was the pitcher's worst nightmare. His livelihood, his arm, was not functioning. It took him more than an hour to get dressed because he had the use of only his left arm. He was, understandably, "real scared."[26]

He absolutely lost his composure, thinking only the worst thoughts imaginable. The only thing that interrupted those depressing thoughts was the excruciating pain from his dysfunctional arm. "The pain stayed so long that it finally numbed my arm. Have you ever seen an old man, a real one, one who hurts so he can hardly move and what he can move is so stiff it don't work very good? That was me. I sweated some more and bit into my lip, but I finally got my shirt on. I didn't even think of trying a coat. I couldn't even think. Nothing like that ever happened to me before. I didn't know what to do so I did the only thing I really knew how to do. I went out to the ballpark."[27]

Paige went straight to the field to seek out the manager and requested that someone give him a baseball. He was asked where his uniform was. Never mind that. Paige was given the ball from the bag and then tried to throw it and found that he could not. The pain hit him so hard that all he "could see was white. Everything in me hurt. Then I could see clear again. The ball was only a few feet from me. My manager came right over. 'What's wrong, Satch? What's wrong?' The ball went nowhere." Paige told him in a frightened tone: "It's my arm." Even the simple, gentle touch of his manager to his arm made him grimace. When his manager said he wanted to try moving it around, Paige yelled at him not to do it. The slightest movement of his arm sent pain that cut clear through his head like a knife. He tried again and again to throw the ball, but could manage only little loopers going a few feet. He was living the pitcher's ultimate nightmare. His livelihood, his arm, was in deep trouble.[28]

The focus was on what could be done. Paige consulted the physicians available in Mexico City. They found nothing wrong, no breakages, no torn tendons, no torn ligaments, just an arm with such excruciating pain that it would not permit him to throw a baseball. He knew full well that his ability to pitch, and especially to deliver his patented fastball, was the thing that brought crowds to the ball games and put money in his pocket. His livelihood was in jeopardy.

Immediately, Paige began receiving the cold shoulder from teams. All of a sudden the Mexican team was no longer interested in him. His pay was based on daily performance. If he could not pitch, he did not get paid. If he did not earn money, he did not eat. He was advised that he should probably return to the States. Paige agreed. It was the only thing left for him to do. In the States he could look for what he hoped would be superior medical help and someone who might be able to tell him what was wrong and, more important, fix it. Without his arm he was nothing, and he knew it. To say that Satchel Paige was frightened is to put it lightly. He was terrified out of his wits because his career looked like it might be over.

The news began to spread like wildfire throughout Mexico, Latin America, and the Caribbean that Satchel Paige might be through as a pitcher. The news reached the States, where fans gasped at the bad news. There were some, however, who said that this was divine retribution for Paige's bad behavior and especially his disloyalty to the Negro Leagues. All may have had a point, but the reality was that Paige was working so hard and putting in so many hours trying to make that money that his arm was overworked and had rebelled in such a way that the consequences were made poignantly clear to him and his entire body.

Satchel Paige was a household name. The Latin world had always been warm and friendly to him. They still showed him respect, were polite, and spoke kindly, but since he could no longer pitch, they no longer needed him. Paige packed up his belongings and headed home to the United States.

Arriving back in Pittsburgh, he did not have to worry about any warrants for his arrest for violating the travel restraining orders. Authorities were not interested in him. Friends and fans greeted him with respect. Many inquired as to how his arm was doing and when he would be pitching again. Those questions tortured him. He was suffering his own private agony and damnation. He began to venture out of the hotel less because he would inevitably be met with questions about his arm. There in his room, his depression grew. When the media finally caught up with him to ask him about his plans, he informed them that he had had enough as an active player and was interested in becoming a manager.[29]

With his arm injured and desperately looking for some means of employment, Paige dashed off a telegram to the Newark Eagles, informing them that he was available and that they should "call me at this hotel Friday at 10 o'clock." No phone call was ever made. If one had, what could he have done? He could not pitch.[30]

He wrote further to Effa Manley, attempting to explain the misunderstandings of the past and that he was anxious to correct all of that and play for the

Eagles. "I wanted to let you hear from me. I am well. At this time and I truly hope when these few lines reach you they will find you in the very best of health. Listen Mrs. Manley I thought I heard someone say that I belong to you. Why do you take so long to send for me. I have been waiting and waiting for you to write me. But it looks like something is wrong. Listen Mrs. Manley it looks like to me when I make up my mind to do right everybody wants to do wrong. So I'm gone to see just what you will have to say about me. So if you get this letter please answer it at once. Yours truly."[31]

The Paige letter to Effa Manley was written in all capitals and without proper punctuation. He gave Pittsburgh as his return address. The master hurler was begging to be picked up by the Newark Eagles during this time of his crisis. Desperation was ruling supreme, and Paige was hoping to somehow stay in baseball by any means necessary. The Eagles, however, were no longer anxious to meet with him. That should have been no surprise. All of black baseball knew of the injury to his pitching arm. Effa Manley replied to Paige and told him that she sent a copy of his recent letter and the earlier one as well to her husband, Abe Manley. She wrote, "I am in receipt of your letter asking why you had not heard from the Eagles. I have sent the letter to Mr. Manley in camp at Daytona Beach Florida, and will let you know as soon as I hear from him, what he has to say." Effa Manley did write to her husband to convey what was going on. The Eagles were no longer interested in Satchel Paige.[32]

Paige remained hopeful, or desperate, and wrote her again, urging that she and the Eagles "please don't give up on me" and not to make the "mistake that some of the owners continued to make when they wait until the last minute then they will try to get a man." He went on to tell Manley that he was not under contractual obligations to anyone. So, as far as he was concerned, he was ready to come to New Jersey immediately if they were interested in his services. He wrote, "Please send me a telegram write back and let me know and I'll have my plane ticket made out for where ever you say. Listen I can come to Chicago or St. Louis. I really want you to be the first this year." He suggested to Manley, "Bring your contract with you and we can get together I will sign up" and said, "I do want to hear from you and I don't think you will waste any money on me this year that is if you don't give up. Listen I want the same thing to go as I say last year. Listen Mrs. Manley don't beat around the bush. I'm a man tell me just what you want me to know and please answer the thing I ask you. So I'll close looking to hear from you at once." The letter was signed Mr. Satchel Paige, with, in parentheses, a drawn-in smiley face.[33]

Being an uppity black could have its consequences. The newfound dilemma facing Paige was, in the eyes of many, a case of chickens coming home to roost—a just reward for his contemptuousness. In late spring of 1938, Satchel Paige was hanging around Pittsburgh with no job prospects. Rumor had it that he might go to Florida and join up with the Homestead Grays, but that never materialized. Rumors and hopes were basically all he had left. Paige was at the bottom of the abyss with a career that had seemingly ended in an instant. How would he resurrect himself, reinvent himself, or just plain earn a living? Baseball was the only thing he knew, and it looked like his days on the mound were over.

Lula Paige, circa 1953 (courtesy of the Paige family)

Aleitha Young, circa 1923, a.k.a., "Mrs. Meannie," who was in fact better known as one of the most beloved teachers in the black Mobile community (courtesy of the Young family)

(Above) Pittsburgh Crawfords, 1932. Standing (left to right): Gus Greenlee, Bennie Jones, L.D. Livingston, S.P., Josh Gibson (in jacket), R. Williams, Walter Canady, William Perkins, Oscar Charleston, John Clark (secretary). Kneeling (left to right): Sam Streeter, Chester Williams, Harry Williams, Harry Kincannon, Clyde Spearman, Jimmie Crutchfield, Bobby Williams, Ted "Double Duty" Radcliffe. (courtesy of Ted "Double Duty" Radcliffe)

(Top left) Alabama Reform School for Juvenile Negro Law-Breakers, 1922 (courtesy of the Jackson Davis Collection, Albert and Shirley Small Special Collections Library, University of Virginia)

(Bottom left) Cornelia Bowen, April 26, 1923 (Courtesy of the Jackson Davis Collection, Albert and Shirley Small Special Collections Library, University of Virginia)

(Above) Bismarck Semi-Pro Championship Team, 1935. Standing (left to right): Hilton Smith, Red Haley, Barney Morris, S.P., Vernon Johnson, Quincy Trouppe, Ted "Double Duty" Radcliffe. Kneeling (left to right): Joe Desiderato, Al Leary, Neil Churchill (owner/manager), Danny Oberholzer, Ed Hendee (dropped before the championship). Not shown: Chet Brewer and Art Hancock. (courtesy of Ted "Double Duty" Radcliffe)

(Left) Janet Howard Paige and Bill "Bojangles" Robinson dancing at the wedding reception, October 26, 1934 (courtesy of Tennie Harris and NoirTech Research, Inc.)

(Above) Kansas City Monarchs, 1941. (Left to right): Newt Allen, Rainey Bibbs, Bill Simms, Allen Bryant, Willard Brown, Jesse Williams, Frank Bradley, Hilton Smith, Frank Duncan, James Greene, John Ford Smith, George Walker, John "Buck" O'Neil, Ted Strong, Clifford Johnson, S.P. Not pictured: William Dismukes, Chet Brewer, Jesse Douglas, Frank Duncan III, Willie Hutchinson, Jack Matchett, Booker McDaniel, Andrew Patterson, Eugene Smith, Sylvester Sneed, Herb Souell, Sam Thompson, Tom Young (courtesy of John "Buck" O'Neil)

(Right) S.P. enjoyed collecting fine silver, crystal, and Chippendale furniture, 1942

NEWS-VIEWS

BASEBALL PITCHER

he CHICAGO DAILY NEWS PICTORIAL SECTION
August 29, 1942

157

(Above) S.P. with boxing great Henry Armstrong, examining Cessna airplane used to ferry S.P. to games, 1943

(Top left) S.P. and Dizzy Dean just before a matchup, May 24, 1942

(Bottom left) Negro World Series, Grays v. Monarchs, 1942. Pictured: Josh Gibson, New York Mayor Fiorello La Guardia, and S.P.

(Above) Heavyweight Champ Joe Louis congratulates S.P. for victory over White Sox in second Major League start, August 13, 1948

(Left) S.P. on the mound for Cleveland, 1948

Teammates, Bob Feller and S.P., 1948

S.P. and Bill Veeck in St. Louis, 1951

S.P. Pitching for the Kansas City Athletics in his
final professional game, September 25, 1965

S.P. and family on "This Is Your Life," January 26, 1972. Visible left to right: John Paige, Jr. (brother), Carolyn (daughter), Lahoma (wife), Linda (daughter), S.P., Pamela (daughter), Rita Jean (daughter), Warren (son), Robert (son). Not visible: Lula Quida (daughter), and host Ralph Edwards. Shirley (daughter) not present (courtesy of the Paige family)

Portrait of Lahoma and S.P. at a Negro Leagues ballgame "dressed to the nines." Pamela Paige O'Neal (daughter) and Robert Leroy Paige (son) are holding the portrait in front of a mural, in Kansas City near Vine Street, done in tribute to S.P. by an anonymous artist (photo by John Puglia)

9

Lazarus

Paige went through a parade of different physicians in hopes of finding a cure for his arm. Their diagnosis was the same. "Oh, yes. I remember him. Real good. I remember him because after he was done poking me, and lifting my arm, and checking my back, he studied and thought for what seemed like an hour. Then he turned and looked long at me." That unnamed physician, like all the rest, gave him the same bad news: "Satchel, I don't think you'll ever pitch again." It was a personal ordeal for Paige, and no less of one for the whole of Negro Leagues Baseball, with the well-being of both at stake and often at odds.[1]

For more than a week, or what seemed like an eternity for him, Paige sat in his hotel room in Pittsburgh contemplating the end to his career and questioning how he would earn a living. He walked back and forth, sat a little, and then walked some more. He took walks at night around the neighborhood, wandering, hoping that people would not recognize him. He thought back to his childhood in Mobile when he had little or nothing and wondered whether he would end up the same way. To say that he was in despair was accurate to the highest or lowest sense of the term. He was a baseball player, and that was all that he knew. If he could not earn his money pitching, there was little else left for him. He sent out word to Negro Leagues teams that he was back in town and wanting to join them in some role, perhaps as a manager or doing something related to baseball. The answers were quite simple and straightforward: if Satchel Paige could not pitch, Negro Leagues Baseball was not interested in him. Paige figured that perhaps they could use his name. "That still drew some fans. But they didn't want it," Paige lamented.[2]

He should not have been surprised by the reactions. There was a great deal of animosity in Negro Leagues Baseball about his jumping to Mexico and South America and the Caribbean for the bigger paychecks and at the expense of Negro Leagues ball. At least that was the way that the owners and some of the fans saw it. Now he was scrounging around the fringes of the game, looking for work. Without that magic arm of his, the doors were shut. "They all seemed to be saying something like, well, Satch, you treated me pretty rough back in 35, or, if you joined my club like you were supposed to in 36, if you'd taking care of me then, maybe I could take care of you now. But things are pretty rough right now. You know how it is?" Paige seemed to forget that, while he was away, there was also the little matter of the Negro Leagues having banned him from participating in either the Negro American League or the Negro National League for at least two years.[3]

He was in deep despair. "I could see the end. Ten years of gravy and then nothing but an aching arm and aching stomach. Oh, I had my car and shotguns and fishing gear and clothes." Those items were fleeting, too, as Paige found himself in a situation where he was counting every penny to try to make ends meet. His expensive custom fishing rods and reels, gun collection, and rings and watches were all expendable in the name of survival. He made countless trips to the local pawnshops. It got so they knew him very well. Actually, they knew him at any rate because he was, after all, Satchel Paige. He was now a frequent customer, coming in on an almost daily basis to hock something for cash. As Paige put it, "I had to. A man got a way of getting used to eating and eating takes money." These were times when he felt hunger for the first time in his life. Ironically, growing up in Mobile in a family of twelve, there was always something to eat, thanks to the diligence of mother Lula. He was never one to eat a great deal and pointed out that he never needed much food in his life. But when the food was not available, like now, he was hungrier than ever.[4]

His whole life seemed to be in turmoil. To make things worse, his relationship with Janet had hit an all-time low. They had separate lives and lived apart. Sequestered in his hotel room, he thought about going back to Janet. The thoughts were out of desperation. He discarded them quickly. It was questionable whether she would have him back. He realized that he could not meet the responsibility of provider for her or for himself. His personal pride would not let him do it, and he did not.

These were some long days for Satchel Paige and some very cold and lonely nights. This was the lowest point in his life. "I was a broken bum just wandering around looking for a piece of bread." He was in hell, and it looked insurmountable to him: "I was beat. I knew it. There was no place to turn. I was a big man who was just falling into that old land where nobody knows you."[5]

Then came the phone call that would make the world of difference. It was J. L. (James Leslie) Wilkinson, the owner of the Kansas City Monarchs, and he had a business proposition for him. That phone call from Wilkinson gave Paige a new lease on life. He dashed off to Kansas City with barely a mention to Janet that he was leaving. What remained of their life together was completely over. He would send her checks on an irregular basis, but that was it. What new life he might have a chance at had just begun.[6]

In 1938 when Paige arrived in KC—the nickname that African Americans dubbed the city—he learned that Wilkinson was not inviting him to join the Monarchs, at least not in theory. He wanted him to be part of a separate traveling squad that would be known as the Satchel Paige All-Stars. Actually, that would be the only way that Paige could be used. The Monarchs were in the Negro American League, and had Wilkinson put him on the main squad, that would have been in direct violation of the ban against Paige. The traveling squad, managed by Wilkinson's son, was supposedly an independent group with no league affiliation. Hence, it was an arrangement that did not technically violate the leagues' ban against Paige.

Wilkinson knew of Paige's arm troubles, as everyone in Negro Leagues Baseball did, and expected no real pitching from him. At one level, one could argue that Paige was going to be a sideshow attraction. The master hurler never saw it that way and never put it in those terms, and neither did Wilkinson. The truth was he could not pitch, and people would be coming to see him because of his name. Nevertheless, there were expectations from fans that they would see some glimmer of the old, original Satchel Paige.

He performed a "pepper show," meaning that he did tricks with the ball, like making it roll across his arm and chest to his other arm and hand, and did a little bit of shadow ball playing. He did slow-motion throws and gags. He was putting on a show the only way he could. But the name Satchel Paige drew fans, and it was a moneymaking proposition for Wilkinson and a livelihood once again for Paige. It was certainly way better than living off charity or making more trips to the pawnshop, especially when he had little left to pawn.[7]

It was a smart move on the part of Wilkinson and his associates to make this business arrangement with Paige. He often brought in several thousand paying customers at a single game. Wilkinson was lauded for his business acumen, including how to effectively market Satchel Paige, bad arm or not. Satchel Paige's All-Stars played against community teams, post office teams, industrial league teams, church squads, Sunday-school teams, railroad-sponsored teams, pharmacy-sponsored teams, and any local nine that came together with enough cash to sponsor the contest, cover their travel expenses, and guarantee a reasonable gate. Just to have him up there on the mound, throwing bloopers, and playing shadow ball was enough to bring them into the stadium and to leave feeling satisfied.

After barnstorming for several months with his all-stars, something amazing happened. Paige had just finished receiving his arm message from Frank "Jewbaby" Floyd, who performed the service before and after each practice and game. He was getting ready on the field to go through the agony of warming up his injured arm to toss the bloopers when he noticed something very unusual—there was no pain. He continued to warm up as he always had, very carefully, and taking every precaution to make sure he was loose. After that his arm still felt good, so he called his catcher over and informed him of what he could hardly believe. He then took it a step further and told his catcher that he wanted to try throwing one with some zip on it. His catcher gave a reasonable response: "Are you sure?" Paige answered in the affirmative.[8]

The master hurler began letting them fly with a fair amount of zip on them. The throws were not his ultimate fastball but fast enough that the faint pop of the catcher's mitt lured the team's manager over. That evening Paige and the manager made a joint phone call to Kansas City to Wilkinson to inform him of the incredible good news. All three men were elated to the heavens. Wilkinson was first to gain his composure and told Paige to take it easy and to stay with the traveling squad through the end of the season. Next season would be a different matter. He told the former king of the mound to get in shape and to join "the" Kansas City Monarchs at spring training for the next season. Wilkinson had not received league approval but felt certain that he would win the case for reinstating Paige because the leagues were weak and Paige was good for all of Negro Leagues Baseball. Also, the two years of the ban, which went into affect in 1938, had only one more year to it, a point Wilkinson felt he could negotiate. Paige had been born again. He rightfully prided himself for having weathered the worst period in his professional life.[9]

Paige's return to form was a triumphant celebration. In 1939 he came on board with the Monarchs, and everything looked bright to him. Black Kansas City was elated to hear the announcement that Satchel Paige would be pitching in future contests. The *Kansas City Call*, the city's black newspaper, trumpeted Paige's triumphant return to form and preeminence. Whether playing in American Association Park or in Muehlebach Park, it was predicted that all of black KC would want to turn out for the Monarchs' games. With Paige on the Monarchs, attendance at the games reached new heights at home and on the road, which helped the organization make it through the remainder of the Great Depression.[10]

Paige and the Monarchs were also powerful role models for blacks in Kansas City. Beyond the dress requirement, players were forbidden to shoot craps on the bus or at the hotel. Star players like Paige spoke at the Young Men's Progressive Club, before YMCA groups, and at other community organizations. Paige fostered a great relationship with the community.[11]

Monarchs baseball games were tremendous social events, a vibrant part of KC's new Negro movement. Black celebrities from the entertainment world were in regular attendance at the games. Joe Louis was there, as were Count Basie, Stepin Fetchit (a.k.a. Lincoln Perry), and Louis Armstrong, to name a few. If they were in town they attended the games, and the players returned the favor, attending a Joe Louis fight, catching Louis Armstrong playing at one of the clubs, or taking in a Shirley Temple movie, to see their friend Lincoln Perry, of whom Paige was a huge fan. The one player whom all the other celebrities wanted to see was Satchel Paige. They all knew him and he knew them.

The Monarchs were also of interest to whites, who turned out in good numbers to see black baseball. They typically numbered 20 percent of the audience. When it was a major game, such as a championship series or a fight for the pennant, whites came out in larger numbers.

Wilkinson did not miss any opportunity to court the African American community, and every component of it, to come out to the games. He solicited the black churches of Kansas City, giving ministers free tickets for themselves and select members of the congregation, and playing benefit games to support the churches. Wilkinson also allowed the black Baptist ministers to hold unity services in the stadium after the conclusion of the Monarchs' games. In short, there was a relationship between baseball and religion. Although Paige was not an overly devout Christian man, he said the right things in the presence of the ministers, and everyone loved him for it. He understood very well the importance of having the churches supportive of the team. After all, the black church was the major foundation in black America. Kansas City was no exception.[12]

Wilkinson knew that you had to use all means to get patrons to the ballpark and then be sure to give them excellent entertainment. Putting on a show, a good show, was the promise of Monarchs baseball. Stunting was a reality of the game, and Paige was second to none at his ability to please the crowd. There were teams like the Miami Ethiopian Clowns and others who took it a bit far, but all of Negro Leagues Baseball was flashy and full of stunts to keep the fans coming and interested once the game began. Wilkinson was the innovator who brought portable lights to make night baseball possible for the Negro Leagues and beyond. Others in the Negro Leagues and the Major Leagues would copy his innovation. The lighting system, which went into effect in 1930, helped the Monarchs survive the Depression. People could come to the games in the evening, be out of the sun, after work (if they were lucky enough to have a job), and have a good time.

The whole of African America rallied to the Monarchs and its star-studded team. The team players on the Monarchs were celebrities throughout the period between World War I and World War II and beyond. The roster was impressive, ranging from Satchel Paige to Hilton Smith, from Newt Allen to Wilber "Bullet Joe" Rogan, from Ernie Banks and Elston Howard to Buck O'Neil and Jackie Robinson.

That fame came with a price, however. Satchel Paige was such a megastar baseball hero that fans in KC and all through the country wanted to see him in every game. The ace hurler was forced, by demand, to resume pitching in at least one or two innings of almost every contest. Black Kansas City, like elsewhere, fixated on "Satchel." In a series in the city, Paige actually pitched in all three games in one day: starting for the first game, pitching in relief in the second one, and starting the nightcap. Incredibly, he won all three.

Black Kansas City could not get enough of him, and he could not get enough of black Kansas City. Entertainment and entertainers, the best of the best, were right down the street. Kansas City was a musical oasis for some of the best jazz on the planet, one of the leading musical centers of the black Renaissance. Eighteenth and Vine was to Kansas City what Lenox Avenue was to Harlem or Thirty-Fifth Street and Forty-Seventh Street were to Chicago or Rampart Street was to New Orleans. It was the lifeblood of the community, with numerous famous jazz spots and nightclubs that let the African American population of Kansas City kick up its heels into the wee hours of the morning. There were great clubs like the Sunset, the Reno Club, the Paradise Club, the Panama Club, the Subway, Lucille's Paradise, Wolf's Buffet, and Eleanor's Restaurant.

Paige loved to hang out at the spots and enjoy the great music, conversation, booze, and all the other cultural trappings. The second coming of the Bennie Moten Orchestra was onstage, Count Basie was blasting away with his swaying big band, or you could catch the great jazz pianist Mary Lou Williams or another of Paige's favorites, Margaret "Countess" Johnson. The Cotton Pickers were one of the hippest bands in Kansas City, and Paige loved them. Paige washed himself in jazz with the legendary Jay McShann Band and pioneer saxophonists Lester Young and the incomparable Charlie "Yardbird" Parker; there were Buster Smith and the deep, gritty sounds of blues vocalist Big Joe Turner. Paige imbibed on the music of Andy Kirk and the Clouds of Joy, another great Kansas City band, and caught the magnificent Mamie Smith, Ethel Waters, Billie Holiday, Kenny Clarke, Thelonious Monk, Coleman Hawkins, Max Roach, and countless other greats when they were in town. He never got enough of listening to Jo Jones on the drums or dancing at the Lyric, Dreamland, or Lincoln dance halls that invited you to dance until you dropped. He was particularly fond of the Lyric and almost a fixture there, showing off his latest dance steps when not on the road playing ball. At one point, the stretch down Vine for several blocks in either direction sported twenty-five clubs.[13]

In KC the entertainers and other upscale African American visitors stayed at the beautiful fifty-room Street's Hotel, located at Eighteenth and Vine, and owned by African American businessmen R. S. Street and funeral director T. B. Watkins. Street's was one of the nicest hotels for blacks in Kansas City. Some said the hotel was the best west of Chicago. You could often find Paige there, relaxing in the spacious lobby, having a cocktail, and holding court with friends and other ballplayers. The Blue Room and the Rose Room at the hotel were favorite gathering places for him and other ballplayers and for community functions.[14]

Street's was known as the hot spot where male entertainment celebrities had more than their fair share of rendezvous. The Monarchs were near or at the top of that list. Players who did not have homes in Kansas City stayed at the Street's Hotel when they had a game. But many of those who did have homes in Kansas City stayed at the hotel from time to time. For many this was a wide-open opportunity for carousing with the opposite sex, whether single or married.

Wilkinson's attempt to keep a lid on these activities fell short. Neither he nor anyone else could have kept young virile men from being young virile men, no matter how many fines were levied. Paige was second to none when it came to social carousing. He was the great Leroy "Satchel" Paige, and starry-eyed women flocked to him. Street's was a jumping place, with sexual liaisons in abundance, especially when the Monarchs were checked in. The opportunity to party seemed to come with the territory of being a ballplayer. Whether it was the white Majors or the Negro Leagues, or for that matter any of the other high-profile sports, athletes had a special advantage as stars in attracting women and being successful in their pursuit of them. Paige was reportedly among the best at this game of "bedding them down." Between the players there was a gentlemen's agreement of sorts, including with the hotel owner, that what happened at Street's stayed at Street's.[15]

Part of Paige's and the Monarchs' success with women may have been due to their uniforms. There were those women who loved a man in uniform. The snappy uniforms of the Monarchs were a plus in the game of hunt-and-seek between men and women. This combined with the salaries they earned, compared to the average male, gave them another advantage over other male suitors. Nature was another factor at play. The Monarchs were a team of active young men in a time that saluted sexual conquests, the more the merrier. They were sportsmen and shared in the mind-set that women were fair game and you proved your manliness by having as many sexual liaisons as possible, balancing as many girlfriends as you possibly could. This was not the case for all of the members of the Monarchs team. There were those who were faithful married men who did not mess around. For so many of the players, however, married or not, the temptations proved too great. Dan Burley of the *Amsterdam News* labeled Satchel Paige a star attraction to the ladies. Burley had just seen Paige in the Big Apple and recorded that the star hurler was "driving a long car, squiring a pretty girl and thinking about signing a Black Yankee contract." There is no official record of how much or how frequent was Paige's cavorting on and off the road, but it was most likely substantial.[16]

Paige was on a roll with his beloved Monarchs. He could rightly boast that after joining the Monarchs, he was the toast of the town whose name recognition saw no bounds. The years were great for him. "That arm of mine never once bothered me during the 1939 season and in 1940, with a whole year pitching behind me, I was even hotter. I must've won about 40 ballgames that season."[17]

The Monarchs with Paige was one of the few black baseball teams that consistently made a profit. The team barnstormed everywhere. Players barnstormed at the end of the season in September, but they also barnstormed during the regular season. The best of the players with the highest name recognition went into Winter League ball. Following that, the best of the best were invited to come to the islands to continue their play. Paige had more invitations than he could possibly meet.

For the winter of 1939 Paige took his marquee name south of the border to his favorite islands. He played in Cuba and was a fixture in Puerto Rico, where he helped pack the stands game after game. Every baseball team south of the border wanted Paige, and everyone adored him. Those who did not have him were envious of the fact. It was reported in Puerto Rico that the policy of the owners of the clubs was to have the American pitchers pitch against the Puerto Rican pitchers, but the other clubs claimed that "the club which has Satchel are using him against all the pitchers."[18]

Paige stole the show in the Puerto Rican Winter League, which opened its first official season in 1939 with teams from Guayama, Humacao, San Juan, Ponce, Caguas, and Mayagüez. Paige won nineteen of twenty-four games and set a record for strikeouts and shutouts for his Guayama team and led them to the pennant, while setting an all-time league record of nineteen games won. His league record for the most strikeouts stood for two decades. Paige was also selected their most valuable player, an honor he would repeat the following year. His two winter seasons in Puerto Rico made him a household name there and throughout the Caribbean that would never be forgotten.[19]

He and the other black ballplayers loved playing in Puerto Rico. Josh Gibson's San Juan team was a good one until they went up against Guayama and their ace, Satchel Paige, on November 5, 1939, and lost by a score of 23–0. Puerto Ricans labeled Paige the best pitcher in the Puerto Rican League and the best pitcher they had ever seen. Paige knew it, too, and loved playing there, the people, the food, the atmosphere, and being able to take in the beach for a nice swim.[20]

They loved him all through the islands and beyond. He played many games in Venezuela, where fans came out in droves to see him, and in Cuba, too, where they compared him to their legendary Jose Mendez. Paige was being paid seven hundred dollars a month plus one thousand dollars in bonus money in the islands. What he and all the players liked about being in the Caribbean, South America, Mexico, and so forth was that said through the years: they were treated royally and in an environment free of Jim Crow. Paige and the other American blacks were national heroes in Mexico, constantly besieged by autograph hounds, their photos dawning the front pages of the local newspapers. The crowds loved them and they loved the people. Paige and the other Negro Leagues stars could only dream that the United States would someday treat them as well.[21]

Paige also enjoyed the special companionship the islands offered. He reportedly struck up a relationship with an attractive older woman named Hattie in Puerto Rico. That relationship soon gave way to his romantic involvement with a woman described as being younger and more beautiful that Hattie, Lucy Figueroa. The two of them were a hot commodity.

When Paige hit the island's nightspots and hotels, it was with Lucy Figueroa close in tow, beginning in 1940. The two were inseparable, and after two years of a winter seasonal romance, they revved their relationship up a notch and decided to come back to the States together. They set sail out of San Juan, Puerto Rico, on the SS *Coamo* on April 25, 1941. It was easy to see how the rumor might have begun that Lucy Figueroa was Satchel Paige's new bride. She was registered on the ship manifest as Lucy Paige. An examination of recorded marriages in Puerto Rico, Kansas City, and throughout the United States shows that no nuptials ever took place between the two of them. Paige had no doubt reasoned that listing her as his wife on the ship manifest and for immigration purposes was the best way to register his companion, especially since they were traveling together and staying in the same cabin. It was, however, merely a face-saving gesture. The ship manifests also listed Lucy Figueroa's age at twenty-one. That may have been her actual age, but she may have been several years younger. One also notes that Satchel Paige listed his own birthday on the *Coamo* manifest as 1908, thus shaving a couple of years off his actual age.

The couple arrived in New York on April 31, 1941, and took the train from there to Kansas City, where Paige set Lucy up in her own little apartment, two miles from his house. The two of them were often seen together in KC, and it was not unreasonable for some to think that she was the new Mrs. Paige. Indeed, there was every indication that Lucy Figueroa identified herself more than once as Mrs. Paige. It made life a little easier for her and her own existence seemingly more honorable. A finite obstacle ensuring that they were not married was that Paige was still legally married to Janet Howard.

The year 1941 was one of conquest for Paige, although he did receive his occasional comeuppance, as he experienced in a game in Hartford, Connecticut. He was pitching under the banner of the Santo Domingo Stars after the formal season with the Monarchs had ended. He and the Stars faced a Hartford team that boasted that it would win because they had a youngster pitching for them who many were saying could outpitch the great Satchel Paige. Paige, hearing this, replied that he would embarrass the youngster from the mound. The youngster overheard it and said to Paige that maybe he should worry a little bit, because "you're not as young as you used to be." It was true that Paige was thirty-five years of age, but he was at the height of his game, and no high school boy was going to outshine him on the diamond. Paige was not at his best in that game, but he turned in a very respectable pitching performance. The only problem was that in the eighth inning, Hartford scored twice off of him, and that was it. The high school boy was sensational and gave up only two hits to the Stars in the last two innings; if he hadn't, he would have had a perfect game. Paige had to admit that although he pitched well, "it was nowhere near as good as that kid did."[22]

He also admitted feeling a touch old and tired. He started wondering to himself if he might not be as good as he used to be. He felt the weight of the world on his shoulders after that embarrassing defeat from the young upstart. As Paige reflected, "You'd never seen an old man if you didn't see me after the game. I ran back to the hotel and locked myself in my room." Might he be over the hill? That was a question he asked over and over. "It's a mighty bad feeling when a young punk comes along and does better than you and you know it. And you know you ain't young like you used to be so you don't have time to get any better." He was depressed for the next few games but pitching anyway, being the consummate professional.[23]

He pitched himself back into mental health and reassurance of his own abilities and that he was not over the hill. "Fact is, I was still pitching long after everybody forgotten what that high school boy done against me." Paige had learned and taught himself the lesson of any true professional: you bounce back after defeat or victory, and you come back strong and consistent. It was not just the ability to win. It was the stability to come back after defeat or victory and play up to one's full potential. Paige had such ability, and even as he put on more years, he would never forget the lesson that the defeat at the hands of the schoolboy taught him.[24]

What was also happening to Paige was a maturing in terms of baseball. He felt at home with the Monarchs and meshed with his teammates and with Wilkinson, whom he considered always "on the up and up."

> Before I went with the Monarchs, I hadn't thought anything about jumping contracts when I felt like it. I guess I never cared about much of anything except myself. I'd made guys like Abe Saperstein, who ran the Harlem Globetrotters, and Gus Greenlee and Candy Jim Taylor and lots of others mad at me because of that. I might have gone on doing that, but after my arm went dead and then came back I started thinking. I wasn't getting any younger and I figured it was about time to take care of some of the boys who was taking care of me. That was easy to do when the guy taking care of you was somebody like Mr. Wilkinson. And Mr. Baird, too. They made Kansas City a real fine home. I sort of settled there. The folks in Kansas City treated me like a king and you never saw a king of the walk if you didn't see Ol' Satch around Eighteenth and Vine in those days, rubber-necking all the girls walking by.[25]

Paige's professional life was a complex picture, with the ongoing fight for his pitching services developing into a baseball war. The impression was looming large again that the whole of Negro Leagues Baseball could not survive without the services of Satchel Paige. The teams were now at odds with his success, his barnstorming with his all-stars that league owners defined as against the best interests of the leagues. Both the Negro National League and the Negro American League came to the decision on June 27, 1940, that, whatever their individual opinions, Satchel Paige needed to be embraced. The two leagues conceded that both leagues had a justified claim on Paige, but the famous pitcher had indicated he would rather stay in Kansas City. He contended that slavery was over and he could play for whomever he pleased. It proved once more that Satchel Paige was bigger than Negro Leagues Baseball. The leagues' owners tried to strong-arm Paige to leave the Monarchs for the Eagles and told him that unless he did that, "there will be a war between the two leagues." Paige and Wilkinson ignored the threats.[26]

The only problem was that there were those who would do anything to try to make Paige suffer for past baseball sins. That mind-set worked against his being allowed to participate in the East-West All-Star Game of 1940. Paige was declared ineligible for the East-West classic. It was no problem for him. He continued barnstorming and then spent the winter playing more ball on the West Coast and then went south to the islands.

The truth was that neither the Crawfords nor even the Newark Eagles wanted Paige when his arm was hurt. It was J. L. Wilkinson who recognized the marquee value of Paige as a draw wherever he played. Wilkinson used his marketing skills quite effectively, embarrassing those who had walked away from Paige earlier.

The Newark Eagles were most determined to have him with them. Never mind the fact that the Eagles had distanced themselves when Paige had his arm problems. Owner Effa Manley of the Eagles became fixated on the notion that she must have Satchel Paige. It became an ugly battle. She expressed anger when Paige went to play winter ball in the islands and continued her assault when he returned and played in nearby New York under rumors that he was considering signing on for a while with the Black Yankees. The *Amsterdam News* reported on Paige's arrival in New York directly from Puerto Rico: "The great Satchel just came in from Puerto Rico where he had been bowling over opposition with his bee ball, and living the life of a molasses-hued Don. From what we could get, Paige is a bit tired of life in the islands, despite the lure of the heavy cash that Latins have been laying on him and would like a turn on the hill in 'Heaven,' that is, he'd like to pitch with one foot on 7th Avenue and the other on the mound in Yankee Stadium." Everyone was aware of the legal fights brewing for Paige's service. "Paige had been mixed up in a lot of litigation" since he left Gus Greenlee's Pittsburgh Crawfords. "Effa Manley of the Newark Eagles once got out an injunction which would have put the eccentric hurler in the hoosegow if he pitched for any team in New Jersey or New York other than the Eagles."[27]

Manley took it a step further. She branded J. L. Wilkinson a thief who had no business contracting Paige when his services were promised to her and the Eagles. She proclaimed that the "Nordic Wilkinson of Kansas City, violated an inter-Leagues covenant and took Satchel away from them." The Newark Eagles, according to her, were the legitimate holders of Paige's contract, and he should be playing for them.[28]

The Negro National League wanted Paige, while the Negro American League, of which the Kansas City Monarchs were members, had him. Thus, the two leagues found themselves at odds. It became one of "the most fiery issues in Negro baseball." Effa Manley and the Eagles argued that they had signed Paige back in 1938 before he left the country, and thus he was contractually obligated to play for them. Manley labeled Wilkinson's actions illegal; furthermore, she reminded everyone that there was a ban against Paige playing Negro Leagues Baseball and he and Wilkinson were violating it.[29]

She further accused Wilkinson and an American League official of conspiring together and using their joint influence to keep Paige in Kansas City to benefit the American League against the Negro National League. She further alleged that the Satchel Paige All-Stars were a way for Wilkinson to play Paige against Negro National League teams. Manley said that "everyone knew that the Satchel Paige All-Stars was owned by Mr. Wilkinson and his people and had been barnstorming all over the country" and that there was an apparent "conspiracy" by Wilkinson and others to "keep Paige away from the Eagles at all cost."[30]

Manley admitted to the business benefits of winning Paige to her team. She most certainly understood why Wilkinson wanted him. What she could not understand was why "the Negroes who have invested so heavily in this business, and the honest white men connected with it, stand for this sort of thing." She also claimed that she had "agreed to pay Paige the largest salary ever paid a Negro ballplayer in the history of the game. He cannot possibly earn anywhere the amount with the team he is now with. There is only one conclusion to reach. I expect each of you to order Wilkinson to send Paige to Newark and immediately this week. If organized baseball is not strong enough to do this, it is not strong enough to call itself organized and anything may happen." She wrote of learning that "Satchel Paige's All-Stars are playing the Clown's in Cincinnati. That is a joke as everybody knows who Satchel belongs to, his name is J. L. Wilkinson." Manley pleaded with her colleagues that "whatever decision you reach remember that there is a big race issue involved, 'Negro Baseball.' It is probably at the crossroads, and its future may depend upon your handling of this present situation. I pray you will have divine guidance at this time." She held strongly to her beliefs and warned her husband, Abe Manley, to "be aware of the Jews," especially promoter and booking agent Eddie Gottlieb and his crowd. "Please don't make any concessions to these niggers, just think of the dirty deal they gave us."[31]

One wonders if this was bluster or sour grapes on the part of Manley, in that the Eagles missed their opportunity and Wilkinson, who took a chance, came out victorious. *Bluster* might be the appropriate term because there was never a contract between Paige and the Eagles. Research into the financial records of the Newark Eagles, available in the New Jersey Public Library Special Collections, failed to uncover any such contract or correspondence between Paige and the Eagles or Effa Manley suggesting that he had agreed to terms.[32]

Never mind that Effa Manley and the Eagles organization could not produce a signed contract between them and Paige. The spirited owner was determined to win this battle and rallied her supporters to the cause. Cum Posey weighed in on the matter and, to no one's surprise, supported his friend Manley and her contention that Paige should either be playing for the Eagles or continue to be banned from Negro Leagues Baseball. In a column titled "Posey's Points," the owner of the Homestead Grays wrote, "The owners of the Newark Eagles are up in arms over the action of the American League clubs playing Satchel Paige's All-Stars. Satchel was claimed by Newark at the joint leagues meeting in New York City on September 28, 1939, and no club disputed their claim." Posey further suggested that the "American League is not living up to the joint agreement, which states no clubs of either leagues will play against any club which harbors a player belonging to any club of either Negro Major Leagues."[33]

The Effa Manley fixation on Satchel Paige started to irritate fans of the Eagles. One of those fans wrote to Manley, expressing her disgust with all the attention paid to Paige:

> So who is Satchel Paige that you should desire him as though he were God himself? Aren't there any other pitchers in this whole wide United States of America, even maybe in South America? There must be some growing up. Maybe if the rest of the team would encourage them, one other pitcher as marvelous as he is supposed to be, would emerge. I don't think he's so marvelous—I guess he too is often too tired from traveling to pitch. He must have been the time he came from Trujillo and pitched against Taylor at the Stadium here.[34]

Some thought that Manley may have finally given up on Paige when in the spring of 1941 she announced a new pitching acquisition. The Newark Eagles were glad to put in a press release that they had just signed Chester McDuffie, right-handed pitcher whom they were touting as better than Paige. In their press release they noted that he had been selected the second most valuable pitcher in the Cuban League and would be joining the Eagles' spring training camp in Virginia. She did digress a bit to throw another jab at Satchel Paige and mention in the release that McDuffie "had beat Paige in 3 championship games out of 4 in Puerto Rico." Manley also pointed out that McDuffie was "born in Mobile, Alabama just like Satchel Paige."[35]

Back in the States, a most satisfying moment for Paige came in July 1941 when he made a triumphant return to Pittsburgh. Paige jumped from team to team for guest pitching appearances, with the full support and blessing of Wilkinson and the Monarchs, to help other teams against strong opponents and, most important, to help both sides make their payroll and turn a profit. He helped the Homestead Grays to defeat the Black Yankees. But before going on to another gig in New York, he was feted at the Crawford Grill. It was like old times as everyone gathered around him, slapping him on the back, applauding his very presence, and listening to every word as he told stories of his triumphs on the mound against not only the best in the Negro Leagues but the greats of the Major Leagues, including Joe DiMaggio and Dizzy Dean. He received nothing but praise and warm wishes from his gleeful audience. It was like he had never left. He could not buy a drink or food for himself. Although Gus Greenlee was conspicuously absent, the event could not have been held without his consent. Perhaps it was too much to ask that the two forget old scores. The Crawford Grill was all abuzz that evening with laughter, good food, drinks flowing, and faces aglow in the presence of Paige, whom black Pittsburgh would forever claim as its own.[36]

On another occasion he was loaned out to the New York Black Yankees in their game against the Philadelphia Stars in Yankee Stadium. Announcement that Paige would be pitching was something the New York fans had heard many times before without the great one actually showing up. This time he was there as promised and in full Black Yankees uniform to start the game against the Stars. With the promise of Satchel Paige there, another important figure kept his promise and attended the event. Mayor Fiorello La Guardia attended the game and threw out the first ball. The attendance that night broke records with a turnout of eighteen thousand, one-fourth of whom were white. Everyone wanted to see Paige. The attendance was even more remarkable in that the Major Leagues' New York Giants were also playing that day at the Polo Grounds.[37]

Paige, to be expected, put on a masterful show for the New York crowd. When he started the first game of the doubleheader for the Yankees, it "sent his cohorts into delirium" as he struck out the first and second batters he faced. In all, he gave up five hits and struck out eight and scored a run himself in the eighth inning as the Yankees went on to win 5–3 behind the show-stealing pitching and performance of Paige. It did not escape the press that more people had come to the game to see Satchel Paige than Mayor La Guardia and that in the unofficial count of those seeking autographs, the requests for Paige's signature far outnumbered those seeking the John Hancock of the mayor.[38]

Next up for the visiting fastballer for hire was either Chicago or Cleveland. He was a man on the move and barnstorming where they needed him to make payroll and so he could bring in cash for himself and his partner, J. L. Wilkinson. In Dayton, Ohio, fans were excited that it had been announced that Paige and the Kansas City Monarchs would be there to battle their local Dayton Frigidaires of the Ohio Indiana League. They expected at least ten thousand to attend the event. After performing more magic in New York and Ohio, Paige flew off to keep his promised date with the East-West All-Star Game in Chicago. Unlike the previous year, fans were promised that Satchel Paige would be present and pitch in the game, and he confirmed the agreement and commitment.[39]

Paige's participation in the 1941 East-West All-Star Game also meant that he had won over the Negro Leagues owners, at least most of them. They could not afford to work against Paige. Effa Manley was furious and so were a few others. The reality was, however, that Paige was bigger than the leagues, and there was no getting around that fact, no matter who wished otherwise. You could leave him out of the contests, and attendance and earnings would be down, as they were in the previous East-West All-Star Games when he did not play.

By the time of the game, Paige had garnered more than 276,000 votes, the largest number ever received in voting a player onto the All-Star squad. Paige was going to play, but he would not start. Fans accepted that promise, although they dearly wanted to have him earlier to ensure a victory. But they would see Paige in action. It was billed as the "Dream Game" Sunday. Both East and West were primed for the ninth annual classic in Chicago and the promise of this being "the most spectacular, colorful, colossal diamond extravaganza in the history of Negro baseball." The reason they dared use such hyperbole was, they proudly proclaimed, because "Leroy Satchel Paige, peerless pitcher of the Kansas City Monarchs, will be playing in the big classic." The *Defender* suggested that it was perfectly valid to advertise Satchel Paige "as the greatest pitcher in baseball." When asked why, their answer was simple: "Because he is." The great hurler "with the million dollar arm and eccentric characteristics is expected to be the difference between victory and defeat in the battle."[40]

The 1941 East-West All-Star classic was full of hoopla and high expectations. Chicago and the nation could not wait to view the great event. Every African American newspaper in the country gave space to announcing the game. They began lining up at Comiskey Park at the crack of dawn, even though the game was hours away. The press had bragged that they expected the stadium would be filled to capacity, with fifty thousand fans. Their prediction was no exaggeration. They were lined up around the blocks, waiting for their chance to get through the turnstiles to see the event and the great master on the mound. He was the drawing card that everybody talked about. What will Satchel do? What inning will they bring him in to shut down the other side? Can Satchel pull it off? Never mind the fact that most pundits thought that the East had the better team that year; somehow the Paige factor, they thought, would neutralize that advantage.

The official count through the turnstiles that Sunday, July 27, 1941, was 47,865, of whom 5,000 were whites who too wanted to take in the action. The stadium was busting at the seams. At least 10,000 people could not gain admission because of the overcrowding and went home to wait for the results, although some lingered around outside of the stadium just to hear that cheering and shouting and to be near the event.[41]

The game itself could not possibly have lived up to the high expectations. It was also one of the more sloppily played of the East-West classics, with nine recorded errors, a record for the event. Most spectators believed that the errors occurred because players were not giving a 100 percent effort. Others thought that perhaps some of the players were a bit too loose and saw the game as merely an opportunity to pose and to collect a nice paycheck. But as the game went on, the crowd became a bit more restless, as the East began dismantling the West in the fourth inning. The East took an early lead because of a couple of unearned runs in the first off of errors in the field. The play of Buck Leonard received high marks, as did the splendid defensive play of Monte Irvin at third base. The fabulous Horacio "Rabbit" Martinez at short was also outstanding. Hilton Smith had started the contests on the mound for the West and completed his three innings, which were not his best performance. Three innings were agreed as the limit for each pitcher. The West next went with Double Duty Radcliffe. You could hear the talk in the stands already. They loved Radcliffe, but everyone wanted to see Paige, and given that the East had already jumped out to a lead, the wisdom of the day suggested that the master hurler was urgently needed to bring a halt to the hemorrhage.

It was in the eighth when fans saw the man they wanted strolling his unforgettable stride toward the mound. The place erupted as Paige made his long-overdue appearance. There was no need for any introduction; everyone knew who was out there at last. The game, however, was safely in the bank for the East, leading by a score of 8–3 with only two innings remaining. But at least they would now see Paige for the West, and he did not disappoint. He went to work and immediately struck out the first two hitters. In his two innings of work to end the game, the master hurler struck out four, walked one, and allowed only one hit. Despite his short appearance on the mound, it gave the fans what they came to see. The debate would go on well after the game as to why Paige was not used much earlier. But in the end, "The public was fairly well satisfied with the game with the exception of those who wanted the West to win."[42]

If Cum Posey had his way, however, fans would have never been treated to an appearance by Satchel Paige in any capacity. Posey was frustrated after he had attended a joint meeting of the Negro National League and the Negro American League and chastised the leagues for abandoning their own edict against players who had jumped to the Latin countries and the Caribbean. It seemed clear to him that the leagues were making the decision that it could not exist without the star players and that the stars could do whatever they wanted to do. He reminded the leagues' representatives that it was agreed that the wayward players would have to pay a specific fine before being officially admitted back into the leagues. But as Posey pointed out in the *Pittsburgh Courier*, there was no record that any fines had ever been paid by these players. He was particularly critical of the leagues' failure to discipline Paige.[43]

No one was listing, with the exception of one other owner, named Effa Manley. The fans, the public, wanted Satchel Paige, and most of the other owners understood this, whether grudgingly or not. In the very same issue of the *Pittsburgh Courier* on August 16, 1941, that Cum Posey's broadside against Paige appeared, another article appeared by John Williams, proclaiming that all of Detroit was eager to see Paige. "Detroit is looking forward to the baseball classic of the season when the Kansas City Monarchs and the internationally famous pitcher, Satchel Paige, play the Chicago American Giants in the doubleheader at Brick Stadium here, Sunday, September 14," Williams wrote in his piece, and he predicted a massive turnout, a capacity crowd of 56,000 to attend the doubleheader, and that all eyes would be there because of the highest-priced pitching ace in Negro Leagues Baseball. Williams saw nothing wrong in his proclamation. He thought all of this was good for black Detroit, good for the community, and good for baseball, black and white. Williams concurred that Paige was the highest-paid ballplayer in baseball and, in his opinion, "worth every penny."[44]

Paige's performance on the field, the fan adulation, his mounting string of victories and praise by most writers in the black press made him virtually invincible—a lesson that Cum Posey finally learned. Less than a month after his August article, Posey found himself retracting his perceived opposition to Paige. In the face of such a tidal wave of support and public adulation for the king of the mound, Posey in his column, "Posey Points," capitulated and wrote, "Satchel Paige without a doubt is making the greatest comeback of Negro baseball history. Satchel was but a shadow of his former greatness in 1939 and 1940. He is now the Satchel of 1934."[45]

Paige by his 1941 performance was pushing his name beyond that of superstar. He was becoming a living legend. Fans agreed that there was little doubt that the two greatest names in African American sport were Joe Louis and Satchel Paige, and it was apparent to most that Paige did not exist in the shadow of Joe Louis or any other sports giant. He was a giant among giants. Wendell Smith perhaps put it best when he wrote, "The most remarkable pitcher in the history of the great American pastime, Satchel Paige." "There is no doubt that Satchel Paige is the most colorful, dynamic athlete in the country," Smith expounded. "No other athlete in sports has the magnetic pull or personal appeal equal to that of the loquacious Leroy. He's Mr. It in the world of sports. And that means he doesn't have to take a backward step for Joe Louis, his greatest rival."[46]

With the end of the regular season, Paige's season was only half complete. It was time to barnstorm full-time. On October 5, 1941, he matched his pitching skills against "Rapid" Bob Feller, the ace of the Major League Cleveland Indians. Feller, some said, was out to prove or to settle a little score with Paige, who had bested him previously and whom many were now calling "the world's greatest pitcher," while others anointed Feller with the title. Both pitched splendid baseball when the two all-star teams met in Sportsman's Park in St. Louis. Paige outpitched Feller and brought home the victory while making his statement for being called the world's best.[47]

10

Double V

There was one critic who stood fast and did not buy into any of the hoop-la and extravagant praises for Satchel Paige. She maintained that his actions were hurtful to Negro Leagues Baseball and that he violated contractual agreements and the spirit of what Negro Leagues ball was all about. She did not think he deserved to play in the East-West All-Star Game or be admitted back into the Negro Leagues without serving his suspension and paying the levied fines. As far as she was concerned, Paige was a pariah, a bird of prey whose wings needed to be clipped before he brought all of Negro Leagues Baseball to its knees. Newark Eagles owner Effa Manley stood her ground.

Manley also thought that Negro Leagues Baseball served a higher purpose, namely, as a symbol of racial pride and black self-assertion. She was a strong, outspoken race woman on every level, and that colored her leadership of the Newark Eagles, her activism in the community, and her steadfastness against Paige. She concluded that Paige was a figment of the imagination and she spoke her mind as a "Negro woman." Ironically, Effa Manley was genetically a white woman who, raised by her mother and black stepfather, embraced African American culture and chose to live her life as a black woman. Satchel Paige, she contended, was basically the creation of a powerful Jewish coalition that was making money off him. In short, Paige, as she would complain to close associates, was a tool in the Jewish conspiracy to control Negro Leagues Baseball. Manley wrote a bitter letter to Cum Posey in which she shared her confidences and severe criticism of Paige and the Jews. Hers was a long-standing, but rarely openly spoken, view that Jews had prominent positions in sports scheduling of athletic facilities and stadia that worked against the best interests of black team owners. Abe Saperstein of the Harlem Globetrotters was one she pointed to. Saperstein was also involved in promoting and scheduling Negro Leagues games and the renting of Major Leagues ballparks for the events. Manley did not like Saperstein, and she was upset beyond words with Ed Gottlieb, whom she considered to be a shady character. Manley told other blacks that she was tired of the control of the white man and especially the Jews. She confided, "Those two white men [Gottlieb and Saperstein] have decided we Negroes are just putty in their hands. I don't know what will eventually be done. After all you all permitted Wilkinson to take Satchel from me, and Gottlieb Yankee Stadium." It was her contention that if the black owners wanted to come together, she invited them to join the Eagles in the effort to "stop Gottlieb, Wilkinson, Leuschner, Saperstein and all the others." She questioned Paige's racial consciousness because he had "not shown his colors." Paige, for his part, completely ignored the accusations.[1]

Manley continued to be dismayed that black owners "don't seem to be able to get together and get their act together while the O-Fays [whites] are all pulling together, and are even lucky enough to have a few of the Negroes pulling with them." She had Paige in mind. Any mention of him angered her. She was especially upset with new evidence that Paige was getting extra compensation from Gottlieb, $542 to be exact, for the most recent game against the Eagles. She felt that money should have been divided among the clubs and not given to any one player. Manley shared with Posey her contention that it was Gottlieb at work as usual: "I told him I would not stand for anything taken out for Satchel," but he did it anyway.[2]

Paige, his Jewish supporters, and the Negro Leagues' male owners all continued to be flash points for Manley as the world went to war. She ended in a letter to Gottlieb, which was dated November 4, 1941, that it did "seem ridiculous that intelligent people cannot come to an agreement about anything, but after all the whole world is arguing at present." Indeed, much of the world was "arguing." In just thirty-four days after her letter, that argument would also fully engulf the United States of America and have a profound impact on Satchel Paige and the Negro Leagues.[3]

The bombing of Pearl Harbor on December 7, 1941, was a jolt to Paige, as it was to all Negro Leagues ballplayers and Major League ballplayers, all Americans, and the world. World War II changed baseball for everyone. Much attention has been given to white athletes, those Major League ballplayers who served the war effort in uniform. The Negro Leagues also contributed players who served in the military during the war. Paige did his patriotic part in a uniform of a different sort. He suited up in his Monarchs uniform and played in games throughout the country that raised money for military relief and supported the payroll savings plan and the buying of war bonds. Paige was not drafted, but one factor was clear—he was a bit too old, even without using the exaggerated dates surrounding his age, which had some thinking of him as older than Methuselah. His war would be fought on the baseball field.[4]

Paige, and like-minded African Americans, hoped that the end result of the war would be a double victory, or "Double V," a triumph over tyranny and injustice abroad and at home. He and his teammates not only participated in games to benefit the war effort, but also participated in games to benefit the NAACP and its Legal Defense Fund. Paige and champ Joe Louis both saw themselves as supporters of the Double V. Their performances in the athletic arena supported the war effort and were significant contributions against the lie of racial inferiority, whether it was Louis knocking his white challengers out cold or Paige dominating white batters and outpitching his white counterparts. These were their statements of demonstrated equality.[5]

Major League Baseball was depredated with the drain on its manpower owing to the war. Joe DiMaggio and Bob Feller were two of the large number of stalwarts from the Major Leagues who answered the call of duty. The shortage in the Majors was, ironically, an advantageous factor in Negro Leagues Baseball. Black baseball had always done well in comparison to the white Major Leagues in terms of attracting fans. The war made it clear to any reasonable spectator that Negro Leagues Baseball was by far the superior ball being offered. Those wanting to see the best baseball through the duration of World War II found it at those games. The stars such as Satchel Paige, Josh Gibson, Cool Papa Bell, and others found a new lease on life and enthusiastic crowds who now had more money to spend because of the positive impact of war on reinvigorating the American economy. Negro ball and Satchel Paige would have some of their best and most profitable years during World War II.[6]

Paige and his Kansas City Monarchs outdrew most competing white Major League teams in the cities they traveled to and played in during the war years. In their own hometown of KC, the white Kansas City Blues could not compete with Paige and the Monarchs in drawing fans. African Americans came out faithfully in KC whenever their Monarchs played. On the road, the Monarchs with their heralded hurler, held drawing power the white Major League teams could only wish for. The Monarchs boasted an attractive roster of great ballplayers with the likes of Newt Allen, Turkey Stearnes, Ted Strong, Willard Brown, Jesse Williams, Joe Greene, and John Buck O'Neil, with the pitching duties being held down by Hilton Smith, Booker McDaniel, Connie Johnson, George Walker, and Paige.[7]

The Monarchs were at the top of the Negro Leagues in terms of profitability and player salaries, which averaged $350 a month. Paige, of course, was in his own category of earnings. He was in a unique bargaining position, and he did not hold back in making his demands. For many games he was getting an extra couple of hundred dollars on the side just for showing up. If it was a major game such as the East-West All-Star classic or the World Series, Paige made an additional $800-$1000 for his presence. He thought it was all quite fair, since he realized that the people were coming out to see him. The press constantly mentioned his name, and he received more coverage than anyone else in Negro Leagues Baseball, including entire teams. Even Major Leaguers fell by the wayside when their names were put up against his, especially with Joe DiMaggio and Bob Feller serving in the military.

Sports columnist Wendell Smith concurred that not only was Paige the "center of attraction at the largest crowd to ever witness a Negro game—50,000—in Chicago at the East-West classic," but he may very "well be the greatest athlete of all time," as he maintained that "magic touch by attracting larger crowds than any other single player."[8]

Chicago organizers had something very special in mind. They had been contemplating it for several months, and all agreed that it was time to make it public that the Windy City was going to pay special homage to the master hurler by giving him his own special day. Word went out that July 26, 1942, would be "Satchel Paige Day" at Chicago's Wrigley Field. This was an extraordinary gesture and a shrewd business move. There was no question about it that Chicago loved Satchel Paige, as did the world, and that it was also good business for the black community whenever he was in town. The thinking among the organizers, with Wilkinson and Abe Saperstein also pushing the idea, was that a special day for Satchel Paige would be good for Negro Leagues Baseball.

It was a splendid turnout for the game, with more than eighteen thousand paying their way into the tribute to Paige. Chicago honored Paige and called him to home plate for photographs and to receive gifts from his adoring public. Edith Chamberlain made a presentation of a huge bouquet of flowers. Among the other gifts that Paige received was a new suit from Chicago Credit Clothing, a gold trophy from Abe Saperstein, a portable radio from Henderson's Chicken Shack—Henderson's announced that it was closed during the game in honor of Satchel Paige—a live band performance from the Music Makers of the Savoy Ballroom, and, finally, a bathrobe from Albert's Men's Shop. James Cashin from the board of the Robert Abbott publishing company, which published the *Chicago Defender,* made the keynote presentation and the gift of an Elgin pocket watch inscribed, "To Satchel Paige, World's Greatest Pitcher, from the Chicago Defender, World's Greatest Weekly."[9]

Satchel Paige Day in Chicago and the other games after that featuring the heralded hurler all served to direct the spotlight on what was forthcoming on

August 16, 1942: the East-West All-Star Game. As the days grew closer to the classic, it was estimated that fifty thousand fans or more would be at the game. Frank "Jewbaby" Floyd, the Monarchs trainer who was now Paige's personal trainer, did extra massage work every day on the master hurler's arm to make sure he was ready. Fans liked what they were hearing. It was promised that Paige would start the game for the West in this tenth annual all-star classic in Chicago. "Tell them I'll be ready," Paige wired the *Chicago Defender*. That was the kind of news that everyone wanted to hear. It promised, fans thought, that Paige would start. He would be backed up by Hilton Smith, who came in second in the balloting. When the final votes for the all-star team were tallied, Paige led the pack with an amazing 235,672 votes. The next closest vote getter was his teammate Hilton Smith, with a little more than 150,000 votes. Verdel Mathis garnered 125,000 votes.[10]

There was also a negative whisper in the air, and sometimes it became an outright open discussion, questioning as to whether Satchel Paige was getting too old to maintain his crown as the best pitcher in Negro Leagues Baseball. Paige resented such remarks. In his heart, however, he worried too that age was catching up with him. The questioning continued: how long could Paige fend off pitchers who were in their twenties when he was, at least, in his midthirties, if not older?[11]

The tenth All-Star Game, played before a packed Comiskey Park, proved not to be one of Paige's finest performances. Neither did he start the game as promised. But when he was brought in, the game stood tied at two runs apiece. It was the seventh inning, and everyone expected the great Satchel Paige to control the East's hitters from that point to the end. To the contrary, it was pitcher Leonard Day for the East who controlled the action from that point forward with his entrance in the seventh inning in relief. He stole the show. Day, who was twenty-five years of age and known for his fastball, struck out five hitters in his two innings of work. Day received the best pitching honors and shoved Paige to the background, as the East triumphed over the West All-Stars and Satchel Paige by the score of 5–2. Day played for the Newark Eagles, and his shinning performance over Paige in the All-Star Game reportedly sent team owner Effa Manley jumping for joy.[12]

Paige offered no excuses for his less than stellar performance. He could have if he had wanted to. The reality was he was pitching too much and far too often. On August 13, just three days before the East-West classic was to take place in Chicago, Paige and the Monarchs took on the Homestead Grays at Griffith Park in Washington, DC, in an evening contest in which Paige pitched the first three innings. Hilton Smith came in for the rest of the way, as the Monarchs whipped the Grays 10–2. It may have been for only three innings, but the point was that Paige was out there pitching even though he did so at a relaxed pace, taking almost a minute between pitches. He nevertheless worked that arm just days before the East-West classic, and he likely paid for it on the day of the big event.[13]

There was another compelling factor that may well have been the ultimate contributor to Paige's lackluster performance. A story had run the week before, stating that he was not in favor of integrating Major League Baseball. Paige had already begun to receive a great deal of serious questioning about his statement and whether it was true. He confided to his close friends his doubts about integration. He personally thought that it meant that Major League teams would take one or two black players on certain teams, and that, in his mind, was not integration. Paige warned that the Majors would siphon off enough black players that the traditional Negro Leagues audiences and loyal fan base would follow them into the Majors. In short, it was all about money, and Negro Leagues Baseball would be the loser, in his opinion. Paige also made it clear that for him to join a Major League Baseball club would not be possible at any rate because he was too expensive, making far more than the average Major League player, some of them making as little as five thousand dollars a year. For Paige, integration into the Majors would mean a substantial pay cut, and that was not something he was interested in and made that point to the media when asked. What everyone apparently focused on was that Satchel Paige seemed to be rejecting the goal of integrating the Majors.

He did an extraordinary thing at the All-Star Game. He asked at the end of the sixth inning if he could have the microphone to speak to the forty-eight thousand fans who were in attendance. Paige was granted his wish, and he told the fans that he had been "misquoted" in the local newspapers. He explained that he was "not opposed to Negroes playing on Major League teams." He went on to say that he "told a reporter that it was all right. But that he felt that it would be better if a complete Negro team went into the Majors." Paige made that point previously, saying that, for example, why not take the Monarchs as a whole team into the Majors? He also suggested that a Negro all-star team be put together and admitted as a whole unit into the Majors. He did not tell the Chicago crowd about his doubts regarding integration. He basically told them he was for it but questioned the best way of accomplishing the goal. Paige's biggest point, as he informed the crowd: "Ladies and gentlemen I would like to take this opportunity to deny a statement that the daily papers credited to me." He made the point repeatedly in his remarks that he wanted to let them "know that I did not say anything against the use of Negro players in the big leagues." The question to him was who would be the winners and who would be the losers in all of this. Paige shared privately with friends like Double Duty Radcliffe and Buck O'Neil that he thought integration would spell the end of the Negro Leagues and that all the Majors wanted to do was to capture the black fans.[14]

There was still a little matter of the Negro World Series, and the Kansas City Monarchs were the Negro American League champions of 1942 and ready to pace off against the Negro National League champions, which was their old nemesis the Homestead Grays. The attendance was barely half that of the East-West contest. Paige started the first game of the World Series and held the Grays scoreless for five innings before relinquishing the ball to Jack Matchett, who took the team home the rest of the way to an 8–0 victory. The Monarchs behind Paige completely dominated the Grays in the first game and went into the second contest ready to do the same.

It was in the second game, the evening of Thursday, September 17, 1942, that a showdown took place that would be forever recorded in the annals of sports history as one of its greatest moments. The contest began with Hilton Smith on the mound for the Monarchs against Roy Partlow pitching for the Grays. The weather had worked against the second game, and a crowd of only fifty-two hundred braved the drizzle and occasional showers that afternoon to be present.

It was the sixth inning, and Hilton Smith had a 2–0 lead and the Grays trying to figure out some way of getting a hit off him. He was showing signs of tiring, and Paige came in to relieve him. Paige reported to the mound and told Smith, "You've been relieving me all these times. Let me relieve you now." Paige retired the side. In the seventh inning he was cruising along well with two outs and needing only one more when the Grays surprised him with a triple into left field. With one man on third and only needing one more out, Paige decided that he wanted to do something a little bit different, and he called over to his friend Buck O'Neil to join him at the mound. O'Neil, who was also one of the managers for the Monarchs and playing first base, walked over to see what the master hurler wanted. Paige said to him, "Nancy, you know what I'm thinking about doing?" O'Neil's reply was, "Oh, no, Satch, don't do it!" Paige said, "But I have to. People have been waiting to see Josh and me settle this thing, and it's about time we do it." O'Neil knew exactly what this meant. It meant that Paige had decided that he wanted to walk the next two hitters to be able to pitch to Josh Gibson for the last out. O'Neil thought this was madness and called to manager Frank Duncan from the dugout to try to dissuade Paige. Duncan quickly shrugged his shoulders and gave up on the matter and went back to the dugout. He basically told O'Neil, "Whatever Satchel wants to do is what Satchel will do. We have a few thousand fans here, and I know that all of them came to see Satchel and Josh." That was it. O'Neil went back to first base, and Paige walked the next two batters so that he could face the incomparable Josh Gibson.[15]

Make no mistake about it: Josh Gibson was the greatest hitter in the history of Negro Leagues Baseball. He hit such mighty home runs that they had already gone into the annals of African American folklore. In a Grays game against the Chicago American Giants in Forbes Field in Pittsburgh, he blasted a homer that folks were still talking about. As the ball cleared the center-field stands, its trajectory continued upward, clearing the park and nearby buildings and still going up as startled fans shaded their eyes as they watched the ball vanish into the distance. Reportedly, as the story goes, three days later Gibson and the Grays were in Chicago to start the remaining games of the series when one of the fans yelled out to a Giants player, "Look up, there's a ball coming!" The startled player did so and witnessed the ball falling out of the sky and caught it. An umpire standing a few feet away from him, looking as startled as the player, looked at the player and the ball and then, scratching his head, looked around for an explanation. He saw Josh Gibson across the way talking to another player. The umpire looked at the ball and looked at Gibson, looked again at the ball, and looked back again to Gibson. Finally, he yelled to Gibson, "Gibson, yes you Josh Gibson. You're out! You're out in Pittsburgh three days ago!"[16]

It was one of those stories that everyone knew was, shall we say, a slight stretch of the imagination, but it punctuated what most thought about the incredible hitting ability and power of Gibson. To think that a pitcher would have the audacity to single him out, and intentionally load the bases to pitch to him, was too much to believe. Paige did exactly that, and the fans went wild in disbelief at what they were about to witness. This was no dream or folktale. It was real. Everyone in the stands was on their feet. No one wanted to miss any detail of this. There may have been only five thousand in attendance, but you would have thought the stadium was full to capacity as the shouts and cheers of excitement rocked the house. Then, a collective hush and total silence took over as Gibson took his stance at the plate with bat at the ready to take whatever Paige was going to dare throw.

What Paige first delivered was his incessant trash talk. He was talking up a storm. He told his old friend and former teammate that they needed to settle the matter once and for all about who would win if the world's greatest hitter faced the world's greatest pitcher. It was something that the two of them had joked about years earlier when they were teammates on the Crawfords, wondering what would happen if they faced each other with the game in the balance. Paige answered his own trash-talking question by saying that "superior pitching always wins over superior hitting." Gibson was a pretty good trash-talker himself and did not take this insult from his old friend without response. He told Paige, "Well, Satchel, when I smack it out of the park you can go fetch it! Or if you like we can continue talking while I run around the bases!" The fans who picked up on the exchange went into a frenzy but were immediately told by others to hush and be quiet.[17]

The audacious Paige next told Gibson what he was going to throw him. "Josh, the first one will be a fastball on the outside corner and it will be coming so fast that there ain't a thing you can do about it." Whiff! "Strike one," the umpire yelled. Paige then continued his diatribe, telling his old friend, "Now Josh, the second one is going to be a strike on the inside corner. It will look like it's a might low but it will be good. And Josh, it will be faster than the first one I threw you." Zip! "Strike two," the umpire called it. The fans went berserk between pitches and then immediately went silent to watch every detail of the next one. Finally, with two strikes on him, the master hurler told the master hitter, "I know you are a great hitter and that's why it would be foolhardy to tell you where the last one is going. I will tell you one thing: it's going to be a whole lot faster than the other two!" Paige did a windmill windup and let loose with a rifle shot that popped in the catcher's glove and echoed across the stadium. The umpire called it loud and clear: "Strike three on you Gibson. You're out!"[18]

It was bedlam. The five thousand went wild, yelling and screaming, the men throwing straw hats onto the field. Buck O'Neil recalled that "Josh never swung at any of the pitches. There was nothing he could do. He slammed his bat down in disgust and walked off." Paige, to all of the accolades, the yelling and cheering, the fans going mad with appreciation, took it all in stride. Did he tip his cap? Did he take a bow? Did he wave to the crowd? No. He did none of those things. He looked straight ahead as he walked leisurely off the field as if it had been just another day at the office. This sent the crowd into even greater hysterics—as if that were possible—as the man of the hour strolled off the field too cool to take a bow. Paige was not perfect for the rest of the game. He gave up several runs, but his teammates scored as well. In the end, the Monarchs and he prevailed, 8–4. It was more than just another sweet victory for Satchel Paige; his showdown with Gibson was the day he stepped into baseball immortality. The Monarchs went on to take the series and another world championship.[19]

Paige and the Monarchs had many seasons full of victories. There was also for them and the rest of Negro Leagues ballplayers the ongoing hope for a Double V. Would World War II live up to its promise of democracy not only over there but over here and give African Americans an equal footing in America for the first time in the nation's history? These were questions on the minds of black folk, including Paige. He was consumed with baseball, but he was well aware of so many other things taking place in black America. There was the question of a segregated American military. Those African Americans who volunteered or were drafted were for the most part relegated to all-black units, despite the utterances of Franklin Delano Roosevelt.

Paige was in a changing world where folks were speaking out and taking action to make a difference. The continuing struggle against lynching moved him. Paige, like his Negro Leagues compatriots, constantly discussed the crisis in lynching and what must be done to stop it. Bill "Bojangles" Robinson fought a never-ending battle to bring about a resolution. He donated to the cause and collected money from others to push and help the struggle for effective antilynching legislation. Paige, like others, saw lynchings as a true Fifth Column. He supported the crusade against lynchings that his good friend Bojangles Robinson was so deeply committed to. Besides giving money, Paige often spoke to other ballplayers, friends, and family about the problem of lynching. He knew the horrible problem only too well as a child of Alabama and, like all other decent Americans, wanted the practice to stop. "Satchel and all the black ballplayers I knew contributed something to help what Bojangles was doing. Most of us were from the South, and we wanted something done," Buck O'Neil reflected.[20]

Paige and the Negro Leaguers were pulled in all sorts of directions. There were the constant racial biases of the media. Satchel Paige was the target more than anyone else because he was so frequently in the news. He stomached such articles as the one that appeared in the *Saturday Evening Post* in which Ted Shane mimicked Paige as speaking in a "Negro dialect" and wrote about what he considered to be Paige's "apelike arms" and his "Stepin Fetchit accent." The venerable *Sporting News* early on did not bother to cover any Negro Leagues Baseball. When it finally did, its early coverage followed all the traditional racial biases for the most part. Time and again the *Sporting News* questioned whether blacks were suited for Major League Baseball and suggested that possible outbreaks of violence might occur if any mixed sporting event took place. The *Sporting News* contended that in a game "before a crowd of the opposite color," any little mishap on the field might have cataclysmic results, because "it might be taken the wrong way." Hence, it was, in the opinion of the publication, best "to leave things as is" and leave blacks "to develop in their own circles. Proper tribute has been paid to Satchel Paige as being a great pitcher. Whether he would be held in such esteem had he attempted to win his laurels elsewhere is problematical. The same is true of other Negro stars. They have blossomed forth with the inspiration and the encouragement and sympathy of their own followers. It is doubtful if the road would have been so easy, otherwise."[21]

There was nothing easy about Paige's professional or personal life. During the war years his "rubbernecking," as he called it, took on an added dimension of complexity and entanglement one Saturday afternoon early in the 1942 season in KC. Paige loved taking photographs and was starting to consider himself something of a semiprofessional photographer. He collected eight different cameras and a wide array of fancy photography equipment. He had run out of 120 film for his Kodak Brownie, his favorite camera at the time, and stopped into Roberts Drugstore to buy some. He was greeted by a very attractive clerk of whom he immediately took special notice. He informed her of his desire to purchase some 120 film. After looking through the drugstore's stock of film, the clerk informed him that they were out of 120 and wondered if he might be able to use a different size. Paige considered the remark tremendously uninformed and told her so. She replied that his was merely an ordinary camera and nothing special and that he should not get all huffy. This outraged Paige, not just because she insulted him and his camera but even more because the young lady did not recognize him. Indeed, the clerk was a rare commodity in Kansas City: she was not a baseball fan and follower of the Monarchs. Hence, she was not impressed that she was speaking to the great Satchel Paige. He was just another customer in her eyes, and a rude one at that.

Paige's ego was bruised more than the fact that the film he needed was not in stock. He yelled for the manager. Hearing the call, the store's manager came from the back. The manager immediately recognized the celebrity customer and apologized profusely for the conduct of his clerk. Paige informed him that the young clerk had basically insulted him by not knowing that one could not put just anything in a camera. He further informed the manager that his clerk needed to be better trained and to have better manners in dealing with customers. The manager offered more apologies to Mr. Satchel Paige and offered to fire the clerk on the spot if he wanted him to.

Paige was taken back by the gesture, but no matter how big of a star he thought he was, he had enough compassion not to want to see someone lose their job, "especially a gal as pretty as this one." He informed the manager that firing would not be necessary but repeated his demand that the manager should teach his clerk manners so that she would know how to speak to people. In the process of this exchange, the manager had mentioned the name of the clerk, referring to her as Miss Brown.[22]

Whatever the laws of chemistry or the attraction of opposites, Paige found himself attracted to the beautiful young clerk. He most definitely had an eye for pretty women and certainly one who was salty and did not know the great Satchel Paige. He returned to Roberts Drugstore numerous times, buying film and other items and always asking to be waited on by the "half smart gal." Miss Brown overheard him and came to the counter to wait on him each time. He figured that if he kept calling her the "half smart gal" that she might sooner or later forget that she had been angry with him and begin to see it as an ongoing joke.[23]

His tactic worked, and each time he bought an item, he struck up a longer conversation with Miss Brown, to the point of his fourth or fifth visit to the drugstore when he inquired as to her first name. He learned that it was Lahoma. Lahoma Jean Brown was young, just like Paige liked them, twenty years of age, born on April 7, 1922, in Stillwater, Oklahoma. Her father, Warren Brown, was a hardworking laborer but unable to read and write and already fifty-two years of age when his wife, Jessie Ouida Brown, thirty-two, gave birth to their youngest daughter, Lahoma. Jessie Ouida Brown had roots in Louisiana and liked the sound of the state's name. Warren Brown felt the same about Oklahoma. They liked the sounds and the sense of roots and combined the two to come up with the name for their daughter, La-homa.

Warren and Jessie Ouida moved the family to Kansas City in the mid-1930s, hoping to escape the Depression and find better economic opportunities for themselves and their children. It was Jessie Ouida who taught Lahoma and the other children to read and write. Both parents had a respect for education and made sure that their children went to school.

Lahoma, as Paige would quickly learn, had four older sisters, Beulah, Nina, Carrie Oletha, and Helen. There had also been a brother, Hulan, who died at age nineteen, and a sister, Della, who succumbed in very early childhood. The four elder sisters kept watchful eyes on Lahoma, and did so for the rest of their lives. Luckily for Paige, the other sisters knew Monarch baseball, knew his name, and, most important, took an immediate liking to him as a suitor for their younger sibling.[24]

Finally, Paige asked Lahoma if she would go out to dinner with him. He was not certain of the answer and rightly so, given his behavior early on and not knowing whether the chemistry between the two had turned into a good mixture or was something that was basically going to explode. The chemical mixture turned out to be a soothing elixir. Lahoma accepted his offer to go out with him for dinner. It may very well be that in the intervening time she had learned from her sisters who her suitor was or would have certainly have heard it more than once from the store manager, or read about him in the newspaper, or heard about him from almost anybody in KC.

They went out to dinner and repeated it countless times during the coming weeks and months. They hit all the best spots to dine in black KC. They took in good music at the Reno Club, ate ribs at Gates Barbecue, made several visits to Club Mardi Gras, and had numerous dining excursions in the top-of-the-line restaurants of Street's Hotel, movies at the Lincoln, and dancing galore at the Lyric.

In only two months Satchel Paige and Lahoma Jean Brown had become an item too in black KC. Paige saw Lucy Figueroa less frequently now, as their relationship wound down. Nevertheless, he was juggling two women in the same town while still having not resolved the little matter of his estranged wife back in Pittsburgh. Paige's juggling act of women became even more complex after the Monarchs' road trip to Sioux Falls, South Dakota. There Paige met a strikingly beautiful Native American maiden by the name of Nancy, and he immediately took a liking to her.

The juggling act escalated on the following road trip to Chicago, which Buck O'Neil humorously referred to as the birth of his nickname as Nancy. Paige had invited the Native American woman, Nancy, to visit him in Chicago, where he and the team would be playing the Chicago American Giants and where she had some relatives whom she wanted to visit. Paige and the team checked into the Evans Hotel. Shortly afterward, Nancy showed up at the hotel to see Paige. He had checked her into a room down the hall from his. Evidently, he had forgotten that he had also invited another young woman to visit him at the same hotel.

While Paige was upstairs with Nancy, Buck O'Neil, who was downstairs in the hotel lobby, witnessed the arrival of Paige's other woman friend. O'Neil immediately went into a defensive mode, greeted her, and suggested that she wait in the lobby with him because Paige had not arrived at the hotel, which was a lie. Meanwhile, he excused himself to find a bell clerk and get him to take a message upstairs to Paige, alerting him to the dilemma downstairs. According to O'Neil, Paige came down via the fire escape in the rear of the hotel and then came around to the front as if he had just arrived. He greeted his other lady friend in the lobby and assisted her too in checking into the hotel.

That night, Paige journeyed down the hotel corridor, wanting to meet with Nancy, who had a room on the same floor at the opposite end, to offer her some kind of explanation. He tapped on her door and called out in a muffled voice, "Nancy, Nancy, Nancy." Nancy was evidently sound asleep, but Paige's other guest, in the room next to his, was not and, despite his muffled voice, recognized it and opened her door to investigate. O'Neil, who was in the room next to hers, heard her door opening and spontaneously rushed into action and poked his head out just in time to defuse the situation by answering his friend: "Yeah, Satchel, what do you want?" With the inquisitive other woman guest looking on, Paige—with a comeback quicker than playing the dozens, a jazz riff, call-and-response in the black church, or his fastball—replied to O'Neil, "Oh, there you are, Nancy. I was looking for you. What time is the game tomorrow?" From that moment on, Paige always referred to his lifesaving-friend, Buck O'Neil, as "Nancy."[25]

Did Paige and the Monarchs win or lose against the Chicago team? That may have been of little importance to him after his hair-raising night at the Evans Hotel. He was glad to get out of Chicago and back to the relative calm of KC. At least there he was actively dividing his time between only two love interests, with some distance between them. There was, however, the matter of his estranged wife in Pittsburgh, and that situation was not improving over time.

Back in KC, his success and thoughts about settling down for real in terms of his personal life led him to purchase his first home. It was no easy matter for him attaining his first house. It was a nice dwelling in an area that blacks were just starting to move into. That meant that there were hesitation and roadblocks to be overcome. He could overcome the most major one in that he had money. Paige was proud of his new home at 2020 East Twelfth Street. He kept it neatly painted and the yard always well trimmed.

What 1942 brought to Paige in terms of glory, 1943 brought to him in terms of pain. The year was one that he would remember not so much for his triumphs as for the agony of defeat. The year started off with a familiar pattern of numerous spring games and traveling and barnstorming everywhere, including great matches with his mutual admirer Dizzy Dean. Paige and Dean took their barnstorming clashes throughout the nation. Dean had always admired Paige's pitching. Most folks failed to realize that Paige felt equal respect and admiration for Dean. In an interview for the *Chicago Daily News,* Paige said that Dean threw the hardest fastball he ever saw in his life and that Dean "made lefthanders look like righthanders, the way that boy pitches. Man, he didn't have no ordinary fastball. He had a sneaky fastball. He throws so hard that it sort of took off past you faster than you'd ever think a ball to travel. That Dizzy Dean," Paige exclaimed, "never saw a man like Dizzy, ever. That boy loved baseball and he had the confidence and he was a ball-playing fool. Bismarck was the finest team I ever played with an Ol' Diz the greatest ballplayer I ever knew."[26]

The year settled into the traditional hectic schedule of mad dashes from town to town for Paige and his All-Stars or when the regular season began with Paige and the Monarchs, or his solo jaunts from team to team with the blessing and percentage cut to J. L. Wilkinson. It was basically déjà vu for Paige, and one wonders how he distinguished one year from the next, one month from the next, and one town from the next.

As the time came to start thinking again about the biggest moneymaker in Negro Leagues Baseball and the biggest turnout of fans, the East-West Game, it was like a replay of 1942, as the good folks in Chicago wanted to have another Satchel Paige Day in the Windy City as a momentum builder to the East-West classic, like before. They announced that Paige would be honored on July 25. Paige would not be playing with the Monarchs; he would be on loan to the Memphis Red Sox for a four-team doubleheader against the New York Cubans Stars. The second game would be between the Birmingham Black Barons, who had won the first half of the split season and the Cincinnati Clowns.[27]

It worked again. Satchel Paige Day in Chicago drew an audience of twenty-five thousand to witness him go up against the Cubans. Paige pitched the first five innings, striking out seven, walking two, and allowing no hits. He relished playing in Chicago, and the town inspired him to give his all. When he concluded the fifth inning, he received a thunderous ovation that seemed to never end.

They halted the contests after the fifth to present Paige with a huge bouquet of flowers, a set of luggage, and numerous other gifts. It was another great day to add to his legacy. Paige was grateful for it. He always had a special place in his heart for the fans, and not just because they were his meal ticket. One of the reasons he was so successful was that he played for the fans, and they knew it. He wanted to please and to be the best of the best for himself and them.

That would have been the end of the story, a great day to remember, if it had ended on that note, but it did not. What captivated the news headlines as much as the brilliant mound performance was the climax to the rumor that had been circulating all week prior to the game. The rumor proved not to be a rumor. Everyone in baseball knew of Satchel Paige's ongoing estranged relationship with his wife, Janet.

Paige was served with divorce papers following the heralded Satchel Paige Day, immediately after the game. The *Chicago Defender* and the *Baltimore Afro-American* both carried the same story, that Janet's decree for divorce of her estranged husband had been granted. Not only that, but the divorce was granted on the terms that Janet Paige wanted. Judge Benjamin Epstein had no empathy for the wayward star. The judge ruled straight down the line in favor of Janet Paige's charges, which included her claim that Satchel Paige made an annual income of forty thousand dollars a year; that he owned a building worth twenty-five thousand dollars in Kansas City, Missouri; that he possessed antiques and curios worth an additional thirty thousand; and that she was entitled to a fair and just settlement. Janet won alimony amounting to one hundred dollars weekly during the baseball season and fifty dollars weekly doing the rest of the year. In addition, Satchel Paige was ordered to pay his estranged wife eighteen hundred in cash and three hundred to cover her attorney fees. As the black press sounded: "Satchel Paige Loses Wife and $1800."[28]

Janet Paige was evidently never aware of the third woman vying for the affections of her estranged husband. Indeed, Satchel Paige was smitten over

Lahoma Brown and devoting more and more of his time exclusively to her. By the end of 1943, Lucy Figueroa had moved on to start a new life in Chicago. Ironically, she chose the same city that Janet Paige chose for her new beginning. After the divorce, Janet too moved to the Windy City and became a greeter and hostess in nightclubs on the city's South Side. She billed herself as Mrs. Satchel Paige and used that name recognition and her attractiveness to forge a place for herself in the black Chicago social scene.

Satchel Paige's affections now focused exclusively on Lahoma Brown. "I am a free man," he told her immediately after being served with the divorce decree. Lahoma told him that she had read about it in the newspaper. The future was to be him and Lahoma. For the first time in Paige's life, he had actually found the woman he truly loved. "She looked real happy about it and we started seeing the town like nobody ever'd done before. I could tell she was the gal for me. I'd never met anybody like her and that slowed me down like no gal'd ever slowed me down before." He began to start thinking seriously about marriage and settling down in the real sense of the word.[29]

"Satchel Paige Day" had worked, and the town was abuzz about the forthcoming East-West classic scheduled for Comiskey Park on August 1. Fans were unable to get enough of Paige. To no one's surprise, when the voting had concluded naming the players to the East-West classic, Paige once again topped the list of vote getters. Now thirty-seven years of age, he was the old man of the game, that seasoned veteran, a household name, the crowd pleaser, and the biggest draw in baseball. His schedule was so hectic by this time that J. L. Wilkinson leased an airplane to get Paige from date to date. Wilkinson's son, a former World War II pilot, captained the aircraft.[30]

The Paige magic was still there for the 1943 classic, with a huge crowd. The final tally at the game was 51,723 out for a perfect afternoon of splendid baseball. The great one once again went into the breach and rose to the occasion with no-hit pitching for the first three innings. Buck Leonard later admitted that the team lost its heart after going up against Paige and being put in its place. The master hurler set the tone, and the West went on to defeat the East before a standing-room-only crowd. The white Majors watched with envy. Few of their games topped the 20,000 mark.[31]

Paige paused only long enough to support the war effort. He considered himself a good American and wanted to do his part. He lent his name and part of his purse on at least fifteen occasions to the selling of war bonds, the patriotic theme and goal that underlined the fifth annual North-South Classic being held in the Big Easy. It was agreed and both teams signed on to the Star-Spangled Banner Pledge of raising one hundred thousand dollars by the end of the season for the war effort. War Board chairman Ernest Wright was at the game and announced the campaign among African Americans and Negro Leagues ballplayers and owners to support the war effort and buy bonds. Paige signed on immediately, as did David Barnhill and most of the other stars from both camps. The war effort was served, as fans also saw a great game of baseball that sweltering late-Sunday afternoon in New Orleans.[32]

Never any time to dwell, Paige hit the road again for another North-South showdown in October and lost this one 6–1. The North won that encounter before 12,165 loyal fans, which included more than 2,000 servicemen and -women. Paige was the victim, but he did not see it that way. In his thinking, the important point was that the military was saluted and entertained and money raised for the war effort. Paige was not a superman. He indeed had his off days, on occasion.[33]

The 1944 East-West classic would not be business as usual. There was controversy that gripped the event early on. It surrounded Paige and a conflict he was having with organizers of the event. Owners, especially at the forefront Cum Posey and J. B. Martin, president of the Negro American League, decided to take a hard line with Paige this time and his requirement of extra compensation for participating in the classic game. The owners and organizers decided, by majority vote, that all players would receive the same amount for their participation in the game.

While the East-West classic was the biggest payday in Negro Leagues Baseball for the owners, it was hardly that for the players. Most of them received less than one hundred dollars each for their participation. The great exception to the rule was Paige, who commanded upward of eight hundred to a thousand for his putting in an appearance. They publicly pooh-poohed Paige's receiving of special payment for his participation over other players and touted their new egalitarian philosophy. They made no mention of how much owners, promoters, and the event's organizers received in compensation.

Paige let it be known immediately that he did not intend to pitch in the next East-West Game unless he was compensated accordingly. Everyone knew that Paige demanded and commanded special fees for his participation. What Paige confided to his friends was more hard-hitting than what he told the press, and that was that he knew full well that the owners made a killing in the East-West Game. On that score, he was correct. The 1943 East-West classic had earned more than three hundred thousand dollars. When one considered that amount, it was not unreasonable that Paige wanted what he considered fair compensation. The owners' biggest expense was the rental of Comiskey Park. The White Sox were doing no favor to the Negro Leagues by renting out the park to them and took the lion's share of the money earned and included control over the concessions. The Negro Leagues all-star ballplayers received the short end of the stick, with the exception of Paige, who was not in any mood to change his ways at this point in his career when his name recognition was greater than ever.

As the controversy grew, the arguments on both sides soured. Paige was publicly accused of thinking only of himself. He did not deny that his first concern was that he be paid accordingly. After that, he expanded his argument to say that all the ballplayers should be paid more. The fans came out to see the ballplayers and not the owners, he said. The black press, especially Fay Young, the sports editor for the *Chicago Defender,* and sports editor Wendell Smith at the *Pittsburgh Courier,* lashed out at Paige for being a one-man show, or at least thinking that he was. J. B. Martin was quite blunt. He did not like Paige attempting to, as he characterized it, dictate terms for his payment and how other players should be compensated.

Paige was losing the propaganda war in the media but then upped the ante when he fired back that the owners and everyone involved should be thinking of the war effort and donate a sizable amount of the profits from the East-West Game to military relief. If not, he suggested that the game be boycotted until they came to their senses to do what was right not just for the ballplayers but for America's gallant military personnel. Martin reminded all of those who would listen to him that he and other owners participated in relief efforts for the military. He resented Paige's raising issues that seemed to make the owners appear unpatriotic and Paige somehow more patriotic. "We don't propose, however, to have Satchel Paige or any other disgruntled ballplayer dictate to us as to when and how this army or navy relief game shall be played," Martin declared.[34]

Fay Young, in a piece published on August 12, just one day prior to the scheduled 1944 East-West classic, berated the master hurler and claimed that he had gotten himself fired from the role as pitcher in the East-West Game. Young told fans to be ready to miss Paige at the game on Sunday and that "the internationally known mound artist will not work the first three innings or any part of the game because of his threats to take a walk and his insinuation that owners of Negro ball clubs were unpatriotic." Young went on to accuse Paige of the worst kind of hypocrisy. He labeled all of Satchel Paige's declarations as nonsense. According to Young, there were other games in which Paige was paid as much as four thousand dollars extra, while the average Monarch player was lucky if he made five hundred dollars a month, and, according to Young, this was "after Pearl Harbor." Young talked about how Paige received twelve hundred for pitching some innings in Chicago for a benefit for Provident Hospital and did not give any part of his earnings to the cause. Moreover, he excoriated, "Paige claims that in San Diego this winter, his heart went out" for the wounded soldiers and sailors in the government hospital who had fought in the South Pacific. The truth is that "Paige's heart is still out," Young concluded.[35]

Paige's media war with the owners over his compensation for the 1944 East-West classic stirred the consciousness of the other black ballplayers. They began to talk among themselves about how little they were being paid for an event that made the owners a substantial pile of money. The players posed questions similar to those of Paige: Who are the fans coming to see? Who should be making the lion's share of the profits from this? What is being contributed by the owners to military relief? The players were restless and felt that they were not appreciated.

At a secret joint meeting of all-stars from the West and East, the players outlined an action plan to at least get "a fairer share of the gate." Double Duty Radcliffe, who always had a penchant for speaking his mind, had to tread softly since speaking out quite boldly in the press, stating how little he had been paid in the past, only twenty-five dollars for the 1943 East-West All-Star Game as compared to Satchel Paige's eight hundred dollars. Radcliffe did most of his talking among the players, since he was now on the Chicago American Giants and under the orbit of the Martin brothers, who led the owners in their recalcitrant position not to pay Paige any more money and not wanting to give any of the other players more money for their participation. "We players struck a deal," Radcliffe reflected. "It would be the East All-Stars who led the way in refusing to play unless they were paid two hundred dollars each for the game. We on the West knew that also would mean that we would have to have our share as well. That's the way we had to play it since we were a little handicapped on the West side because of the Martins," Radcliffe reminisced.[36]

The fans had no idea that the 1944 game was up in the air about actually being played at all. The matter was settled just prior to the teams taking the field for their warm-ups. The East All-Stars had led the way in the verbal demand that they would have to be paid two hundred dollars per man or would not play. The deal was struck because the owners had no choice or the All-Star Game might have been canceled and more than forty thousand fans left furious and demanding their money back. The players won their demand for the extra money on both sides.

When Paige learned of this, he felt vindicated. He never begrudged other players making more money. He felt an extra sense of satisfaction since he knew how much the owners hated to give up that money. There was also a promise made by the owners and the players that there would have to be and indeed would be future contests, future games, played to benefit the military relief fund. Paige's demand for his usual extra compensation had evolved into the first labor action on the part of Negro Leagues ballplayers and ended with positive results. His 1943 appearance would be his last time on the mound at the East-West All-Star Game for many years. There were forty-six thousand who attended the 1944 game, played without Satchel Paige, a decline of five thousand from the previous year.[37]

The *Sporting News* had no idea what was going on behind the scene. What was happening in black baseball and the life of Satchel Paige was part of the changing dynamics in American society. Paige, Negro Leagues Baseball, and the Major Leagues were on the cusp of the dawning of the new era of postwar America, where deaf ears were no longer acceptable to those demanding fair treatment.

The war years also prompted some Major League owners to begin rethinking the color line. They were basically no different from the Negro Leagues owners in that they wanted to sell tickets, fill the stands, win games, and turn as large a profit as possible. It was all about having the superior product that attracted consumers. This led Major League owners back to the basic question of why they were not filling the stands. Wendell Smith offered them a succinct answer: "Unfortunately, the Majors have no Satchel Paige—for there is only one Satchel Paige, and he plays in Negro baseball. Nor do the Majors have a Josh Gibson, Buck Leonard, Sammy Jethroe or Ray Dandridge. And that combination in itself makes the Negro classic much more appealing than the big leagues 'Dream Game.'"[38]

11

Integration

According to Paige, integration destroyed the Negro Leagues. He was defending himself, no doubt, but his early retrospective offered a chilling assessment of what happened to Negro Leagues Baseball after the signing of Jackie Robinson: "Even with those guys jumping off, the Negro Leagues didn't come close to busting up. That bust-up came when the Major Leagues started raiding Negro clubs and just giving them a few pennies or nothing and killing off attendance. If the Major Leagues turned the Negro Leagues into a good minor league, those owners who squawked at me never would have gone out of business."[1]

The pillars of Paige's world began shifting dynamically in the 1940s and more with the end of World War II. There was something else that for Negro Leagues Baseball, the Major Leagues, the world of sports, and American race relations was of earth-shattering significance. It was the stunning announcement of President Hector Racine of the Montréal Royals on October 23, 1945, of the signing of Jackie Robinson. The contract was for five thousand dollars, and it was with the Montréal Royals, the farm team of the Brooklyn Dodgers, but it was unmistakable: the color bar was broken, and a black had been signed to Major League Baseball. It was the shot that was heard around the world. Branch Rickey had done it, and Robinson was going to be given the opportunity to make the grade and earn a spot on the Brooklyn Dodgers.

When Satchel Paige was hit with the news, the press, white and black, could not wait to hear what he had to say. They asked him if he was bitter that it was not him selected. He said, "No he was not bitter that his time had passed." They asked if he thought Robinson could make it, and his answer was a resounding and powerful yes. Paige went on to say, "They didn't make a mistake by signing Robinson. They couldn't have picked a better man." When asked what about himself, Paige reiterated, "Of course I'm too old now."[2]

In private to family and close friends, Paige shared his disappointment in that so many of the great ballplayers he had known, and that included himself, were not given this opportunity in their prime. He also knew that there were still many other black ballplayers out there who had a number of good years left. But Paige was skeptical about the process of the Major Leagues, which he thought was the taking of potshots at Negro Leagues clubs and taking players here and there from them. He went back to a point he had made many years earlier that he felt a Negro Leagues ball club or two should be brought into the Major Leagues as a whole unit. Failing that, he, along with virtually all the Negro Leagues players and owners, questioned why the Negro Leagues clubs at least could not be signed on as farm teams for the Major Leagues. This would have provided them with some financial relief rather than the monetary gestures made at the discretion of white Major League owners to compensate them for players they would most certainly start recruiting if Robinson proved successful.

Wilkinson, Baird, and the Monarchs organization were not compensated for Robinson, and when it seemed that they were complaining about what was going on, they were harshly criticized in the African American press for thinking of themselves rather than the advancement of the race. They quickly backed off. They were saying quite simply that Negro Leagues teams should be compensated if the Majors were going to start taking their players from them. Wilkinson and Baird went on record that they would do nothing to stop the progress of black ballplayers who might get a chance to play in the Major Leagues, like their former player Jackie Robinson, who was with them only one year before being tagged as "the one" by Branch Rickey to bring into his Dodgers organization as the great experiment to integrate Major League Baseball.[3]

For Paige, there were serious questions that needed to be answered rather than just jumping on the integration bandwagon. First of all, he was not convinced even by 1945 that parts of the nation, especially the South, were ready for this. He had talked about it and been interviewed countless times, sometimes making statements that seemed contradictory but with several points that loomed large. Paige had never said, as some attributed to him, that blacks were not ready for big league baseball—of course not. That would have been to say that he too was never ready to play in the Majors. What he had, in fact, said was that big league baseball was not ready for blacks. If you have an integrated team, Paige questioned, how would that work in the South? He concluded that it would not work because no hotel in Dixie would accept blacks and whites rooming together, and most of the hotels would not accept blacks on any basis. There was a question of restaurants that he knew only too well would not serve blacks, no matter how prominent they were or in the company of whites.

Paige was unequivocal in private in his criticism of the color line. He did not believe that America was ready for integration in general and not in its cherished sport of baseball. He questioned what integration actually meant. He had suggested back in 1942, for which he was roundly condemned, that blacks should not be siphoned off one by one into the Major Leagues but that an entire black team should go into the Majors, and he kept reiterating that point. No one took him up on the idea, certainly not the owners of Major League Baseball, and they were not doing so now with the signing of a lone Jackie Robinson.[4]

Neither did Paige think that the Majors were interested in improving the quality of play by adding superior black talent. If it was a matter of quality, it would and should have been done years ago. There were those managers in years past, such as "Doc" Prothro of the Philadelphia Phillies, who had said that he would have used blacks like Satchel Paige: "I certainly would, if given permission I would jump at the opportunity to sign up a good Negro ballplayer." The Majors, as Paige reckoned, were interested now because they wanted to increase attendance. The novelty of a black player on a Major League team would do that at several levels, attracting curious whites and winning over the black fan base away from the Negro Leagues.[5]

Not only did Paige understand this, but one of his long-standing critics echoed exactly the same concern in the clearest possible voice. Effa Manley of the Eagles thought that integration would be a disaster for the Negro Leagues and that the leagues needed to push home the point to the African American community that black baseball was black owned, for the most part, and that in most cases the money that Negro Leagues teams generated stayed in the black community. She readily predicted that the moment Robinson put on a Dodgers uniform, one could start counting the days to the death of the Negro Leagues. It could be likened to the old adage that it's not over until the fat lady sings. She had not sung in 1945 when Robinson signed on with Montréal but she was warming up in her dressing room.[6]

Cum Posey, who previously disagreed with Paige on many issues and was not particularly fond of the independent-minded hurler, was largely in agreement with him on the integration question. Posey urged black America to rethink the notion of integration and what could be the negative impact on black-owned businesses such as Negro Leagues Baseball. "After all," Posey stated, "it doesn't make much difference to us in the Negro National League whether two, three or the frequently mentioned ten or a dozen players go up to the Majors. We're more concerned about the 200 other colored players in this league and with our own investments. I think the colored players themselves feel the same way."[7]

Buck O'Neil, Double Duty Radcliffe, Cool Papa Bell, and Buck Leonard were a few of the many Negro Leagues players who were questioning what integration might mean in terms of its negative impact on their livelihood. The great stars, who were too old to think realistically of being eventually drafted into the Majors, were at least making a living in Negro Leagues Baseball. Those players who were not superstars and were unlikely prospects for the Majors at any point were also making a decent living in Negro Leagues Baseball.

The African American community, however, including most of the blacks sportswriters and pundits, was locked in on the ideal of integration and rarely discussed or considered the possible negative consequences of integration. Would the African American community benefit by having some number of black players in the Major Leagues, or would black folk as a race benefit more by having Negro Leagues teams continue as the source of the highest-quality baseball? What commitment, if any, would Major League Baseball make to the African American community?

The danger, as Paige's experience confirmed, was that speaking out might be perceived as critical of the goal of integration. Buck O'Neil would live long enough to really question that goal and to state emphatically, "We should have supported our Negro Leagues teams and then gone on and found a way, as Satchel had said, to take whole teams into the Majors or at least make the Negro Leagues part of the farm system of the Majors."[8]

Just prior to the announced signing of Jackie Robinson, an interesting exchange occurred between sports columnist Wendell Smith and Satchel Paige. It was one of those rare instances when Paige actually wrote his thoughts for publication in the newspaper. He addressed the issue of black ballplayers finally being given the opportunity to try out for some Major League teams. What he did not know was that in a few months, the Dodgers organization would be signing Robinson. It is not known whether he could see that the gates were about to open to allow some folks of color to enter Major League Baseball, but he offered his opinion that May 12, 1945, in his letter to Smith, who published it in his column, "Sports Beat," under the subtitle of "Satchel Takes Pen in Hand." Paige articulated how Major League Baseball, in his opinion, was not genuinely interested in bringing blacks into the game:

> I see in the *Courier* where the Major Leagues are trying out some colored players. Please listen to me—the Negro will never break into the Majors like

that. You see, the owners and managers will always have a way to find fault with our very best players. The only way I see we can make it is to pick an All-Star club of our own to play their best club and let the whole world see. This must be a big game, not just a spring training contest where only 25 or 30 people will see it. Some say we do not have many good Negro players—at least good enough for the Major Leagues. This is not true. What is wrong with Booker McDaniel, Kansas City pitcher; Josh Gibson of the Homestead Grays and Buck Leonard of Kansas City? Too old? Listen, there are a lot of big leaguers now playing that are over 30 years of age. The men I have named and plenty of other Negro players, are just as good and better than a lot of big leaguers the same age. Pal, I haven't started training yet. However, I'm going to Hot Springs and getting in good condition. I'll be right in there when the sun comes smiling through. By the way, let anyone who wishes to read this letter do so. Sincerely, your pal Satchel.[9]

Paige was ambivalent in his thinking about integration and whether in fact he wanted to play in the Majors. He always wanted to play in Major League Baseball. He, like his fellow African Americans, accepted the notion that Major League Baseball was the epitome of baseball, and no matter how many fans the East-West classic and other Negro Leagues games outdrew the Majors, they found themselves tacitly or unconsciously accepting the superiority of Major League Baseball. It is not that he or other African Americans doubted the ability of black folk to play superior-quality baseball; they simply could not convince themselves and the black community that the integration of Major League Baseball was less important than support of Negro Leagues Baseball.

Immediately after Robinson signed with Montréal, Paige lost consecutive games pitching against Bob Feller. Those back-to-back losses said that something was distracting him. It is easy to believe that his heart and mind were not on the games and that he was reeling from the announced signing three days earlier of Robinson to be the first player with the opportunity to break the color line in the Majors. Paige denied this and said that Bob Feller simply outpitched him on those particular days. He quickly added that he believed when he looked at the count he had won more games over Feller than he lost. No matter what he said, something was wrong, and one could easily understand how Paige, as the anointed star of Negro Leagues Baseball, was distracted by the signing. He had been passed up for a younger man who certainly did not have a track record that in any way equaled his.

Paige, however, was always supportive of Robinson, although at the same time he blamed Jim Crow for keeping him and his talent from shining under the ultimate spotlight, center stage in the white arena. "Almost twenty years after I fired my first trouble ball as a full-time professional, Jim Crow'd gotten busted on the nose," he confided to his autobiography. "I hadn't thought it'd

ever happen, but it had. The colored ballplayer'd made his first dent in organized baseball. After all those years of fighting, it'd finally happened. It hadn't
happened to me, but it'd happened. They'd signed my old teammate, Jackie
Robinson. Somehow I always figured it'd be me. But it hadn't. Maybe it'd happened too late and everybody figured I was too old. Maybe that was why it was
Jackie and not me." It was a bittersweet pill that he had to swallow. "But signing Jackie like they did still hurt me deep down," Paige admitted. "I'd been the
guy who'd started all that big talk about letting us in the big time. I'd been the
one who'd opened up the Major Leagues parks to the colored teams. I'd been
the one who the white boys wanted to barnstorm against. I'd been the one who
everybody'd said should be in the Majors. But Jackie'd been the first one signed
by the white boys and he'd probably be the first one in the Majors."[10]

There was an instant decline in attendance at Negro Leagues games after
the signing of Robinson, but Paige as an attraction continued to be a major draw. He would have to travel farther and faster to reach his public. The
Monarchs organization decided to use him even more as a solo act in addition
to the games played with his traveling All-Stars. Wilkinson leased an airplane
to fly Paige and his All-Stars from game to game and him to solo dates, since
often the distances were too great to make in a timely fashion by automobile,
even if you drove as fast as Paige. Thus, there was Paige with his own airplane
with the big lettering on it reading, "Satchel Paige."[11]

The first plane was a Cessna single-engine job. Richard Wilkinson, son of
the team's owner, took command of the flying duties and responsibility of
getting the fireballer for hire to and from engagements. Theoretically, this
opened up more possibilities for Paige to pitch three or four innings here and
there and to make more money. "I guess I was the first pitcher ever to have his
club buy him his own plane for traveling," Paige figured. Actually, the aircraft
was not brand-new and rented, not purchased.[12]

Richard Wilkinson was an excellent pilot, but not all airfields were of the
best quality. Despite what might be the challenges of tricky landings and
sometimes less than reliable instrumentation, there was also the unpredict-
able nature of the weather. The day after the plane was delivered, Paige and
Richard took off for a game in Madison, Wisconsin, where the in-demand
hurler was scheduled to pitch three innings. Paige had pitched three innings
in Kansas City the previous evening and was well rested and looking forward
to the adventure of the flight, or so he thought. It turned out to be a very
smooth ride, and the experience of the first leg of the flight almost convinced
him that flying might be better than driving. He also realized that with the
use of the airplane, he could indeed make more money by making more engagements. But the return flight from Madison would make him rethink his
desire to be airborne.

Paige received a call at the ballpark in Madison from Richard, urging him to get back to the airport as soon as he could after the game because inclement weather was predicted and he thought it best that they leave as soon as possible to avoid the storm. Paige was unconcerned. "I'd never been worried about storms so I didn't see any reason to worry now. I just didn't know airplanes." He told Richard, "That old weather don't scare Satch. It's just a lot of noise." He would later regret what he had said and chastised himself for not heeding Richard's urging.[13]

No sooner were they airborne than they ran smack into a major storm system. The plane bounced up and down like a roller-coaster ride. Richard had warned as they took off that the flight might be a little rough but that they would be okay. The roller-coaster ride continued all the way to Kansas City. "Man, when we hit that storm, Dick had me upside down half the time. You trying to kill me? I yelled at him. Get me out of here!" But there was nothing that Richard could do to control the wrath of Mother Nature. Luckily, they pulled through and Richard was able to make a nice, smooth landing, but that in no way took away from the harrowing flight that left Paige promising that he would never fly again, no matter what.[14]

Yet there were miles to go and promises to keep. Moreover, there was money to be made, and the very next day Paige was scheduled to play in Oklahoma. There was no way for them to get there in time unless he was willing to brave the skies once more. Paige's answer was emphatic: he would not do it under any circumstances. Richard informed him that he was to be paid five hundred dollars for the game and questioned whether he was willing to miss that opportunity. "I ain't flying again," Paige emphatically stated, "but that $500 was mighty tempting." In the end, the five hundred dollars won out. Paige was simply not able to skip that amount of money and thought that perhaps Richard's assurance that nothing else could possibly go wrong might be the case. He told him that they simply ran into some bad weather last time and that the weather looked fine for the flight to Oklahoma. Against his better judgment, Paige took to the air once more.[15]

The flight out was great. There were no storms, and they made it there in time for Paige to play his three innings and collect his five hundred dollars. But on the way back, the two intrepid air travelers were not as fortunate. This time it was not inclement weather that was the bad guy; it was a mechanical problem. Oil began leaking from the engine and accumulating on the windshield. Paige sheepishly asked Richard, "What's that black stuff?" Richard in a very calm voice told him it was just a minor oil leak and nothing to worry about. Paige's knowledge as an avid car driver told him otherwise. He knew full well that when his automobile leaked oil that there was a problem and that the engine was usually involved. On the road that was bad enough, but in the air, he figured correctly, this could have more serious consequences. He recalled that he was never more frightened in his life during those last few hours to Kansas City, worried all the way whether they were going to make it.[16]

Upon landing, he kissed the ground and told Richard in no uncertain terms that he would never get him into that little thing again. Richard did not try to persuade him otherwise. He knew there was no use. After only two flights in two days, the Cessna idea was abandoned and the plane returned to its place of rental. Paige's flying days, however, were not over. The Monarchs ownership leased a larger plane in which to carry the star performer and his "Satchel Paige All-Stars." The fact that it was a much bigger plane with two engines and that the entire team would be flying gave Paige a new sense of daring, and he capitulated and flew. On one of those flights, Paige noticed as they were coming in for a landing that fire trucks and ambulances were parked along the runway with their emergency lights flashing. He asked what was going on and was told that it was simply a welcoming party for Satchel Paige and his All-Stars. He was not informed that the flight was experiencing problems with the landing gear and that the pilot was not certain until the last minute whether the wheels were going to come down. They had radioed for emergency personnel to stand ready. The pilot knew better than to tell Paige the truth. Paige did not learn otherwise until years later and confirmed that if he had known, he would never have flown again.[17]

Paige's popularity when coupled with his desire to make money, have the good life, and love of the game made for an incredibly hectic schedule. Nevertheless, the more he gave, the more that was demanded and the greater the expectations. Even the most faithful Satchel Paige supporters started questioning his age and ability to go the distance. This irked him not only when he read it in the press but also when he heard it from fans. Most athletes were long since retired from the game, or should have been, by their thirties. Here he was, in his forties, and still *the pitching man*. But could he go the distance? The detractors wanted to know. In some sense, he wanted to know as well. It had been a long time since he had pitched a full game or even attempted to go nine innings. He had something to prove to himself, and to the doubters, and decided he would as the regular season was drawing to a conclusion.

The Monarchs were scheduled to play the Indianapolis Clowns, and a huge crowd was expected for the scheduled doubleheader that would start off in St. Louis a seven-game series, taking the two teams on to Kansas City, Indianapolis, and Columbus, Ohio. The Monarchs had not played in St. Louis in a number of seasons, and folks wanted to see Paige and the stellar perennial champion Monarchs. It was announced that the master hurler would start the second game of the doubleheader against the Clowns. He informed manager Frank Duncan that he wished to go the distance if he felt good. Duncan agreed. The question was whether Paige could do it.

The game drew a respectable twenty-three thousand fans. There in Sportsman's Park in St. Louis, Paige was going to answer to his critics and to himself the question of whether he could still go nine innings. He took extra time warming up and being by himself, getting his mind strictly into the game and for the long haul he planned to endure. When his team took the field, he followed with his trademark slow stroll to the mound to the roaring ovation that only he could command. No trademark double and triple windups this time. After a few warm-up throws, he was ready to get straight to business. That afternoon fans were treated to the grand master at work, at full throttle. In the second inning, he struck out three Indianapolis hitters in a row, including his good friend Goose Tatum. He was not in a charitable mood. Every hitter was the enemy, and Paige treated him as such. The only damage to his performance that night came in the fourth inning, when Indianapolis finally scored a run. When the contest ended, Paige stood for a minute or more on the mound, soaking in the accolades for the triumphant 6–1 victory. It was an especially good moment for him because he had gone a full, grueling nine innings and had prevailed. He paid the price for that, however, later on, with a sore arm, back pain, leg cramps, and aching feet. But he felt good. He showed the naysayers and himself that the old man still had it and could go the distance. He gave up only six hits and one run and retired seven by way of strikeout.[18]

There was a growing chorus of voices urging that Paige be given his opportunity in the Major Leagues, despite his age. The *Philadelphia Tribune* added its voice to the increasing outcry for Paige to be given his chance. It was, to be sure, not his fault that he was barred from Major League Baseball during his prime because of his color. The *Philadelphia Tribune* pronounced shortly after Paige's nine-inning performance in St. Louis: "Even the National Negro League fellows are beginning to believe Paige was getting too old to go the route when he waited until the last week of the season to pitch nine innings. Most of his job in 31 games had been for three and four inning stints. He showed the boys something a week ago when he fired his fastball the full distance in clinching the pennant in a game at St. Louis." The paper concluded in a headline, "Satchel Paige Wants Chance in Majors," and argued that he should be given that chance.[19]

Paige and the Kansas City Monarchs had a good year in 1946, winning their league and going on to face the Newark Eagles in the Negro Leagues World Series. That series may have been one of the best played in league history. In game 1 at the Polo Grounds in New York, Hilton Smith started on the mound for the Monarchs and was doing just fine until the sixth inning, with a man on first and nobody out. He had walked the dangerous Larry Doby in Kansas City's hope to hold on to its 1–0 lead. Smith was dead tired, and Paige was summoned to relieve him.

Paige took, even for him, an undue amount of time to stroll to the mound. The fans, however, loved it, as he finally arrived there and then took additional time with warm-up tosses to his catcher before signaling that he was ready to play ball. But when he said he was ready, he was ready and commenced to striking out the heralded Monte Irvin, who was the Negro National League's leading hitter. After Larry Doby stole second, Paige struck out Lenny Pearson. Johnny Davis, however, touched him for a single to right, and Doby blasted home to tie the score. When Davis attempted to steal second base, he was thrown out. It had not been an auspicious beginning for Paige in relief at that point. But the grand master rose to the occasion from the next inning onward and did not allow Newark another score. Not only that, but in the seventh inning Paige hit for a single off Rufus Louis, and when Doby made a bad throw, Paige took second. His Monarchs teammate Herb Souell slammed a nice hit, and Paige showed he had some youth left in those legs as he sprinted home for what proved to be the winning run, as the Monarchs took the first game of the series by the score of 2–1. However, the highly talented Eagles in the end won the series four games to three over Paige and the Monarchs. Effa Manley was overjoyed in her team's victory and especially the handing of the recalcitrant Paige his comeuppance. She loved it.[20]

Paige did not have time to sulk about losing the World Series. It was time to hit the road with his All-Stars to face Bob Feller and his All-Stars and a series of twenty games that would take the two clubs across the nation in competition before more than two hundred thousand by the time they were finished. The Feller-versus-Paige matches were the highlight of the Major versus Negro Leaguers with Dizzy Dean's retirement, this time for real. The younger Bob Feller was the anointed best pitcher in Major League Baseball in the postwar years. Having them tee off against one another from the mound was what folks really wanted to see. The Sporting News said it quite plainly: "Can a good Major League club beat a good Negro team?" In the minds of many, if not most, that question had been answered definitively many years earlier and certainly with the Paige-versus-Dean traveling tours and in many previous encounters between Paige and Feller. The rhetoric made for good entertainment, and the challenge never failed to draw crowds.[21]

The tour opened at Forbes Field in Pittsburgh and was played before a crowd of forty-six hundred in uncomfortably cold conditions on September 30, 1946. Paige and his All-Stars took the first game in the series 3–1. In the next game in Youngstown, Ohio, Feller and his Major Leaguers trounced

Paige and his compatriots 11–2 before an audience of three thousand. That same evening the two teams met again at Municipal Stadium in Cleveland in front of a sold-out audience of ninety-seven hundred, with Feller, assisted by Major League ace Bob Lemon with the mound work, taking the contest 5–0. Feller and crew repeated their victorious way next in Chicago's Comiskey Park on October 3 before an audience of twenty thousand.

In each one of the losses Paige typically pitched the first three innings and in most cases never gave up more than one hit and no runs. Feller for the most part equaled him, with his teammates being a bit stronger when it came to hitting off the other Negro Leagues pitchers. Feller and his All-Stars had won the majority of the games thus far over Paige and his All-Stars. When Paige and company won 3–2 over Feller and his mates in Kansas City, the black press took special joy in reporting the outcome. The two stars met again before a jampacked audience of more than twenty-two thousand in Los Angeles in October.

Feller and team won that one as well in a thrilling contest that ended 4–3. Feller struck out seven in his five innings of play. Paige matched him with the same number of strikeouts, but when he left the contest his teammates gave up four runs. The series of twenty games ended with Feller and his All-Stars winning thirteen and Paige and his All-Stars winning seven. When one looked at the pitching performances of Feller and Paige, Paige actually outpitched Feller, giving up the fewest number of hits and runs over the course of the series. What was again demonstrated to everyone, despite Paige and his All-Stars coming up short in the overall count of victories, was that these were competitive games, and it was hard to make the case that anyone out there was better than Satchel Paige.

Bob Feller, however, expressed reservations about whether black ballplayers could make it in the Majors. When Jackie Robinson was signed, Feller raised serious doubts. "If Robinson were a white man, I doubt if they would consider him big-league material," said Feller. "I hope he makes good. But I don't think he will." In the last stretch of the series against the Paige All-Stars, Feller was asked point-blank about his experience playing against Satchel Paige and his team and other "colored teams as well. Do you think they'll make the big league grade?" Feller continued in his reply: "Haven't seen one—not one," he said. "Maybe Paige when he was young. When you name him you're done. Some are good hitters. Some field pretty good. Most of them are fast. But I have seen none who combine the qualities of the big league ballplayer." The questioner asked of Bob Feller, "Not even Jackie Robinson?" Feller replied, "Not even Jackie Robinson."[22]

Guarded praise from Feller aside, Paige wanted to play in Major League Baseball, despite not being in his prime. He wanted the chance, despite what he also knew that Jackie Robinson was going through on the Montréal farm team. That first spring training for Robinson was a nightmare in many respects, as historian Jules Tygiel has written. Robinson was prepared to pay the price. He wanted to not only advance his career but also open the door to Major League Baseball to others and advance the cause of racial progress in America, which he dedicated himself to and in a very real sense gave his life to. Paige too was willing to do his part for racial and professional advancement, if given the opportunity. The question was whether he would ever be given the chance.[23]

Those who knew Paige knew he was engaged in and always felt himself connected to the African American struggle, even within the rarefied circles of Negro Leagues Baseball. The trappings of stardom at one level would make Negro Leagues players appear to be far more than the average black person, but, as he knew, he was always black in the eyes of those who judged him by the color of his skin. Paige was a very prideful man about himself and his race. When on the road, O'Neil recalled how Paige often spoke about "what we were up against" and how they had to be strong and show folks what they could do. "All of us knew this," O'Neil retorted. "All the black men knew that they had to be strong and that you were always being evaluated. We knew where we came from." Paige and he often spoke about "the prejudice we had to deal with every day. But we did it. We got through all of that."[24]

Paige supported a number of causes, protest efforts, and fund drives to benefit black folk. He gave his support to numerous initiatives against discrimination in housing and employment opportunities. He also boldly put his name on petitions circulated in Chicago, New York, and elsewhere protesting against the ban against blacks in the Major Leagues long before the signing of Robinson and after the signing.[25]

The heightened sensitivity in black consciousness during the war years and in the aftermath was something that Paige shared directly and indirectly. His name appeared frequently in the black press as pundits struck out against the color line in Major League Baseball with greater vigor through the war and postwar years. He was in a real sense the poster child for the wrongs of segregation and color restrictions in America's favorite pastime. Lester Rodney, the editor of the *Daily Worker*, the newspaper of the Communist Party of America, constantly wrote pieces condemning Major League Baseball for banning black players. Rodney and the communist newspaper often listed the name of Satchel Paige in their condemnation. It was that constant association of the name Paige in the communist newspaper and in the African American press with the ongoing struggle that made the heralded hurler a person of interest to the Federal Bureau of Investigation.

J. Edgar Hoover ordered the FBI field offices to place Paige under surveillance and continued to monitor his actions for a decade. The bureau wanted to know if Paige was a communist. They saw his name mentioned repeatedly and were well aware of his condemnation of the ban against blacks in Major League Baseball. The FBI field offices reported with snippets especially from the *Daily Worker,* and Paige's name was front and center. In a field report the bureau expressed its concern that the Communist Party and the trade union movement were both condemning segregation in baseball and citing the accomplishments of Satchel Paige to bolster their case and public appeal. The bureau conveyed the following in its report: "Whereas, many outstanding athletes in big-league baseball, past and present, have voiced their opinions that Negroes such as Satchel Paige, Josh Gibson, Ray Brown, and Bankhead could make and bill any big-league All-Star team; Dizzy Dean, Joe DiMaggio, Bob Feller and Joe McCarthy who have toured and played exhibitions with them have constantly praised their character, sportsmanship and ability."[26]

The FBI was very concerned in its report that a Chicago African American newspaper praised the *Daily Worker* for challenging racism in baseball. The FBI's extraction from the *Daily Worker* was conveyed to headquarters and placed in the Satchel Paige file:

> Chicago Negro newspaper compliments *Daily Worker* on battle against Jim Crow. An edition of the *Chicago Bee,* a Negro weekly, congratulated the *Daily Worker* upon its campaign to lift the ban on Negro baseball players in the Major Leagues. The *Daily Worker* has gone all out for Negro baseball leagues in the big leagues. Now I am not a communist, but those Reds have something there. After watching Satchel Paige and the Kansas City Monarchs perform, it struck us that both the Cubs and the White Sox could use to good advantage every one of the stars in their lineup.[27]

In the field reports on Paige there were also references to organized labor and other activist organizations that were evidently seen as threatening to America's interests. The FBI reported that an unidentified woman who called the Communist Party headquarters said that on a labor-union protest petition she collected "the signature of all the baseball players including Satchel Paige and Paige was asked to speak and he said that he would do his best."[28]

The Unified Furniture Workers of America published a broadside titled "Furniture Workers Convention Demands End to Baseball Jim Crow" and went on to mention "Satchel Paige and many others" as possessing the skills but being discriminated against because of their color. Despite this being a very pro-American statement and supportive of America's lofty goals of democracy, the FBI evidently saw the organization as possibly subversive.[29]

The bureau's field agent reported that in a talk in Ohio, the communist spokesperson "pointed out . . . Satchel Paige, one of the greatest pitchers in the past 20 years," and said that his denied freedoms were "a blight on American democracy indicative of American imperialism." The name Satchel Paige was mentioned at the Civil Rights Congress of Michigan and in picketing actions and demonstrations against police brutality, with protesters carrying signs saying "Satchel Paige, Jim Crow Must Go!" It was of great concern to the bureau, as its confidential informant reported, that the *Daily Worker* and other Communist Party publications seemed to be using this issue for effective propaganda with "articles concerning Satchel Paige, Negro baseball pitcher."[30]

Paige was no communist, but he did believe in equality of opportunity and fair play. It was not his choice that Major League Baseball banned him and his kind from participation and had engaged in that practice over the past half century. He welcomed the new opportunity, a chance at the Majors, at least for Jackie Robinson with his signing on with Montréal. But Paige, like others, wondered if Robinson would get a chance beyond that and to actually join and play for the Dodgers.

Paige, the Negro Leagues, and all of America and the world received the answer to the question of whether Robinson would be brought up from the Minors when he was asked to report to the Dodgers for the 1947 season. It had happened. Jackie Robinson had broken the ultimate color line in Major League Baseball. The news spread around the nation and the world, headlining most newspapers with the announcement that Robinson would play for the Dodgers in New York. The black press and the *Daily Worker* and its editor, Lester Rodney, celebrated this moment of inclusion, even though it was just one team and one player who had gained entrance to the hallowed sanctum.

The reaction to the announcement of Robinson being called up to the Dodgers manifested itself at two levels for Paige. When asked by the press what he thought about this, he lavished more praise on Robinson and said how he knew "he would make it." He touted Robinson's abilities and what he had seen in him when he was on the Monarchs and said of him that he was "a fine man, and a great athlete." Paige told the media that he thought Robinson was a superb choice to break the color line, that he was young, talented, educated, and smart and would "do us all proud."[31]

He shared with friends and family his intimate thoughts regarding how he felt passed over and unappreciated. In a very real sense, it was his right. Any sense of fairness would concur that Paige deserved to be in the Majors. He apparently was a generation too late and too old as the doors finally started to open. He told the story over and over to friends and family. It was almost therapeutic for him to do it and to share his disgust for being denied. He had demonstrated that he could still produce and strike people out while going the distance. He very much wanted the chance in the Majors. At the same time, Paige would not have gone to the Majors for the peanuts they were paying

Robinson. There was no compromise on that point. That aside, he wanted what was just, and he was hopeful that he might yet get the chance: "That was my right. I should have been there. I got those boys thinking about having Negroes in the Majors, but when they get one, it wasn't me. That bothered me plenty, but I wasn't going to fold up and quit. I promised myself I'd keep throwing until somebody figured they needed me bad in the Major Leagues. Before that arm of mine gave out, I was going to taste that major league living."[32]

Paige leaned on the one shoulder he had learned to rely on the most, the warm embrace and reassurance of Lahoma. She was his touchstone, his rock of Gibraltar, his dry-weather port in the storm. Right now, he was facing considerable turbulence with his conflicted emotions about Robinson's entrance into the Major Leagues and his own failure to get a serious nod from any of the big league teams. He confided to Lahoma that it hurt really bad and that the pain was unbearable. Paige was not sleeping very well at this time as he mulled over why it was that Robinson was chosen rather than him. It always came back the same answer: Robinson was young and he was old.

Lahoma reassured him nonstop that he was as good as and better than anyone out there and what he needed to do was to keep on doing what he always did: to play great baseball, pitch great games, and sooner or later some team would come calling. It was in her reassurance, her devotion, and her unshakable faith in him that Paige came to the conclusion that both of them had earlier hinted about but that now he was absolutely certain needed to happen. He asked Lahoma Jean Brown to marry him, and she accepted.

Leroy Robert Paige and Lahoma Jean Brown were married on October 12, 1947, in a quick jaunt to a magistrate in Hays, Kansas. It was what the both of them wanted, a quiet ceremony out of the public eye, without fanfare and media coverage. That was the moment that Satchel Paige started to reinvent himself as a "homebody." It did not mean that he was giving up on baseball or never taking notice of a pretty woman again. But it did mean that his life would have at its center a home with a devoted wife and that he could take notice of the pretty girls out there but take no action. There would be a lot of controversy among many writers on the private life of Paige and his pursuit of the opposite sex. Part of that can be attributed to the rumor mill among Negro Leaguers and other men. There has long been a tendency to boast and lie outright among fellows regarding their female conquests. There was no proof or other evidence of the master hurler pitching more than the occasional flirtatious remark. The gallivanting Satchel Paige, the fastballer for hire, the quintessential traveling man, was slowing down in every sense of the term.[33]

He loved his new life with Lahoma. She had been married previously to Christopher Brown and had a daughter, Shirley, from that marriage who was three years of age. In a sense, Paige became an instant father, although Shirley's biological father lived in Kansas City and his daughter would often spend time with him. Paige became a father in his own right in early 1948 with the birth of his first child, Pamela. This was that very special moment in his life when he actually realized that there was more to life than baseball. Paige reveled in being a new dad, showing off his baby girl to teammates and friends at the ballpark and with the parade of guests who came through his home.

At the same time, the realities of family life had not changed much since his first marriage with Janet in that funds were needed to maintain a household. What was new on the horizon was that his income-making ability was starting to taper off right at the time that he was settling into family life. The impact of Jackie Robinson playing with the Dodgers was felt by all the Negro Leagues ballplayers, and now even Paige. Attendance at games continued downward. Competing teams that used to attract crowds of twenty thousand were lucky now if they could get five thousand to attend their games. Even the great Satchel Paige was not enough to bring fans out to the ballpark in the numbers he once commanded. Why see Paige and Negro Leagues Baseball when you could see the Majors with Robinson playing? Branch Rickey's decision to break the color line was a mammoth success at the box office of the Dodgers. Attendance at Dodgers games rose by 40 percent.

Paige as family man would need to hustle even more games, drive farther from town to town at those breakneck speeds, or hop a plane to those places and fans removed from the center of baseball and unable to get to the Dodgers' games to see Robinson. There were still tickets to be sold and games to be played before grateful audiences, but the numbers of those were rapidly declining thanks to the "integration" of baseball.[34]

Bob Feller hatched an interesting plan with Paige for their scheduled touring game pitting the Kansas City Royals, the team composed of Kansas City Monarchs players and a few others, headlined by Satchel Paige, against Bob Feller and his Major Leagues All-Stars scheduled for November 2, 1947, in Los Angeles. Feller came up with the idea that they should bill this as a grudge match between the two master hurlers. Paige readily agreed and thought that Feller had devised a wonderful marketing tool, especially if it worked and put more people into the seats; it could mean a bigger payday for all concerned.

What happened next was unexpected. Feller was able to garner considerable press coverage with his promoting of the game as a grudge match between him and Paige to settle once and for all who was the best pitcher. Paige went along with it, saying the same to the press when he was interviewed. Paige remembered how "Feller told the papers I might have an edge on him in those few innings we'd pitched against each other, but I was too old to stand up against him if I tried to go nine innings." Tickets sold like hotcakes to the November 2 challenge match between the two aces. But something strange happened. Paige began to take to heart the whole notion of the challenge about his age and the question again of whether he could go nine innings. As the showdown drew closer, he became more serious about making a good showing. It was getting to Paige that "some of those reporters were saying I was so old I probably couldn't even go nine, much less win" against Feller.[35]

Fans had a short memory about Paige earlier going a full nine. It proved the old adage that you were only as good as your last game. But the reality was that most of the media chose not to remember that last game. By the time November rolled around, Paige was as serious as one could be about putting out his best effort. "That game stopped being just another old game for me then. I decided it was time for those writers out there to see a man who still could throw, throw hard enough to tear the glove off the catcher's hand. All I had to do was go nine, I kept thinking. Sure, I was pushing into my forties, but they thought I was fifty and even if they believed that, it never seemed to worry them before."[36]

He and Lahoma made the West Coast engagement into a honeymoon of sorts. However, there was a matter of a little pitching work to do against the anointed best pitcher of the times in the Majors, Bob Feller. Paige settled in to his work routine, with Lahoma telling him that his game against Feller could be another opportunity to show the folks out there what they were missing by not having him in the Majors. All eyes were on "Feller versus Paige" in the grudge match in Los Angeles.[37]

When game day came Paige was at 100 percent in energy level, concentration, and desire to win. He had a good, solid pregame rubdown for more than an hour to make sure, as he explained it, that those juices were flowing. He put on his uniform and put on his extra pair of socks, which he routinely did to try to make up for how skinny his legs were. He disliked what they called him at Mount Meigs—the Crane—and ever since then had worn two pairs of socks to give bulk to his slim legs.

Paige took his time coming out to the field and his place on the mound. He purposefully skipped doing his warm-ups and had decided instead that taking them on the mound would be the best course of action to save every bit of his arm, which he would need to go nine. What had started out as a publicity stunt to get the fans to the ballpark was now a full-fledged matter of honor, at least for Paige. He was there to go the distance and to defeat Feller.

After enough tosses to his catcher, he signaled to the umpire. "I was ready," Paige declared. "I fired my hard one and kept firing it." He varied his pitches with a beautiful change of pace and a deceptively good curveball. When he needed it, he overpowered the batter with his blistering fastball. But he knew he was up against top talent from the Major Leagues and could not do it all with fastballs. The mix and match he did that day showed anyone watching the game that Paige was an extraordinary master pitcher, with a full arsenal at his disposal. "Pitching in a manner to belie his length of service in baseball," the *Philadelphia Tribune* reported, "Satchel Paige, right-handed pitching ace of the Kansas City Monarchs, struck out 15 batters as his touring Kansas City Royals won an 8–0 verdict over Bob Feller's All-Stars."[38]

He had done it. He had gone the distance and shut them out. Paige was completely spent at the end of the game. The victory felt good, but "boy was I tired. And my stomach hurt, hurt like it always did. And my feet were sore. But I'd showed them." In the locker room, Paige had a beer and sat there soaking in the accolades of his teammates and continued sitting there after they left the building. It felt good to him to savor the victory as long as he could. "I'd shown them out there, but as tired as I was I couldn't help wondering how many more years I could keep doing it. I'd gotten to wondering that more and more. They'd been asking me for four or five years when I was going to quit, but I just kept on winning, winning more games each year than most pitchers win in two or three. But now I was beginning to feel the soreness."[39]

He started finally to rise to his feet and go to take a shower when the towel boy came over and said to him, "Mr. Paige, they got Jackie Robinson in the Major Leagues and they brought up some of those other guys, but they are nothing like you. Why, you're kind of like Babe Ruth. How come they took those guys and not you?" Paige gave the youngster his standard answer, that he would cost the Majors too much money and that they did not want to pay him what he was worth. But deep in his heart and soul he did not possess a definitive answer. The truth of the matter was that he wanted to play so badly in the Majors now that he could taste it: "That old major-league bug was biting me harder than ever and I was looking around for an offer." The towel boy, not hearing of course what Paige was saying to himself, concluded with a positive thought that he offered to the great hurler: "Maybe somebody'll offer you enough one of these days, Mr. Paige."[40]

Paige was the featured story throughout the black press, and those who did not read the columns nevertheless talked about the Feller-Paige grudge match in Los Angeles and what Paige had done. They talked about it in the streets of Los Angeles, Chicago, Philadelphia, Pittsburgh, Birmingham, New York, Canada, Mexico, Puerto Rico, the Dominican Republic, and Cuba. There was a general consensus that "Satchel still had plenty of stuff left in that old arm of his, and the white boys took an 8–0 drubbing."[41]

Despite the physical pain after the game, Paige was walking on cloud nine. He had without a doubt proved the critics wrong. Nothing could dampen his triumph that day, not even a possible lawsuit that Melton Jones, a car dealer in Kansas City, was promising to file against Paige for damaging the Cadillac that the star hurler rented for the trip to the West Coast and returned with considerable engine damage. Paige would later settle the lawsuit out of court. It was not the first car whose engine met demise through his heavy-footed practices, nor would it be the last. Neither was he perturbed by the discussion in the media as to whether it was he or his good friend professional footballer Claude "Buddy" Young who had the best performance in sports that week. His thoughts were on his own performance and nothing else, having gone the full nine innings against some of the very best of the Major Leaguers and nearly equaled the Major Leagues' strikeout record for a single game, which, at that time, was sixteen and held by none other than Bob Feller, whom Paige completely outpitched that day.[42]

Interviewed by the media after the game, Paige was asked the familiar question of what was his true age. He was not interested in perpetuating the old gimmick anymore. He answered truthfully that he was forty-one. He knew that was old enough if not too old for a chance in the Majors, but it was his true age, and he hoped it would not count against his getting the chance. If African American sportswriter Al Moses had his way, it would not. "On all sides folks inquire of me how old is Satchel Paige? Unfailingly I come back with his sworn statement which adds up to 41 years. But chippie or old man, the fire on his blazing 'hard one' remains to mystify and embarrass many of baseball's budding young stars as well as seasoned white veterans of Major League stature. In short, Leroy (Satch) Paige earns the right to be listed as one of America's all-time great moundsmen."[43]

Paige could only hope for the best. He confided later to Lahoma that he wondered if anybody had taken serious notice of what he had just accomplished in Los Angeles or if anyone really cared. She did. She had made the trip with him to Los Angeles only in part as a honeymoon. She knew how important the game had become for him, and she wanted to be there to cheer him on with the conviction that he could still go nine and win. Lahoma reassured her husband too that someone in the Majors surely took notice and would have to give him his chance.[44]

Meanwhile, he kept doing what he did best: to barnstorm and provide his pitching skills wherever the opportunity presented itself. In the spring of 1948 he was busy putting together his own independent touring team and announced that beginning shortly, he and his players would be barnstorming everywhere and that he was planning to play no fewer than 117 games during the coming season. That plan, however, was about to be altered for a most compelling reason. It might not have rivaled his marriage to Lahoma or the coming of his first child, but it was the epic opportunity of his life.

12

Center Stage in the White Arena

July 5, 1948, became one of the happiest days in Satchel Paige's life, for this was the day, late in the afternoon, that he received a letter from Abe Saperstein asking him, How soon can you be in Cleveland for a tryout with the Indians? Paige and Lahoma danced all over the house and into the night, doing the jitterbug and hully gully; laughing, joking, her repeatedly congratulating him; him toasting with his favorite bourbon while she did hers with some apple cider. They talked about what was happening, the opportunity finally being afforded him, and what it all meant. They were as proud as two human beings could be. Satchel Paige felt complete euphoria. When that feeling subsided, what crept into his mind were the lost years and that he was going to have to go up there and audition at age forty-two. But he quickly pushed those thoughts to the back of his mind. He was a positive thinker and believed absolutely that he was still one of the best pitchers ever and would go to Cleveland and show them.

Those who knew him best outside the immediate family, and with whom he shared the news, recalled how Paige was able to maintain a sense of "low-key excitement" to them. "I got the call" was how he put it. Family, friends, and countless baseball fans were excited for him and did not hold back. In so many cases, that euphoria quickly settled into a kind of consensus of "it's about time."[1]

Paige, traveling with Abe Saperstein, arrived in Cleveland on Wednesday, July 7, 1948, and went straight to the ballpark for his debut tryout. When

Paige arrived at the facility, Cleveland owner Bill Veeck was there along with manager Lou Boudreau and the rest of the Cleveland team. Paige and Veeck chatted for a while, and then one of the trainers showed him to the locker room and gave him a Cleveland uniform to change into.

Paige was feeling pretty good, having donned a uniform of a Major League Baseball team for the first time. He brought his own glove and shoes. The trainer had both at the ready, but Paige, like any seasoned veteran, went with his own. There would always be time later to break in a new pair of shoes once he had made the team and even a new glove, although he did not have that in mind at all. He was dressed and ready and strolled leisurely onto the field and reported to the team owner. Standing there side by side, Veeck told him to show the folks what he could do and then went on with a quick pep talk to which Paige could see that the owner was nervous for him. Paige told him, "Don't worry, Mr. Bill—as he looked out at the pitcher's mound—I've been there before." Veeck then called over Boudreau and stepped aside.[2]

Boudreau invited Paige to do some laps to get warmed up. Paige ran about fifty yards at a moderate speed once or twice and then came back over to Boudreau to let them know that he felt that he had done enough running. In Paige's mind a lot of exercise was a waste of time and would have done nothing but take strength away from his legs. He was never one in those later years for doing wind sprints and unnecessary training. To put it mildly, he contended that he kept his legs in good-enough shape through dancing and actually playing baseball games at such a clip and elongated schedule that more exercise was not necessary. No doubt Paige would have run additional sprints if it had been required of him, but Boudreau had mercy and could see that he was a seasoned veteran and was likely the best judge of what warmed him up.

Accepting Paige's pronouncement that he was ready, Boudreau himself donned the catcher's mitt, chest protector, and face mask to catch Paige. The master hurler started out easy, making sure to absolutely get the arm warmed up properly. As Paige liked to say, he needed to get "those juices flowing." After about fifteen minutes of light to moderate tosses, he was ready. Page threw ten or twelve pitches; all of them would have been good for strikes. For a more realistic test, Boudreau took off his catcher's paraphernalia to take on the role of hitter, with another Cleveland player called in to the plate to do the catching. Bill Veeck summed up what happened next:

> As ridiculous as it was for Satchel Paige to be on trial, that was precisely the situation as he went out to the mound to throw to Boudreau who, at that moment, was leading both leagues with a batting average of almost .400. Against Paige, he batted .000. Satch threw twenty pitches. Nineteen of them were strikes. Lou swung nineteen times and he had nothing that looked like a base hit. After

a final pop fly, Lou dropped his bat, came over to us and said, "Don't let him get away, Bill. We can use him."[3]

It was an impressive performance. Paige was asked to go ahead and change in the locker room while Veeck, Boudreau, and Saperstein talked things over. It was not a long conversation. Veeck invited Paige to come over to his office, telling him that they wanted him on the Cleveland Indians, and offered him a contract there on the spot. There was no further discussion; the grateful hurler signed the document "real quick." After all, "Paige almost missed the boat," the African American press reported, "but he sure grabbed the gang plank before it was hoisted up." It was an amount too that he was quite happy with. It was not thirty or forty thousand dollars, but it was twenty-five thousand dollars of steady money, and, considering that he was joining the team midseason, it was quite acceptable to Paige. It was a respectable paycheck, and that still left him the off-season of winter ball to make additional funds barnstorming. At any rate, he was not complaining. He felt great. He was too glad to be a part of the Major Leagues, and as he would later tell family members, twenty-five thousand for half a season of work was nothing to sneeze at. It was more than the average ballplayer made, although it was a long way away from the eighty thousand dollars that Bob Feller reportedly earned. Paige was not concerned about that. He was in the Majors now, a ballplayer who would participate at the pinnacle of his profession. Not only that, but Cleveland was in a tight pennant race, and he was going to be given the opportunity to contribute immediately. He could not wait.[4]

Some of the harshest criticism of the signing of Satchel Paige came from *Sporting News*. The paper angrily lashed out at Veeck, accusing him of having "gone too far in his quest of publicity, and that he has done his League's position absolutely no good in so far as public reaction is concerned." The sporting Bible went on to say that Paige was far too old to be brought into the Majors and was being treated special because of his race. "To sign a hurler at Paige's age is to demean the standards of baseball in the big circuits," the *Sporting News* charged. "Further complicating the situation is the suspicion that if Satchel were white, he would not have drawn a second thought from Veeck."[5]

The pressure was on Paige to deliver, and his first opportunity came in an exhibition game against the Brooklyn Dodgers at Cleveland Municipal Stadium on July 15, 1948. It was not an accident that 64,877 fans showed up for an exhibition game on a Wednesday night. Veeck and any of the other smart promoters knew that the large turnout was because of the presence of Satchel Paige. And it was Paige who "gave the Cleveland fans their biggest thrill" that night. The crowd witnessed "a brilliant two-inning relief chore by Paige, ageless Negro hurler recently signed by the Tribe." Paige came in to take the mound in the seventh inning and threw a total of twelve pitches and struck out the side. He retired Gil Hodges with four pitches, took out Irvin Palica with three, and blasted Tommy Brown out with a combination of fancy curves and sonic fastballs. He then struck out three other would-be hitters in the eighth to conclude his magnificent strikeout performance for the night. The crowd went wild. Cleveland took the contest 4–3.[6]

It was no easy ride for Paige in the Majors. There were countless confrontations with Jim Crow on and off the field. He, for the most part, dismissed the racial epithets and pretended he did not hear them, but he did. His baptism was similar to what Jackie Robinson experienced—the yells of "nigger" and "watermelon." There were the taxis that refused to transport blacks, such as in Texarkana, Texas, where Paige, Larry Doby, and Orestes "Minnie" Minoso were late getting to the ballpark because no taxi would take them. There were also the continued problems with hotel accommodations that inevitably came up. It made things easier for Paige and Doby that they were roommates together on the road and that the team's owner was a man sensitive to the housing problem and did as much advance work as possible in making arrangements with hotels that would accommodate all of the team's players.[7]

Paige and Doby were truly a study in contrasts. They were the perfect Mutt and Jeff. Paige had the big-name recognition, was superconfident, and was outgoing. Doby was rather reserved and moody. As Paige found, he would talk to him about baseball all day and night and then the next day not even speak to him. It also made Doby uneasy when he learned that Paige not only collected guns but often carried one on the road. Doby also had a problem with Paige's cooking in their hotel room. He was probably also embarrassed by the smell of frying catfish and knowing that his white teammates were taking notice. Doby was trying to separate himself from his South Carolina roots and those dishes that were commonplace for black folk, like catfish, chitlins, hog maws, and watermelons, all of which were on Doby's list to avoid at all costs or risk authenticating the prevailing stereotype about blacks.[8]

Paige was just the opposite. He carried with him his little portable Coleman with which he could bake or fry. He, indeed, loved to cook fish, especially if he had an opportunity to go out and catch it himself. If not, he would buy from the market. Paige took great pride in his recipe for catfish, which featured the liberal sprinkling of Duff Gordon Number 28 and expensive sherry. He always offered Doby some of whatever he was cooking, which the roommate always refused with a passion.[9]

Paige's storytelling was a source of embarrassment for Doby. Paige would often have the entire locker room laughing with stories from his barnstorming adventures. Doby felt that Paige might be shining his white teammates on too much. He also thought that they were laughing at Paige rather than laughing

with him. According to Doby, Jackie Robinson also thought that Paige's stories were distasteful. Both evidently thought that Paige did too much clowning and that some experiences were best left unshared.

On one occasion, finding Paige's antics too much, Doby advised him that
he would not want to be clowning around like he did in the Negro Leagues,
or people would take it the wrong way. Doby told Paige that he was in the
big leagues and that he should reframe from Negro Leagues antics. "None of
that show off stuff you got away with on the exhibition circuit. You're in the
Majors now." Paige believed baseball was baseball no matter what league you
played it in. He answered Doby, "You're talking to a fellow who knows something about this baseball business." For Paige, that meant that you needed to
always blend a bit of entertainment into the game. When Paige, in the presence of Doby, was telling a reporter about the first baseball lights he ever
experienced, he impressed upon him that they were pretty good lights and
there were no serious problems with them, that they lit things very well. Doby
chimed in, disagreeing. He said, "They may have been fine with you because
you're a pitcher. I'm glad I never had to bat against you under those lights."
Paige retorted instantly, "Wouldn't made no difference, son. Wouldn't made
no difference. Day or night, good lights or bad lights. I strike you out every
time." These differences between the two men easily explained why they never
became good friends.[10]

Doby was perceptive in his observation that Paige did not bow to white
folks or accept second-class status. "Satchel never dealt in black and white,"
according to Doby. "He was a star. He never took a backseat to Dizzy Dean
or Bobby Feller. Satchel would say, 'get out of my face.'" Doby was also cogni-
zant of Paige's use of humor to disarm whites. From all outward appearances,
and from what Paige confided to his autobiography and to friends and family,
he got along quite well with his white Cleveland teammates. He sometimes
played his ukulele to relax before game time. He put together a barbershop
quartet featuring him and several of his white teammates who harmonized
before the rest of the team with some classics like "Old Man River." Paige and
his teammates had a good time with it. It was difficult to imagine a player
who did not get along with Satchel Paige, white or black, but that was always
the possibility given the times. Paige made no mention of any racial clashes
between him and his teammates. Moreover, Bill Veeck set the tone for the
Cleveland organization, and the maverick owner was progressive far beyond
the mainstream of organized baseball.[11]

Paige would likely have downplayed any minor racial incident with teammates or personally defused the situation if it occurred. But he was neither an
Uncle Tom nor a buffoon. To the contrary, he simply did not wear his racial
pride and sensitivity on his sleeve. He also preferred not to have everyone

know exactly what he truly thought. Be that as it may, there was clearly no love affair between him and manager Lou Boudreau. They all got along well enough as professionals. On a personal level, Paige liked Bill Veeck, and the respect was mutual. They were both professionals who were in sync in their thinking and treatment of baseball as a business and entertainment. Theirs was a winning combination as far as both men were concerned.

Jackie Robinson, better than anyone, understood the pressure that Paige and other blacks were under who dared to cross the color line. There was no one happier to see Paige in the Majors than Robinson, who expressed being overjoyed to see his old teammate "finally get a chance to make the grade in the big leagues. While we worked together at Kansas City I became aware of the greatness of the man." Robinson hailed Paige as one of the best pitchers he had ever seen and with a true competitor's heart that was second to none. "At Kansas City," Robinson said, "it was generally known that when we had to have a ballgame Satchel would be the man that got the call, and as a rule there was very little doubt about the outcome." Neither did Robinson have any doubt that Paige would help Cleveland in its drive for the pennant. He also agreed with Cleveland's use of Paige, largely in a relief role. He had seen Paige at work in three of four innings to save ball games, and he could testify that the master hurler was extraordinarily hard to hit. He also went on to make note of how pleased he was to see that the Dodgers organization had brought in Roy Campanella and that he was already adding substantially to the team.[12]

Paige proved immediately that he was worth every penny Cleveland was paying him, and more. Bob Lemon had done a fine job against St. Louis but was starting to tire. Manager Boudreau signaled for Paige. The master hurler strolled from bullpen to the glare of the announcement: "Satchel, Leroy, Paige, number 29, now pitching for Cleveland." A substantial portion of the crowd of 34,748 rose to its feet with applause and cheers. It was widely reported that the increased attendance was a result of those who came out in the hope of seeing Paige in action. They were now going to get that chance. He warmed up on the mound and then did what the team needed: stopped St. Louis and brought home the victory.[13]

A historic milestone took place on July 21, 1948, when Cleveland took on the Brooklyn Dodgers and the game brought together the four black players in the Major Leagues: Larry Doby and Satchel Paige for Cleveland and Jackie Robinson and Roy Campanella for the Dodgers. The game drew an audience of 65,000, half of whom were African American.

By the end of July most baseball enthusiasts were starting to come to terms with Bill Veeck's hiring of Satchel Paige. Paige's performance vindicated Veeck's decision. Almost every time Paige took the field, he delivered. The elderly star hurler of Negro Leagues ball was more than a gate attraction. He was helping Cleveland in its march to the pennant.

Cleveland maintained its faith in Paige, and good news came quickly. There were those who predicted that it would eventually happen, and others who were not so sure. But it had. Paige was going to do more than relief work. Bill Veeck announced that Paige would be starting the game in Municipal Stadium as Cleveland took on the Washington Nationals in a night game. The national press jumped on the story, announcing that "the lanky hurler, who has caused national wide controversy because of his belated entry into Major League Baseball, has already established himself as an able relief hurler since donning the Cleveland Indians uniform and will now attempt to make the grade as a starting hurler. If successful, manager Lou Boudreau announced that he will be called upon to pitch once a week."[14]

Paige was going to make sure that his first shot as a starter in Major League Baseball was going to be successful. He went home to Lahoma, and together they talked about the upcoming game and what it meant and tried to spend some quiet time with one another, which was almost impossible given the family and friends who all wanted to wish him well in his debut as a starter in the Majors. When Paige returned to Cleveland, it was not that he was a changed man, but he was completely focused, more so than usual for him. He was still his relaxed self in outward appearance as he joked with teammates. He brought his ukulele into the locker room and played and sang tunes to relieve the tension. These were the little things that had made his transition smooth into the otherwise white-only club, with just him and Larry Doby adding the mixture of color. All of his teammates, including Doby, gave him plenty of room the day of the game and engaged him in conversation only if he said something to one of them. Ballplayers know that you give pitchers all the space they want when they will be taking the mound.

It was Tuesday night, August 3, 1948, and Paige was ready to start. There had been all kinds of predictions in the media that the stadium would probably see a very large audience. Those predictions proved to be way off the mark. The stadium would see one of the largest audiences in its history. Fans began pouring in at nine in the morning for the evening game. Before the game even began, concessionaires had sold out, and some were running around to local stores to try to replenish their supplies to take advantage of the huge market at their disposal. Most of them knew better and stayed put. The odds were not good that you would be able to regain admission into the ballpark. The traffic was backed up for miles. Streets were jammed for hours with automobiles. Those who walked considerable distances to avoid the traffic found that there were equal jams of human capacity at the turnstiles. The crush of the crowd at every entrance point was presenting a safety factor, and the fire marshal was demanding that the entrances be closed and no more people allowed into the stadium. The conservative estimate was that between ten and fifteen thousand fans had to be turned away.

Paige could hear his teammates talking as word spread in the locker room of the incredible number of spectators who were pouring into the stadium for the game. No one told Paige directly. Everyone was avoiding him at all costs. As the teams took the field for warm-ups, the stadium rocked with applause and cheers. All eyes were on Paige and everything he did in warm-ups, watching every one of his limbering-up exercises, every ball he threw, and any exchange he had with his catcher.

Finally, the moment came. The visiting Washington Nationals were up first, and Cleveland took the field. Paige was in his element and did what he had done in countless Negro Leagues games. He took the field last, strolling leisurely to the mound as the stadium erupted with cheers, clapping, and stomping. The noise was deafening. Those who were present said that you could not hear yourself think. Everyone there had come with the excitement of seeing Paige in his first start.

He stood there on the mound, ready to deliver some limbering-up throws to his catcher but unable to do so because the game was being delayed to allow the huge gathering of photographers at home plate to finish taking their photographs. The umpires had decided on this extraordinary action, given the historic circumstances. After a while, the umpires began asking the press to please clear the field to allow the game to begin. They complied.

The master hurler then took three relaxed throws to his catcher and nodded to the umpire that he was ready. He had the juices flowing, as he liked to say. It was game time. Announcer Jack Graney trumpeted the historic words, as if there was someone who was not aware that the person now pitching for Cleveland was Satchel Paige. The fans, however, acted like it was a surprise, and Municipal Stadium exploded in one collective roar, punctuating the moment. They finally settled down when the home umpire said those magic words to play ball.

Paige, the iceman, was off target on his first two pitches. Perhaps it was because of the delay to allow the photographers those extra minutes to get their pictures. More likely, it was the incredible pressure of the moment that even the master hurler could not immediately shake off. He was center stage in the white arena with all eyes on him in a pressure situation that had to make him think back to his struggles over the years and all the other sacrifices, trials, tribulations, and the many miles barnstorming through every city, small town, and hamlet throughout the United States and abroad to get him to this moment. Beyond that, he was the symbol for an entire race of people, and he knew they were counting on him. If he failed, all of black America failed. He was a sports and racial icon. He was more than the sum of the parts. Like his friend Joe Louis, he could either be a credit to his race or let them down at the moment of truth. Jesse Owens had likewise proven to the world what the American black could achieve in the sports arena. It was now Paige's turn to deliver before one of the largest crowds in sports history. The pressure had to be incredible.

He calmed down a tad and started firing his fastball and got his first strike-out. But then he allowed two walks and a triple that brought in two runs. It was not an auspicious beginning. He walked the mound, took his time, shook his arms and limbered up more, rotated his head and neck, and shook his backside, which brought some in the crowd to laughter. He was finding his rhythm; he was finding himself. He pulled his thoughts together and took a deep breath and relaxed, telling himself that he had done this many times before and it was time to show them who was the master of this game. Paige settled in and reached into that reservoir where his greatness resided. His very next pitch to Mickey Vernon forced him to pop up to Joe Gordon for an easy out and did the same to Tom McBride, with an easy one to Lou Boudreau. He got out of the first inning, having given up two runs. He knew he had to do much better work in the following innings.

To start the second inning, Paige walked Mark Crispin, which was not the best start of things. He then walked the mound one more time and placed his hands on his hips. An old friend of his in the stands, Double Duty Radcliffe, knew what it meant. He knew that Paige was ready to pitch now. If he need-ed any more touchstones, he knew too that Lahoma was with him in spirit back in Kansas City, taking care of their new daughter and glued to the radio broadcast of the game. If he was ever going to pitch his best, the time was now. With all of these things going through his mind in successive order or all at once, those who knew him and heard what he said later about his experience knew that baseball was a mind game and that the first mind that had to be under control was his own.

Paige started talking trash to the next hitter, letting him know that he was going to have to strike him out and start striking out all these other boys to let folks know that they were up against Satchel Paige. Perhaps it was that trash-talking, his bravado, that conveyed to opposing batters that he was de-termined to rule the plate. Steve Early was up next, and he faced a succession of fastballs, followed by Earl Wynn and Eddie Yost. They all went down in succession as Paige took command.

His Cleveland teammates Doby, Ken Keitner, and Boudreau did their parts at bat, as did Allie Clark and Jim Hogan, with a home run blast in the sixth in-ning. Cleveland scored its fifth run in the seventh inning. Paige had done fine mound work after his shaky first inning. Boudreau decided that he needed a pinch hitter, and that meant that Paige would have to be replaced on the mound for the start of the seventh inning. He left the mound to thunderous applause. His team was ahead 5–3, and he had pitched excellent baseball. His replacement kept things in check for the final two innings, and Satchel Paige had his first win as a starter. He mastered the Nationals without the use of his much-celebrated "hesitation pitch," which the American League had in the previous month permanently banned as a balk. It was only one pitch of his arsenal of many, as he demonstrated to the Nationals that August evening.[15]

As he strolled from the field, he was serenaded with a loud, continuous one-word chorus of "Satchel." He did his usual as he had done in other big games, as he had done his starring role in the East-West All-Star Game in 1934, and as he had done when he loaded the bases in order to face Josh Gibson. Paige looked straight ahead and strolled off the field to the thunderous accolades without making any acknowledgment. His body language conveyed to the appreciative multitude that it was just routine work for him.

The first African American to start as pitcher in a Major League Baseball game had not only won that game but likely won the respect of those who had witnessed it. Satchel Paige walked off the field that evening and into the pages of sports history, into American legend, and into the iconic embrace of an especially grateful African American people.[16]

The next showing for Paige was at Chicago's Comiskey Park against the White Sox. His presence pushed ticket sales through the roof. It was clear forty-eight hours before the game that there would be no more seats available. At least 15,000 fans were turned away by the time the game started. Comiskey Park had people standing in the aisles, with a crowd of 51,013, which set a new record for a night game in Chicago. Everyone who was anyone in black America was at the game, including Paige's good friend Joe Louis, who was still celebrating his recent victory over Jersey Joe Walcott to retain his heavyweight title. Louis wished Paige all the best in the game, shaking his hand during warm-ups and telling him to "knock 'em dead." Paige promised to do exactly that, and he did. He went to work with masterful pitching, allowing the White Sox only a few scattered hits in an otherwise flawless performance, going the distance of a full nine innings for a 5–0 shutout and another Cleveland win. Louis congratulated him on the victory.[17]

It was a bitter irony that the Negro Leagues' East-West All-Star Game was to be played in Chicago three days later. The turnout for the classic was 42,000, with the press lamenting, "The 16th Annual Classic Drew Less than Satchel Paige Did Here August 13." Paige, the once major attraction of the East-West classic, was now the magnet drawing fans to Major League games in record numbers.[18]

When word went out that Paige would be starting once again in Cleveland against the White Sox, tickets went like hotcakes. The entire Cleveland community and beyond was energized to go out to the game. Back in Cleveland, the organizers were determined to be better prepared than last time at Municipal Stadium. They beefed up security and added additional personnel at the ticket windows and turnstiles, and concessionaires brought in extra supplies of everything. They were right in their expectations. The game drew a new all-time attendance record for a night game of 78,382, with thousands more having to be turned away. Sportswriter Doc Young summed it up well when he reported, "The 44 year old star of the Negro American League and hero of two East versus West games may be destined to fill the shoes of the once great Babe Ruth who died Monday of last week. Surely no single player, not even Lou Gehrig, Ruth's teammate who passed before the Bambino, has been able to pack 'em in as has Paige." Young was correct about Paige's drawing power and in his comparing it to the public appeal of Babe Ruth and Lou Gehrig. He was mistaken in listing Paige as forty-four years of age. He was old enough at forty-two and pulling off miracles that few even half his age could claim. Paige was now the biggest draw in Major League Baseball.[19]

The public's insatiable appetite for Satchel Paige expanded in 1948. They could not get enough of him. Paige's experience in Major League Baseball was quite interesting. The public wanted to know what kind of person he really was. Beyond the games, about his age, they wanted to know more about him as a person. It was like America, or at least some in white America, was discovering Satchel Paige for the first time. Black folk did not need a crash course. They had known him for decades. But he was center stage in the white arena now, with the nation's eyes on him. The *Sporting News* decided to devote itself to a series on Satchel Paige that appeared in two parts in September 1948, titled "Life in the Majors with Paige." Ed McAuley, who reported for the *Cleveland News,* traveled with the Cleveland Indians and was selected to pen the two-part series. Sport enthusiast Hal Lebovitz that same year published *Pitching Man: Satchel Paige's Own Story.*[20]

In the interviews conducted of Paige for the series, he told some tall tales. He was playing along with the media and dishing out stuff that he thought they would want to hear. It was fact mixed with fiction, and it was up to the reader to discern which was which. Paige, for the most part, took the light approach in both publications. He joked about his age and his stomach ailments. He was known for being gaseous and having to take bicarbonate soda even while pitching and letting out huge burps to punctuate the moment that also happened to bring smiles and laughter to the fans. He told McAuley that he started having problems with his stomach during the winter in Venezuela.

"Nobody there could say bread," Paige recounted. "I didn't know any Spanish words, and when I asked for bread, all I got was a polite grin. One day, I heard a fellow say something." They brought him a plate of liver. "For the next two months, I kept saying that same thing. I had liver for breakfast, dinner and supper. It was better than starving. But I've been spouting gas ever since." Paige knew how to keep them laughing, engaged, and interested in him.[21]

The McAuley series on Paige was successful, and most readers thought it quite positive on the whole. But the black athlete always had a tenuous relationship with the white media and many of its writers and would sooner or later end up as the butt of a joke. McAuley was no exception. A few days after his last installment of the series, he added a piece called "McAuley Learns Why Train Was Held—It Was Satch." He went on to recount what he said had occurred at the Cleveland train terminal on a date in September, three minutes after the scheduled departure time of the team's train for Detroit. McAuley said that he thought for sure that he had missed the train but went down to the platform to find that it was still there, and so was the anxious team secretary, Spud Goldstein. McAuley then thanked Goldstein for holding the train for him, to which he received the reply, "I wasn't holding it for you. I figured you were a cinch to miss it. I was holding it for Satchel Paige." McAuley concluded his piece, "The Negro pitcher finally came shuffling down the steps and the conductor waved 'All aboard.'"[22]

Cleveland celebrated like it had never celebrated before as the pennant race came to a conclusion and their team clinched the banner. Paige was riding high and it was well deserved. He saved or won sixteen games for Cleveland in a tight race, performing brilliantly in coming through in the clutch. What he looked forward to now was to play on the biggest stage in all of baseball—the World Series.

The coming of the World Series was one good fortune after another for Paige. He could hardly believe that he was not only on a Major League team, had helped it win its league's crown, and was going to play in the World Series. All of this had happened to him in the brief span of a few months. He traveled to Boston with great expectations and with the whole world watching along with his throngs of fans, especially African American ones, waiting for him to pitch in the World Series.

He did not get his chance in the first game either as a starter or in a relief role. In the second game Bob Lemon started for Cleveland, and it looked to Paige that it would be his chance, as Lemon began to fade in the latter innings. He was hoping that he would get the nod from Boudreau to warm up. The command never came. Paige heard the fans, the Cleveland faithful and Boston fans alike, yelling that they wanted Satchel. The "We want Satchel" chant continued off and on. Finally, Boudreau signaled for Paige to warm up.

He started getting ready, taking his time and reserving his energy but getting the juices flowing and the arm ready. Paige played it cool, although he was dying to get in the game. Lemon, however, dug himself out of the hole and led the team to a 4–0 win, which evened the series at one game each.

Heading back to Cleveland for game 3 of the series, Paige overheard Boudreau's answer to reporters as to who would be the starting pitcher. The answer was Gene Bearden. All Paige could hope for was that he might be brought in for some relief work. He kidded with his teammates and tried to enjoy the train ride back. He had a friendly exchange with Spud Goldstein about the traveling arrangements and whether he could get a lower bunk. Paige found that Goldstein was pleased and proud to let him know that "we have nothing but roomettes on our train. Remember, Mr. Paige, you're with a big-League club now." Paige was likely embarrassed but quickly recovered and played the moment for all it was worth, replying to Goldstein in as serious a tone as he could, "If you boys ain't all careful, you all are gonna give me a swelled head."[23]

Paige thought he might have a chance to get in the third game in a relief role and looked forward to that possibility. He became more hopeful when Boudreau, walking down the train, gave Paige a friendly slap on the shoulder and told him that if Lemon had not settled down, he was about to pull him and put the master hurler in the game. Paige was sure that he was going to get some playing time in game 4. Gene Bearden was solid in the third game, and Cleveland came away with its second win in the series.

There was always game 4. Paige was hopeful, believing for certain that Boudreau was going to ask him to start that one. When he heard the announcement that Steve Gromek would be starting on the mound for Cleveland for that game, Paige felt sick. He wondered if he would see any action at all. There was the outside chance that Gromek could have a bad day and need some help. The help was not needed, and Gromek led the team to its third victory.

Paige was more desperate than ever and went to Boudreau and asked him if he was going to get a chance to start for the next game. The manager did not give him an answer. Boudreau later informed the team and the press that Bob Feller would be starting the next game. Paige's heart nearly stopped, because he knew Feller was a true ace and might very well not need any help in the game. If that held true, it meant that his dream of pitching in the World Series would not materialize. "I felt low as anybody ever felt. The papers were on my side. They kept asking why Mr. Lou was pitching Bobby instead of me." Several reporters wrote that they thought that Paige deserved the opportunity to pitch. He was ready, better rested than Feller, and had earned the right, given his performance in the pennant race.[24]

Feller started game 5 and was not his typical brilliant self for the early going. "I didn't want Bobby to get hit," Paige confessed, "but I guess deep down I was pulling against my own team. I wanted in that World Series awfully bad. I didn't show it. I didn't want anybody saying I was against my own team." It looked like Paige might be called upon to do some relief work as Boston jumped out ahead 4–1 by the end of the third inning. Then Cleveland rallied in the fourth inning to go up one run. It looked like Feller had found his old rhythm. Boston came back and tied the score. Feller looked like he was starting to fade. Paige's hopes grew large that he would have to be called in. He had proved himself to be the team's ultimate closer, and they needed him. With Feller wavering, Boudreau signaled for his bullpen to warm up. Paige felt certain that he was going to get the call. He did not. Boudreau sent for Ed Kleiman.[25]

Boston got to Kleiman quickly, but Boudreau went next to Russ Christopher, leaving Paige still warming up in the bullpen. The fans' cry of "We want Satchel! We want Satchel!" seemed to fall on deaf ears. Boston jumped on Christopher quickly as well, and manager Boudreau had only one pitcher left for relief duty. Boston had an 11–5 lead and the game well in hand. "Maybe that's why they called me in," Paige quipped later, "because we already were so far behind." At any rate, Paige finally received the nod. He strolled toward the mound to a deafening ovation, by far the loudest cheering the crowd had done through the entire game.[26]

He was center stage in the World Series arena. He was there, at the pinnacle of Major League Baseball. With a man on first and one out, the master hurler went to work. But the moment he wiped his hand on his uniform, the home plate umpire called for the ball to examine it. His first pitch was called a balk. Paige was called for halting, or "hesitating," in motion for his next pitch. Boston was yelling "Balk!" because he was not throwing in one continuous motion. Managers from both sides rushed up to the umpire. Boudreau stormed the plate to argue against the call. The umpire's decision was, of course, not reversed. After that was over, Paige just went to his fastball. He dispatched Warren Spahn. But as he wound up to throw to the next batter, the first base umpire called a balk, and the runner on first was awarded second base. Although angry beyond belief, Paige controlled it and went to his blistering fastball to get the next hitter out of there to mercifully bring the inning to a conclusion. Boudreau took Paige out and put in another pitcher to finish the game, which Boston won. Cleveland took the next game, however, 4–3— without Paige seeing any action—to win the World Series.[27]

It was a great day for Cleveland. Paige, however, was understandably dismayed about his performance and that he saw action only in two-thirds of one inning. Nevertheless, he was the first African American to pitch in a World Series game. That, combined with being the first African American pitcher to start a Major League game, guaranteed his place in baseball history. He finished the year with six wins, one loss, and an ERA of 2.17.[28]

Fans went wild in Cleveland over the team's first national championship in twenty-eight years, and the hometown planned on welcoming them back in style. An extra forty-eight policemen were put on special duty for the team's arrival. Citizens were concerned because pistols were being fired into the air in celebration. Huge likenesses of Boudreau and Feller were hung over statues and storefronts to honor the heroes. The city was having a good time in celebration of its new champions. The Cleveland Indians returned home to a massive parade, the streets lined with more than two hundred thousand fans to welcome back their diamond heroes. Paige, however, was not present.[29]

For public consumption, the master hurler said that he was not skipping the parade because he was angry at not getting the opportunity to start in the series or at least to put in some respectable relief work. "I didn't even feel mad at Mr. Lou any more." He lied. Paige harbored some ill feelings regarding Boudreau's decision to take him out of the game. Whatever the reasoning behind the manager's decision not to leave him in the game or to let him start one of the games in the series, Paige was not happy about it. The master hurler's decision not to show for the victory parade spoke volumes.[30]

Paige's dilemma was that he was more than that public caricature. In many respects, he was a private man once he left the ballpark. Yet as a public figure, he was blazing the trail in what would become commonplace for the sports celebrity and other famous people, of trying to have both a public and a private life. His task was made all the more difficult because he was also attempting to have a life of equality at a time in the nation's history when for African Americans such a thought was typically a dream deferred.[31]

Paige thought about these things and many others as he reflected on his treatment in the World Series. It was for all of these reasons that he decided that he would forgo the victory parade that was planned for the team in Cleveland. He left Boston early the next morning by plane rather than take the train back with the team. That plane ride took him to Kansas City, where he could be with Lahoma and his new daughter, Pamela, who was born during his epic season. He was a hero to them and all of black America. What helped soothe his bruised ego was the bonus money for winning the series. Paige received a full share, which amounted to $6,772 per player. The Boston squad received $4,000 each. By the standards of the time, the World Series was very financially rewarding for all involved.[32]

The end of the 1948 season had also brought with it the invariable comparison of Jackie Robinson and Satchel Paige. Both gave stellar performances during their first year in Major League ball. Jackie Robinson took home the "Rookie of the Year Award" for his 1947 debut season. Now there was serious talk about whether Paige deserved to be "rookie of the year" given his stellar performance in 1948. Bill Veeck wrote several letters to the editors and to the venerable *Sporting News,* which had traditionally selected the rookie of the year until the procedure was changed, championing the case for Satchel Paige. Veeck, in one letter, reminded the *Sporting News* that they had criticized him for bringing in Paige. His choice, however, proved to be a superb one. The *Sporting News* conceded that Veeck had been right and stated that "whatever may be the opinion as to the motives of publicity expert Bill Veeck in signing Paige, there is no question that old Satch has brought a lot of color into the Majors—and we don't mean black. It's the red on the faces of American League officials" as Paige gave "lessons to the batters and other pitchers." When told that he was being considered for the Rookie of the Year Award, Paige said that he found that rather ironic. "I've been in baseball for more than 20 years and am hardly a rookie."[33]

Veeck was hailed as a genius for taking a team in two years since purchasing it in 1946 to win the pennant and the World Series. He made the doubters eat their words with his most controversial decision of bringing in forty-two-year-old Satchel Paige. It proved to be a master stroke economically as well. Veeck, utilizing the Paige drawing power to its fullest, filled Municipal Stadium, the largest baseball stadium in the world at the time, and set a new single-season home-attendance record of two-and-a-half-million paying fans.

As Paige, Robinson, Doby, Campanella, and other black ballplayers became a part of the Major Leagues, the shift in allegiance and fan base portended the demise of the Negro Leagues. Effa Manley reported that her team lost more than twenty thousand dollars in 1948, which she blamed on integration. She announced that she was going to close down the Eagles organization because it was impossible to go forward. "Organized Negro baseball has been ruined in the metropolitan area," Manley proclaimed. "It still thrives in Baltimore, Birmingham and Memphis but in the North, where it suffers from the competition of the Majors with Negro players in their lineups, it is finished. And all because of the very few Negro players in the Majors—Doby, Satchel Paige, Jackie Robinson and Roy Campanella." Those four were apparently enough to lure the African American fan base away from Negro Leagues ball. She would lament the lack of "racial pride" that she felt that blacks exhibited in not supporting their own leagues. The cause and effect were undeniable, as black baseball was clearly no longer the game that was center stage and most important to people of color. The Branch Rickeys and Bill Veecks had won. Whether Paige liked it or not, his move to the Majors took black fans along with it.[34]

Larry Doby did not agree with Effa Manley's assessment of the impact of integration on Negro Leagues Baseball. He thought that his former club owner had missed the mark and what the public wanted. Doby thought that it was unfair of Manley to claim, "Negro fans are guilty of deserting Negro Leagues games to watch a handful of their people in the Majors." Doby saw the whole thing differently: "I think Negro fans just have become acquainted with a better brand of ball and preferred to see it. Jackie Robinson, Satchel Paige, Roy Campanella and myself—we're just part of the picture." He did acknowledge that there was a decline in attendance at Negro Leagues ball games that hurt the clubs and the approximately four hundred Negro Leagues players. "It is not good, of course," Doby concurred. "There's something that has to be done about it. The whole thing needs to be worked out by both sides. Maybe the solution would be for the Majors to give the Negro clubs help, like they do with minor league farm clubs. Maybe the answer would be for some of the younger white players to get their seasoning in the Negro Leagues. This would give the Negro games a novelty that would boost the gate. I don't know the whole answer. Nobody does."[35]

Despite the challenges and likely blowback, Paige and the other first crossers of the color line in the Majors saw no alternative for them except to press forward. Paige wanted to stay with Cleveland. He announced at the end of the season that he hoped to be with the team next season. "I'd like to stay in the Majors and especially with Cleveland," Paige responded to questioning. "If they'd use me often, I believe I could win 20 games next year. For next year I'm going to ask for two things—a raise and a chance to make a regular pitching turn. I think I can win 20 or 25 games that way."[36]

Before the nameplate was set on the World Series championship trophy, Paige was getting ready to go barnstorming. He planned on hitting the road where they still enjoyed Negro Leagues Baseball or at least recognized the name Satchel Paige and would come out to see him and other headliners. He announced in October that he would headline an all-star team that would be an integrated squad of Negro Leagues ballplayers and players from the American League and that they would oppose a team being put together for an exhibition game in California at the end of the month. He promised to announce further games and more about his tour as the schedule developed. Paige continued to be able to draw audiences on the road, but barnstorming and Negro Leagues Baseball were declining.[37]

He hit the road nevertheless. On October 17, 1948, he put on an exhibition in Los Angeles, with his Cleveland teammate Bob Lemon starring for the opposing side of white Major Leaguers against Paige with his All-Stars composed primarily of Kansas City Monarchs. Paige and the Monarchs lost to the Lemon squad 4–2. The consensus was, however, that Paige outpitched Lemon during their three innings each on the mound. The audience measuring ten thousand witnessed them go at it.[38]

Paige and Jackie Robinson squared off against each other on several occasions with their competing touring teams. That certainly helped attendance. When Robinson was booked for the game in Oakland, California, on the team run by Gene Bearden, he was afforded the opportunity to take on the Kansas City Royals with Paige on the mound. Robinson did quite well, getting hits every time at bat. Robinson, however, gentleman that he was, said that anyone could tell that it was an off day for Paige. "It was one day Satch didn't have it," Robinson explained.[39]

Paige was already on the road to the next engagement. He was a sizzling commodity in the aftermath of the 1948 championship season. His name was soaring higher than ever. He had become such an American icon that there was serious talk in Hollywood about producing a film based on the "Satchel Paige story." The well-known and controversial comedic actor Lincoln Perry, better known as Stepin Fetchit, was thinking seriously of starring in the film and expressed great interest in moving forward with the project. Perry saw similarities between his life and that of Paige. First of all, he admired Paige and referred to him as the greatest pitcher who ever lived. Perry was also struck by Paige's duality of existence. He well understood Paige's stunting to entertain his fans, but he also knew that Paige was nobody's fool. Perry very much related to this notion because, for him, that was the essence of his own life. His Stepin Fetchit character made him well known throughout the world, but it did not represent who he was: a highly talented actor who preferred to play serious roles if given the opportunity. Only the roles of comedy, buffoonery, or menials were open to him and most blacks in the movies. Perry believed that he had the perfect sensitivity to convey Paige's life story on the screen with the complexities and seriousness it deserved. The Satchel Paige story starring Lincoln Perry did not happen. Many felt, however, that it was a project whose day would eventually come.[40]

Black folk were always limited or pigeonholed one way or another during Satchel Paige's lifetime. This was true whether it was Lincoln Perry wanting to be more than Stepin Fetchit or Paige wanting to be more than the famous entertainer on the mound. The snubbing of Paige in the World Series—and that was how he saw it—left a lingering bitter taste in his mouth. Neither did he forget how he was stopped at the gate for the first World Series game in Boston. He told the guard to inform the manager that he was going home and that they could carry on without him. "He was just about ready to give up and return to his hotel to listen to the game over the radio when another player came along and vouched for his identity." Paige took it somewhat in stride, used comic relief, and played the dozens: "Can you imagine that? That fellow must have thought I was Jackie Robinson, for he said I was too young to be Satchel Paige." Paige knew full well that it was because of the color of his skin

that he was denied admission while his white teammates had no such problem and one of them had to vouch for him.[41]

The affable and easygoing manner that Paige displayed to the media and
the public did not mean that there was not fire in his bosom, a constant burning and smoldering because of racism in America. Paige defined himself as a
black man in America rather than exclusively as a ballplayer. He was for civil
rights and equality and hated every moment of Jim Crowism, even when it
was subtle. Edward Burns, in his attempt to dig a bit deeper into Paige's thinking through a series of interviews in 1948, found the master hurler to have
some very definite opinions on race and civil rights. "Satchel Paige may not be
as fuzzy as some about civil rights, poll tax controversies or even anti-lynch-
ing filibusters and Jim Crow enforcement but he has a lot of pride in his race
and a very definite dignity," Burns concluded. He learned that Paige resented
many things that the media and the establishment said about him, that he was
offended by the "cabin-in-the-cotton stories of his origin and early life and all
the sketches written about him and what he claims is unauthentic dialect, and
probably is unauthentic, inasmuch as it consists largely of 'Sho nuff,' and 'Ah
sho is a-goin' to do such and such.'"[42]

Paige did not like how some in the media, white and black, made fun of
his nickname, Satchel, and often just made up anything that they thought was
funny and claimed it as the origins of his nickname. He was "not pleased with
the moniker, and prefers Leroy in the several social sets in which he moves.
Furthermore, he disapproves pointedly with the widespread explanation of
the origins of the nickname. It seems most fans think he originally was called
Satchel because of the shape and size of his feet. His main rebuttal to that is
that he wears a number 11, triple A, dress shoe. This is, for instance quite a
little leather short of Primo Carnera's No. 16 triple D, making Satchel's mocca-
sins virtually pity-pats in contrast." The name had nothing to do with his shoe
size, and he did not like anyone calling him "Satchelfoot."[43]

Paige's star status in no way diminished his consciousness of the ongoing
race problem in America and the never-ending struggle to fully integrate and
reform Major League Baseball. Most treatments of Paige failed to credit him
as a "race man." He was never satisfied with the small number of blacks in
the Major Leagues and on his own team. He often jokingly put it to owner
Bill Veeck, "Mr. Veeck, you need to get some more Negroes in here." Veeck
typically replied that he was trying, and "if you see a really good one just let
me know." Paige often did just that. Such was the case of Dave Hoskins, who
played in the Texas League and whom Paige had faced off against a number
of times. He had also become familiar with Hoskins's struggle in Texas and
deeply empathized with his situation. Having been the first black to play in
the Texas League, Hoskins received death threats during the season. Despite

that, he won twenty-four games on the mound for his Dallas team. Paige was impressed with the youngster's hitting and pitching ability and brought him to the attention of Veeck. The rest, as they say, was history. Hoskins was eventually brought in and performed marvelously well for the Indians. It was Paige who had worked behind the scenes to get a fellow African American ballplayer his chance in the big leagues, and a pitcher at that. Some would have seen that as helping a fellow who might later be a competitor for your job. Paige did not see it that way.[44]

Paige was no saint. He was tough-minded and self-confident, as one would expect of a highly competitive and successful athlete. The master hurler also knew that he had the advantage of standing on the shoulders of others and should try to open doors for those coming behind him. He saw the signs and newspaper ads proclaiming him "the greatest pitcher in the world." He must have reflected on the elder statesmen of black baseball who were never given their opportunity. He was of a generation that understood that you needed to learn from the experiences of those who came before you. Satchel Paige stood in the shadows of other iconic black pitchers, including Rube Foster, Walter Ball, Bullet Joe Rogan, John Donaldson, Smokey Joe Williams, Big Bill Gatewood, Jose Mendez, and Dick Redding, who struck out Babe Ruth three times in the same game when the Sultan of Swat was at the height of his hitting prowess. Redding's later years were spent tending bar on Fifth Avenue in New York. The same fate befell Smokey Joe Williams, who many said had a fastball equal to Paige's.[45]

Jackie Robinson also tried to open doors for those coming behind him. He continued to do his part and spoke out against the racial barriers in Major League Baseball. Robinson criticized the New York Yankees directly for not having any black ballplayers. Apologists for the Yankees lambasted Robinson and chided him for being ungrateful. The apologists nevertheless admitted that ten of the sixteen teams in the Majors were yet all white and hoped to win that way. They attacked Robinson, arguing that his assertive approach would not yield positive results for those wanting integration. Robinson's critics argued that his direct approach would not work and pointed out that Paul Robeson used that tactic, and it had yielded no positive results for the integration of baseball. Back in 1943, Robeson, the singer, actor, former All-American football player at Rutgers, and activist, was, with others, granted a meeting with Commissioner Landis and the Major League owners at their December gathering at the Commodore Hotel in Manhattan. Robeson and his companions spoke for fifteen minutes, offering an eloquent plea for the integration of baseball. The owners seemed attentive and polite and raised no questions or comments for Robeson. He concluded his remarks and left. The meeting resumed as if Robeson had never been present. Opponents of Jackie Robinson's assertiveness in accusing the Yankees of prejudice alluded to what they considered to be a better way of doing things, the better way being that of "Larry Doby or Luke Easter or Satchel Paige or Roy Campanella or any of a dozen others who have discovered that a reliable bat and an able arm will advance the cause more rapidly than all the soapboxes ever nailed together." It was the old try at racial divide and conquer. Robinson and Paige did not fall for it; they persisted in their own ways to advance the race in baseball.[46]

13

Ninth Inning

Paige did a fair amount of barnstorming after the 1948 World Series, riding high on his name recognition, which was huge in the afterglow of the championship season and his anointment by the white Major League. He was a hot item. But, overall, the barnstorming circuit was in a downward spiral. The exceptions were those teams that barnstormed in the Midwest and South, or out West or in the Caribbean and South America during the winter, and featured one of the black stars from the Majors, either Paige, Robinson, Doby, Campanella, or Don Newcombe. The number of African Americans attending Major League Baseball games more than quadrupled in the two years following Robinson's signing. All eyes were turning to the Majors rather than the remnants of Negro Leagues ball. Paige played conflicting roles in that shift.

He needed to barnstorm. He certainly needed the money. Paige celebrated the championship by buying himself a new white Cadillac to go with his Willys station wagon and his DeSoto, several new shotguns, a couple of new hunting dogs, some new custom fishing equipment, a new motorboat, and new camera equipment for his photography hobby and added to his collection of Chippendale furniture. At that clip, the championship earnings did not last very long. Saving money was not his forte, despite Lahoma's urging him to the contrary. Paige was never that good at financial investment for the future. He earned it and he spent it, which meant that he experienced bouts of feast and famine. He basically lived from paycheck to paycheck, from gate to gate, which could make daily life somewhat challenging.[1]

When he received his new contract to be with Cleveland for the 1949 season, he signed right away, and for the same amount he had previously earned—twenty-five thousand dollars. He had hoped to see a contract of fifty thousand or at least forty thousand dollars. His contract for 1948 was for half the season. Hence, his expectation or hope was that the new contract would be double the amount. It is unlikely he made Bill Veeck and co-owner Hank Greenberg aware of his wish. Paige knew only too well that he was on borrowed time. He readily admitted that his fastball was not as fast as it used to be, although, as he liked to say, it was plenty good enough. He mastered other pitches that made him a complete pitcher and able to go the distance. But going the distance was becoming more difficult. He was a pitching machine, but even the greatest machine eventually shows wear and tear, and Paige was human. He also sensed that team manager Boudreau was not thoroughly convinced of his value to the team, despite his overall performance the previous year. All of these factors played a part in Paige's thinking.

He got off to an ominous beginning in spring training for the new season with a disastrous exhibition series. The hustle and bustle of spring training in the Majors was something that Paige was not up for, particularly at this late stage in his career. He did many of the drills, exercises, running, and other conditioning, but not with enthusiasm. He would rather have danced himself into shape. But that was not the way it was on the Cleveland squad and certainly not for Boudreau. Paige informed him of his wish not to overindulge in exercise: "I didn't have any desire to kill myself. I didn't believe in all of that exercise stuff especially at my age."[2]

The master hurler described his problem as "having the miseries." Paige suffered from stomach problems the entire spring training. The digestive difficulties could no longer be blamed on fried foods. By this time he was baking everything, including his beloved catfish. One observer noted that Paige, in his opinion, usually ate sandwiches and candy bars rather than having steaks, like his teammates. Those observations were accurate. One could have added to that Paige's bad habit of chain-smoking. He had started smoking when he was a child in Mobile and continued the habit, advancing to a pack a day before he was thirty years of age. It was, of course, par for the times, and most of the ballplayers smoked, chewed tobacco, or dipped snuff. The sophisticated look of the times dictated that to be suave and debonair necessitated a cigarette dangling from the mouth. The smoking combined with his eating habits and the constant pressure he was under—whether he knew it or admitted it—contributed to his "miseries."[3]

The ultimate culprit, however, proved to be his teeth. It is not known when he first or last visited a dentist. It was likely when in reform school at Mount Meigs, since dental exams and physicals were annual requirements.

He did not maintain any sort of regular program of visits to the dentist during his adult years. The poor condition of his gums and teeth, combined with the other issues, gave him the digestive problems. It was only a partial gag when Paige would delay a game and call from the mound to have the trainer run out from the locker room to bring him a bicarbonate of soda. That dated back to the days of active Negro Leagues ball, and he did it more than once in the Majors. Paige was a showman, and there was no getting around that. That showmanship may have belied the seriousness of his digestive difficulties.

Desperate to find a solution, he finally bowed to Lahoma's urging and went to see a physician. Like most men, or so they said around the Paige household, he would not go in to see a doctor unless his life depended upon it. His life might have been in the balance; certainly, his professional career was in jeopardy as a result of his ailments. The physician diagnosed his digestive problems as being caused by bacterial infection in his mouth due to long-term dental neglect.

The dentist confirmed the diagnosis and recommended that all of his teeth be extracted. The mouth problems also explained why he had settled for sandwiches rather than steaks. Chewing for Paige was immensely uncomfortable. He made the right decision when he told the dentist to go ahead and pull them all out. A month or two afterward he became able to chew, and as time progressed he was chewing better than any time he could remember in his life. The stomach ailment, the miseries, went away.

Paige called Bill Veeck to let him know that the stomach problem was resolved. He thought that he would hear words of encouragement as he explained to Veeck that the problem was with his teeth, and to solve that problem and to make sure that he would be ready to go back and do well for Cleveland, he had had them all pulled. He assured the Cleveland owner that he was ready to play first-rate baseball and could contribute to the team. Veeck was reassuring. He and Paige had become friends. The problem was that Veeck was being bought out at Cleveland and unsure of his own baseball future.

Paige ended the 1949 season with a disappointing record of four wins, seven losses, and an ERA of 3.04. It was his last stint with Cleveland. Veeck had sold his interest in the club and was out of baseball and in no position to leverage any influence on behalf of his former hurler. Paige wrote in his autobiography that he received an unexceptional contract for the 1950 season from Hank Greenberg, the new controlling owner of the Cleveland ball team. Paige evidently told Lahoma that he received a contract offer of nineteen thousand dollars, six thousand less than he was paid in 1949, an amount unacceptable. There are no records to confirm what Cleveland offered him, if they offered him a new contract at all. The available evidence suggests that he received nothing from Cleveland. This was the reason that he called Greenberg to ask about his future with the team. It was during that call that Greenberg informed him that he had discussed the matter with the manager and that "his services were no longer needed."[4]

Whatever the actual scenario of events and ultimate cause and effect, Cleveland did not see Paige as a part of its future. The organization was going with youth. Paige was not a part of the equation. He found it ironic: "They used to say, 'if you were only white you could be in the major leagues.' Now it was 'if you weren't so old you could be in the major leagues.'"[5]

The greatest hurler who ever lived was in need of employment. He sought out J. L. Wilkinson, who contacted Abe Saperstein and Ed Gottlieb. Paige, despite the negative assessment some held of the two men, saw them as pretty fair promoters. He was certainly open to virtually any involvement that might help him to keep his career in baseball going. In a few weeks, a tentative tour schedule emerged, and the fastballer for hire hit the road with a vengeance. Wherever the team or town that would pay the price, they could gain the services and name of Satchel Paige. He had his name, and he could pitch a pretty good ball. The people in the small towns and hamlets most certainly wanted to see him. He made a good living during 1950. Even as the nation entered the Korean War, there was need for recreation, and Paige was there on the road to give them the entertainment of good baseball with flair.

Meanwhile, his friend Veeck was engaged in negotiations to purchase the St. Louis Browns. He had promised Paige that if he picked up another baseball team, that he would have a job. Veeck knew the value of Satchel Paige and steadfastly believed in his pitching ability and gate appeal.

In the spring of 1951, Veeck finalized his deal to purchase the Browns. He immediately gave the master hurler a phone call and asked him if he was ready to come to St. Louis. Veeck's purchase of the St. Louis team gave Paige a new lease on life. There would be some obstacles to overcome since the city of St. Louis expressed early on its resentment of even having tryouts for black players to join the team. Veeck did not let that deter him. He maintained that baseball, professional baseball, was about winning, and St. Louis was certainly not a winner and needed to do those things necessary to win games and bring out the fans. He called for Satchel Paige.[6]

Veeck was putting a lot of faith in Paige. With the exception of the master hurler, he did not plan on bringing in any more African American ballplayers at the moment. It meant that Paige's success or failure in St. Louis would spell the future for other blacks on the club. Veeck also figured that Paige was the one black ballplayer that St. Louis would accept. With the master hurler on board, Veeck proclaimed, "Sportsman's Park is open for business under new management."[7]

Paige was ecstatic that he was back in the Majors. Another factor that made joining the St. Louis franchise attractive to him, besides the fact that it was under the ownership of someone he could trust, was that it was in driving distance of his Kansas City home. His new job, to his way of thinking, was down the street, since it was only 250 miles from his home on East Twenty-Eighth Street in KC to Sportsman's Park in St. Louis. A round-trip of 500 miles meant for him that he could stay at home and still be a member of the St. Louis team without moving his family. He loved it. It was during this period of time that Paige earned more traffic tickets than any other time in his life—at least fourteen citations in two years for speeding. Most of those came on his trek from Kansas City to St. Louis. He tended to go a little slower on the return leg.

The presence of Paige on the Browns stirred serious interest in the squad. This coupled with fireworks displays, women's night, free beer on occasion, roving bands that played in the stands, and comedic antics around the dugout brought fans back to the games. Several of the Browns players formed their own band and entertained the fans during the seventh-inning stretch. The players' band consisted of Ed Redys on accordion, Al Widmar on bass, Johnny Berardino on conga and vocals, and Satchel Paige on snare drum and vocals. All of these stunts and gags in combination, "Fun, Food, and Fireworks," made for good times and an entertaining outing at the ballpark. There was never to be another dull moment at a Browns game after Veeck purchased the team. Paige was the key ingredient in his promotional package, which meant a chance for the Browns to show a profit for the first time in many years.[8]

He, as usual, jelled smoothly with his white teammates, especially with Ned Garver, the team's talented young ace hurler who sat with Paige on the train rides and bus trips, always talking baseball and picking the master hurler's brain for all he could learn about the game. Paige enjoyed this and was pleased to share his knowledge with other pitchers who sought his advice.[9]

On the road there were many familiar problems. Jim Crow was alive and well, whether it was the South or the Midwest. Veeck shrewdly guided the team to miss most of the racial pitfalls by having a Pullman porter car for the team with their own individual sleeping compartments. When it was a matter of a hotel stay, Veeck had his people do advance scouting months if not years in advance. He attempted to secure guarantees or at least gentlemen's agreements with the hotels in question that they would not invoke the color line and would accommodate the entire team.

But the off-season was another matter altogether. Paige was barnstorming with some of his Browns teammates when he found himself again confronting Jim Crow. It was on a trip for a game in a small town in Indiana. Paige was experienced at handling Jim Crow, but he admitted that he thought it had died down with the advent of blacks into Major League Baseball, at least to some degree. "But after that newness wore off," Paige said, "those mean folks started acting up again, started letting that meanness run out again. All those years I put in taught me how to handle that kind of trouble real easy, but when it surprised me I could blow up with the best of them."[10]

It hit him right in the face in that little town. "It wasn't even down South, but I still couldn't go anywhere. There wasn't any food, any rooms, nothing. They finally got me in the back room of some kitchen and got me some food. But I had to stand to eat. That really shook me up." Yet when Paige pitched in the game, he was cheered, and afterward townsfolk approached him, wanting to get his autograph. He refused. "Go to hell" was what he told them. They wanted his autograph, but he was not good enough to stay in their hotel or to be served in their restaurants. Paige recalled how the whole thing was "eating up my insides over the way they treated me like an animal."[11]

Veeck's scouting of appropriate hotels evidently failed in another town where the team was staying, as the hotel desk clerk refused to acknowledge Paige's presence as he waited to be assigned a room. When the clerk did "see him," he turned his head away and continued on with what he was doing. Finally, Paige spoke out that he would like a room. The clerk did not look up at him. Paige repeated his requests, getting louder each time. Finally, the clerk turned around, frowned, and said, "We don't serve niggers here."[12]

Paige somehow managed to keep his composure and said to the clerk that he was with the Browns and had been informed that he could stay at this hotel. "I was trying to sound quiet and not cause troubles, but I couldn't. I was getting louder." The clerk just simply ignored him, to which Paige grabbed the edge of the desk and squeezed it in an effort to keep "from boiling over" and "to keep from hitting that man. I didn't hit him. I just turned around and walked out of the hotel." Paige was so angry he kept on walking and then took a cab to the airport and caught a flight to Washington, DC. Never mind that was not his choice of destinations, but that was where the plane was going and he wanted out.[13]

Someone evidently recognized him at the airport or one of his teammates learned what had happened and sent word to the manager, who called the airport and had a message relayed to Paige on the airplane to please get off at the next town. "I must've cooled off some on that plane because if I hadn't, I don't think I'd have done what my manager said. But what happened back in Charleston didn't seem too bad anymore. Things like that happened before. You just got to take them."[14]

After the plane landed, Paige called his manager, who told him that the man who ran the hotel had apologized and that the clerk had not been told about the arrangements. Paige was asked to take a taxi and return to where the team was staying. He decided that he would. He was the consummate professional, a black ballplayer who was used to all kinds of trials and tribulations and racism in America, and he did not want "to disappoint those fans just to get even with the meanness in somebody else. I went back."[15]

Paige's record on the mound for 1951 was three wins and four losses with a 4.79 earned run average. That was a reasonable performance, considering that the team he played for was in last place. It was acceptable too because Paige contributed in so many other ways, particularly gate attraction. Veeck offered him a contract for 1952. Immediately, the press started talking about Paige's age and how they noticed that in interviews with the master hurler, he seemed each time to be getting younger by the years and dates he gave to the reporters. Veeck loved it, as did the media and the fans.

There were guessing games about Paige's salary, too. The press seemed desperate to learn how much he was being paid. It was estimated that Paige's salary was twenty-two thousand for the coming season. Paige joked with the press about the amount and told them that he "made lots more in 1950 barnstorming for J. L. Wilkinson of Kansas City, my manager, and Eddie Gottlieb." Paige said that back then he made about fifty thousand a year. It was, of course, an exaggeration. Then he turned and looked directly at Bill Veeck and said, "I need a raise on this contract." The press conference filled with laughter.[16]

Veeck, always searching to get more publicity, sent out a challenge to his old friend Hank Greenberg in Cleveland that centered on Paige. Veeck, along with quite a few others, believed that the master hurler in 1952 at the age of forty-six had a fastball second to none. Veeck was willing to put his money where his mouth was. He challenged Greenberg to send out his best pitchers to take on Paige in a speed test. They would use the newfangled machine that recorded Bob Feller's fastball at more than ninety miles an hour. Paige's ball had been clocked in a practice session back in the 1940s as well with one of the early elementary timing devices. Page was called in from warm-ups on the other side of the field and asked to throw a few fastballs. He obliged. He then asked if they were finished with him. They said yes, and he went back to what he was doing. The man operating the timing gun, with others gathered around in amazement, yelled out to Paige, "Satchel, that pitch of yours was over a 100 miles an hour!" Paige yelled back to him, "If I'd known you were timing me, I would've thrown hard!"[17]

The combination of Veeck, Abe Saperstein, and Paige was very successful. Saperstein and Veeck were partners in the ownership of the St. Louis Browns, and Saperstein would visit the city from time to time to check on his holdings and their number-one asset, Satchel Paige. Saperstein was there for opening day for the 1952 season and participated in the opening stunt with Veeck, which was the burning up at home plate of old write-ups on the Browns and their last-place finishes. Basically, all the Browns could do was joke about their consistent dwelling in the cellar. They were promising new results for the coming season, and Saperstein felt he needed to be on hand for this promotional kick. Much of this promised success was premised on Paige.

Veeck was an excellent motivator and knew how to get the best out of his players, including Paige. He often rewarded a player for outstanding performance in a game. If you hit the game-winning home run, you might find the grateful owner purchasing a dozen new shirts for you. An outstanding pitching performance might earn you a new suit of clothes or something along those lines. For Satchel Paige, the doling out of new clothes was what he appreciated most. He was without a doubt the best-dressed player on the Browns team, if not all of Major League Baseball. He never forgot those humble Alabama roots and his scarecrow childhood wardrobe. He made up for it every chance he got, and Veeck knew it. Urging his star hurler for a great game in Washington against the Senators on the evening of June 3, 1952, Paige delivered and was rewarded with a new tailor-made suit courtesy of Veeck.[18]

There was a human problem on the team for Paige, at least one. He would later describe it as one of the worst experiences for him in the Majors. He got along exceedingly well with the players, but that did not include his relationship with Rogers Hornsby, who was brought in to manage the Browns in 1952. Most of the players disliked Hornsby. It was not surprising that the manager of the Browns had issues with Paige. Hornsby's racial views were problematic. It was long rumored that he had been, and perhaps still was, a member of the Ku Klux Klan.

That spring training he put the Browns through their paces and at such a clip Paige thought he was going to die. They were forced to do so much exercising that everyone on the squad was complaining. Finally, Paige went over to Hornsby to ask him if he was trying to "kill him," because, as Paige explained, "I'm an old man, too old for this." These tactics, minus possible underlying racial motives against the sole black player, could be easily justified given the last-place finish of the Browns. Hornsby was whipping them into shape. Paige would later admit that he was in the best shape of his life in that 1952 season and that it came in handy in some of those late-inning games. It did not change the end results for the team that season. The *Sporting News* in its evaluation of Hornsby and his failure to use Paige at the right times editorialized, "There were games lost in the late innings that the front office believed might have been saved if Hornsby had used Satchel Paige more frequently. The suggestion, of course, was that the hard-headed son of Texas didn't want to lean too heavily on the Negro."[19]

Hornsby did not last very long as manager of the Browns. Veeck later admitted that he made a mistake in going with Hornsby and that he would not make such an error again. The St. Louis Browns' new manager, Marty Marion, had a very different attitude toward his players and his aging master hurler. When up against the Washington Senators again later in June in a Friday-night contest, Paige was brought into the game in a relief role with the score tied at five each. Little did anyone know that he was going to have to go ten innings in a contest that went eighteen innings before the game was called at one o'clock in the morning, ending in a 5–5 tie. Paige was nothing short of brilliant for his ten innings in relief in which he struck out five, walked two, and allowed only five scattered hits and no runs. That next morning he was late for the team meeting scheduled for eight o'clock. He readily admitted that he overslept. Reporters wanted to know if manager Marion was going to fine him, as was the tradition for being late for any team meeting. Marion did not. He basically concluded that Paige had earned an extra hour or two of sleep and ignored his Saturday-morning tardiness, given his Friday-night performance.[20]

Veeck knew that Paige was a good promotional idea, the major attraction that meant the chance for the team to show a profit. Veeck, however, never overlooked the baseball abilities of Paige, and he was right. The heralded hurler came through in grand fashion in the 1952 season. As late as June, Paige had not allowed a run in more than twenty-six innings pitched in eleven games. He repeatedly demonstrated that he was one of the best, if not the best, relief pitcher in Major League Baseball.[21]

Then there was the game against the Boston Red Sox in Beantown on the night of June 11, 1952. Paige was doing well, keeping the Sox under control and maintaining his team's 9–5 lead. Then came the last of the ninth inning when the wheels fell off the wagon, and it was because of one Jimmy Piersall, the Boston outfielder.

Paige was always the one who talked trash to hitters, but before he could open his mouth, Piersall was already dancing and raving and yelling at Paige, telling him about how he was going to get on base because of his cunning and prowess. Not only that, but Piersall made gestures, screamed defiantly at Paige, virtually swearing to him that he was going to bunt and get on first base, yelling it out repeatedly. He took Paige off his game and undoubtedly broke the master hurler's concentration. He threw one up there, and sure enough, Piersall bunted and then beat it out to first base a step ahead of Paige, who was behind him, covering first.

Then the show really began with Piersall on first. He quacked like a duck and imitated Paige's every pitching move. Piersall gave his impression of Paige's windmill windup and high kick. The fans roared with laughter as Piersall continued his antics, making a mockery of the great Satchel Paige.

Paige's pitches lacked their usual precision and zip. Piersall's gyrations, his flapping his arms like a big bird and jumping around on first, caused the

Browns manager to complain, but nothing was done. The result was disastrous for the master hurler, as the Red Sox nailed him for hits and a grand slam off his curveball that won the game for Boston, 11–9.

That ninth inning was a nightmare performance for Paige. When interviewed later, he denied that Piersall got to him or that he was in any way distracted. "Piersall's shenanigans didn't bother me, but that swing at a curve ball did." Eyewitnesses said something different. Piersall's carrying on had definitely affected Paige, as it did many other players in the league. It was not long before Boston realized that their star outfielder was not just acting up and clowning for the fans in order to win ball games. He had deeper psychological problems that would become apparent later that season and that he eventually made public in his autobiography, *Fear Strikes Out*.[22]

Despite Paige's setback in the Boston game, manager Marion lost no faith in the master hurler's abilities. He called upon him again and again during the season, and Paige rose to the occasion. Interestingly enough, Marion had doubts early on when he took charge of the team of whether Paige was going to be an asset or a hindrance. He was completely unimpressed with Paige's performance during spring training, finding him loafing through practice sessions and avoiding workouts as much as possible. "I doubted that Satchel was the great pitcher everyone said he was," Marion admitted. "Today, all I can say is that I only wish I could've seen him pitch 20 years ago." Paige was named as one of the top-ten "comeback players" for the 1952 season in a poll of sixty-one baseball writers by the Associated Press. The compliment to his pitching ability that was dearest to his heart came when Ted Williams publicly proclaimed that Paige along with Bob Feller were the two toughest pitchers he had ever faced. Casey Stengel announced the selection of Paige to the 1952 All-Star team. Stengel concluded that Paige was one of the very best relief pitchers in all of baseball. "This completes everything in baseball for me," Paige said about his selection to the All-Star team.[23]

In honor of Paige's selection, Veeck, never one to miss an opportunity for greater promotion, had a contour chair placed out in the bullpen for Paige to rest upon. That alone attracted fans to the stadium to glean the ageless wonder sitting comfortably in his special chair. On several occasions the chair was actually moved and placed next to the dugout. It was a gag, of course. Some, in more recent days, would view it as demeaning, but Paige never did, nor did the black and white fans who went to Browns games. Paige always wanted to participate in promotional stunts and anything that would help sell tickets as long as it did not go too far. To his thinking the contour chair was a blessing, since he hated sitting on the hard bench and could enjoy a comfortable seat to rest his aging bones. After all, he had complained of how hard the bench was out there. Others argued that he did not need the chair because he was always coming into the game in relief work, another reason Stengel tapped him for the All-Star team. Inclement weather spoiled the All-Star Game. It was Paige who summed it up best when he said, "It was a day for a fellow to get in out of the rain." But nothing could diminish his accomplishment.[24]

His name was everywhere as sport icon, ageless wonder, and entertainer extraordinaire that the public wanted to know more about. There was talk again, scuttlebutt that Universal Pictures might be interested in developing a script around Satchel Paige's life and further talk that Lincoln Perry (a.k.a. Stepin Fetchit) might get the nod for the starring role to portray Satchel Paige. Supposedly, there had been a studio bid of seventy-five thousand dollars for the Paige story, but in real life much of this was Hollywood hoopla rather than fact. There would, more than a decade later, be a movie made that was based very loosely on Paige's life, but not in 1952.[25]

As some doors opened, other doors were closing. The 1953 season started off with a bang for Paige, but little did he know that it would be his last hurrah in the Majors. Veeck expressed optimism about the forthcoming season with Paige and Marlin Stewart in relief. Paige was off and running. In Chicago he helped his team beat the White Sox 6–4 in relief. But as quickly as the good start had begun, his performance and that of his team rapidly faded. It had pundits speculating as early as June that in the case of Paige, "he seemed to have run out of gas," as St. Louis lost to Los Angeles. He came back momentarily with a short winning streak for the Browns and was given credit for his assistance. As Marion pointed out, he "suddenly showed a reversal in form, began to pitch winning ball for us and we found ourselves in a winning streak." They were working Paige to death, however. He appeared in eleven games in only seventeen days. That was too much for any man, young or old. When Paige failed to show up for the Washington Touchdown Club's fourth annual baseball luncheon of the season with his Browns teammates, Bill Veeck quipped, "The old boy pitches for us every night and he really rates a day off."[26]

The spotlight that was on Paige generated substantial public interest. He was colorful, a miracle of age, affable, funny, and a success story, despite the recent win-loss record. Americans, black and white, wanted to know more about this incredible athlete. Collier's announced that in a few months it would do a full spread on Satchel Paige. The piece, which contained a number of factual errors, appeared on newspaper stands and in homes around America on June 13, 1953. The article, titled "Satchel Makes the Majors," traced the life of the "middle-aged and fabulous Leroy Paige." The article talked a bit about his background in Mobile and made a brief mention of the Negro Leagues. The primary focus was on Paige in the Majors. The article recounted his duels against Dizzy Dean and Bob Feller, who later was his teammate in Cleveland. The article made special mention of Paige's victories over Joe DiMaggio and other great hitters.[27]

Paige was asked in the *Collier's* interview the seminal question, "Who was the best hitter you ever faced?" He needed no time to think about the many great hitters he went up against in his career, which included the Major Leagues. His answer was unequivocal: "Josh Gibson was the best hitter I ever faced." Some might have thought of it as an answer given by a race man. Perhaps it was. One did not have to bring race into the equation to give Paige's answer legitimacy. He would later say throughout his life to family and friends that he saw many great hitters in the white Majors and equally good hitters in the Negro Leagues and that without a doubt, "Josh Gibson was better than all of them, way better."[28]

Roy Campanella concurred. He said that Josh Gibson was the greatest hitter. He also offered an assessment of Paige, whom he believed to be the greatest pitcher in the world. Campanella said that Paige was "the greatest pitcher I ever saw—by far" and added that he swung against Paige in many games and "didn't get a hit off him until they faced each other in the 1953 All-Star game."[29]

Richard Donovan, author of the *Collier's* article on Paige, offered an insightful assessment of the "real Satchel Paige." Donovan came to the conclusion that "Paige's real character, as opposed to his character when tardy, is an arresting blend of warmth and reserve, humor, cunning, dignity, slapstick and competitive drive—all governed by one of the most penetrating, though unschooled, intelligences in or outside baseball."[30]

Donovan went on to explain what he meant by that when he recounted an example of Paige's exceptional thinking in his discussions of the legendary hurler's interactions with others. "Paige thinks creatively in almost any field," Donovan found, "which is to say that even though he may not know what he is talking about on some subject, what he says nevertheless sounds more factual than the facts. Recently, for example, Paige told one teammate how to make straw hats. The man, who had once worked in a straw hat factory, came away convinced that he had spent years laboring in error."[31]

Collier's thought it should share with its readers some of Satchel Paige's wisdom on "how to stay young" and published his six pearls of wisdom that Dr. Robert Clark, professor of medicine at the University of Illinois, had brought to public attention following his interview with Paige to find out how he was able to perform so well physically at his age: "1. Avoid fried meats which anger up the blood. 2. If your stomach disputes you, lie down and pacify it with cool thoughts. 3. Keep the juices flowing by jangling around gently as you move. 4. Go very light on the vices, such as carrying on in society. The social ramble ain't restful. 5. Avoid running at all times, and 6. Don't look back. Something might be gaining on you."[32]

When it came to Paige's private life, he enjoyed presenting his children with gifts and having quiet time to himself. Family life, the *Collier's* editor discovered, was sacred territory. Lahoma Paige did not approve of mixing her illustrious husband's baseball career with his family life. In short, she and the children were off-limits. *Collier's* was at least able to persuade the Paige family to grant them a photograph, of which Lahoma approved, gathered around the piano with their four children at that time: Pamela, age five; Carolyn, two and a half; Linda, one and a half; and Robert Leroy, who was six months.[33]

The Browns continued to use Paige at a breakneck pace. By early July, he was set to break the all-time relief record. One wondered if he was being brought in just to please the crowds, given the dismal record of the team. On the other hand, he was desperately needed to try to shore up the weaknesses in fielding and overall play of the St. Louis club. The hope was that his superb pitching might at least halt or slow down the hemorrhages. It all meant that the ageless hurler was terribly overplayed.[34]

Paige was the workhorse on a dismal Browns team. His record midseason was one win and six losses. Nevertheless, Casey Stengel selected him to the 1953 All-Star team. Paige's performance in that game turned out to be one of the lowest points in his career. With the American League trailing in the game 3–0 in the eighth inning, Stengel brought in Paige to stop the onslaught. The critics at the game could not believe that he chose "the old man" over such heralded pitchers as Bob Lemon and Johnny Sain. Stengel did and it was a disaster. In one inning, Paige was burned for two scores, three hits, and a walk. The critics contended, "It might have been a sentimental gesture to show Paige to a National League crowd, but pitching this old fellow" was, in the opinion of many, a terrible mistake that "ruined the Americans' last chance. It meant that when they started their rally in the ninth they had to play for five runs to tie instead of three."[35]

Paige's star seemed to be dimming through the rest of the season. The Detroit Tigers took his measure again in July in the opener of a doubleheader in Brick Stadium. Paige was on the mound with the bases loaded, and not only did he fail to get the batter out, but his great control also failed him, as he walked Steve Souchock with the bases loaded and Souchock would score the winning run. In another contest, Paige's control left him again, as he hit Minnie Minoso with the pitch. Luckily for Minoso, it was not a Paige fastball that caught him on the shoulder.[36]

Most objective observers were predicting that this year would be Paige's last season in the Majors, especially since his benefactor, Bill Veeck, sold his interest in the ball club and the team was being moved to Baltimore, where it would be renamed the Baltimore Orioles. The organization was going for youth, and there would be no place for a pitcher, in a relief role or any other capacity, who was on the cusp of fifty years of age. There were, however, those who stood firm in their belief that Paige could still pitch, that he could help some team in relief. Most thought that at his age, those were unrealistic judgments. Paige had a remarkable run, but, they predicted, it was over.

He did not go gracefully into that good night. Paige thought he had more to offer the Major Leagues and hoped until the last minute that the Orioles were going to put him under contract. He concurred in his autobiography that 1953 had been a disastrous year for him on the mound. "No matter how much I looked around that season, I just couldn't find those wins. I finished up with a 3 and 9 record. That was the worst year I've ever had. It upset me. But I guess it upset Lahoma even worse. Don't you worry, I told her, trying to ease her mind. They not gonna drop me just for one bad year. I still can throw and I'll have me my job back. Just don't you worry."[37]

Paige's days in the Major Leagues were over. He no doubt told Lahoma what he did regarding a contract being forthcoming to put her mind at ease. They had a growing family to feed, and if he was not playing baseball, it meant that he was not earning a paycheck. The old master revved up to do what he did best. He tried hitting the road again barnstorming.

14

Extra Innings

By the end of 1953 the handwriting on the wall was written in indelible ink. There was no debate among Major League team owners, with, perhaps, the exception of one, that the clock on the wall had run out on the great fireballer, as it does for every athlete sooner or later. In Paige's case, it had been much later, which afforded him an inordinate amount of time to dazzle the public with a career that impacted beyond the boundaries of baseball.

His longevity on the mound, for one thing, became the focal point for serious discussions on age discrimination and the rethinking of mandatory retirement. Paige defied conventional wisdom about how long an athlete could perform, and he became a role model for senior practitioners who contemplated continuing their careers. He was the seminal pioneering example for athletes who wanted to control their own bodies and destinies, and he showed the sporting world that "it's never over until it's over," to paraphrase one of his admirers. The combination of necessity, ego, and ability was a force that prompted him to continue. In the end, he was part of the movement to make baseball rethink itself, as American society did in the late 1950s and 1960s, and beyond. It was never over for Satchel Paige, even when he threw out his last baseball.

With a wife and four children to provide for, and more youngsters on the way, Paige continued with what he knew best, the nomadic life of barnstorming wherever they would pay the price for his baseball talents as fastballer for hire. Before the 1953 season was completely over, he was already thinking ahead with other members of the Browns and old friends from the remnants of the Negro Leagues, especially the Monarchs, about the possibility of hitting the road again. He became "a globetrotter" figuratively and literally. He announced that he had worked out a deal with Abe Saperstein for the spring and would be appearing along with the Harlem Globetrotters in a barnstorming tour that would feature basketball but also feature Satchel Paige.[1]

Interests, however, were changing, as were sensitivities. Consciousness was growing in the African American community. *Amos 'n' Andy* was starting to draw criticisms from elements in the black community concerned with the negative racial stereotypes that the program fostered. Even the vaunted Harlem Globetrotters were starting to draw criticism from some elements of the community concerned about too much clowning.

The winds of change blew strongly. Charles Hamilton Houston's dream of someday defeating *Plessy v. Ferguson* was carried forward to its final conclusion in the hands of the NAACP and its lead attorney, and Houston's former student, Thurgood Marshall. The momentous *Brown* decision of 1954, striking down *Plessy v. Ferguson*—at least on paper—did not escape Paige and the other black ballplayers. They discussed the implications of the decision, as did most African Americans and Americans in general. Paige, Buck O'Neil, Goose Tatum, Booker McDaniel, and Frank Duncan always found time to get together in Kansas City and to chat, whether it was at Paige's home on Twenty-Eighth Street or at their favorite watering hole over on Vine. "You bet we discussed the *Brown* decision and what it meant to black folk, and what the new dream might be," Buck O'Neil recounted. "Satchel thought about these things just like the rest of us did, and we talked about it. Sure we did."[2]

The vicious slaying the following year of fourteen-year-old Emmett Till in Money, Mississippi, angered Paige. He and Lahoma talked about it and commiserated about the value of black life in America. Black folk in every walk of life were shocked, saddened, and outraged by the Till murder. "What they did to the Till boy, I tell you," O'Neil reflected for himself and on behalf of his friend Paige. "What kind of human beings would do something like that? All of us were angry. NAACP memberships went up that year, I know that. What a place. Good old Mississippi. Good old Mississippi."[3]

The 1950s were a trying period in every aspect of Paige's life. There was no denying the reality of resources, which were starting to dwindle, and Lahoma knew this as well as he did, if not better. She was the one at home with the children while he was barnstorming. She had the support of her older sisters, who routinely helped with the babysitting. Paying the household bills was another matter. The new house that Paige bought at 2626 East Twenty-Eighth Street was spacious, with high ceilings, three floors, and a service elevator that his son in particular enjoyed playing on. It was expensive to maintain, and

Paige's income was not what it used to be. He decided to sell the old house on Twelfth Street rather than continue using it as a rental property.

He was glad to receive calls from anyone interested in contracting the services of the ageless fireballer for hire. Paige continued to tell family and friends that he might be brought back into the Majors because he believed Bill Veeck, sooner or later, was going to own another baseball team and that he would then be receiving a phone call. It is doubtful whether Lahoma believed what she heard, but she went along with it as if she did.

In April 1956, Paige received a phone call from none other than Bill Veeck. His old friend and former boss was now part owner of the Miami Marlins of the International Baseball League, and he was calling because he needed a good relief pitcher. Most people had dismissed Veeck's earlier remarks as merely a gesture of respect for a once-great ballplayer and friend when he answered the question of which active players he would put on a baseball dream team, and he answered that he would choose Satchel Paige as his number-one relief pitcher. He was true to his word. "Everybody kept telling me he [Paige] was through, but that was understandable," Veeck expounded. "They thought he was only human."[4]

Paige and Lahoma loaded up the big Cadillac with as many of the essentials as they could take with them and took Linda and Robert Leroy, leaving Pamela, Carolyn, and Shirley with Lahoma's sisters Beulah and Nina. Pamela, Carolyn, and Shirley were attending school, and the parents did not want to disrupt their education. They would bring them down later. They were off to the Sunshine State and the promise of a very interesting tenure with the Miami Marlins.

Paige took up temporary quarters in the Sir John Hotel in Overtown, in the black section of Miami, since his pitching services were needed right away. He would later join Lahoma and the children at their temporary home, a villa in West Palm Beach, courtesy of Dr. John O. Brown, the first African American ophthalmologist in Miami, a leading civil right activist, and cousin of Lahoma Jean Brown Paige.[5]

Veeck had things all set up for Paige's grand entrance to the first game of the Marlins. The pregame festivities included a high-wire tightrope walker and a juggling act to get the crowd in the right mood. Then he hit them with the big surprise for the start of the game: the arrival of Satchel Paige. It was one incredible entrance, as Paige was delivered to midfield by helicopter. The cheering could be heard for miles, and discussions about Paige's grand entrance continued long after the game began and ended. Paige stepped out of the helicopter, in full Miami Marlins uniform, with glove in hand, and the announcer broadcasting in full volume: "The Old Man Himself Has Arrived, Satchel Paige!" He then strolled slowly over to the dugout, where there was a rocking chair waiting for him and, pretending to dust it off first, took his time before sitting down, crossed his legs, and started to rock. The stadium of eight thousand in attendance rocked as well with cheers, applause, and laughter. "Miami fans went crazy." Veeck's stunt had worked, and "big-time." Most fans in attendance could hardly remember the outcome of the game, yet they would never forget the grand entrance of Satchel Paige.[6]

Veeck pulled out all the stops in bringing in fans. He was determined to set a new attendance record for the International League at the Marlins' scheduled game against Columbus at the Orange Bowl in Miami on August 7, and he promoted the game with all the pomp and circumstance and entertainment features one could imagine. He brought in Cab Calloway and his band and singer Ginny Simms. There would be juggling, acrobatics, fireworks, musical entertainment galore, he promised the Miami fans.

The effort worked, as 57,713 showed up for the game, highlighted with the promise that Satchel Paige was going to do his very best to win it. Paige started the contest. Veeck loved for him to put on a show, and he did exactly that, doing double- and triple-windmill windups and fancy throws of every variety, overhand, sidearm, and one behind the back to first base for the out.

He had the crowd in stitches with the excitement he produced on the field. Paige was telling the world that "I am Satchel and I do as I do." Richard Donovan captured the aura of Satchel Paige when he wrote, "Doing as he does, Paige communicates his personality to whole ballparks full of fans with theatrical ease. Every time he rises from his bullpen-seat, even to get a drink, an excited murmur runs through the stands. When he starts his slow, slightly bent, sadly comic amble to the mound to save a game, fans get the impression from him that the whole situation is too simple for concern. This unconcern is the essence of Paige and always causes the crowd to explode in appreciation."[7]

Paige responded to Florida's adulation. He and Lahoma took great pride when he was able to make contributions to the African American community. He was, for example, the guest of honor in Pompano, Florida, where he tossed out the first pitch for the inaugural game marking the dedication of a new hundred-thousand-dollar athletic venue for the African American community, a facility to which he personally contributed.[8]

The Paiges connected with black Miami. After school was out in Kansas City, the rest of the children joined them in Miami. Lahoma had already been back and forth to the Magic City numerous times to get the family all settled in. The home base was the very nice villa in West Palm Beach, a one-hour drive north, or considerably less in driving time for Satchel Paige. Off and on through much of the first season, Paige stayed at the Sir John Hotel, an icon establishment of the African American community of Overtown, just west of downtown Miami on Sixth Street and Third Avenue. Overtown was an all-black community and largely self-contained. It boasted its own grocery stores, cleaners, barbershops and beauty parlors, restaurants, hotels, and theatrical house, the Lyric Theater. There was the pool at the Sir John Hotel, which the Paige family put to regular use, or they often frequented Virginia Key Beach, Miami's only black beach. These were the times of Jim Crow, and African Americans were banned from the use of beaches except for their one designated African American beach, Virginia Key. Golf courses were segregated, as were most facilities downtown. This was the discrimination and color line that the civil rights movement in Miami targeted under the leadership of individuals such as the Reverend Theodore Gibson, Thelma Gibson, Patricia Stephens Due, John Due, and Lahoma's cousin Dr. Brown.[9]

Although Overtown was a relatively small enclave compared to the African American communities of KC, Chicago, or New York, it had experienced its own version of the new Negro movement and continued to be a mecca for many of the leading black entertainers in the world, including Satchel Paige. Major headliners such as Duke Ellington, the Mills Brothers, Billie Holliday, the Ink Spots, Lena Horne, Ella Fitzgerald, Dinah Washington, Nat King Cole, Red Foxx, Pearl Bailey, Lionel Hampton, and Sammy Davis Jr. were some of the performers who took the stage at the Sir John Hotel. The Sir John could not afford to hire them at their regular rates. They would be in town to entertain at one of the big hotels on Miami Beach. Those same great black entertainers were not allowed to stay at the hotels on Miami Beach because of their color, despite the *Brown* decision. After their performance, they headed back to the Sir John, where they were staying. What also happened was that they inevitably took the stage at the Sir John in protracted after-hours sets that lasted into the wee hours of the morning. These jam sessions, with these major black headliners, became well known to those looking for fantastic after-hours entertainment. Not only did the black community turn out to see them, but adventurous whites trekked over to the Sir John or Mary Elizabeth Hotels to partake in this fabulous late-night reveling. In that way, the color line was broken in Overtown as a result of segregation on Miami Beach.

Paige and Lahoma were part of the after-hours cultural milieu of Overtown. Lahoma was a very protective mother and steadfastly refused to trust her young children to the care of any local babysitter. When her sister Nina and her husband, Lester, came down to visit, which they did on many occasions, given the lure of Miami, especially in the winter, that freed Lahoma and her famous hurler husband to go out together and partake of the late-night scene. Paige already knew most of the headline musicians since he was a household name and typically mingled in that rarefied company. He and Lahoma spent many a great evening dancing to the world's best music right there at the Sir

John and often just sitting and listening or chatting over cocktails with the likes of Sammy Davis Jr., Billy Eckstine, Cab Calloway, Arthur Prysock, and Sarah Vaughan—courtesy of segregation.[10]

Back on the baseball diamond, all was going well for him, as he continued to be a productive member of the Marlins. He showed spunk throughout the next season, too, and many questioned whether he would ever get too old to pitch. When challenged about his age or his pitching, the fire was still in his belly, as Carlos Paula found out when he impugned Paige's pitching ability. Paula fashioned himself a superb hitter and told Paige, "Old man, you don't throw balls hard like the last time I saw you pitch." Paige fired back, "In the first place you ain't never seen me pitch before. In the second, I can throw hard enough to get a nothing hitter like you out any day." Age had not dimmed his trash-talking ability or confidence in his pitching. He went 11-4 that season, a brilliant performance.[11]

Paige was back in form for the 1957 season and dictating his own terms in terms of schedule and training. The Marlins allowed him to have his way because they knew his ability to perform on the mound and its importance at the gate. Paige announced that he was ready to go for the new season and had contacted his old Native American friend out West for more of the secret elixir for his shoulder. He also acknowledged that the Marlins had agreed to his training schedule. The Marlins' manager, Don Osborn, was basically unconcerned about how Paige trained or did not train as long as he could continue to save games for the team. By the manager's count, the ageless master hurler had saved no fewer than fifteen games during the past season. He could train however he pleased.[12]

Paige took the new liberties to the extreme. He lived out the embodiment of his rule to avoid running at all times. That seemed to also mean that he could arrive whenever he wanted to for training sessions. He showed up late for most of them. Osborn's gentle criticism of Paige for his tardiness was to tell the master hurler that he should train at least a bit, and suggested to him, "You've got to devote as much time to spring training as you do to fishing." Osborn then thought about what he had said to Paige and toned it down a bit, adding, "Well, almost as much time."[13]

When Paige reported for the 1958 season, he seemed early on to be his typical self. Asked by a reporter if he and his famous right arm were ready for another year of work, Paige quipped, "All I have to do is shake hands with the catcher and I'm ready to go." The season would prove to be his last in a Marlins uniform. He was doing yeoman service for the team, but in truth his relationship with management had been in steady decline ever since Bill Veeck sold his interest in the Marlins two years earlier and left town. The situation was growing worse. Paige had received a salary cut. His current contract promised him only nine thousand dollars. Attendance at Marlins games was also dropping off. The team seemed to draw best when on the road. Some suggested that Miami was simply not a baseball town and likely would never be one.[14]

Even with the salary cut, Paige thought he might be able to work it out. As the season drew on, the tensions between him and the new team manager and the front office deteriorated. The management was not solely to blame, as Paige was consistently late and showed signs of uninterest in what was taking place on the field. In his defense, he basically argued that he was giving a half effort since he was receiving half a paycheck, a sort of "part-time play for part-time pay." On August 2, 1958, Paige was so angry with his treatment by the Marlins that he "quit the team" right at the scheduled departure time of the flight out of Rochester, New York. He said that the management of the Marlins owed him sixty-five dollars for meal money and that he had not received it. The management countered that Paige failed to show up when the funds were handed out and that he would have to wait to receive the money. Management also argued that it had given him advances on his salary throughout the season and that he was in debt to them. At any rate, they were able to solve the problem momentarily and get him back on the plane to make the return trip to Miami.[15]

The situation came to a head when the Marlins' new manager, Kerby Farrell, placed Paige on the inactive list. He told the aging hurler that he had done so because he felt that he would likely not want to pitch much when the team played games in the colder climates of New York and Montreal. Paige was outraged by the decision. That in combination with his lower pay was absolutely it for him. He told Lahoma that he was finished with the Marlins, and the real question was whether he could last through the end of the year. Lahoma did not take this decision easily. They had five children now, and there was a real question of how they would survive. "The kids. What will we do?" Lahoma questioned her dejected husband. Paige had reached the point of no return and said it was a matter of pride. He did not report to Miami for the 1959 season, which was just as well because Miami was no longer interested in him. Paige claimed that the Marlins owed him thirteen hundred dollars. The Marlins contended that they owed him nothing and that he was cut from the team; they were going with youth. He and the Marlins parted ways, with sour notes and accusations flying from both sides.[16]

What to do next was a serious question. There had been a rumor floating around about his being offered a job in motion pictures, but it was only a rumor. He had asked Veeck, who was spending much of his time in Los Angeles these days, to please shop his name around for a possible role. What started off as a rumor actually ended up as reality. Paige received a call from United Artists. The studio thought he would be perfect for a part they had in mind in the new picture *The Wonderful Country*, starring Robert Mitchum and Julie London, along with the much-heralded Mexican actor Pedro Armendeiz. Satchel Paige was on his way to Hollywood and the big screen.

The filming had already begun, and they needed Paige to report within the next two weeks on location in Durango, Mexico. Paige and Lahoma were excited, as was their daughter Shirley. There was the matter of their youngest arrival, Lula Ouida, who was less than a year old. They needed to move quickly on their travel plans. Lahoma had made up her mind, and daughter Shirley concurred, that they were going to Mexico. Lahoma saw this as an opportunity for at least this part of the family to be together, since Paige would be in one place and not traveling all over Mexico like in his barnstorming days. They applied and received their passports and were ready to go in short order: Paige, Lahoma, Shirley, and little baby Lula Ouida.

Satchel Paige was the toast of Durango. They knew him all over Mexico from his barnstorming prowess, and the Mexicans loved baseball. He also got along exceedingly well with Robert Mitchum, who went out of his way to make sure that Paige and family were comfortable. It turned out that Mitchum was a longtime Satchel Paige fan. If Veeck was the one responsible for getting Paige the role in the film, it was certainly not a hard sale, since Mitchum was involved in handpicking the supporting cast.

The off-the-screen shenanigans there in Durango were so wild that they impacted on the production of the film. Robert Mitchum had a long history of loving to booze it up and would spend many a late night into the early morning carousing around Durango with a woman in one hand and tequila in the other. Paige was a family man now and went with them only one time to have a few drinks and found that Mitchum could drink him and everybody else under the table. In addition, there was the little matter of Lahoma, Shirley, and Lula Ouida. Paige stayed at home with the family when not on the set. The film was eventually made. It did not do well at the box office.

Paige briefly contemplated a possible career in films. It was all talk, and his filmmaking days were gone as quickly as they began. The money he made in his Hollywood debut would last the family only a few months, as he, and certainly Lahoma, realized. It meant that he needed to find permanent work, and that was becoming more tricky given his age, the demise of black baseball, and the public interest in sports that was beginning to show signs of a shift of interest toward other pastimes, including a growing interest in collegiate and professional football and basketball.

There was only one thing to do, and Satchel Paige said those familiar words again and hit the road once more barnstorming. It seemed that he would pitch forever or at least attempt to do so. It was with that in mind that writer David Lipman contacted the ageless hurler with the idea of doing a book focusing on his life story. The resulting work was *Maybe I'll Pitch Forever* by Leroy (Satchel) Paige, "as told to David Lipman," which was published in 1961. The sales of the book were moderate, with Lipman receiving the larger percentage of the royalties. In total, Paige was compensated a mere pittance of less than two thousand dollars for his life story and so-called autobiography.[17]

Paige was not happy about that, and neither were his family members. He was never one to dwell on what might have been or be consumed with negatives. The times were changing, in some respects, and he was doing his best to change right along with them and to continue to make a living playing ball.

His staying power made sportswriters around the country start to reevaluate their thinking about age and athletic performance. The *Chicago Defender* led the way in its reassessment. "It's becoming more and more apparent that we need to revise our judgment on the relationship between athletic prowess and age," the *Defender* concluded after looking at Paige's longevity. Paige was proving the old adage concerning age, or, as he philosophized, "Age is a matter of mind over matter. If you don't mind it don't matter."[18]

He became a point of discussion around dinner tables, in sport training facilities, and among the elderly population, who referenced him as a counterargument to those who set age limitations. In government circles, Paige's name came up as an example of "living proof that the employees' retirement age should be raised." In Chicago they were having serious debates as to whether to increase benefits from municipal employees retiring at age fifty-five. The argument was made that a person at age fifty-five could do virtually anything someone younger could do and may, in fact, do it better. The argument went: "Today a man of 55 is still in his prime. Look at Satchel Paige. Nobody knows how old he is, but it's agreed he's over 50." Elroy Hirsch, better known as "Crazy Legs" Hirsch, the football star running back who at age thirty-three was still able to woo crowds and make the long, breathtaking receptions and jitterbug runs from scrimmage, decided that he just might have some good years left and that he was too young to retire. "The way I feel now I don't know how long I'll keep on," Hirsch answered his critics. "Maybe I'll even get my third wind like Satchel Paige."[19]

Boxing great Archie Moore defied age much like Paige, and when asked how old he was, Moore quipped, "How old is Satchel Paige?" When Sugar Ray Robinson, at the old age for a boxer of thirty-five, defeated a much younger Carl Olson, witnesses reflected on how they thought they would never be referring to Robinson as an old man at the same time that "Jersey Joe Walcott and Satchel Paige were defying signs of senility." When the age of Diomedes Olivo, a new relief pitcher for the Pittsburgh Pirates, was brought up, the management answered that it did not matter and added, "How old is Satchel Paige?" When asked a hypothetical question of what active players today would he put on a baseball dream team, Bill Veeck, in naming his relief pitcher for that team, again listed Satchel Paige. Veeck said that he was convinced that Paige could still deliver, even at his present age.[20]

There were much more important issues than his age, as far as Paige was concerned. The winds of change since the *Brown* decision, Emmett Till, the Montgomery bus boycott, the killing of Medgar Evers in Mississippi, and the church bombing that took the lives of four little girls in Birmingham continued to gain momentum and resonance that were being felt by society, Satchel Paige, and Major League Baseball. As the number of black players grew in the Majors, so did the demands by them for equal treatment. One problem that drew heated criticism from black ballplayers was the continuing Jim Crow treatment they received in the South. Jackie Robinson experienced the color line when he traveled with the Dodgers into Dixie. Roy Campanella and Don Newcombe were flat out refused accommodations in the team's hotel in many southern locations. They resented it and spoke out against it, pushing the Dodger organization to make arrangements with hotels that did not practice Jim Crow. Hank Aaron voiced his displeasure with being Jim Crowed right there in Atlanta: "It was bad in the early days and got ugly as I closed in on Ruth's record." In St. Louis, the Chase Hotel was well known for its restrictions against blacks. Blacks knew the hotel as a bastion of racism, a hotel that not only refused blacks as guests but would not hire them as bellhops or use them in any menial positions, including as janitors or maids. Paige and Buck O'Neil, along with other blacks in Missouri, gave the Chase the nickname "Old Dixie."[21]

Black Major League ballplayers made more demands on their teams, refused to stay in hotels that would not give them full and equal access, and pushed team management and owners to adopt the policy of "one for all and all for one." If a hotel would not properly house all of the team's members, then none would stay there—a course of action that Paige and his Bismarck teammates took two decades earlier. The Chicago White Sox came up with an innovative way of handling the discrimination against its black players during spring training in Florida. The White Sox organization purchased the Sarasota Terrace Hotel in Sarasota, Florida, with the public pronouncement that "now all of our players can live under the same roof during training season."[22]

In many respects, baseball, thanks to its African American players, was being prodded to take a leading role in the modern civil rights movement. Along with Satchel Paige, Willie Mays, Hank Aaron, Leon Wagner, and Roy Campanella all expressed their pleasure in the changes being made in baseball thanks to the civil rights movement. Their own activism from within baseball also helped. Ernie Banks, who was gaining the nickname of Mr. Cubs, while complimenting his Chicago team for having improved dramatically in race relations, recalled how in St. Louis his team could stay in the Chase Hotel but he could not eat in the restaurant. All of that was starting to change. "That's all a thing of the past, now," Banks noted. Lee Mays of the Cleveland Indians put it this way: "I know the brothers and other professional sports and, from what I can tell, baseball has come the farthest in race relations—with fans and players. But there always will be some resentment, or quiet crack now and then. And some unfairness still exists."[23]

Paige had a racial consciousness that predated the 1960s and that continued to evolve. He shared with Buck O'Neil his thinking on race and the condition of black folk in many conversations. O'Neil vividly recalled the time they were barnstorming together in South Carolina and Paige said to him, "Come with me, Nancy. I want to take you somewhere." The place he took him to was Drum Island, which had been a major slave port and market. It was Paige who knew about the history of the place. They chatted about it for more than a half hour, and then Paige said, "This is where they brought us. This is where they sold us." After a long pause and complete silence, as they contemplated the significance of their location and its importance in the experience of black Americans, Paige confided to his teammate and friend, "You know, your grandma and my grandmother and -father could have been sold right here. You know what, Nancy? Seems like I've been here before." O'Neil answered him, "Me too, Satchel." "That was Leroy Robert Paige," O'Neil concluded. "A little bit deeper than most people thought." He continued, "That was a part of Satchel that a lot of people did not know."[24]

Consciousness was one thing; eating was another. Paige joined the Indianapolis Clowns in the 1960s, but with an understanding and agreement with Saperstein that he would wear his uniform from the Cleveland Indians and never don a grass skirt or put on war paint or blackface. Paige played on the opposing team that traveled with the Clowns, which posed as "the local team" or a group of "baseball all-stars." That team wore regular uniforms and played the "straight man" in the skits of the Clowns.

The stunting, in combination with the second-class travel of the team, the fleabag hotels they were forced to stay in, and the dwindling size of the crowds, got to Paige more quickly than even he would have predicted. At a game in Beloit, Wisconsin, he felt so demeaned that he refused to pitch. He had once again started driving his own car to games rather than ride on the dilapidated team bus and made it to Telfer Park in Beloit a few minutes before game time. When he asked where the team's locker room was, he was informed that there was none. Paige was outraged. He yelled at the manager, "Where do you want me to dress, under the stands!" The audience of six hundred could hear the argument going on and his complaining about the facilities and the turnout. The manager finally persuaded Paige to change on the bus. It was easy to tell that Paige was just interested in his paycheck and pitched that way. The size of the crowd disappointed him, the facilities disappointed him, and the play of his team aggravated him. The fans sensed his displeasure and showed their displeasure with him. For the first time in his career, Satchel Paige was roundly booed.[25]

Neither did he jell with his teammates. Most of them knew of the legendary ageless hurler, but thought of him and his pitching as nothing special. The generational gap worked both ways. His young teammates did not show him homage, and he showed them disdain and aloofness for what he considered to be a bunch of amateurs. In short, the chemistry between Paige and the rest of the team was not good. As reported, "Paige isn't very popular with most of his teammates. The Clowns and Stars are composed mostly of young men hoping for pro careers." His stint with the Clowns was short-lived. After a few more games, he quit. After touring the 1965 winter season with the Harlem Globetrotters, Paige intimated that his days with that team were coming to an end.[26]

Along with the growing racial consciousness was a heightened sense of self-worth and a demand for independence—traits that Paige symbolized his entire career and that were now at the center of the challenge to the owners' hold on Major League Baseball. Curt Flood led the way, as he took on the reserve clause. He objected to being traded without having any say in the matter. As the issue heated up in August 1965, supporters of management and of the traditional way of doing things spoke out in favor of preserving the reserve clause, contending that it allowed teams in minor markets to better compete with those in the major cities. Without it, they predicted huge salaries and that baseball teams with the most power at the gate would get all the best players. They predicted that big-city teams such as those in Chicago, Boston, and New York "would not be interested in the game unless they could develop and keep for the fans of the city such players as Ernie Banks, Willie Mays and Ted Williams. The few big stars would get all the money. It would be Mays in San Francisco one year and Chicago the next in Boston the next. And eventually the game would degenerate into a few road-show teams headed by the big stars in the way Satchel Paige and Josh Gibson once roamed the country." Flood saw it quite differently and rejected the whole notion that he could be summarily traded away by St. Louis to Philadelphia without his consent. He argued that this was a new form of slavery. When his opponents pointed out that he was earning one hundred thousand dollars a year in baseball, Flood fired back, "I am a one-hundred-thousand-dollars-a-year slave." Paige was on the list to testify in support of Flood's effort, if called. Flood lost the suit, but it was just a matter of time before the reserve clause would, in principle, be struck down.[27]

Paige was preoccupied with his own financial situation and how he was going to support his family as the decade rolled on and his earning capacity continued to diminish. Unfortunately, he could not qualify for a Major League pension because he had not been in the Majors long enough. His was the dilemma of the character Yossarian in Joseph Heller's novel *Catch-22*. In Paige's case, he had not been in the Majors long enough to qualify for a pension because the Majors had not allowed him in for most of his career because of his color. Dick Young, writing in his sports column, chastised the great hurler for calling baseball prejudiced and characterized Paige's criticism of big-league ball as the "sad ranting of an old, embittered man." Young said Major League Baseball was "not prejudiced." Evidently, Young discarded Paige's history of having not been allowed to enter baseball until he was forty-two years of age because of the color of his skin. Young said that Paige should ask himself, "Is he any darker now than he was when baseball hired him?" The real issue, Young posited, was Paige's age. "Society is prejudiced, unfortunately," Young concluded, "against the old, more than against the Negro. No man of 65 is sought by industry, be they black, white or striped." Young suggested that Paige think about what President Lyndon Johnson had said in his State of the Union address, in which he told the nation that we must eliminate by law the unjust discrimination against employment because of age. Young reiterated, "Satchel Paige has a case. He is being discriminated against, but he does not know the reason. The injustice to Satchel Paige is the injustice done to all older people."[28]

When Charles Finley announced that he had signed Paige in September 1965 to pitch for the Kansas City Athletics, shock waves reverberated throughout the Majors. Numerous pundits jumped all over Finley for this "novelty number." Others called it justice. Bill Veeck waded in to say that he thought it was a great idea because it would give Paige the required amount of time in the Majors to qualify for a pension and that he hoped Finley was doing this more than for a publicity stunt to get people into the park. Paige was pretty silent on the matter except to say that he was ready to go and glad to have the opportunity. Those who knew Paige best said that he was absolutely convinced that he could pitch with the best of them even then. At the age of fifty-nine, Paige became the oldest player in the history of Major League Baseball when he took the mound against Boston on September 26, 1965.[29]

His brief stint with the Athletics only helped him dent the time requirement to be eligible for the pension. In August 1968, Bill Bartholomay, president of the Atlanta Braves, invited Paige to join their organization and offered him a contract. The Braves had decided to do the right thing and bring sixty-two-year-old Paige in to enable him to earn the remaining time needed to qualify for a pension. The Braves organization, however, said it was not doing this for charity. "We expect Paige to be of great help, not only this year but in helping to condition our young players next season," President Bartholomay explained. "We're giving fans in this area a chance to see a living legend." Those who predicted that attendance at Braves games would increase were absolutely correct. After the signing of Satchel Paige, conservative estimates indicated that attendance at Braves games jumped at least 20 percent.[30]

There were those who were concerned about Paige's ability to mesh well with the Braves' superstar slugger, Hank Aaron. No such worry was necessary. Paige and Aaron hit it off from the very start. Aaron loved to play the dozens with Paige, ribbing him from time to time, and Paige wisecracking back at him, with both of them laughing and admiring the other's retort. This friendly signifying between the two was a tension breaker in the Atlanta clubhouse that made everyone loosen up with the pleasant vibes coming off of Paige and Aaron. "He was a good teammate," Aaron recalled. "It was great having him around."[31]

The Atlanta Braves kept Paige on long enough to qualify for his pension. He started receiving his steady paycheck in 1969. It helped to stabilize the home front and relieve a bit of the financial pressure. He could sit back a little and enjoy his position as elder statesman of baseball and a homebody.

Paige loved being at home now on a relatively regular basis. He had not given up barnstorming completely, however. He was spokesperson for the Red Birds, the farm team of the St. Louis Cardinals. That gave him the opportunity to rev up the Cadillac—off to wherever they needed him to be the public face. He loved it. He was still the traveling man, but with considerably less traveling these days.

The family always greeted him with that explosion of joy when he returned from the road. The trips now were of considerably shorter duration. There were times during the heyday of his barnstorming and with the Majors that he was gone as long as nine months of the year, with only periodic stops home. The family dutifully checked on him. The children phoned him on many occasions when he was on the road to make sure things were all right. Pamela fondly remembered from her earliest days calling local sheriffs and police and state troopers in all the little towns all over America to find out what her dad was doing. They had his calendar on the wall at home and knew where he was playing and wanted to touch base with him. She would phone the law enforcement headquarters wherever he was and ask them, "Do you know if there's a ball game being played there today?" She could hear someone in the background say, "Yeah, there's a game over in such-and-such field, I think." She would then ask them, "Would it be possible for someone to give a message to my dad? He's playing in the game, and we need for him to call home to make sure that he's okay." Someone would then answer back, as they did in Lima, Ohio, "What's your dad's name?" She would reply, "His name is Satchel Paige." There would always be an immediate reaction. Pamela found that there was not one town in America that refused to send an officer over to tell her father to please call home. That her dad's name was Satchel Paige might have had something to do with it.[32]

At home, Paige's day started with the children bringing him his cup of Sanka decaffeinated coffee, prepared with just the right amount of sugar and cream and carefully placed on the night table next to the bed. Next came the feeding of the animals. The Paige's backyard reminded one of Noah's Ark in that they had a small menagerie of animals. "My dad's pride and joy were his hunting dogs," Robert Paige reminisced. "He paid a lot of money for them and had all kinds. He had his red tick and blue tick coonhounds." Next came the serious southern-style family breakfast at the Paige household of scrambled eggs, rabbit and gravy, rice, biscuits, and sorghum molasses. Paige loved freshly made biscuits. He also loved his rice, cooked just right.

The remaining chores for the children constituted the next item of business during the day. They had to keep the front yard just right, with their illustrious dad supervising their manual labor. He was a good supervisor but was not the family disciplinarian. Lahoma was the one who disciplined the children. Paige never spanked any of his children. He, no doubt, vividly recalled his encounters with "the switch" and refrained from ever having one of his children go and fetch one. His temperament was extremely relaxed at home. He was an older dad with a wife who was sixteen years his junior.[33]

Not only that, but Lahoma beat him at fishing. This was one of the great sources of constant amazement to him and joyful jousting around the Paige household. There he was with all of his expensive fishing gear and her with one rod or a pole, and she consistently caught the biggest fish and more of them. The children rolled with laughter, poking fun at their illustrious dad. Paige went along with the joke and contended that Lahoma beat him fishing only because she had a special relationship with the fish.

There seemed to always be visitors at the Paige home. It was required that a pot of rice and a large pot of greens be at the ready all day long, not just for him to enjoy. He was, after all, Satchel Paige and folks, in the African American tradition, were sure to drop by the house, and you needed to be able to offer them something good to eat. Uncle Brig (short for "Brigadier General"), as the children nicknamed their dad's older brother Wilson, was a frequent visitor, having moved up from Mobile for a better life in KC. The children called him Uncle Brig because he was always so matter-of-fact and calculating in the advice he gave to them on navigating their way through life. Paige and Wilson enjoyed numerous afternoons together at the house on Twenty-Eighth Street.

The Paige home was the stopover for many of the who's who in African American entertainment. Everyone from individual celebrities to the entire Harlem Globetrotters basketball team dropped in when in town. Goose Tatum was a close friend and was often over at the house to visit with Paige, sitting, watching a game on the television, or playing cards with the rest of the guys. Old teammates, like good friends Booker McDaniel and Frank Duncan, often stopped in. The list was endless.[34]

Old Negro Leaguers who were down on their luck always found an open door at the Paige house, as the old master hurler insisted. There were times that players were making their way through Kansas City and ran out of money and needed to stay over until funds arrived. There was always a spare bedroom or room on the couch in the living room, but no one was turned away. There was a community understanding back then among black folk that helping one another was the key to group success.

Paige was also the family's in-house comedian and life of the party. He seemed to always come up with something funny. He told jokes about when barnstorming and the various players he had come up against. When the children were young and the many visitors were stopping at the house, they greeted them at the door, introduced themselves, and then immediately went upstairs. In those days, children were best seen and not heard. In later years son Robert often found himself playing the role of a gofer, as he would be summoned to fetch ice for their drinks or run a quick errand to the store and pick up a pack of cigarettes or some more food to keep his father's gathering hordes supplied after what was in the house was depleted.

Satchel Paige's friends took in many a game of dominoes, with their host holding court with stories and liquor. He favored Old Crow bourbon whiskey and liked to drink it out of an old jelly jar. Pamela found this appalling and in later years bought her father some top-of-the-line bourbon and scotch and a set of Waterford crystal from which to drink the more refined liquor. It did not work. He preferred Old Crow out of the jelly jar.[35]

The 1960s brought two of the most difficult moments in Paige's life. In 1965 his brother Wilson died. The children of the Paige household saw something they had never witnessed before—their father crying. He wept openly at the passing of his brother. If that was not enough, the following year, on Thursday, January 4, 1966, his mother, Lula Coleman Paige, passed away in Mobile. He did not weep openly at her death. Perhaps it was because he found solace in what he had been able to provide her while she was alive. One of the greatest satisfactions in Satchel Paige's life, and one he always cherished, was when his success enabled him to get his mother out of the old shotgun house on Mobile's South Franklin Street and buy her a lovely new home. She lived in that house for the rest of her life thanks to her son, who made good.[36]

He may also have found some relief in the belief that, at her death, Lula Paige was reportedly 104 years of age. The surviving family members had many decades earlier accepted her recollection of her own age. That, of course, made sense. The only problem was that public records indicated through the US Census reports, including the information Lula Paige personally provided the census takers of the reports for 1910, 1920, and again in 1930, that she was, in fact, born in 1874. If the US Census reports were correct, Lula Paige died at the age of 92, not 104. It would not have been the first time that the US Census got it wrong, despite what the interviewee provided, yet the births of her husband and her children matched their reported ages, which included her son, the master hurler, as having been born July 7, 1906. If Lula Paige had been playing the age game, then that was something else that she and her illustrious son had in common.[37]

Satchel Paige had become a living legend and the measure of great pitching. Robert Hieronimus, who played against him in the fading years of the Negro Leagues, asserted, "Satchel Paige, I mean there aren't there I don't know of any white Major League pitcher that could go up—and his team could go up—against Satchel Paige in his prime and beat 'em. He was just impossible to beat; throwing the ball at a hundred miles an hour consistently and with such accuracy." Jackie Robinson perhaps said it best in 1966 in his praise for Sandy Koufax, who he thought was the best pitcher in baseball at that time. Robinson went on to say, "However, I think that Satchel Paige would have given Koufax competition for the honor if accorded the opportunity in his prime."[38]

It was understandable that a movement commenced in earnest to get Paige inducted into the Baseball Hall of Fame. African American newspapers and then a growing list of the white dailies came on board. The *Chicago Tribune* came out in favor of Paige's being inducted into the Baseball Hall of Fame. The *Saturday Evening Post* endorsed the idea that Paige deserved to be in the hall. A major piece was published by Bob Feller in which he argued that it was patently "unfair" that Satchel Paige, among others, could not be selected to the Hall of Fame.[39]

A committee was established in 1962 called the "Hall of Fame for Paige Committee," headed by Judge John Henry Norton of Fairfield, Connecticut. The group advertised and collected letters supporting the induction of past Negro Leagues greats, especially Satchel Paige. All letters were to be bound together and eventually sent to the Hall of Fame in Cooperstown. Bill Veeck wrote that Paige had already been inducted into the Kansas City Sports Hall of Fame and needed to be in the one in Cooperstown. He went on to say, "Had Leroy had an opportunity to pitch in the majors when he was in his prime, he would have been baseball's greatest pitcher." Veeck even took it a point further when he declared, "If Satchel Paige had been brought into the Majors in his prime, today's 'Cy Young Award' would be known as the 'Satchel Paige Award.'"[40]

The public outcry, media blitz, petitioning, personal letters, pleas, and prodding pushed the National Baseball Hall of Fame and commissioner Bowie Kuhn into action. A special ten-member committee was established in 1968 to devise a process for the induction of selected players from the Negro Leagues into the Baseball Hall of Fame. There would be many long meetings, discussions about process, debates about statistics and athletic performance, and talk about how to authenticate the stats. There was considerable discussion about future selections to the hall and whether, at some point, managers and owners and coaches would be considered for induction. In the end, there was very little debate about what player would be the first inductee. The committee unanimously selected Leroy Robert "Satchel" Paige. He would be a member of the class of 1971.

The Paige household celebrated the phone call from commissioner Bowie Kuhn and the head of the selection committee giving the master hurler the official word of his selection to the hall and inviting him and his wife to dinner in New York at Toots Shor's restaurant, where the official announcement would be made on February 9, 1971. It was a dream come true. The poor boy from Mobile, Alabama, had risen to the very pinnacle of sport. All of Kansas City drew a deep breath of relief, as did Satchel Paige fans throughout the country and beyond. The significance of his selection did not escape any who appreciated the importance of baseball and what selection to the Hall of Fame meant and represented. The official letter informing Paige of his induction arrived at his home in early July and, noticeably, was dated July 7, Paige's birthday. It was the perfect gift.[41]

Unfortunately, there were problems. The selection committee recommended that the plaques and likenesses of the Negro Leaguers be placed in a separate wing of the hall. This decision elicited an immediate negative reaction that reverberated throughout the African American community and the sports world. People said, "Why was Paige being segregated?" and "These black ballplayers who suffered through the racism and discrimination of the past would now be Jim Crowed in the Hall of Fame." There were also black members on the selection committee who, in a sense, defended the decision of using a separate wing for the Negro Leaguers. Sam Lacy thought it was the best that could be done at this time and that at some later date perhaps the rules could be changed and the hall more fully integrated. Most folks were not so forgiving and voiced strong displeasure with the "segregation" of those Negro

Leagues players selected to the Hall of Fame. Doc Young called it shameful. He referred the committee to Conrad's cartoon in the *Los Angeles Times,* which depicted a white man shaking hands with a black man and telling him, "Congratulations. I hope you won't mind sitting in the back of the dugout."[42]

The firestorm as to where the likenesses of the Negro Leaguers would be placed in the hall did not die down. Major League Baseball concluded that it did not need any more of the negative publicity from its bad decision and reversed itself. Commissioner Kuhn and the selection committee proudly announced that the likenesses of Satchel Paige and all future inductees from the Negro Leagues would be placed in the main hall along with all other inductees from Major League Baseball.[43]

Satchel Paige's induction on August 9, 1971, was a day of tremendous joy and satisfaction for him and his family. His two sons would be present, Robert and Warren. Robert, who was in the military at the time, was on leave to attend his father's induction. On the trip there he shared a cab with two other gentlemen. During the ride the two other passengers talked constantly about the players being inducted, and, of course, they spoke about Satchel Paige. They talked about how great he was, how this was the right thing to do, and went on and on in their praise of the master hurler. Little did they know that the other rider in the taxi with them was Satchel Paige's son, since the passengers never introduced themselves. Robert took pleasure in hearing all the great things said about his father, this coming from two white men with no idea of his family connection. When he checked in at the hotel desk and gave his name, Robert Leroy Paige, the two men turned in surprise and awe.[44]

Upon induction, Satchel Paige was given a few minutes to address the audience and spoke eloquently, acknowledging his old boss and friend Bill Veeck who was sitting inconspicuously several rows back in the audience among the hundreds attending the event. Paige hit all the right notes of gratitude, humility, and personal pride, and he touched on race and age. Pointing again to Veeck, Paige said, "I finally got you off the hook today." Paige was referring to his old boss's having brought him into the Majors under a great deal of early criticism for that decision. Paige talked about the integration of baseball and how he initially thought he should have been the first black in the Majors. On further reflection, he told the audience, he thought Jackie Robinson was a better choice.[45]

Paige returned to KC to the glare of the news media's coverage of their hometown hero. There was ongoing discussion over whether Paige would be the one and only player from the Negro Leagues elected to the hall, a rumor that was quickly dispelled. There were those who questioned why he was the first rather than someone like Rube Foster, the founder of the Negro Leagues. When would the Latin ballplayers such as the great Martin Dihigo get in? The discussions were healthy because they further prompted the committee to get on with what it had earlier decided, and that was to bring in other inductees. There was also the desire to see more than one inductee per year, or at that rate, as Doc Young argued, it would take fifty years to induct a significant number of the many qualified players, owners, managers, and coaches from the Negro Leagues. Paige would not be the last one. He was the beginning.[46]

One might have thought that nothing else could happen in 1971 to make it a more memorable year in the life and career of Leroy Satchel Paige, but it did. Paige accepted an invitation to speak at a veterans hospital in New York in October. He gladly accepted the opportunity to use whatever name recognition and a bunch of his favorite stories to hopefully cheer up wounded veterans of the Vietnam War. After all, his son Robert was serving in the US Air Force, and anything he could do to help the troops he was certainly glad to do. Little did he know that this was a ruse, as set up by Ralph Edwards and his people. Edwards was the host and producer of the popular television series *This Is Your Life,* and Satchel Paige had been chosen for the distinction.

As Paige walked around the group of wounded Vietnam veterans, shaking hands and getting ready to speak, he was surprisingly interrupted by Ralph Edwards, who ushered him over to take the seat center stage and watch as his life story unfolded with special guest appearances. It seemed absolutely clear that Paige was caught totally off guard by this, or if not he was a marvelous actor. One by one they came from offstage to greet him with a little humorous story before moving on and allowing the next surprise guest to come forth. Frank Duncan, his old battery mate and good friend came first; followed by Wilbur Hines, childhood friend from Mobile, Alabama; William Lowe, another former teammate; and Chester Arnold, who received the most enthusiastic bear hug from Paige. Their friendship went all the way back to their childhood days throwing rocks in the streets of Mobile. Next came Ted Page, followed by Newt Allen, and Lou Boudreau, whom Paige likely had some mixed feelings about. The grand entrance was the arrival of Paige's wife, Lahoma, followed by the arrival of Pamela, Carolyn, Linda, Lula, Rita, Warren, and, finally, Robert, who was in the US Air Force at the time and flown in special for the event. Paige was in seventh heaven.

The most emotional moment came when his eldest brother, John, and his wife arrived. John was obviously in declining health and walked with a cane, but he had made the journey from Mobile to honor his famous younger brother. Paige began to tear up; they were tears of joy. At the very end of the program, star African American pitcher Vida Blue of the San Francisco Giants anchored the event and told a nationwide audience what Satchel Paige meant to him, that he was the role model that all young pitchers looked up to. The program aired on January 26, 1972, and brought Paige's story to the attention of new generations who might not have been as familiar with the living icon. To the older generations, it was recognition that was long overdue. No group was happier than African Americans to see *This Is Your Life: Leroy "Satchel" Paige,* although the diehard baseball fans of every ethnicity were a close second.

A biographer later wrote that Paige's mother, "the now ninety-eight-year old Lula Paige," was also one of the surprise guests on the program. If the writer had reviewed the program, he would have seen that Paige's mother was not one of the guests. If she had been, it would have, indeed, been a great "surprise" to Paige and the rest of the family since his mother, Lula Coleman Paige, died in 1966, five years before the program was taped.[47]

There were many honorary dinners and special-recognition ceremonies for Satchel Paige. He, however, still needed to make a living. He had the pension, but additional income certainly would help. There were very few barnstorming gigs now, but he had the name that everyone recognized. He was able to land a job as a deputy at the Jackson County Jail. It was not the best work in the world, but it did not involve any heavy lifting, and Paige kept it light around the facility, with stories and jokes that made things easier for the guards and inmates.

He was approached by a faction of the Democratic Party that wanted to put his name forward as a candidate for the Missouri House of Representatives. Paige accepted and did a bit of campaigning, with family members pitching in. Robert helped him distribute flyers all over town. Paige was serious about the run, and with his name recognition there were some who thought he might actually have a chance, but he lost.

ABC Television announced that it was going to produce a film about Satchel Paige. The film was based on the writings of Dave Lipman, who was managing editor of the *St. Louis Post-Dispatch.* Paige, who was looking frail and in obvious declining health, was brought in as a special consultant for the movie in which he showed up only at the beginning of the first shoot to have his picture taken with Lou Gossett Jr., the star of the film and playing him; George C. Scott, who directed the film; and members of the supporting cast, which included Beverly Todd, Cleavon Little, and Ozzie Davis. Paige received five thousand dollars for his alleged consulting work and use of his name. The film, *Don't Look Back: The Story of Leroy Satchel Paige,* aired in 1981 to mixed reviews.

He was making more frequent trips to the physician these days. His emphysema was worsening. While on a short road trip Paige reported feeling faint and having some difficulty breathing. He was taken immediately to the emergency room, where he was admitted to the intensive care unit and was there for three days before being pronounced healthy enough to go home.

That scare in St. Louis clearly indicated that his traveling days were over. By the end of 1981 his condition required that he use a portable oxygen tank and be confined to a wheelchair. The once confident, invincible, trash-talking, entertaining fastballer for hire, "The World's Greatest Pitcher," knew that he was in the bottom of the ninth and that he would not be able to win it in extra innings.

Fortuitously, the last in-depth interview with Paige was conducted by Bill Ford, a sports reporter with the *Cincinnati Inquirer* and an African American. Ford asked pointed questions, and Paige was in the mood for some good straight talk. The chemistry between the two was evidently right, and, as Ford would later say, it was in part because Ford was asking the questions that needed to be asked and there was a feeling of a mutual understanding too between two black men talking frankly.

Paige, who had reached the plateau of the racial mountain he was climbing, had no other peaks to conquer in his twilight years. Hence, with Ford hitting with the right questions, Paige batted back to him the straight answers. There was no need to sugarcoat things and play the diplomat; that game was over, and he had some points he wanted to make clear. Paige talked about the experiences barnstorming and the problems with accommodations in the fleabag hotels, with "a lot of bedbugs around, I can tell you that, and we used to keep the light on all night. And you had to sleep on paper. That was really the only way you had of scaring them off, it was the rustling of the paper."[48]

When Ford asked him about his experience playing in the Majors and why he thought the color line had been there for so long, Paige was forthright. He thought that he, Jackie Robinson, and the others who were in that first group to break the color line had made a difference, because "we had to show we didn't have tails; that we were as good as anybody; we could do things other people did."[49]

Paige also pointed out that during the years barnstorming, playing those little towns and other locations that basically had never seen black folks before, he suffered every abuse imaginable. "But back then," he told Ford, "they would announce to the world at the ballpark: well we have here today, nigger Satchel Paige and nigger Perkins catching. You understand me? Now would you have took that? How bad could that be? All right, we went on and played, we've been playing all through that kind of mess and that's way before Jackie."[50]

Referring further to Robinson, Paige again stated that he would not have been able to go through what Jackie experienced because his temperament was different. Paige also noted that he came up in an earlier time than Robinson and that it was much tougher than what Jackie experienced. "Jackie didn't have to go through half the back doors as me, nor be insulted for trying to get a sandwich as me, nor be run out of as many places as me. No, there is no baseball player in America that took as much as me, if you want me to tell you the truth." Paige said it was better that Robinson than him had gone first into the Majors and that if it had been him instead, he "might have set the race back 50 or some more years. Because I wouldn't have put up with what Jackie took." Paige also added in support of Robinson that it should not have been that way for him or any of the other black ballplayers: "It shouldn't have been so bad for Jackie either."[51]

When asked to reflect on the early contention at the Hall of Fame that they were going to have him and all the Negro Leagues ballplayers placed in a separate wing upstairs, Paige told Ford that he would not have accepted being in a separate wing, that he would not have accepted being inducted into the Hall of Fame. "No, I wouldn't, I don't think I would have went upstairs, no. I can tell you that now, no. Because—you know I can say it now—I figured and I know I was just as greater pitcher as they ever had in the United States, I know that. And why should I go upstairs by myself when the people—the public—was always saying anyhow, without me being in there at all, that I was the greatest pitcher they ever seen." The two ended their interview, shaking hands and embracing.[52]

The invincible hurler made his last public appearance on Saturday, June 5, 1982, at a KC ballpark that was being named in his honor. Two days later a *derecho* hit the city and other parts of the Midwest. The powerful straight-line storm, with gusts exceeding eighty miles per hour, took off roofs, smashed businesses, caused extensive flash flooding, knocked down trees and power lines, and left more than one hundred thousand residents in KC without electricity, the Paige household among them. It would be four to five days before power was restored to most homes. That Tuesday, June 8, Lahoma made a trip to where ice was being distributed to get some to help her husband cool off a bit since he was complaining of being too warm. When she returned she found him sitting on the side of the bed. She asked him if he was still too warm. He told her no, that, in fact, he was feeling a little chilly. She put her jacket around him. He stretched out on the bed and soon went motionless. Lahoma sensed something was wrong and tried to revive him. He was unresponsive. She called the paramedics and applied cardiopulmonary resuscitation until they arrived. Paige apparently suffered heart failure due to the emphysema. He was rushed to the hospital, where at 1:30 p.m. he was pronounced dead.

Lahoma and the rest of the family had expected the patriarch's demise, given his deteriorating health over the past few years. Nevertheless, when it finally came, it was no less easy to take. He was gone, and the family's sense of loss echoed throughout KC and the entire sporting world. Satchel Paige's death was reported in virtually every newspaper in America, including most small towns. The loss was felt across the borders in Canada, Puerto Rico, Cuba, Venezuela, the Dominican Republic, Mexico, the Philippines, Japan, and the many other ports of call he barnstormed through during his miraculous career spanning four decades.[53]

Funeral services for him were held on the afternoon of Saturday, June 12, 1982. In attendance were family, friends, representatives from the former Negro Leagues, Minor League ball, the Major Leagues, and Missouri local and state governmental officials. Satchel Paige left behind his wife, Lahoma Jean Brown Paige; his daughters, Shirley Long Miller, Pamela Paige O'Neal, Carolyn Paige Mason, Linda Sue Paige, Lula Ouida Paige, and Rita Paige Rogers; and his sons, Robert Leroy Paige and Warren James Paige. He also had two surviving sisters, Palestine Caldwell and Inez Burrington; a niece, Vera Petteway; along with fourteen grandchildren and countless friends and admirers.

Those making remarks at the services included Senator Thomas F. Eagleton, Monte Irvin, Ray Smith of the Red Birds, and John "Buck" O'Neil. The Reverend Emanuel Cleaver, the Paige family minister, delivered the eulogy. The speakers, in their heartfelt condolences, attempted to, somehow, briefly explain the significance of Paige's life. What they were all saying in their own way was what the nation and much of the world had come to understand. Leroy Robert "Satchel" Paige made baseball better and America better along the way. He did that, and it meant so much to so many of us—and still does.

Notes

Warm-ups: A Prelude

1. Interviews with Theodore Roosevelt "Double Duty" Radcliffe, July 1999 and July 2001, Chicago. Other Negro Leaguers expressed similar sentiments: interviews with John "Buck" O'Neil, November 2005 and follow-ups, Negro Leagues Museum, Kansas City, Mo.; and interviews with Hank Aaron, Samuel Allen, George Altman, Jimmy Armstead, Otha Bailey, Ernie Banks, William Barnes, Herbert Barnhill, William Bell, Joseph Black, William Blair, Robert Boyd, William Breda, Sherwood Brewer, Clifford Brown, Ernest Burke, William "Ready" Cash, Henry Clark, James Cohen, James Colzie, Charlie Davis, Ross Davis, Felix Delgado, Wesley Lewis Dennis, Eugene Doby, Larry Doby, Joseph Douse, Mahlon Duckett, James Dudley, William Dumpson, Melvin Duncan, Henry Elmore, Lionel Evelyn, William Felder, Albertus Fennar, Wilmer Fields, John Gibbons, Louis Gillis, Harold Gordon, Harold Gould, Willie Grace, Acie Griggs, Arthur Hamilton, Charles Harmon, Isaiah Harris, Lonnie Harris, Willie Harris, Wilmer Harris, J. C. Hartman, John Head, Neale Henderson, Joe Henry, Francisco Herrera, Carl Holden, Ulysses Holliman, Gordon Hopkins, Cowan Hyde, Monte Irvin, James Ivory, Verdell Jackson, Clarence Jenkins, James "Pee Wee" Jenkins, Sam Jethroe, Clifford Johnson, Curtis Johnson, Donald Johnson, Ernest Johnson, Louis Johnson, Mamie Johnson, Ralph Johnson, Thomas Fairfax Johnson, Cecil Kaiser, Larry Kimbrough, Willie James Lee, Larry LeGrande, William Lindsay, William Little, Anthony Lloyd, Lester Lockett, Carl Long, Ernest Long, Lee Mabon, Raydell Maddix, Josef Marbury, Rendon Marbury, Frank Marsh, Edward Martin, Henry Mason, Willie Mays, Nathaniel McClinic, Clinton McCord, Walter McCoy, William McCrary, Ira McKnight, John Miles, Minnie Minoso, Jesse Mitchell, John Mitchell, James Moore, Robert Motley, Emilio Navarro, Don Newcombe, Orlando O'Farrill, Andrew Porter, Merle Porter, William Powell, Henry Prestwood, Marvin Price, Charlie Pride, Mack Pride, Henry Robinson, James Robinson, William Robinson, Jesse Rogers, Thomas Sampson, James Sanders, Ed Scott, Joseph Scott, Robert Scott, Pedro Sierra, Al Smith, Eugene Smith, George Smith, Quincy Smith, Alfred Surratt, Ron Teasley, Donald Troy, Thomas Turner, William "Cool Breeze" Van Buren, Ernest Westfield, Eugene White, Davey Whitney, Jimmy Wilkes, Clyde Henry Williams, Eli Williams, Eugene Williams, Willie Young, and Jim Zapp.

2. Exclusive interviews with Robert Leroy Paige, February 2006 and follow-ups in 2007–9, O'Fallon, Mo.

3. I had the pleasure to serve as moderator for a session on "Past Time: Baseball as History" at the annual meeting of the Organization of American Historians in Los Angeles in 2001. The session focused on Jules Tygiel's new book of the same title as the session. We had a very distinguished group of discussants: Stanley Cutler of the University of Wisconsin; James Murrin of Princeton; Sharon Robinson, director of Jackie's Nine and daughter of Jackie Robinson; and Jules Tygiel of San Francisco State University. After the well-attended session concluded, I was afforded the opportunity to chat with Sharon Robinson at length about the legacy of her father and her current work. A recent news item had pointed to an interview with a star African American ballplayer in the Major Leagues, who, when the name Jackie Robinson was mentioned to him in the interview, replied, "Who is he?" When the questioner responded back with "the Jackie Robinson," the ballplayer admitted that he had never heard of Jackie Robinson. Sharon Robinson confirmed that most of the Major League ballplayers of color she had come in contact with through her work, whether foreign born or born in the United States, had no knowledge of Jackie Robinson. She hoped to help educate the players, children, and larger public about her father's legacy through the continuing work of her foundation.

4. Exclusive interviews with R. L. Paige; exclusive interviews with Pamela Paige O'Neal, April 2007 and follow-ups, Kansas City, Mo.; interviews with O'Neil.

5. Leroy Satchel Paige (as told to David Lipman), *Maybe I'll Pitch Forever*, 34–35. Paige sometimes called the bat wood or weight. Interviews with Radcliffe.

6. Paige's favorite sayings are compiled in David Sterry's collection, *Satchel Sez: The Wit, Wisdom, and World of Leroy "Satchel" Paige.*

7. See Chapter 6, "How the West Was Won," for full coverage and contextualization.

8. Consult Chapter 11, "Integration," for discussion of the FBI interest in Paige, the Communist Party, and the civil rights movement.

9. Chapter 7, "Baseball Diplomacy," provides a detailed examination of what becomes an involved foreign policy issue.

10. Donald Spivey, "Satchel Paige's Struggle for Selfhood in the Era of Jim Crow," 93.

Chapter 1. Without a Satchel

1. Jerome Cochran, MD, *History of the Small-Pox Epidemic in the City of Mobile, 1874–5, with Mortuary and Meteorological Tables, Also Notes and Reflections upon Diphtheria and Typho-Malarial Fever; Together with an Ordinance to Secure the Public Health,* 3, 6–7, 11, 12, 14–18; Eric D. Duke, "A Life in the Struggle: John L. LeFlore and the Civil Rights Movements in Mobile, Alabama, 1925–1975," 2, 8–13, 15, 17, 24; John L. LeFlore and the civil rights movement in James L. Dixon, *Pictorial History of Mobile Civil Rights: Civil Rights Movement to the 1960's Black Revolution,* 12; David E. Alsobrook, "The Mobile Streetcar Boycott of 1902: African American Protest or Capitulation," 2; *Mobile Southern Watchman,* 8 September 1900; Charles Grayson Summersell, *Mobile: History of a Seaport Town,* 1–81.

2. US Census (1880), Beat 1, Choctaw, Ala., Roll T9, 7, Family History Film 1254007, p. 266.1000, Enumeration District 19; US Census (1880), Albemarle, Va., Roll T9, 1352, Family History Film 1255352, p. 134.3000, Enumeration District 6; US Census (1900), Garritys, Mobile, Ala., Roll T623 32, p. 3B, Enumeration District 116; US Census (1910), Mobile Ward 10, Mobile, Ala., Roll T624 27, p. 11B, Enumeration District 116; US Census (1920), Mobile Ward 9, Mobile, Ala., Roll T625 35, p. 5B, Enumeration District 126; US Census (1930), Mobile, Ala., Roll 42, p. 5B, Enumeration District 84; US Census (1920), Mount Meigs, Montgomery, Ala., Roll T7625 37, p. 4B, Enumeration District 135; *Social*

Security Death Index, Death Master File, Social Security Administration, Citation Number 497-14-0755, Issue State Missouri, Issue Date before 1951; Verification of Birth Record for Leroy Page, 7 July 1906; Issued 5 February 1954, Office of Vital Statistics, County Health Department, Mobile, Ala.; Spivey, "Paige's Struggle for Selfhood," 91–93; Phil Musick, *Hank Aaron: The Man Who Beat the Babe,* 28; Paige, *Maybe I'll Pitch Forever,* 15, 25.

3. Interview with Robert Leroy Paige, February 2006 and follow-ups, O'Fallon, Mo. See also sources listed in note 2.

4. Paige, *Maybe I'll Pitch Forever,* 15–16.

5. Ibid., 16.

6. Ibid.

7. Ibid.

8. Ibid., passim; Leroy Satchel Paige (as told to Hal Lebovitz), *Pitchin' Man: Satchel Paige's Own Story,* xiv, 18–29. See also Henry Louis Gates Jr., *Signifying Monkey: A Theory of African-American Literary Criticism,* 52, 56, 99–101; and Robin D. G. Kelley, *Yo' Mama's Disfunktional: Fighting the Culture Wars in Urban America,* 1–2, 32–35.

9. Paige, *Pitchin' Man,* 17.

10. Interviews with Theodore Roosevelt "Double Duty" Radcliffe, July 1999 and July 2001, Chicago.

11. Paige, *Maybe I'll Pitch Forever,* 17–18; "Satch Got Hesitation Pitch in 'Brick Wars' as a Tyke," *Miami Herald,* 2 October 1971, clipping in Ashland Collection.

12. Ibid.

13. Minutes of the Meetings of the Board of School Commissioners, Mobile, Ala., 13 November 1913, as cited in Bessie Mae Holloway, "A History of Public School Education in Mobile, Alabama, for the Child under Six Years of Age, 1833–1928," 28, 43, 161–164; George Edmund Haynes, "Conditions among Negroes in the Cities," 110; Petition, Interdenominational Ministers Union of Colored Clergymen to the Mayor and Board of Commissioners, 10 January 1913, Records of the Mobile City Commission, Mobile Municipal Archives, as cited in Alsobrook, "Mobile Streetcar Boycott of 1902," 7, 11; Henry C. Williams, *A History of Mobile County Training School,* 1–14; Marilyn Mannhard, "The Free People of Color in Antebellum Mobile County, Alabama," 15, 39, 41, 43; Miscellaneous Books of the Probate Court, Books C and D, 1837–45; *U.S. Census Reports, 1840, 1860, 1880, 1890,* Mobile Public Library; Willis G. Clark, *History of Education in Alabama, 1702–1889,* 220, 262, 269. The first school to train colored teachers in Alabama was the Huntsville Colored Normal School in 1875. In 1878 W. H. Council was the principal. W. Clark, *History of Education in Alabama,* 277. See also Paige, *Maybe I'll Pitch Forever,* 19.

14. Paige, *Maybe I'll Pitch Forever,* 23.

15. Ibid., 20.

16. Ibid., 15, 16.

17. Ibid.

18. Interviews with Radcliffe; Minutes of the Meetings of the Board of School Commissioners, Mobile, Ala., 13 November 1913, as cited in B. M. Holloway, "History of Public School Education," 28, 43, 161–164; Haynes, "Conditions among Negroes in the Cities," 110; Petition, Interdenominational Ministers Union of Colored Clergymen to the Mayor and Board of Commissioners, 10 January 1913, Records of the Mobile City Commission, Mobile Municipal Archives, as cited in Alsobrook, "Mobile Streetcar Boycott of 1902," 7, 11; Williams, *History of Mobile County Training School,* 1–14; Mannhard, "Free People of Color," 15, 39, 41, 43; Miscellaneous Books of the Probate Court, Books C and D, 1837–45; *U.S. Census Reports, 1840, 1860, 1880, 1890,* Mobile Public Library; W. Clark, *History of Education in Alabama,* 220, 262, 269. The first school to train colored teachers in Alabama was the Huntsville Colored Normal School in 1875. In 1878, Mr. W. H.

Council was the principal; W. Clark, *History of Education in Alabama*, 277. See also Paige, *Maybe I'll Pitch Forever*, 19.

19. Paige, *Maybe I'll Pitch Forever*, 22.

20. Interviews with Radcliffe.

21. Frank W. Crenshaw to Booker T. Washington, 6 January 1913, and Washington to Crenshaw, 10 January 1913, Booker T. Washington Papers; Paige, *Maybe I'll Pitch Forever*, 15.

22. Crenshaw to Washington, 6 January 1913, Washington Papers.

23. Ibid.

24. Ibid. For further discussion of the "uppity Negro" issue and the dynamic of racial tensions, the best analysis is still Joel Williamson, *A Rage for Order: Black-White Relations in the American South since Emancipation*. See also Tim Tyson, *Radio Free Dixie: Robert F. Williams and the Roots of Black Power*; and, specifically relating to the issue of sport, Randy Roberts, *Papa Jack: Jack Johnson and the Era of White Hopes*; and Al-Tony Gilmore, *Bad Nigger: The National Impact of Jack Johnson*.

25. Williams, *History of Mobile County Training School*, 18–21; Council Traditional School, Miscellaneous File Clippings, Mobile Public Library; Paige, *Maybe I'll Pitch Forever*, 23–24; "Satch Got Hesitation Pitch in 'Brick Wars' as a Tyke," *Miami Herald*, 2 October 1971, clipping in Ashland Collection.

Chapter 2. On the Mount

1. *Steele v. Louisville & Nashville Ry. Co., No. 45, Argued Nov. 14, 15, 1944, Decided Dec. 18, 1944*, 322 US 192, 193 (1944). For further discussion of Houston and the L&N case, see Genna Rae McNeil, *Groundwork: Charles Hamilton Houston and the Struggle for Civil Rights*, 162–71; and Hugh Williamson, "The Role of the Courts in the Status of the Negro." See also Charles B. Castner, *A Brief History of the Louisville and Nashville Railroad*, 1–5; and John B. Scott Jr., *Memories of the Mount: The Story of Mt. Meigs, Alabama*, 126–28, 155–57, 191–94.

2. Paige, *Maybe I'll Pitch Forever*, 16.

3. *Annual Report of the Alabama Reform School for Juvenile Negro Law Breakers* (1918–19), 271; *Annual Report of the Alabama Reform School for Juvenile Negro Law Breakers* (1922), 278–79; *Colored Alabamian*, 14 March 1908, 1, 25 July 1908, 3; photographs and notes pertaining to 1922 and 1923 site visits to the Alabama Reform School for Juvenile Negro Law-Breakers, Jackson Davis Collection.

4. "The 25th Anniversary of Mt. Meigs Colored Institute," *Colored Alabamian*, 19 April 1913, 1; "Great Meeting State Federation Colored Women," *Colored Alabamian*, 13 July 1912, 1; US Census (1910), Mount Meigs, Montgomery, Ala., Roll To24 28, Page 15A, Enumeration District 123; US Census (1890), Tuskegee, Macon, Ala., Roll T9 21; Family History Film 1254021, p. 442.1000, Enumeration District 119; US Census (1910), Mount Meigs, Montgomery, Ala., Roll T624 28, p. 4B, Enumeration District 123; US Census (1920), Mount Meigs, Montgomery, Ala., Roll T625.37, p. 3A, Enumeration District 135; A. Simms, Principal, *Annual Report of the Alabama Reform School for Juvenile Negro Law Breakers* (1918–19), 271; *Annual Report of the Alabama Reform School for Juvenile Negro Law Breakers* (1922), 278–79; Cornelia Bowen to W. H. Stovey, 5 June 1902, Washington Papers; US Census (1910), Mount Meigs, Montgomery, Ala., Roll T624 28, p. 4B, Enumeration District 123; Booker T. Washington, ed., *Tuskegee and Its People: Their Ideals and Achievements*, 211–23; Cornelia Bowen, "The Mission of the Negro Woman," *Colored Alabamian*, 24 July 1915, 2; "The Women, God's Police Force," *Colored*

Alabamian, 1 August 1908; "Reformatory Boys Picnic, Mt. Meigs, Ala., Sept. 25, 1908," *Colored Alabamian,* 1; "Cornelia Bowen," in *Notable Black American Women,* edited by Jessie Carney Smith, 45–48; Jerome A. Gray et al., *History of the Alabama State Teachers Association,* 71–72; Floris Barnett Cash, "Kinship and Quilting: An Examination of an African-American Tradition," 36; "Cornelia Bowen," photo negative no. 2368, Davis Collection; "Mount Meigs Reform School for Juvenile Negro Law Breakers, Main Building, 26 September 1922," photo negative no. 6329, Special Collections, University of Virginia Library; "Party Visiting Cornelia Bowen's School Montgomery County Training School, 26 April 1923," photo negative no. 2369, Special Collections, University of Virginia Library; Benjamin Brawley, *Women of Achievement: Written for the Fireside Schools under the Auspices of the Women's American Baptist Home Mission Society,* 12; *Annual Report, 1993–1997,* State of Alabama.

5. "The 25th Anniversary of Mt. Meigs Colored Institute," *Colored Alabamian,* 19 April 1913, 1.

6. Mary Church Terrell, "The Progress of Colored Women," Presidential Address, National Association of Colored Women, 18 February 1898, 5–6, Library of Congress.

7. See Cornelia Bowen to W. H. Stovey, 5 June 1902, Bowen to Washington, 5 June and 31 July 1903, and Washington to Bowen, 11 December 1912, Washington Papers; photographs and notes pertaining to 1922 and 1923 site visits to the Alabama Reform School for Juvenile Negro Law-Breakers, Davis Collection.

8. "Great Meeting State Federation Colored Women," *Colored Alabamian,* 13 July 1912, 1; Simms, *Annual Report of the Alabama Reform School for Juvenile Negro Law Breakers* (1918–19), 271; *Annual Report of the Alabama Reform School for Juvenile Negro Law Breakers* (1922), 278–79; Cornelia Bowen, "The Mission of the Negro Woman," *Colored Alabamian,* 24 July 1915, 2; "Sixty-One Boys in Reformatory," *Colored Alabamian,* 13 July 1912, 1.

9. "The Women, God's Police Force," *Colored Alabamian,* 1 August 1908.

10. "Great Meeting State Federation Colored Women," *Colored Alabamian,* 13 July 1912, 1. See also *Social Betterment among Negro Americans: A Social Study Made by Atlanta University, under the Patronage of the Trustees of the John F. Slater Fund,* 53–57.

11. *Annual Report of the Alabama Reform School for Juvenile Negro Law Breakers* (1922), 279; *Annual Report of the Alabama Reform School for Juvenile Negro Law Breakers* (1923), 232–33; Edgar W. Knight, Survey Staff Director, "A Study of Higher Education in Alabama," Montgomery, Ala., June 1940, 6, SG13206, Alabama State Archives; "The 25th Anniversary of Mt. Meigs Colored Institute," *Colored Alabamian,* 19 April 1913, 1. The Alabama Reform School for Juvenile Negro Law-Breakers at Mount Meigs was created, according to the State of Alabama, "to provide for the training of juvenile negro law breakers" (Ala. Acts, 544, p. 802 [1923]). In 1931 the law was amended to retain girls at Mount Meigs as well. At the end of the juvenile's sentence the inmate was discharged on the approval of the Board of Trustees or the Executive Committee of the school and the governor. Bylaws and Rules and Regulations of the Alabama Reform School for Juvenile Negro Law-Breakers, Article V, p. 13 [1916]); "Closing Session, Department of Public School Instruction, State Reform School for Negro Boys, Mt. Meigs, Alabama, May 19, 1916, Program," SP 362, Alabama State Archives; Washington to Bowen, 11 December 1912, Washington Papers.

12. Ibid.; US Census (1920), Mount Meigs, Montgomery, Ala., Roll T625.37, p. 3A, Enumeration District 135; Simms, *Annual Report of the Alabama Reform School for Juvenile Negro Law Breakers* (1918–19), 271; *Social Betterment among Negro Americans,* 53–57.

13. See US Census (1920), Mount Meigs, Montgomery, Ala., Roll T625.37, p. 3A, Enumeration District 135. Note the corrections the bureau had to later make to the spelling of his name and information regarding age.

14. See sources in note 12; Paige, *Maybe I'll Pitch Forever,* 24–27. See also photographs and notes pertaining to 1922 and 1923 site visits to the Alabama Reform School for Juvenile Negro Law-Breakers, Davis Collection.

15. Paige, *Maybe I'll Pitch Forever,* 24.

16. Washington to Bowen, 11 December 1912, Washington Papers.

17. Ibid.; Paige, *Maybe I'll Pitch Forever,* 24–27. See also *Annual Report of the Alabama Reform School for Juvenile Negro Law Breakers* (1922), 279; *Annual Report of the Alabama Reform School for Juvenile Negro Law Breakers* (1923), 232–33; Knight, "Study of Higher Education in Alabama"; and "The 25th Anniversary of Mt. Meigs Colored Institute," *Colored Alabamian,* 19 April 1913, 1.

18. "Closing Session, Department of Public School Instruction"; *Colored Alabamian,* 25 July 1908, 7. The tradition and pattern were clearly established.

19. Ibid.

20. Exclusive interviews with Robert Leroy Paige, February 2006 and follow-ups in 2007 and 2008, O'Fallon, Mo.; Paige, *Maybe I'll Pitch Forever,* 25.

21. Richard Dittmer, "An Exploration of the Motivating Forces behind Brig. General R. H. Pratt's Creation of the Indian Industrial School at Carlisle, Pennsylvania," 2, 7, 12, 27; Vine Deloria cited in ibid., 27; Chief Spotted Tail cited in Linda F. Witmer, *The Indian Industrial School, Carlisle, Pennsylvania, 1879–1918,* 14. For Pratt's own words, see Richard H. Pratt, *Battlefield and Classroom: Four Decades with the American Indian, 1867–1904,* 220, and "The Indian No Problem," 9 May 1904, 1–2, 18, Richard H. Pratt Papers. See also Michael L. Cooper, *Indian School: Teaching the White Man's Way;* Mark O. Hagenbuch, "Richard Henry Pratt, the Carlisle Indian Industrial School, and U.S. Policies Related to American Indian Education, 1879 to 1904," 61, 66; Samuel Chapman Armstrong, "Indian Education in the East," *Southern Workman,* November 1880, Armstrong Family Papers; Donald Spivey, *Schooling for the New Slavery: Black Industrial Education, 1868–1915,* 23, 13–41; Jorge Noriega, "American Indian Education in the United States: Indoctrination for Subordination to Colonialism"; Mike Bynum, ed., *Pop Warner, Football's Greatest Teacher: The Epic Autobiography of Major College Football's Winningest Coach, Glenn S. (Pop) Warner,* 17; Glenn S. Warner, *Pop Warner's Book for Boys,* 7, 13, 20, 35, 36–51; and "Reformatory Boys Picnic, Mt. Meigs, Ala., Sept. 25, 1908," *Colored Alabamian,* 1.

22. F. C. Lane to Washington, 13 January 1913, and Washington to Lane, 21 January 1913, Washington Papers. See also Bowen to Washington, 31 July 1903, Washington Papers; Booker T. Washington, "William Henry Lewis," 34–37; Washington to Bowen, 12 December 1903, Washington Papers; Booker T. Washington, "Signs of Progress among the Negroes"; *Colored Alabamian,* 18 March 1911, 3; Wayne Stewart, *Babe Ruth: A Biography,* 4–6; John B. Holway, *Josh and Satch: The Life and Times of Josh Gibson and Satchel Paige,* 2; and Roberts, *Papa Jack,* 5–6, 97–98, 112–114.

23. Lane to Washington, 13 January 1913, and Washington to Lane, 21 January 1913, Washington Papers.

24. Frank C. Caffey, "Give the Young Afro-American in the Southern Industrial Schools an Athletic Chance," *Colored Alabamian,* 13 February 1909, 6.

25. "The 25th Anniversary of Mt. Meigs Colored Institute," *Colored Alabamian,* 19 April 1913, 1. See also Lane to Washington, 13 January 1913, Washington to Lane, 21 January 1913, and Bowen to Washington, 31 July 1903, Washington Papers; Washington, "William Henry Lewis"; Washington to Bowen, 12 December 1903, Washington Papers; Washington, "Signs of Progress"; and *Colored Alabamian,* 18 March 1911, 3.

26. "Reformatory Boys Picnic, Mt. Meigs, Ala., Sept. 25, 1908," *Colored Alabamian*, 1. Unfortunately, the *Colored Alabamian* had ceased publication by the time Paige entered Mount Meigs. During his time on the Mount, he likely followed the same program that had become a tradition.

27. Ibid.

28. Ibid.; Dialogue with community leaders at Waugh Baptist Church, February 1999 and June 2006.

29. Paige, *Maybe I'll Pitch Forever*, 26; US Census (1920), Mount Meigs, Montgomery, Ala., Roll T625.37, p. 3A, Enumeration District 135.

30. Paige, *Maybe I'll Pitch Forever*, 25.

31. Mark Ribowsky states that "the Mount's coach, Edward Byrd, whose simple but valuable instruction made Leroy Page whole. At Byrd's insistence, Satch began to kick his front foot high into the air." Ribowsky, *Don't Look Back: Satchel Paige in the Shadows of Baseball*, 34. Ribowsky provides no documentation to support his claim, and the entire book is without footnotes. Byrd is fictitious. See *Annual Report of the Alabama Reform School for Juvenile Negro Law Breakers* (1922), 279; *Annual Report of the Alabama Reform School for Juvenile Negro Law Breakers* (1923); Knight, "Study of Higher Education"; "The 25th Anniversary of Mt. Meigs Colored Institute," *Colored Alabamian*, 19 April 1913, 1; US Census (1920), Mount Meigs, Montgomery, Ala., Roll T625.37, p. 3A, Enumeration District 135, and US Census (1930), same district; Simms, *Annual Report of the Alabama Reform School for Juvenile Negro Law Breakers* (1918–19), 271; *Annual Report of the Alabama Reform School for Juvenile Negro Law Breakers* (1922), 278–79; Cornelia Bowen, "The Mission of the Negro Woman," *Colored Alabamian*, 24 July 1915, 2; Bowen to Washington, 31 July 1903, and Washington to Bowen, 11 December 1912, Washington Papers; and interviews with Theodore Roosevelt "Double Duty" Radcliffe, July 1999 and July 2001, Chicago.

32. Bynum, *Pop Warner*, 17. See also Warner, *Pop Warner's Book for Boys*, 7, 13, 20, 35, 36–51; and "Reformatory Boys Picnic, Mt. Meigs, Ala., Sept. 25, 1908," *Colored Alabamian*, 1.

33. Paige, *Maybe I'll Pitch Forever*, 26.

34. Ibid.

35. Andrew Dietz, *The Last Folk Hero: A True Story of Race and Art, Power and Profit*, 4–8; Johnny Bodley, *These Eyes*, 42, 43, 44, 53; *Selma Times*, 17 December 2002, 2–4; Scott, *Memories of the Mount*, 126–28, 155–57; Stewart, *Babe Ruth: A Biography*, 4–6 and passim.

36. Paige, *Maybe I'll Pitch Forever*, 26; *This Is Your Life: Leroy "Satchel" Paige* (Ralph Edwards Productions, taped 22 October 1971, aired 22 January 1972).

Chapter 3. "If You Were Only White"

1. "Satchel Paige as Told to William Dismukes," Ashland Collection; Paige, *Maybe I'll Pitch Forever*, 29; Joe Cuhaj and Tamra Carraway-Hinckle, *Baseball in Mobile*, 9–14, 20–33, 65, 68; exclusive interviews with Robert Leroy Paige, February 2006, O'Fallon, Mo.

2. Ibid.

3. Interviews with John "Buck" O'Neil, November 2005 and follow-ups, Negro Leagues Museum, Kansas City, Mo.; interviews with Theodore Roosevelt "Double Duty" Radcliffe, July 1999 and July 2001, Chicago. Booker McDaniel, a pitcher with the Kansas City Monarchs in the 1950s and lifelong friend of Satchel Paige, confirmed the power and accuracy of Paige's pitching on many occasions in conversations overheard by Paige family members in later years. Exclusive interviews with R. L. Paige, February 2006 and follow-ups in 2007–9; exclusive interviews with Pamela Paige O'Neal, April 2007, Kansas City, Mo.

4. Interviews with O'Neil.

5. Ibid.

6. Paige, *Maybe I'll Pitch Forever,* 34–35.

7. Ibid., 32.

8. Ibid.

9. Paige, *Pitchin' Man,* 27–28.

10. Ibid.

11. Exclusive interviews with R. L. Paige; exclusive interviews with P. P. O'Neal.

12. Interviews with O'Neil; interviews with Radcliffe; exclusive interviews with R. L. Paige. Many players who faced Satchel Paige said much the same in interviews and in various print sources. See, for example, *The Negro Leagues Players' Reunion Alumni Book;* and Lawrence Hogan, *Shades of Glory: The Negro Leagues and the Story of African-American Baseball.*

13. Paige, *Maybe I'll Pitch Forever,* 40–41.

14. Donald Spivey, "The Sports Front," in *Fire from the Soul: A History of the African-American Struggle,* 245–59; Spivey, "Paige's Struggle for Selfhood"; Donald Spivey, "End Jim Crow in Sports: The Leonard Bates Controversy at New York University, 1940–1941," revised and reprinted in *Sport and the Color Line,* edited by Patrick Miller and David Wiggins, 147–66; Paige, *Maybe I'll Pitch Forever;* interviews with Radcliffe. For further examination of the notorious "hot bed" in the African American experience, see the classic Roi Ottley and William J. Weatherby, *The Negro in New York: An Informal Social History, 1628–1940,* 266–67.

15. Ibid.

16. Ibid.

17. See note 14.

18. Chattanooga African American Museum, *Black America Series: Chattanooga,* 6–9, 73–88; James Livingood, "Before and after Jim Crow," in *Chattanooga: An Illustrated History,* 99–104; US Census (1920), Chattanooga; Gilbert E. Govan and James Livingood, *The Chattanooga Country, 1540–1976,* 404–6; Charles A. McMurry, *Chattanooga: Its History and Geography,* 140–41; Paul Oliver, *Bessie Smith,* 2–7.

19. For a reliable report of Paige's stats, see Dick Clark and Larry Lester, eds., *The Negro Leagues Book,* 328.

20. William Price Fox, *Satchel Paige's America,* 42–43. Fox offers some interesting quotes from Paige based on a series of interviews he did with him thirty years ago. The interviews were not recorded, and Fox jotted down his notes from memory after each interview. The book does not contain an index. For an intriguing discussion of stunting and showboating in African American cultural tradition and in the world of Louis Armstrong, see Gerald Early, *Tuxedo Junction: Essays on American Culture,* 298–300.

21. Ibid.

22. Dale Somers, *The Rise of Sports in New Orleans, 1850–1900,* 130–31, 274, 284–86; Jack V. Buerkle and Danny Barker, *Bourbon Street Black: The New Orleans Black Jazzman,* 5, 18–20, 24; Alan Lomax, *Mister Jelly Roll;* Ilse Storb, *Louis Armstrong: The Definitive Biography,* 3, 13–21; Paige, *Pitchin' Man* and *Maybe I'll Pitch Forever,* 44 and passim.

23. Ibid.

24. Ibid.

25. Bell said that he and Paige were driving through the South when Paige got the forty-dollar fine for speeding and gave the magistrate eighty. Interview with Cool Papa Bell as cited in Jim Bankes, *The Pittsburgh Crawfords,* 88; interviews with Radcliffe; interviews with O'Neil; exclusive interviews with R. L. Paige.

26. Ibid.

27. John Haddock and Steven Ross, *Black Diamonds Blues City: Stories of the Memphis Red Sox*; Larry Nager, *Memphis Beat: The Lives and Times of America's Musical Crossroads*, 24, 14–31; Robert Palmer, *Deep Blues: A Musical and Cultural History of the Mississippi Delta*, 120–23, 152, 225–27; Keith Wailoo, *Dying in the City of the Blues: Sickle Cell Anemia and the Politics of Race and Health*, 27–35 and passim; W. C. Handy, *Father of the Blues: An Autobiography*, 91; Fox, *Satchel Paige's America*, 37–52.

28. Ibid.

29. Ibid.

30. Handy, *Father of the Blues*, 89–121, 178–85.

31. Paige, *Maybe I'll Pitch Forever*, 44.

Chapter 4. Turning the Paige

1. William Moore, "Serving the Black Barons," *Birmingham Reporter*, 11 June 1927, 3.

2. *Financial Chronicle*, 23 September 1865, 387; *Financial Chronicle*, 11 November 1865, 612; *Financial Chronicle*, 20 January 1866, 68; *Financial Chronicle*, 20 June 1868, 262; *Financial Chronicle*, 11 September 1886, 302; *Birmingham Daily News*, 20 April 1894; US Census (1912), 1870–1900: Population; Herbert Gutman, "Black Workers and Labor Unions and Birmingham, Alabama," unpublished manuscript (1971); US Senate Committee on Education and Labor, "Testimony before the Committee to Investigate the Relations between Capital and Labor 4 (Washington, DC: US Government Printing Office, 1885), 47, 483; C. Vann Woodward, *Origins of the New South, 1877–1913*; Ethel Ames, *The Story of Coal and Iron in Alabama*; Spivey, *Schooling for the New Slavery*, 70–73; Christopher Fullerton, *The Story of the Birmingham Black Barons*, 1–94.

3. Fullerton, *Story of the Birmingham Black Barons*, 3–5.

4. Player comments captured in *Birmingham Black Barons* (1995), Peabody Collection, #96004DCT. This is a valuable documentary film on the Black Barons. Bill Ford interview with Satchel Paige, "Looking Back, Paige Relates Good and Bad," *Cincinnati Inquirer*, 24 June 1981, D4, 46, copy also in Ashland Collection.

5. Ibid. See also William A. Nunnelley, *Bull Connor*, 11, 108–17; Andrew M. Manis, *A Fire You Can't Put Out: The Civil Rights Life of Birmingham's Reverend Fred Shuttlesworth*, 12–14, 80; and "South Must Solve Race Problem Says Alexander," *Birmingham Reporter*, 7 May 1927, 1.

6. *Birmingham Reporter*, 23 April 1927, 1.

7. "Near Riot at St. Louis When Donaldson Removes Pitcher," *Chicago Defender*, 2 July 1927, 4.

8. "Fight at St. Louis Park Hall's Third Game; Near Riot as Mitchell Chases Paige with Bat," *Birmingham Reporter*, 2 July 1927, 3.

9. Ibid.

10. "Black Barons Divide Couple with Monarchs," *Birmingham Reporter*, 20 August 1927, 7.

11. "Black Barons in Front of League Race," *Birmingham Reporter*, 17 September 1927, 7.

12. "Black Barons Take Lead in National League Race," *Birmingham Reporter*, 17 September 1927, 7.

13. "Playoff to Open Monday in South Land," *Chicago Defender*, 17 September 1927, 5; "Playoffs between Barons and American Giants Will Resume in Chicago," *Chicago Defender*, 24 September 1927, 4; "American Giants Cop Playoff from Birmingham Barons," *Chicago Defender*, 1 October 1927, 5.

14. "Detroit Has Hard Time to Beat Barons," *Chicago Defender,* 15 September 1928, 8.

15. Fullerton, *Story of the Birmingham Black Barons,* 41. See also "Records of Leroy 'Satchel' Paige," in *The Negro Leagues Book,* edited by D. Clark and Lester.

16. *Chicago Defender,* 9 August 1930, 8.

17. William Dismukes, "Ye Olde Stove League," *Pittsburgh Courier,* 5 January 1929, 1.

18. John B. Holway, *Josh and Satch: The Life and Times of Josh Gibson and Satchel Paige,* 18 and passim; Adrian Burgos Jr., *Playing America's Game: Baseball, Latinos, and the Color Line,* 164–73.

19. Ibid.

20. Fullerton, *Story of the Birmingham Black Barons,* 42; James H. Bready, *Baseball in Baltimore,* 166–69.

21. Bready, *Baseball in Baltimore,* 166–69; "Inspired Black Sox Win Two," *Pittsburgh Courier,* 9 August 1930, 5; "Black Sox Here This Weekend," *Pittsburgh Courier,* 13 September 1930, 4; and see Chapter 5, "Blackballing the Great Depression."

22. Russell Cowans, "Through the Sport Mirror," *Chicago Defender,* 30 August 1930, 8.

23. "Inspired Black Sox Win Two," *Pittsburgh Courier,* 9 August 1930, 5.

24. *Chicago Defender,* 20 September 1930, 8.

Chapter 5. Blackballing the Great Depression

1. Paige, *Maybe I'll Pitch Forever,* 56–57.

2. "Satchel Twirls 10–2 Cleveland Win over Cincy," *Chicago Defender,* 25 July 1931, 8. See also "Tom Wilson to Operate Baseball Team in Cleveland," *Chicago Defender,* 2 May 1931, 9; "Detroit Stars Grab Three from the Cleveland Cubs," *Chicago Defender,* 4 July 1931, 8; Bill Gibson, "Hear Me Talkin' to Ya," *Baltimore Afro-American,* 22 August 1931; "Southern Stars: Tom Wilson and His Elite Giants," *Black Ball News,* June 1992, 1–8; Richard Bak, *Turkey Stearnes and the Detroit Stars: The Negro Leagues in Detroit, 1919–1933,* 50–59, 63, 67–68, 76, 92–144, 177; Brad Snyder, *Beyond the Shadow of the Senators: The Untold Story of the Homestead Grays and the Integration of Baseball,* 36, 41, 44, 51, 113, 129.

3. Bill Gibson, "Hear Me Talkin' to Ya," *Baltimore Afro-American,* 22 August 1931; Bak, *Turkey Stearnes and the Detroit Stars,* 50–59, 63, 67–68, 76, 92–144, 177.

4. *Pittsburgh Courier,* 20 June 1931, 4; interviews with Theodore Roosevelt "Double Duty" Radcliffe, July 1999 and July 2001, Chicago; *Pittsburgh Courier,* 16 July 1932, 5; "No-Hit, No-Run Hero," *Pittsburgh Courier,* 16 July 1932, 4; *Baltimore Afro-American,* 16 July 1932, 14; "Craws Pitchers' Records," *Pittsburgh Courier,* 27 August 1932, 4; Bankes, *The Pittsburgh Crawfords,* 19–22; Larry Lester and Sammy J. Miller, *Black Baseball in Pittsburgh,* 25–53; *Pittsburgh Courier,* 16 July 1932, 5; *Baltimore Afro-American,* 16 July 1932, 14; *Pittsburgh Courier,* 23 July 1932, 9; "Craws Pitchers' Records," *Pittsburgh Courier,* 27 August 1932, 4.

5. "Paige Stops Grays as Crawfords Cop," *Pittsburgh Courier,* 8 August 1931, 5. See also *Pittsburgh Courier,* 16 July 1932, 5; "No-Hit, No-Run Hero," *Pittsburgh Courier* 16 July 1932, 4; *Baltimore Afro-American,* 16 July 1932, 14; *Pittsburgh Courier,* 23 July 1932, 9; "Craws Pitchers' Records," *Pittsburgh Courier,* 27 August 1932, 4; "Spirited Rally by Monroe Nipped as Paige Wins Classic," *Pittsburgh Courier,* 10 September 1932, 5; and *Pittsburgh Courier,* 17 September 1932, 5.

6. "Paige Stops Grays as Crawfords Cop," *Pittsburgh Courier,* 8 August 1931, 5.

7. Interviews with Radcliffe.

8. "Posey's All-American Ball Club," *Pittsburgh Courier,* 10 October 1931, 5.

9. Janet A. Howard, US Census (1920), Pittsburgh Ward 5, Allegheny, Pa.; Roll T625

1520, p. 18, Enumeration District 388; Luella C. Howard, US Census (1930), Pittsburgh Ward 5, Allegheny, Pa.; Roll 1971, p. 14B, Enumeration District: 1; George H. Howard, US Census (1930), New York; Roll 1576, p. 194, Enumeration District 1003; Paige, *Maybe I'll Pitch Forever*, 74; "Crawfords Win Dixie Opener," *Pittsburgh Courier*, 7 April 1934, 4; "Foster Beaten, Paige Is Winner," *Pittsburgh Courier*, 19 May 1934, 4; *Pittsburgh Courier*, 2 June 1934, 7; interviews with Radcliffe.

10. This is a composite. Paige was treated like a king in Pittsburgh after defeating the Grays. See Paige, *Pitchin' Man*, 30–33 and passim; Paige, *Maybe I'll Pitch Forever*, 52–72 and passim; interviews with Radcliffe; and Bankes, *The Pittsburgh Crawfords*, 3, 21–35.

11. *Pittsburgh Courier*, 7 May 1932, 5.

12. Ibid.; interviews with Radcliffe.

13. *Pittsburgh Courier*, 7 May 1932, 5.

14. Ibid.

15. Interviews with John "Buck" O'Neil, November 2005 and follow-ups, Negro Leagues Museum, Kansas City, Mo.

16. Interviews with Radcliffe.

17. *Pittsburgh Courier*, 16 July 1932, 4.

18. Paige, *Maybe I'll Pitch Forever*, 82.

19. Ibid.; "West Wallops East," *Chicago Defender*, 16 August 1933, 8. For more on the lead-up to the game, see also "Big Crowd to Watch Chi-Craw Battle," *Pittsburgh Courier*, 22 July 1933, 5; "Giants Nip Craws in 15th," *Chicago Defender*, 29 July 1933, 8; "Betting Even on Big Game If Foster and Paige Start," *Chicago Defender*, 9 September 1933, copy in Ashland Collection; and Al Monroe, "Speaking of Sports," *Chicago Defender*, 19 August 1933, 8.

20. "Satchel Paige Is Free Agent," *Chicago Defender*, 28 January 1933, 8; *Chicago Defender*, 18 March 1933, 8; *Chicago Defender*, 15 April 1933, 8; "Satchel Paige Is Warned to Report," *Chicago Defender*, 22 April 1933, 8; *Chicago Defender*, 17 June 1933, 8; *Chicago Defender*, 8 July 1933, 8; *Chicago Defender*, 15 July 1933, 8; *Chicago Defender*, 22 July 1933, 8; "Stage All-Star Game at Sox Park," *Chicago Defender*, 5 August 1933, 9; *Chicago Defender*, 18 August 1933, 8; "Satchel Paige May Quit Craws," *Chicago Defender*, 19 August 1933, 8; *Chicago Defender*, 26 August 1933, 9; *Chicago Defender*, 2 September 1933, 8; *Chicago Defender*, 4 September 1933, 9; "20,000 See West Beat East in Baseball Game of Games," *Chicago Defender*, 16 September 1933, 24; "S. Paige Keeps Winning Pace on the Coast," *Chicago Defender*, 11 November 1933, 8; "Paige's Streak Is Finally Broken, 4–1," *Chicago Defender*, 2 December 1933, 8; "Paige Holding Usual," *Chicago Defender*, 30 December 1933, 8; Paige, *Maybe I'll Pitch Forever*, 83.

21. "Paige Hurls No-Hit Classic," *Pittsburgh Courier*, 7 July 1934, 1, 4.

22. "1934 Was Satchel's Biggest Year, Belief," *Pittsburgh Courier*, 17 November 1934, 4.

23. "Says Satchel Paige," *Pittsburgh Courier*, 11 August 1934, 4; "East-West Classic at Comiskey Park Sunday, August 26," *Pittsburgh Courier*, 14 July 1934, 5; "1934 Was Satchel's Biggest Year, Belief," *Pittsburgh Courier*, 17 November 1934, 4. For complete coverage of the East-West All-Star Game, see Larry Lester, *Black Baseball's National Showcase: The East-West All-Star Game, 1933–1953*. See also Leslie Heaphy, ed., *Black Baseball and Chicago*, 173–98.

24. "As Speedball Satchel Paige Ambled into the East-West Game and Simply Stole the Show," *Pittsburgh Courier*, 1 September 1934, 4; interviews with Radcliffe.

25. Interviews with Radcliffe.

26. Ibid.

27. Ibid.

28. Ibid.

29. "Paige Beats Foster in Great Mound Duel," *Baltimore Afro-American,* 1 September 1934, 16; "Wilson Single Scores Bell as 25,000 Thrill," *Pittsburgh Courier,* 1 September 1934, 5; "Looking Back at the East-West Classic in Chi," *Pittsburgh Courier,* 8 September 1934, 5; "Southern Fans Eye All-Star Game," *Chicago Defender,* 4 August 1934, 16; *Chicago Defender,* 25 August 1934, 17; "Paige and Foster to Open Big Game," *Chicago Defender,* 25 August 1934, 17; *Chicago Defender,* 18 August 1934, 16; *Chicago Defender,* 1 September 1934, 17; "East Beats West in 1–0 Thriller," *Chicago Defender,* 1 September 1934, 16; "1934 Was Satchel's Biggest Year, Belief," *Pittsburgh Courier,* 17 November 1934, 4.

30. Ibid.; Lester, *Black Baseball's National Showcase,* 46–62.

31. Donald Spivey, ed., *Union and the Black Musician: The Narrative of William Everett Samuels and Chicago Local 208,* 38–42, 47, 94.

32. "Earl Hines Band Joins National MCA," *Chicago Defender,* 14 January 1933; "Bill Robinson Here in Route to Louis's Fight," *Chicago Defender,* 22 June 1935, 2; "Bill Robinson Passes through One Way to Fight," *Chicago Defender,* 29 June 1935, 7; "One Mayor to Another," *Chicago Defender,* 29 June 1934, 18; "Loop Hotels Bar Robeson, Noted Singer," *Chicago Defender,* 16 November 1935, 12; *Chicago Defender,* 7 January 1; *Chicago Defender,* 18 March 1933, 5; "And Welcomed Them to Chicagoland," *Chicago Defender,* 15 July 1933, 12; "Cab Calloway to Greet You at the Picnic," *Chicago Defender,* 25 August 1934, 15; "Duke Ellington's Band Thrills Bub's Guests," *Chicago Defender,* 25 August 1934, 15; "Other Bands Play," *Chicago Defender,* 1 September 1934; "Spectacular 'O, Sing a New Song' Draws 60,000 to Soldier Field," *Chicago Defender,* 1 September 1934, 5; "Two Tired but Happy Boys Sat in the Grand Hotel Café Sunday Evening and across from Them Was Satchel Paige, Ace Pitcher for the Crawfords, Whose Dazzling Hurling Enabled the East Team to Win," *Chicago Defender,* 1 September 1934, 15; "The Color Line within the Race," *Chicago Defender,* 5 May 1934, 11; Jack Ellis, "The Orchestras," *Chicago Defender,* 25 August 1934, 9; *Chicago Defender,* 1 September 1934, 9; "Earl Hines Band to Play for Us at the Regal," *Chicago Defender,* 1 September 1934, 15; "Tiny Bradshaw's Band," *Chicago Defender,* 18 August 1934, 8; "Going Backstage with the Scribe," *Chicago Defender,* 15 September 1934, 8; Jim Haskins and N. R. Mitgang, *Mister Bojangles: The Biography of Bill Robinson,* 57–58, 78, 140–42, 190–91, 234; Spivey, *Union and the Black Musician,* 22–23, 32–35; Mark Naison, *Communists in Harlem during the Depression,* 57–94, 213–14, 299–300; Rob Ruck, *Sandlot Seasons: Sport in Black Pittsburgh,* 122, 139–40, 149–54; "National Auditions Still Taking Country by Storm," *Chicago Defender,* 14 April 1934, 1; *Chicago Defender,* 12 May 1934, 1; "Noble Sissle Raves over National Auditions Plan," *Chicago Defender,* 26 May 1934, 1; "Auditions Parade to Be Biggest Event in City," *Chicago Defender,* 4 August 1934, 1; "A Day at the Fair," *Chicago Defender,* 11 August 1934, 11; "Recalls Chicago's First World's Fair Back in 1893," *Chicago Defender,* 25 March 1933, 10; "World's Fair to Be Mecca for Artists," *Chicago Defender,* 25 March 1933, 4; "Jim Crow Must Go before Worlds Fair Comes," *Chicago Defender,* 22 April 1933, 3; "Entire Nation Rallies to Big Pageant," *Chicago Defender,* 25 August 1934, 2. For grounding in the importance of the World's Fair and mega events in Chicago cultural life, see Robin F. Bachin, *Building the South Side: Urban Space and Civic Culture in Chicago, 1890–1919;* and Steven A. Riess, *City Games: The Evolution of American Urban Society and the Rise of Sports.*

33. Ibid.; exclusive interviews with Robert Leroy Paige, February 2006 and follow-ups in 2007–9, O'Fallon, Mo.; exclusive interviews with Pamela Paige O'Neal, April 2007 and follow-ups, 2008–9, Kansas City, Mo.

34. Ibid.

35. Paige, *Maybe I'll Pitch Forever,* 84–87.

36. Ibid.

37. Ibid., 86.

38. "Help Scottsboro Victims," *Chicago Defender*, 6 May 1933, 1; "Local NAACP Preparing for and Wrote Cabaret Party at Grand Terrace, Café," *Chicago Defender*, 3 June 1933, 7; National Urban League News, *Chicago Defender*, 28 December 1929, 2; A. Philip Randolph, "What the Universal Economic Depression Has Meant to Members of the Race," *Chicago Defender*, 14 January 1933, 8; "Says Prejudice Hurts Women in Industry," *Chicago Defender*, 5 August 1933, 11; "NRA—Negro Removal Act," *Chicago Defender*, 7 October 1933, 11; Dr. Du Bois Pens Own Statement of Flight with NAACP Program: Tells Why He Quit as *Crisis* Editor," *Chicago Defender*, 21 July 1934, 11; "Hunger Army Battles Police," *Chicago Defender*, 16 January 1932, 1; "Reds Pick Party Candidates," *Chicago Defender*, 4 June 1932, 3; "Race Workers Out of Jobs Add to Ranks of Relief Rolls," *Chicago Defender*, 9 June 1934, 11; "Alabama to Burn 9 in Chair," *Chicago Defender*, 6 January 1934, 1, 2, 11; "Is This the Voice of the South? Dixie's Sentiment on Race Problem Is Aired in Nation," *Chicago Defender*, 6 January 1934, 11; "Ask Reversal in Scottsboro Case," *Chicago Defender*, 13 January 1934, 1; "Scottsboro Hearing Postponed to February 24," *Chicago Defender*, 3 February 1934, 4; "Claude Rains Plays Lead in Play about Scottsboro Case," *Chicago Defender*, 10 February 1934, 5; "Scottsboro Case Stirs Cubans," *Chicago Defender*, 10 February 1934, 1; "French Citizens Appeal for Scottsboro Boys," *Chicago Defender*, 17 February 1934, 16; "Intellectuals Take Lead in the Fight to Create the Sentiment," *Chicago Defender*, 17 February 1934; "Writer Sees Hope for Race under Soviets," *Chicago Defender*, 3 March 1934, A5; "Scottsboro Case Onstage Recalls Uncle Tom's Cabin," *Chicago Defender*, A10; *Chicago Defender*, 10 March 1934, 13; "Dean Kelly Miller Denounces Communism," *Chicago Defender*, 17 March 1934, 2; "Scottsboro Protestants on Trial in New York," *Chicago Defender*, 7 April 1934, 24; "Scottsboro Boys Are Mistreated," *Chicago Defender*, 14 April 1934, 13; "Uncover More Details of Scottsboro Boys Torture," *Chicago Defender*, 28 April 1934, 13; "Scottsboro Mothers Honored," *Chicago Defender*, 12 May 1934, 4; "President Refuses to See Mothers of Scottsboro Boys," *Chicago Defender*, 26 May 1934, 1; "Alabama High Court Weighs Fate of Two Scottsboro Boys," *Chicago Defender*, 2 June 1934, 16; "Is the NAACP Retreating?" *Chicago Defender*, 30 June 1934, 10; "Initiate Drive for Scottsboro Appeal Funds," *Chicago Defender*, 14 June 1934, 2; "Alabama to Disbar Scottsboro Lawyers," *Chicago Defender*, 21 June 1934, 1; "Scottsboro—1934," *Chicago Defender*, 21 July 1934, 12; *Chicago Defender*, 11 August 1934, 1; "Society Makes Plans for Big Benefit Dance," *Chicago Defender*, 11 August 1934, 6; "Indians Aid Fight for Scottsboro Boys," *Chicago Defender*, 18 August 1934, 2; "Clubs Are Rallying to Support Mammoth Benefit Dance," *Chicago Defender*, 18 August 1934, 6; "Society," *Chicago Defender*, 1 September 1934, 7; "High Court Rules Scottsboro Boys Must Die," *Chicago Defender*, 13 October 1934, 24; "Scottsboro Case to US Court," *Chicago Defender*, 20 October 1934, 1; "U.S. Supreme Court Gets Appeal in Scottsboro Case," *Chicago Defender*, 8 December 1934, 10; "Pardon the Scottsboro Boys," *Chicago Defender*, 22 December 1934, 14; "Brutal Lynching of Claude Neal Spurs New Demand for Anti-Mob Legislation," *Chicago Defender*, 17 November 1934, 11; "Race Fares Badly in US Employment," *Chicago Defender*, 11 March 1933, 9; "Our People at the Fair," *Chicago Defender*, 29 July 1933, 14; "No Color Line in NRA—FD Roosevelt," *Chicago Defender*, 7 October 1933, 1; "Secretary of Labor Hits Race Issue," *Chicago Defender*, 25 November 1933, 4; "Race Suffering Is Not Reduced by New Deal," *Chicago Defender*, 3 February 1934, 11; "Jim Crow Practices Exposed in East," *Chicago Defender*, 3 March 1934, A4; "Fight to Hold Teams in Baseball Leagues: East-West and Southern Sets Both Hard-Hit," *Chicago Defender*, 2 July 1932, 8; John Buck O'Neil, *I Was Right on Time: My Journey from the Negro Leagues to the Majors*, 120–23; interviews with Radcliffe; interviews with O'Neil.

39. "Brutal Lynching of Claude Neal Spurs New Demand for Anti-Mob Legislation," *Chicago Defender,* 17 November 1934, 11.

40. "Says Prejudice Hurts Women in Industry," *Chicago Defender,* 5 August 1933, 11.

41. A. Philip Randolph, "What the Universal Economic Depression Has Meant to Members of the Race," *Chicago Defender,* 14 January 1933, 8; "Says Prejudice Hurts Women in Industry," *Chicago Defender,* 5 August 1933, 11; "NRA—Negro Removal Act," *Chicago Defender,* 7 October 1933, 11; Dr. Du Bois Pens Own Statement of Flight with NAACP Program: Tells Why He Quit as *Crisis* Editor," *Chicago Defender,* 21 July 1934, 11; "Hunger Army Battles Police," *Chicago Defender,* 16 January 1932, 1; "Reds Pick Party Candidates," *Chicago Defender,* 4 June 1932, 3; "Race Workers Out of Jobs Add to Ranks of Relief Rolls," *Chicago Defender,* 9 June 1934, 11; "Brutal Lynching of Claude Neal Spurs New Demand for Anti-Mob Legislation," *Chicago Defender,* 17 November 1934, 11; "Race Fares Badly in US Employment," *Chicago Defender,* 11 March 1933, 9; "Our People at the Fair," *Chicago Defender,* 29 July 1933, 14; Paige, *Maybe I'll Pitch Forever,* 86–87.

Chapter 6. How the West Was Won

1. "Paige Allows 3 Hits; Giants Win," *Chicago Defender,* 23 January 1932, 9; "Local Team to Tour the South Early in March," *Chicago Defender,* 27 February 1932, 2; "The Tour Evidently Failed to Materialize," *Chicago Defender,* 27 February 1932, 9; "Leroy Satchel Paige Ranks with the Best," *Chicago Defender,* 30 April 1932, 9; "Paige Trips All-Stars in Coast Battle," *Chicago Defender,* 5 November 1932, Ashland Collection; "Elite Giants Top All-Star Nine by 8–1," *Chicago Defender,* 19 November 1932, 9; "Paige, Davis Win Coast Ball Games, Elites Lead League," *Pittsburgh Courier,* 24 December 1932, sec. 2, p. 4; "Hail Accomplishments of 1932 Athletes," *Chicago Defender,* 31 December 1932, 8; Jose M. Alamillo, "Peloterros in Paradise: Mexican American Baseball and Oppositional Politics in Southern California, 1930–1950," 1, 10; Michael A. Messner, *Power at Play: Sport and the Problem of Masculinity,* 17–23; Yoichi Nagata, "The Pride of Lil' Tokyo: The Los Angeles Nippons Baseball Club, 1926–1941," in *More than a Game: Sport in the Japanese American Community,* edited by Brian Niiya, 100–109; "Daily Writer Tells What Is Wrong with Baseball," *Chicago Defender,* 10 August 1935, 13.

2. Ibid.

3. Ibid.

4. "Plan 'Satchel Paige' Day on Coast after Great Victory," *Pittsburgh Courier,* 11 November 1933, sec. 2, p. 5; "They All Look Alike to Paige When He's O.K.," *Chicago Defender,* 18 November 1933, 9. Winter League ball proved so inviting that Paige had difficulty leaving to return back East. "Satchel Must Join Camp or Be Ousted," *Pittsburgh Courier,* 13 April 1935, sec. 2, p. 5; *Pittsburgh Courier,* 4 May 1935, sec. 2, p. 4; "Baseball's Curtain Falling on Season," *Pittsburgh Courier,* 15 September 1934, 4; "Big Turnouts Herald 'New Day' in Negro Baseball," *Pittsburgh Courier,* 15 September 1934, 5; "Big Moments in Baseball," *Pittsburgh Courier,* 22 September 1934, 4; "Paige and Willis Close Winter League with Win," *Chicago Defender,* 20 January 1934, 9; "Ho Hum! Elites Win Another Contest from Big Leaguers," *Chicago Defender,* 3 February 1934, 9; "Lock 'Em Up Boys, They're a Bunch of Jumping Players," *Chicago Defender,* 16 June 1934, 16; "Satchel 'Stepin Fetchit' Paige Is No Movie Star to Big League All Stars," *Chicago Defender,* 6 October 1934, 16; "Coast Winter Loop Anxious to See Mr. Satchel Paige Play," *Chicago Defender,* 10 November 1934, 17; "Satchel Paige and Willis Win in Winter Loop Games," *Chicago Defender,* 8 December 1934, 17; "Satchel Paige Whips Stars, 7–1," *Chicago Defender,* 15 December 1934, 16; "Hold Annual Baseball Meeting," *Chicago Defender,* 12 January 1935,

14; "Satchel Paige Unbeaten on Coast; Hero of League," *Chicago Defender,* 2 February 1935, 17; "Great Negro Athlete Pitches Bismarck to Title," *Bismarck Tribune,* 28 August 1935, 1; "All Hail Bismarck's Fist National Championship Team," *Bismarck Tribune,* 28 August 1935, 1; *Chicago Defender,* 2 February 1935, 17; "Everybody Wants Satchel Paige, Nobody His Salary," *Chicago Defender,* 9 February 1935, 16; "Speaking of Sports," *Chicago Defender,* 13 April 1935, 16; "Satchel Paige's Contract to the House of David," *Chicago Defender,* 27 April 1935, 17; "Fans, Meet Baseball's Greatest Figure," *Chicago Defender,* 4 May 1935, 10; "Daily Scribe Speaks of Jim Crow in the Majors," *Chicago Defender,* 13 July 1935, 13; "Coast Newspapers Work to Get Race in Majors," *Chicago Defender,* 10 August 1935, 14; "Los Angeles, Aug. 9—Winter league baseball is going to take on a new significance this year, due to the recent bold demands made by famous local sports writers that the Race baseball player be given recognition in the major leagues." "Daily Writer Tells What Is Wrong with Baseball," *Chicago Defender,* 10 August 1935, 13; *Chicago Defender,* 9 May 1936, 13; "Satchel Paige Stars in California Winter Loop," *Chicago Defender,* 23 November 1935, 14. Paige, of course, had his bad days too. "Satchel a Flop in Frisco," *Chicago Defender,* 30 May 1936, 14.

5. Ibid.

6. "Satchel Must Join Camp or Be Ousted," *Pittsburgh Courier,* 13 April 1935, sec. 2, p. 5; "Satchel Paige Returns to Crawfords," *Pittsburgh Courier,* 25 April 1936, sec. 2, p. 4; "Los Angeles Wild over Satchel Paige," *Bismarck Tribune,* 22 November 1933, 1.

7. The marketing was quite effective and the game booked to capacity. The announcement that Paige would be pitching was a guarantee of brisk ticket sales and a good payday for everyone involved. "Satchel Paige Unbeaten on Coast; Hero of League," *Chicago Defender,* 2 February 1935, 17; "Everybody Wants Satchel Paige, Nobody His Salary," *Chicago Defender,* 9 February 1935, 16; "Speaking of Sports," *Chicago Defender,* 13 April 1935, 16; "Satchel Must Join Camp or Be Ousted," *Pittsburgh Courier,* 13 April 1935, sec. 2, p. 5; "Satchel's Back in Town," *Pittsburgh Courier,* 9 May 1936, 4.

8. "Paige Day on Coast Is Also Whitewash Day; Ace Wins," *Chicago Defender,* 25 November 1933, 9; "Satchel Has His Day on Cast, Larry French Pirate Ace, Beaten, 5–0," *Pittsburgh Courier,* 25 November 1933, 4; "Homer by Wells Wins for Paige," *Chicago Defender,* 9 December 1933, 9; "Satchel Fans 13, but Finally Loses in Coast Ball Classic," *Pittsburgh Courier,* 2 December 1933, 5; "Satchel Outpitches Thurston," *Pittsburgh Courier,* 23 December 1933, 4; "Paige, Willis Win for Elite Giants," *Pittsburgh Courier,* 5 June 1935, 4. Paige did not win every contest, of course. "Satchel Paige Loses; Willis Wins on Coast," *Pittsburgh Courier,* 6 June 1934, 5; "Paige, Willis Beat All-Stars," *Pittsburgh Courier,* 10 February 1934, 5. Paige won the first game, and Willis pitched and won the second for the black all-star team. "Paige, Willis Win Again for Elite Giants," *Pittsburgh Courier,* 17 February 1934, sec. 2, p. 5. Paige's performance out West headlined: "Satchel Paige Has 16 Wins, Fans 229," *Pittsburgh Courier,* 24 February 1934, 4; "Another Big Season Looms for Satchel Paige," *Pittsburgh Courier,* 14 April 1934, 5; "Los Angeles Wild over Satchel Paige, Lanky Bismarck Hurler, Smoke-Baller Throws Spell over City," *Bismarck Tribune,* 22 November 1933, 6. See also *Fresno Bee,* 23 March 1936, 1; "Modesto Will Play Colored Giants Here To-day; Negro Star Will Work on Mound, Satchel Paige Is Slated to Pitch," *Modesto Bee,* 29 March 1936, 8; "Negro Pitcher Strikes Out 17, Santa Barbara, Calif., March 18, Satchel Paige, the Santa Barbara Cubs' Negro Pitcher, Shut Out the Seattle Indian Yannigans in a Game Here Yesterday, Fiving the Cubs and 8–0 Victory Paige Struck Out Seventeen Men, Allowing Three Hits," *Oakland Tribune,* 18 March 1937, 8; *Oakland Tribune,* 29 May 1937, 9.

9. Ibid.

10. "Satchel Paige Has 16 Wins, Fans 229," *Pittsburgh Courier,* 24 February 1934, 4.

11. "Colorful Bismarck-Jamestown Baseball Series Will Open Tonight," *Bismarck Tribune,* 2 September 1933, 1; "Bismarck Nine Claims State Championship after Routing Jamestown," *Bismarck Tribune,* 5 September 1933, 1; "Foster Loses to Paige in Tourney," *Chicago Defender,* 9 September 1933, 9.

12. Whether welcoming Paige to town or when Bismarck celebrated its first national championship thanks to him, they could not stay free of the racial caricatures. See "Great Negro Athlete Pitches Bismarck to Title," *Bismarck Tribune,* 28 August 1935, 1; and "All Hail Bismarck's First National Championship Team," *Bismarck Tribune,* 28 August 1935, 1.

13. Paige, *Maybe I'll Pitch Forever,* 88.

14. Ibid. See also Scott Roper, "'Another Chink in Jim Crow?': Race and Baseball on the Northern Plains, 1900–1935," in *Out of the Shadows: African American Baseball from the Cuban Giants to Jackie Robinson,* by Bill Kirwin, 81–83, 86–87.

15. *Bismarck Tribune,* 29 March 1934, 5.

16. "Satchel Paige Will Be Here Next Week He Tells Managers," *Bismarck Tribune,* 29 March 1934, 5.

17. Paige, *Maybe I'll Pitch Forever,* 89. For further discussion, see pp. 89–101; and Roper, "Another Chink in Jim Crow?," in *Out of the Shadows,* by Kirwin, 82–83.

18. Kyle McNary, *Ted "Double Duty" Radcliffe: 36 Years of Pitching and Catching in Baseball's Negro Leagues,* 80; interviews with Theodore Roosevelt "Double Duty" Radcliffe, July 1999 and July 2001, Chicago; Paige, *Pitchin' Man,* 48–52; *Bismarck Tribune,* 2 September 1933, 1; "Satchel Paige Will Stay with Bismarck," *Bismarck Tribune,* 5 September 1933; "Paige, Dusky Star, to Carry Pitching Burden for Locals," *Bismarck Tribune,* 5 September 1933, 2–3; *Bismarck Tribune,* 6 September 1933, 1; "Triple-Threat Ace Got Loose Despite Special Defensive," *Bismarck Tribune,* 7 September 1933, 1.

19. "Paige's Arm Wins $5,000," *Chicago Defender,* 18 August 1934, 16; "Satchel Paige's Contract to the House of David," *Chicago Defender,* 27 August 1935, 17; "Nebraska State," *Chicago Defender,* 21 September 1935, 20; "Satchel Paige Whips House of David Nine," 21 September 1935, 14; "Bismarcks in Trouble When He Comes In," *Chicago Defender,* 21 September 1935, 14; "Bismarck's Semi-Pro Team of 1935 Greatest, Says Satchel Paige," *Bismarck Tribune,* 16 June 1943, 6; *Bismarck Tribune,* 3 September 1935, 1; "Paige Answers Call for Help from Bismarck, Helps Churchill Back Up Threat," *Bismarck Tribune,* 16 June 1943, 1; Joel Hawkins and Terry Bertolino, *The House of David Baseball Team,* 9, 33, 35, 47, 50, 75–76, 83, 113; Don Gitersonke, *Baseball's Bearded Boys: A Historical Look at the Israelite House of David Baseball Club of Benton Harbor, Michigan,* 1–9.

20. "Satchel Paige's Contract to the House of David," *Chicago Defender,* 27 August 1935, 17.

21. Ibid.

22. Interviews with Radcliffe; Scott Roper, "Uncovering Satchel Paige's 1935 Season: A Summer in North Dakota," 51–54; Paige, *Maybe I'll Pitch Forever,* 93.

23. Interviews with Radcliffe.

24. Ibid.

25. McNary, *Ted "Double Duty" Radcliffe,* 99–100; interviews with Radcliffe.

26. Paige, *Maybe I'll Pitch Forever,* 97–98.

27. Interviews with Radcliffe.

28. McNary, *Ted "Double Duty" Radcliffe,* 107.

29. Ibid., 108–9.

30. Ibid., 108.

31. Ibid., 107.

32. Ibid.

33. Interviews with Radcliffe; McNary, *Ted "Double Duty" Radcliffe*, 108.

34. Ibid.

35. "Great Negro Athlete Pitches Bismarck to Title," *Bismarck Tribune*, 28 August 1935, 1; "All Hail Bismarck's Fist National Championship Team," *Bismarck Tribune*, 28 August 1935, 1; interviews with Radcliffe.

36. Doug Feldmann, *Dizzy and the Gas House Gang*, 61–62, 72, 151, 165–66, 173–74; Robert Gregory, *Diz: Dizzy Dean and Baseball during the Great Depression*, 278, 376.

37. "So Satchel Paige Shows Dizzy Dean How to Pitch, 4–1," *Chicago Defender*, 3 November 1934, 16.

38. John Sickels, *Bob Feller: Ace of the Greatest Generation*, 54, 151; Fay Young, "The Stuff Is Here," *Chicago Defender*, 23 April 1938; Eddie Murphy, "Daily Scribe Tells Majors of Value of Satchel Paige," *Chicago Defender*, 8 February 1936, 13; "Giants Eye Paige, Champion Pitcher," *Chicago Defender*, 28 March 1936, 14; "Major Leagues Jim Crowed: Suffer by Policy which Bars Members of the Race from Sport," *Chicago Defender*, 30 May 1936, 14; "White Sports Writer, Backed by N.Y. Daily, Fights for Race Players in Major Leagues; Scribe Jimmy Powers Turns on 'Heat' Down East; Owners Reported Squirming; Draws Comparison with Olympic Records Made by Owens, Metcalfe, Corny Johnson, Etc.," *Chicago Defender*, 15 August 1936, 13–14; "The sensational pitching of Satchel Paige and the catching and hitting of young Josh Gibson, would increase the gate by 150,000 in any major league park. Paige has the praise of such major leaguers as the Warner brothers, the Deans and numerous others who played with him in the Winter League on the Pacific coast." "Umpires Put Race Entry into Major Leagues; Up to J. Louis Comiskey; Send Him Letter on Situation," *Chicago Defender*, 22 August 1936, 14.

39. Quoted in Arthur Daley, "Sport of the Times," *New York Times*, 8 July 1948, 30; "Satchel's Marks Excel Modern Day Hurlers," *Chicago Defender*, 30 May 1959, 24; Paige, *Maybe I'll Pitch Forever*, 106.

Chapter 7. Baseball Diplomacy

1. "Great Colored Hurler Coming Here Next Week," *Winnipeg Free Press*, 17 May 1934, 18; *Winnipeg Free Press*, 18 May 1934, 16; "Wesley Park Opens for Season with Two Games," *Winnipeg Free Press*, 23 May 1934; *Winnipeg Free Press*, 18 May 1934, 16; "Whiskered Ball Team Plays Bismarck Here," *Winnipeg Free Press*, 30 June 1934, 23.

2. "Satchel Paige Fans 17 While Brewer Turns Back 13 Batters," *Winnipeg Free Press*, 7 June 1935, 16; *Winnipeg Free Press*, 8 June 1935, 25; "Touring Teams Break Even on Game Saturday," *Winnipeg Free Press*, 10 June 1935, 15; *Winnipeg Free Press*, 21 June 1935, 16; "Illustrious Satchel Paige and His Bismarcks," *Winnipeg Free Press*, 21 June 1935, 17; "Star Pitchers Meet an Afternoon Game at Osborne Stadium," *Winnipeg Free Press*, 20 July 1935, 21; "Big Ball Tourney at Portage on Monday," *Winnipeg Free Press*, 3 August 1935, 23; "Satchel Paige Star Hurler," *Winnipeg Free Press*, 28 August 1935; "All-Star Teams Here This Week," *Winnipeg Free Press*, 17 August 1937, 14; *Winnipeg Free Press*, 9 October 1937, 23; "Negro Teams to Play Regular League Game in Bismarck Sunday," *Winnipeg Free Press*, 20 July 1939; *Winnipeg Free Press*, 17 August 1940, 21; "Watching the Great Satchel Paige Pitch," *Drumheller* (Alberta, Canada), 1 August 1940, 2; *Winnipeg Free Press*, 17 August 1940, 21. See also Barry Swanton, *The Man Dak League: Haven for Former Negro League Ballplayer, 1950–1957*.

3. Paige, *Maybe I'll Pitch Forever*, 109–11; *Pittsburgh Courier*, 27 April 1940, 16.

4. Ibid.

5. "Los orientales siguen a la cabeza del Campeonato de Base-Ball al vencer al team Santiago en su primer choque," *Listin Diario*, 5 April 1937; *Listin Diario*, 12 April 1937;

"Los Players Perkins y Peiz, llegaron per avion el Domingo 18," *Listin Diario,* 19 April 1937, 6.

6. Rob Ruck, *The Tropic of Baseball: Baseball in the Dominican Republic,* 58; German E. Ornes, *Trujillo: Little Caesar of the Caribbean,* 100.

7. Paige, *Maybe I'll Pitch Forever,* 117–18.

8. "National Olympic Games in the Dominican Republic," Donald D. Edgar, Secretary of Legation, Dominican Republic, to US Secretary of State Cordell Hull, 12 April 1937, 1–4, Central Files, Record Group 59, M-1272 (1934–1939), Dominican Republic, 839.40631/1–839.406.34, National Archives and Records Administration, Archives II.

9. Ruck, *Tropic of Baseball,* 9, 32.

10. "Los Derroto Joe Louis," *Listin Diario,* 9 February 1937, 6; "Jimmy Braddock con Joe Louis," *Listin Diario,* 17 April 1937, 6; *Listin Diario,* 5 February 1937, 6; *Listin Diario,* 27 February 1937, 7; *Listin Diario,* 18 March 1937, 6; "En Ciudad Trujillo Habra juego todos los sabados," *Listin Diario,* 19 March 1937, 6; "Los Players De Ciudad Trujillo," *Listin Diario,* 25 March 1937, 6; *Listin Diario,* 18 February 1937, 6; "Campeonato Nacional de Base-Ball 1937–1938," *Listin Diario,* 2 February 1937; *Listin Diario,* 10 March 1937, 6; *Listin Diario,* 2 April 1937, 6; *Listin Diario,* 5 April 1937, 6; "Base-Ball, Boxeo, Basket Ball," *Listin Diario,* 6 April 1937, 6; "Un Famoso Player Americano Llega Hoy Para El Ciudad Trujillo," *Listin Diario,* 14 April 1937, 6; "Base-Ball Reeleccion Presidente Trujillo," *Listin Diario,* 14 April 1937, 6; "En 2 sensacionales juegos con un total de 21 innings las Estrellas Orientales se llevan las victorias sobre las Aguilas," *Listin Diario,* 19 April 1937, 6; "Los Players Perkins y Peiz, llegaron per avion el Domingo 18," *Listin Diario,* 19 April 1937, 6; "Paige y Perkins se inscriben para jugar en el Ciudad Trujillo—Mucho entusiasmo para los juegos proximos," *Listin Diario,* 22 April 1937, 6; *Listin Diario,* 24 April 1937, 6; "Satchel Paige," *Listin Diario,* 26 April 1937, 6; *Listin Diario,* 28 April 1937, 6; "Satchel Paige y Cy. Perkins," *Listin Diario,* 30 April 1937, 6; "El Campeonato Nacional de Base-Ball 1937–38 fue puesto bajo los auspicios del llustre Presidente de la Republica, Generalisimo Dr. Trujillo Molina—Comenzara posiblemente el 27 de Febrero," *Listin Diario,* 2 February 1937, 1.

11. "Paige y Perkins se inscriben para jugar en el Ciudad Trujillo—Mucho entusiasmo para los juegos proximos," *Listin Diario,* 22 April 1937, 6; "Los Players Perkins y Peiz, llegaron per avion el Domingo 18," *Listin Diario,* 19 April 1937, 6.

12. Ruck, *Tropic of Baseball,* 38–41; Paige, *Maybe I'll Pitch Forever,* 120.

13. Ibid.

14. "How Satch Saved the President," *Pittsburgh Courier,* 5 February 1938, 16.

15. Documents File Note 311.3921 Nina and Mendez: "Practice of Inducing Negro Baseball Players to Break Contracts in the United States," 29 May 1937, Central Files, Record Group 59, M-1272 (1934–1939), Dominican Republic, 839.40631/1–839.406.34, National Archives and Records Administration, Archives II.

16. Ferdinand Q. Morton to Robert F. Wagner, 24 May 1937, Central Files, Record Group 59, M-1272 (1934–1939), Dominican Republic, 839.40631/1–839.406.34, National Archives and Records Administration, Archives II.

17. Ibid.

18. Wagner to Ruth Shipley, 4 June 1937, Central Files, Record Group 59, M-1272 (1934–1939), Dominican Republic, 839.40631/1–839.406.34, National Archives and Records Administration, Archives II.

19. Morton to Wagner, 24 May 1937, Central Files, Record Group 59, M-1272 (1934–1939), Dominican Republic, 839.40631/1–839.406.34, National Archives and Records Administration, Archives II.

20. Republic of Santo Domingo File (1937), Pan-American Airlines Collection.

21. Morton to Wagner, 24 May 1937, Central Files, Record Group 59, M-1272 (1934–

1939), Dominican Republic, 839.40631/1–839.406.34, National Archives and Records Administration, Archives II; Pan-American Airlines Collection.

22. Secretary of State Cordell Hull to Senator Robert F. Wagner, 14 June 1937, Central Files, Record Group 59, M-1272 (1934–1939), Dominican Republic, 839.40631/1–839.406.34, National Archives and Records Administration, Archives II.

23. Representative Matthew Dunn to Secretary of State Cordell Hull, 17 June 1937, National Archives and Records Administration.

24. Representative Henry Ellenbogen to the State Department, 24 June 1937, and Hull to Ellenbogen, 6 July 1937, National Archives and Records Administration.

25. "Statement of Grievances of the Negro National League," 1–7, State Department file copy 839.40634/14, Central Files, Record Group 59, M-1272 (1934–1939), Dominican Republic, 839.40631/1–839.406.34, National Archives and Records Administration, Archives II.

26. Ibid.

27. Ibid.

28. Attorney Ira Hurwick to Representative Matthew A. Dunn, 12 June 1937, National Archives and Records Administration.

29. "Resolution of the National Association of Negro Baseball Leagues," 12 June 1937, State Department file copy, Central Files, Record Group 59, M-1272 (1934–1939), Dominican Republic, 839.40631/1–839.406.34, National Archives and Records Administration, Archives II.

30. Ibid.

31. "Majors' Baseball Bar Drove Paige to Cuba," *Chicago Defender*, 28 May 1937, 12; "Dixie Whites Would Not Quit Big Leagues If Our Men Could Play," *Chicago Defender*, 25 June 1938, 9; "Resolution of the National Association of Negro Baseball Leagues," 12 June 1937, State Department file copy, Central Files, Record Group 59, M-1272 (1934–1939), Dominican Republic, 839.40631/1–839.406.34, National Archives and Records Administration, Archives II.

32. "Resolution of the National Association of Negro Baseball Leagues," 12 June 1937, National Archives and Records Administration.

33. Ibid.

34. Ibid.

35. Ibid.

36. Ibid.

37. Representative Eugene Keogh to Secretary of State, 17 June 1937; Ira Hurwick to Representative Eugene Keogh, 12 June 1937; Hull to Keogh, 21 June 1937; Hull to Representative Herman Kberharter, 21 June 1937; Hull to Senator Royal Copeland, 22 June 1937; Franklin B. Atwood, American Chargé d'Affaires ad interim, Ciudad Trujillo, 24 June 1937, to Hall; Representative Edward O'Neil to Secretary of State, 22 June 1937; Report of the Department of State Division of the American Republics, 21 June 1937; Ellenbogen to Department of State, 24 June 1937; Hull to Ellenbogen, 6 July 1937; Representative Edward O'Neil to Department of State, 7 July 1937, Central Files, Record Group 59, M-1272 (1934–1939), Dominican Republic, 839.40631/1–839.406.34, National Archives and Records Administration, Archives II.

38. Ibid.

39. Atwood, Ciudad Trujillo, 24 June 1937, to Hull, National Archives and Records Administration.

40. "Dominican Republic," Memorandum of the Department of State Division of the American Republics, 21 June 1937, State Department file, 839.40634/11, National Archives and Records Administration.

41. "Statement of Grievances of the Negro National League," 1–7, State Department file copy 839.40634/14, Central Files, Record Group 59, M-1272 (1934–1939), Dominican Republic, 839.40631/1–839.406.34, National Archives and Records Administration, Archives II.

42. "Statement of Grievances of the Negro National League," 5, National Archives and Records Administration.

43. Memorandum of Meeting June 29, 1937, Department of State, Division of Latin American Affairs, State Department file, 839.40634/14, National Archives and Records Administration; Effa Manley to Attorney Richard Carey, 8 May 1940, Newark Eagles Papers.

44. Ibid.

45. "Statement of Grievances of the Negro National League," 6, National Archives and Records Administration.

46. "Statement of Grievances of the Negro National League," 7; Department of State, Division of the American Republics to Mr. Duggan, 16 July 1937; Confidential State Department Memorandum to Senator Joseph Guffey, 16 July 1937, Document 839.40634/16, National Archives and Records Administration.

47. William F. McNeil, *Baseball's Other All-Stars: The Greatest Players from the Negro Leagues, the Japanese Leagues, the Mexican League, and the Pre-1968 Winter Leagues in Cuba, Puerto Rico, and the Dominican Republic,* 18–19. African American culture was warmly embraced abroad ever since the transplanting of jazz to France and other nations of the world around 1915 and the era of World War I. Paige was part of the early planting of baseball abroad. The State Department would eventually make more formal effort to use sport and music, in particular, to bolster America's image abroad. See, for example, Penny Von Eschen, *Satchmo Blows Up the World: Jazz Ambassadors Play the Cold War.*

Chapter 8. The Fugitive

1. Paige, *Maybe I'll Pitch Forever,* 121.

2. Ibid.

3. Ibid., 122.

4. "Paige's All-Stars Win Denver Tourney," *Chicago Defender,* 21 August 1937, 21.

5. "All-Stars to Play before Legionnaires—Satchel Paige to Appear in Big Game at the Polo Grounds," *Chicago Defender,* 11 September 1937, 21.

6. "All-Stars to Play before Legionnaires—Satchel Paige to Appear in Big Game at the Polo Grounds," *Chicago Defender,* 11 September 1937, 21; "Paige's Star Team in Polo Grounds Tilt," *Chicago Defender,* 18 September 1937, 20.

7. Al Monroe, "It's News to Me," *Chicago Defender,* 25 September 1937, 20; "Paige Is Best," *Chicago Defender,* 25 September 1937, 20.

8. "Satchel Made Victim of No-Hit Contest," *Chicago Defender,* 25 September 1937, 20.

9. "Paige Beats Taylor, 9–5, in Star Tilt," *Chicago Defender,* 2 October 1937, 19.

10. Cum Posey, "Posey's Points," *Pittsburgh Courier,* 5 March 1938, 17.

11. Chester Washington, "Satchel Paige, Star Speedball Pitcher on the Craw Roster," *Pittsburgh Courier,* 19 March 1938, 16.

12. *Pittsburgh Courier,* 23 April 1938, 17.

13. Ibid.

14. Ibid.

15. "Satchel Paige Not Wanted," *Chicago Defender,* 17 December 1938, 9.

16. "Satchel Paige Restrained from Going to S. America," *Pittsburgh Courier,* 30 April 1938, 17.

17. *Pittsburgh Courier,* 21 May 1938, 16.

18. Ibid.

19. "Satchel Paige Barred from N.N.L. for Life," *Pittsburgh Courier,* 28 May 1938, 17.

20. *Pittsburgh Courier,* 27 August 1938, 17.

21. "Diz Says Paige Is Best Pitcher in Baseball," *Pittsburgh Courier,* 24 September 1938, 17.

22. John Clark, "The Rise and Fall of Greenlee Field," *Pittsburgh Courier,* 10 December 1938, 17.

23. Ibid.; Wendell Smith, "Plans to Rebuild Famous Craws," 27 April 1940, Wendell Smith Collection.

24. Steven A. Riess, "The Profits of Major League Baseball, 1900 to 1956"; *Pittsburgh Courier,* 18 March 1939, 17.

25. Paige, *Pitchin' Man,* 57–58.

26. Paige, *Maybe I'll Pitch Forever,* 125.

27. Ibid.

28. Ibid., 125–26.

29. Wendell Smith, "Smitty's Sport Spurts," copy in the Smith Collection.

30. Paige to Manley, Western Union telegram, Manley Correspondence, Newark Eagles Papers.

31. Paige to Manley, n.d., Manley Correspondence, Newark Eagles Papers.

32. Paige to Manley, and Manley to Abe Manley, n.d., Manley Correspondence, Newark Eagles Papers.

33. Paige to Manley, Manley Correspondence, Newark Eagles Papers.

Chapter 9. Lazarus

1. "Satchel Paige Joins K. C Monarchs," Ashland Collection; Paige, *Maybe I'll Pitch Forever,* 127.

2. Paige, *Maybe I'll Pitch Forever,* 127.

3. Ibid., 128.

4. Ibid.

5. Ibid., 129.

6. Paige, *Pitchin' Man,* 57–59.

7. Ibid.

8. Paige, *Maybe I'll Pitch Forever,* 128–36; Paige, *Pitchin' Man,* 57–59.

9. Ibid.

10. Interviews with John "Buck" O'Neil, November 2005 and follow-ups, Negro Leagues Museum, Kansas City, Mo.; Larry Lester, "J. L. Wilkinson: 'Only the Stars Come Out at Night,'" in *Satchel Paige and Company: Essays on the Kansas City Monarchs, Their Greatest Star, and the Negro Leagues,* edited by Leslie A. Heaphy, 110–43.

11. Ibid.

12. Ibid.

13. Interviews with O'Neil; Lester, "J. L. Wilkinson," in *Satchel Paige and Company,* edited by Heaphy, 110–43; Janet Bruce, *The Kansas City Monarchs: Champions of Black Baseball,* 44, 49; Frank Diggs and Chuck Haddix, *Kansas City Jazz from Ragtime to Bebop: A History,* 30–31, 166–68; Nathan W. Pearson, *Goin' to Kansas City,* 1–87; Douglas Henry Daniels, *Lester Leaps In: The Life and Times of Lester "Pres" Young.*

14. Ibid.

15. Interviews with O'Neil; Bruce, *Kansas City Monarchs,* 43.

16. Dan Burley, "Confidentially Yours," *Amsterdam News,* 3 May 1941, 18; interviews with O'Neil.

17. Paige, *Maybe I'll Pitch Forever,* 139.

18. *Pittsburgh Courier,* 23 December 1939, 16.

19. W. McNeil, *Baseball's Other All-Stars,* 137–38.

20. Ibid., 9, 193.

21. See Holway, *Josh and Satch,* 13, 154; W. McNeil, *Baseball's Other All-Stars,* 50. See also Joseph L. Arbena, ed., *Sport and Society in Latin America: Diffusion, Dependency, and the Rise of Mass Culture,* 64–65, 113–36; Alan M. Klein, *Sugar Ball: The American Game, the Dominican Dream,* 21–23; Alan M. Klein, *Baseball on the Border: A Tale of Two Laredos,* 74; Burgos, *Playing America's Game,* 164; Ruck, *Tropic of Baseball.*

22. New York Passenger Lists (1941), Microfilm Serial T715, 6541, New York Port Authority; Paige, *Maybe I'll Pitch Forever,* 140–41.

23. Paige, *Maybe I'll Pitch Forever,* 140–42.

24. Ibid.

25. "Award Satchel Paige to American League," *Pittsburgh Courier,* 29 June 1940, 16.

26. Dan Burley, "Famed Hurler Quits Kaycee to Come Here," *Pittsburgh Courier,* 3 May 1941, 19.

27. *Pittsburgh Courier,* 8 June 1940, 17.

28. Ibid.

29. Manley to Dr. J. B. Martin and Mr. Thomas T. Wilson, Chairman of the Negro National and American League Respectively, 2 June 1940, Manley Correspondence, Newark Eagles Papers; "Baseball War Brews over Satchel Paige as Two Teams Claim His Services," *Pittsburgh Courier,* 1 June 1940, 17.

30. Manley to Abe Manley, n.d., Manley Correspondence, Newark Eagles Papers.

31. Ibid.

32. A thorough check of the financial files of the Newark Eagles uncovered no records, contracts, or monetary exchange between Effa Manley and Gus Greenlee for the services of Satchel Paige. Though no contract existed, their financial logs are quite thorough. Financial Files of the Newark Eagles, Newark Eagles Papers.

33. "Posey's Points," *Pittsburgh Courier,* 1 June 1940, 17.

34. Hazel Wigden to Manley, 22 June 1940. See also Earl M. Barnes to Manley, 28 June 1940, Manley Correspondence, Newark Eagles Papers.

35. Newark Eagles Press Release 3-2641, Newark Eagles Papers.

36. "The Mighty Satchel Comes Home," *Pittsburgh Courier,* 26 July 1941, 16.

37. "Paige Is Master, Tops N.Y. by 5 to 3," *Pittsburgh Courier,* 17 May 1941, 16.

38. Ibid.; "Satchel Still a Big Attraction," *Pittsburgh Courier,* 24 May 1941, 17.

39. *Pittsburgh Courier,* 2 August 1941, 16.

40. Chester Washington, "With Satchel in, East-West Game Is Believed in the Bag," *Pittsburgh Courier,* 5 July 1941, 17; "Paige Will Pitch in the East-West Game," *Chicago Defender,* 26 July 1941, 4. See also *Pittsburgh Courier,* 19 July 1941, 16; *Chicago Defender,* 5 July 1941, 23; "Baseball's Dream Game Sunday," *Pittsburgh Courier,* 26 July 1941, 17; *Chicago Defender,* 2 August 1941, 1, 12, 23; and "East Batters Radcliffe in the Fourth to Win Dream Game," *Pittsburgh Courier,* 2 August 1941, 17.

41. *Chicago Defender,* 2 August 1941, 1, 12, 23.

42. Ibid.

43. Cum Posey, "Posey Exposes Case of Satchel Paige," *Pittsburgh Courier,* 16 August 1941, 16.

44. "Large Crowd Expected to See Satch," *Pittsburgh Courier,* 16 August 1941, 17; "Record Throng to Watch Satchel," *Pittsburgh Courier,* 30 August 1941, 17.

45. "Posey's Points," *Pittsburgh Courier,* 13 September 1941, 16.

46. W. Smith, "Smitty's Sports Spurts," 13 September 1941, Smith Collection.

47. "Paige to Face Feller," *Pittsburgh Courier,* 4 October 1941, 16; *Sporting News,* 2 October 1941, 6.

Chapter 10. Double V

1. Death Index, 1940–1997, SSN 145-16-0572. For further discussion of Effa Manley, see James Overmyer, *Queen of the Negro Leagues: Effa Manley and the Newark Eagles;* Manley to Posey, 1 August 1941; Cum Posey to Sports Editor, 8 August 1941; and Ed Gottlieb to Manley, 28 September 1941, all in Manley Correspondence, Newark Eagles Papers.

2. Manley to Posey, 13 October 1941, Manley Correspondence, Newark Eagles Papers.

3. Manley to Gottlieb, 4 November 1941, Manley Correspondence, Newark Eagles Papers.

4. "Kansas City to Battle Soldiers' Team in Benefit Game," *Pittsburgh Courier,* 18 July 1942, 16; Sam Lacy with Moses J. Newson, *Fighting for Fairness: The Life Story of Hall of Fame Sportswriter Sam Lacy,* 53; Gary L. Bloomfield, *Duty, Honor, Victory: America's Athletes in World War II,* 23–25, 83; Steven R. Bullock, *Playing for Their Nation: Baseball and the American Military during World War II,* 45; interview with Bob Feller, April 2007.

5. "Baseball Stars Aplenty in Big Benefit Game," *Pittsburgh Courier,* 21 July 1934, 4; "Kansas City to Battle Soldiers' Team in Benefit Game," *Pittsburgh Courier,* 18 July 1942, 16; Donald Spivey, "Sport, Protest, and Consciousness: The Black Athlete in Big-Time Intercollegiate Sports, 1941–1968"; Spivey, "Paige's Struggle for Selfhood," 107–8; Spivey, "End Jim Crow in Sports," 282–83, 302–3.

6. *Amsterdam News,* 29 November 1941, 19.

7. Bruce, *Kansas City Monarchs,* 98–100.

8. *Pittsburgh Courier,* 3 January 1942, 17.

9. "Chicago Fans Honor Satchel Paige Who Wins 4–2," *Chicago Defender,* 1 August 1942, 19. Paige pawned the watch some years later. A gentleman eventually purchased the watch from the pawnshop for less than one hundred dollars. That same watch was valued at twenty thousand on *Antique Roadshow* in 2006.

10. *Chicago Defender,* 1 August 1942, 20; *Chicago Defender,* 8 August 1942, 8.

11. "Yes Sir, Mr. Paige Will Be in Shape," *Chicago Defender,* 15 August 1942, 19; *Pittsburgh Courier,* 15 August 1942, 17.

12. "48,000 Watch East Turn Back the West All-Stars," *Baltimore Afro-American,* 22 August 1942, 22; Press Release, Newark Eagles Baseball Team, Newark Eagles Papers; *Chicago Defender,* 22 August 1942, 1, 19; *Chicago Defender,* 5 September 1942, 22.

13. *Philadelphia Tribune,* 15 August 1942, 14; *Pittsburgh Courier,* 15 August 1942, 17.

14. "Was Misquoted, Says Satchel," *Pittsburgh Courier,* 22 August 1942, 17; *Chicago Defender,* 22 August 1942, 1, 19.

15. Interviews with John "Buck" O'Neil, November 2005 and follow-ups, Negro Leagues Museum, Kansas City, Mo.; "Satch Paige Fans Josh Gibson with Three on the Bases," *Baltimore Afro-American,* 19 September 1942, 31; J. O'Neil, *I Was Right on Time,* 130–32. Buck O'Neil also repeated the showdown between Paige and Gibson for the Ken Burns series *Baseball,* episode 5, "Shadow Ball." See also Paige, *Pitchin' Man,* 46–47. The Paige-Gibson showdown, with various additions, along with countless humorous

anecdotes about Gibson's hitting ability, was repeated to me by many of the Negro Leagues players that I interviewed.

16. Ibid.

17. Ibid.

18. Ibid.

19. Ibid.

20. Interviews with O'Neil.

21. Cited in Neil Lanctot, *Negro League Baseball: The Rise and Ruin of a Black Institution*, 227, 229; "No Good from Raising Race Issue," *Sporting News*, 6 August 1942, 4.

22. Paige, *Maybe I'll Pitch Forever*, 142–43.

23. Ibid.

24. Ibid. See also Lahoma Brown, US Census (1930), Stillwater, Okla., Roll 1925, p. 5A; Missouri Marriage Records, 2 September 1939, 12 October 1947, Bureau of Vital Statistics, State of Missouri; exclusive interviews with Pamela Paige O'Neal, April 2007 and follow-ups, Kansas City, Mo.

25. J. O'Neil, *I Was Right on Time*, 15; interviews with O'Neil.

26. *Sporting News*, 17 June 1943, 13.

27. *Chicago Defender*, 17 July 1943; *Chicago Defender*, 24 July 1943, 11.

28. *Baltimore Afro-American*, 14 August 1943, 22; *Chicago Defender*, 24 July 1943, 1; *Sporting News*, 8 July 1943, 22; *Sporting News*, 19 August 1943, 18; *Sporting News*, 2 September 1943, 18; *Sporting News*, 28 October 1943, 11; *Sporting News*, 4 November 1943, 9.

29. Paige, *Maybe I'll Pitch Forever*, 156. Janet Howard Paige had already begun making her move to Chicago, where she would take up permanent residence at 4609 South Parkway on the famous South Side black belt of the Windy City. She would later make her permanent residence there in Chicago. She never forgot the city since she and her former husband had visited it during his stellar performance for the 1934 East-West classic that made him a household name. It is unclear how long Janet Paige received alimony after the divorce; it was likely for two to three years. She never remarried and always called herself Mrs. Satchel Paige. That helped her in establishing herself as a socialite in Chicago circles. She held positions as official greeter and hostess at some of the swankier black nightspots, lounges, and clubs. Hers was a hectic life. Janet Howard Paige died in the 1960s.

30. *Chicago Defender*, 24 July 1943, 1, 11.

31. "Record Crowd Sees West, Paige Tame East, 2 to 1," *Chicago Defender*, 7 August 1943, 1.

32. *Pittsburgh Courier*, 28 August 1943, 18; *Pittsburgh Courier*, 2 October 1943, 16. See also "L.A. Enjoys Winter Ball," *Sporting News*, 11 November 1943, 15; and Wendell Smith, "Paige Thumbs Nose at His Public Here," copy in Smith Collection.

33. "Satchel Paige Sparkles before 15,000 in Chicago," *Pittsburgh Courier*, 10 June 1944, 12; *Pittsburgh Courier*, 8 July 1944, 12; *Pittsburgh Courier*, 15 July 1944, 12; "Dean, Paige in Louisville Duel," *Sporting News*, 20 July 1944, 26; *Pittsburgh Courier*, 22 July 1944, 12; "Lefty Mathis Beats Paige," *Pittsburgh Courier*, 5 August 1944, 12; *Pittsburgh Courier*, 30 September 1944, 12; "North Blasts Satch," *Pittsburgh Courier*, 7 October 1944, 12.

34. *Chicago Defender*, 12 August 1944, 7. See also *Pittsburgh Courier*, 29 July 1944, 13.

35. Ibid.

36. Interviews with Theodore Roosevelt "Double Duty" Radcliffe, July 1999 and July 2001, Chicago.

37. "Players Strike Almost Halts All-Star Game," *Chicago Defender*, 19 August 1944, 1; "Ted Radcliffe of Birmingham, Catching for the West, Hit a Home Run in the Big Fifth Inning. Satchel Paige Was Dropped from the West Roster Because of His Attempts to

Disrupt the Playing of the Game Several Weeks Ago, and Paige Did Not Appear," *Sporting News,* 17 August 1944, 25; interviews with Radcliffe.

38. Wendell Smith, "Smitty's Sports Spurts," 22 July 1944, 5 August 1944, 19 August 1944, *Pittsburgh Courier,* copies in Smith Collection.

Chapter 11. Integration

1. Paige, *Maybe I'll Pitch Forever,* 118.

2. "Baird Says Monarchs Will Not Impede Robinson—Bramham Joins in 'Raid' Charges," copy in Ashland Collection; Jules Tygiel, *Baseball's Great Experiment: Jackie Robinson and His Legacy,* 70–95.

3. Ibid.

4. *Hartford Courant,* 7 August 1942, 17; "Paige Says Negroes Not Ready for Big Leagues," *Chicago Defender,* 15 August 1942, 21.

5. *Pittsburgh Courier,* 29 July 1939, 16; *Pittsburgh Courier,* 12 August 1939, 16.

6. Effa Manley and Leon Hardwick, *Negro Baseball before Integration,* 56–57, 93–95.

7. *Pittsburgh Courier,* 29 August 1942, 16.

8. Interviews with John "Buck" O'Neil, November 2005 and follow-ups, Negro Leagues Museum, Kansas City, Mo.; *Pittsburgh Courier,* 29 August 1942, 16.

9. "Satchel Takes Pen in Hand," *Pittsburgh Courier,* 12 May 1945, 17.

10. Paige, *Maybe I'll Pitch Forever,* 172–73; Tygiel, *Baseball's Great Experiment,* 71–95.

11. Bruce, *Kansas City Monarchs,* 105; Larry Lester and Sammy J. Miller, *Black Baseball in Kansas City,* 59.

12. Paige, *Maybe I'll Pitch Forever,* 176.

13. Ibid.

14. Ibid., 176–79.

15. Ibid.

16. Ibid.

17. Ibid.

18. "Satchel Paige Wants Chance in the Majors," *Philadelphia Tribune,* 10 September 1946, 3; *Chicago Defender,* 7 October 1946, 11; *Chicago Defender,* 31 August 1946, 11, B19; *Chicago Defender,* 7 September 1946, 11; *Chicago Defender,* 10 August 1946, 11; *Chicago Defender,* 24 August 1946, 11; *Chicago Defender,* 14 September 1946, 11.

19. Ibid.

20. "Negro World Series," *Pittsburgh Courier,* 21 September 1946, 27; Press Release, Newark Eagles World Champions, Newark Eagles Papers.

21. Interview with Bob Feller, April 2007; "Feller-Paige Tour Test for Colored Aces," *Sporting News,* 2 October 1946, 9; "Paige's and Feller's Teams Launch Series," *Philadelphia Tribune,* 1 October 1946, 10; *Pittsburgh Courier,* 5 October 1946, 24; "Feller's Stars Away to Lead," *Sporting News,* 9 October 1946, 30; "Many Stars with Feller, Paige," *Pittsburgh Courier,* 21 September 1946, 25; Sam Lacy, "Looking 'Em Over," *Baltimore Afro-American,* 12 October 1946, 17; Sam Lacy, "Satchel's All-Stars Twice Beat Major Leaguers in Sunday Bill," *Baltimore Afro-American,* 12 October 1946, 17; *Chicago Defender,* 19 October 1946, 11; Fay Young, "Through the Years," *Chicago Defender,* 19 October 1946, 11; *Chicago Defender,* 26 October 1946, 11; "Paige and Feller," *Pittsburgh Courier,* 28 September 1946, 26; "Feller's All-Stars Attract 148,2000 in 15 Exhibitions," *Sporting News,* 16 October 1946, 23; *Pittsburgh Courier,* 5 October 1946, 24; *Pittsburgh Courier,* 12 October 1946, 15; *Pittsburgh Courier,* 19 October 1946, 25; "Feller's Stars Play to 22,577 in Los Angeles," *Sporting News,* 23 October 1946, 23; "250,000 See Feller-Paige Teams Play," *Sporting News,* 30 October 1946, 9.

22. As cited in Tygiel, *Baseball's Great Experiment,* 160.

23. Interview with Bob Feller, April 2007; "Feller-Paige Tour Test for Colored Aces," *Sporting News,* 2 October 1946, 9; "Paige's and Feller's Teams Launch Series," *Philadelphia Tribune,* 1 October 1946, 10; *Pittsburgh Courier,* 5 October 1946, 24; "Feller's Stars Away to Lead," *Sporting News,* 9 October 1946, 30; "Many Stars with Feller, Paige," *Pittsburgh Courier,* 21 September 1946, 25; Sam Lacy, "Looking 'Em Over," *Baltimore Afro-American,* 12 October 1946, 17; Sam Lacy, "Satchel's All-Stars Twice Beat Major Leaguers in Sunday Bill," *Baltimore Afro-American,* 12 October 1946, 17; *Chicago Defender,* 19 October 1946, 11; Fay Young, "Through the Years," *Chicago Defender,* 19 October 1946, 11; *Chicago Defender,* 26 October 1946, 11; "Paige and Feller," *Pittsburgh Courier,* 28 September 1946, 26; "Feller's All-Stars Attract 148,2000 in 15 Exhibitions," *Sporting News,* 16 October 1946, 23; *Pittsburgh Courier,* 5 October 1946, 24; *Pittsburgh Courier,* 12 October 1946, 15; *Pittsburgh Courier,* 19 October 1946, 25; "Feller's Stars Play to 22,577 in Los Angeles," *Sporting News,* 23 October 1946, 23; "250,000 See Feller-Paige Teams Play," *Sporting News,* 30 October 1946, 9; discussion with Sharon Robinson, daughter of Jackie Robinson, at the annual meeting of the Organization of American Historians in Los Angeles in 2001. Sharon Robinson strongly contended that her father's health issues and untimely death were a result of the extraordinary pressure he suffered as the first African American in modern Major League Baseball.

24. Interviews with O'Neil.

25. FBI file on Leroy Satchel Paige, Document Number 100-702-A.

26. FBI file on Leroy Satchel Paige, Document Numbers 61-7563-A, 100-702-A, 100-3-74-4673, 100-6343-8, 100-3-1-218, 100-3-60-142, 100-361611-2.

27. "Chicago Negro Newspaper Commends Daily Worker on Battle against Jim Crow," in FBI file on Paige, Document Number 61-7563-A.

28. FBI file on Paige, Document Number 100-7002-A.

29. FBI file on Paige, Document Number 100-3-74-4673.

30. FBI file on Paige, Document Number 100-3-1-218. For further discussion of the role of the Communist Party in the integration of baseball, see Irwin Silber, *Press Box Red: The Story of Lester Rodney, the Communist Who Helped Break the Color Line in American Sports,* especially 46–82, 112–23. See also Naison, *Communists in Harlem.*

31. *Sporting News,* 8 November 1945, 23; *Sporting News,* 17 July 1946, 30; *Sporting News,* 8 December 1948, 16.

32. Paige, *Maybe I'll Pitch Forever,* 181; interviews with O'Neil; interviews with Theodore Roosevelt "Double Duty" Radcliffe, July 1999 and July 2001, Chicago; exclusive interviews with Robert Leroy Paige, February 2006 and follow-ups, O'Fallon, Mo.; exclusive interviews with Pamela Paige O'Neal, April 2007 and follow-ups, Kansas City, Mo.

33. Exclusive interviews with P. P. O'Neal; exclusive interviews with R. L. Paige.

34. For a fuller discussion of the contributing factors to the decline of the Negro Leagues, see Lanctot, *Negro League Baseball,* 300–397.

35. Paige, *Maybe I'll Pitch Forever,* 188–89.

36. Ibid., 189.

37. Interview with Bob Feller, April 2007.

38. "Satchel Paige Fans 15 in Beating the Feller," *Philadelphia Tribune,* 4 November 1947, 10; *Baltimore Afro-American,* 8 November 1947, 14; *Chicago Defender,* 15 November 1947, 10; *Baltimore Afro-American,* 15 November 1947, 15, 17; *Philadelphia Tribune,* 11 November 1947, 8; "Jackie to Quit Baseball after Three Years," *Chicago Defender,* 1 November 1947, 11; Paige, *Maybe I'll Pitch Forever,* 190.

39. Paige, *Maybe I'll Pitch Forever,* 191–92.

40. Ibid., 192.

41. "Satchel Paige Fans 15 in Beating the Feller," *Philadelphia Tribune,* 4 November 1947, 10.

42. Ibid.

43. *Philadelphia Tribune,* 11 November 1947, 8.

44. *Sporting News,* 21 April 1948, 21; exclusive interviews with P. P. O'Neal.

Chapter 12. Center Stage in the White Arena

1. This was a sentiment that every Negro Leagues player expressed. Most made special mention that there were many more of the ballplayers before and during the time of Satchel Paige who deserved their shot at the Majors but were denied it because of their color. The change was long overdue. Interviews with Hank Aaron, Samuel Allen, George Altman, Jimmy Armstead, Otha Bailey, Ernie Banks, William Barnes, Herbert Barnhill, William Bell, Joseph Black, William Blair, Robert Boyd, William Breda, Sherwood Brewer, Clifford Brown, Ernest Burke, William "Ready" Cash, Henry Clark, James Cohen, James Colzie, Charlie Davis, Ross Davis, Felix Delgado, Wesley Lewis Dennis, Eugene Doby, Larry Doby, Joseph Douse, Mahlon Duckett, James Dudley, William Dumpson, Melvin Duncan, Henry Elmore, Lionel Evelyn, William Felder, Albertus Fennar, Wilmer Fields, John Gibbons, Louis Gillis, Harold Gordon, Harold Gould, Willie Grace, Acie Griggs, Arthur Hamilton, Charles Harmon, Isaiah Harris, Lonnie Harris, Willie Harris, Wilmer Harris, J. C. Hartman, John Head, Neil Henderson, Joe Henry, Francisco Herrera, Carl Holden, Ulysses Holliman, Gordon Hopkins, Cowan Hyde, Monford Irvin, Monte Irvin, James Ivory, Verdell Jackson, Clarence Jenkins, James "Pee Wee" Jenkins, Sam Jethroe, Clifford Johnson, Curtis Johnson, Donald Johnson, Ernest Johnson, Louis Johnson, Mamie Johnson, Ralph Johnson, Thomas Fairfax Johnson, Cecil Kaiser, Larry Kimbrough, Willie James Lee, Larry LeGrande, William Lindsay, William Little, Anthony Lloyd, Lester Lockett, Carl Long, Ernest Long, Lee Mabon, Raydell Maddix, Josef Marbury, Rendon Marbury, Frank Marsh, Edward Martin, Henry Mason, Willie Mays, Nathaniel McClinic, Clinton McCord, Walter McCoy, William McCrary, Ira McKnight, John Miles, Minnie Minoso, Jesse Mitchell, John Mitchell, James Moore, Robert Motley, Emilio Navarro, Don Newcombe, Orlando O'Farrill, Andrew Porter, Merle Porter, William Powell, Henry Prestwood, Marvin Price, Charlie Pride, Mack Pride, Henry Robinson, James Robinson, William Robinson, Jesse Rogers, Thomas Sampson, James Sanders, Ed Scott, Joseph Scott, Robert Scott, Pedro Sierra, Al Smith, Eugene Smith, George Smith, Quincy Smith, Alfred Surratt, Ron Teasley, Donald Troy, Thomas Turner, William "Cool Breeze" Van Buren, Ernest Westfield, Eugene White, Davey Whitney, Jimmy Wilkes, Clyde Henry Williams, Eli Williams, Eugene Williams, Willie Young, and Jim Zapp; interviews with John "Buck" O'Neil, November 2005 and follow-ups, Negro Leagues Museum, Kansas City, Mo.; interviews with Theodore Roosevelt "Double Duty" Radcliffe, July 1999 and July 2001, Chicago; interview with Bob Feller, April 2007; exclusive interviews with R. L. Paige; exclusive interviews with Pamela Paige O'Neal, April 2007 and follow-ups, Kansas City, Mo.

2. Bill Veeck, *Veeck as in Wreck: The Autobiography of Bill Veeck,* 184.

3. Ibid.

4. "Reach Goal on Long Road of Curves," *Sporting News,* 14 July 1948, 11; "Satchel Hurls for Cleveland Indians," *Chicago Defender,* 17 July 1948, 10; exclusive interviews with R. L. Paige.

5. Taylor Spink, "The Ill-Advised Moves," editorial, *Sporting News,* 14 July 1948, 8.

6. "Shuffling Satchel Fans 3 Dodgers in Row on 12 Pitches," *Detroit News,* 1948; "At Long Last Satchel Paige," Ashland Collection.

7. Lacy with Newsom, *Fighting for Fairness*, 70–71, 79.

8. Ibid., 69; Robert Smith, *Pioneers of Baseball*, 149–76.

9. Joseph Thomas Moore, *Pride against Prejudice: The Biography of Larry Doby*, 14, 30, 73, 77, 78–79, 88–89, 167–76; Lacy with Newsom, *Fighting for Fairness*, 69; R. Smith, *Pioneers of Baseball*, 136–49.

10. Ed McAuley, "Life in the Majors with Satchel Paige," *Sporting News*, 29 September 1948, 14. See also Moore, *Pride against Prejudice*, 168.

11. Moore, *Pride against Prejudice*, 175; interview with Bob Feller, April 2007; exclusive interviews with R. L. Paige.

12. Jackie Robinson, "Jackie Says," *Pittsburgh Courier*, 17 July 1948, 9.

13. *Pittsburgh Courier*, 17 July 1948, 10.

14. *Pittsburgh Courier*, 24 July 1948, 9; *Pittsburgh Courier*, 31 July 1948, 9.

15. "Paige Jinxes Senators and New York Yankees," *Chicago Defender*, 14 August 1948, 11; "Paige Is Baseball's Greatest Drawing Card," *Chicago Defender*, 28 August 1948, 11; *Chicago Defender*, 17 July 1948, 10; *Chicago Defender*, 14 August 1948, 11; "16th Annual Classic Draws Less than Satchel Paige Did Here August 13," *Chicago Defender*, 28 August 1948, 10; *Pittsburgh Courier*, 14 August 1948, 12; *Sporting News*, 21 July 1948, 9, 17, 24; "Tribe Raises Turnstiles Sights, Now Aims at Two Million Gate," *Sporting News*, 11 August 1948, 6; *Chicago Defender*, 21 August 1948, 1, 11; Ed McAuley, "Chicago's Surge to See Ol' Satch Collapses Gates," *Chicago Defender*, 28 August 1948, 4, 6; *Sporting News*, 28 August 1948, 8; "Starter Paige Packs 'Em," *Sporting News*, 1 September 1948, 29; *Sporting News*, 8 September 1948, 9; *Sporting News*, 15 September 1948, 10, 13.

16. Interviews with Radcliffe; interview with William Everett Samuels, July 1976, Chicago; interview with Alex Gayles, February 1999, Chicago; interview with Bob Feller, April 2007; "Paige Is Baseball's Greatest Drawing Card," *Chicago Defender*, 28 August 1948, 11; *Chicago Defender*, 17 July 1948, 10; *Chicago Defender*, 14 August 1948, 11; "16th Annual Classic Draws Less than Satchel Paige Did Here August 13," *Chicago Defender*, 28 August 1948, 10; *Pittsburgh Courier*, 14 August 1948, 12; *Sporting News*, 21 July 1948, 9, 17, 24; "Tribe Raises Turnstiles Sights, Now Aims at Two Million Gate," *Sporting News*, 11 August 1948, 6; *Chicago Defender*, 21 August 1948, 1, 11; Ed McAuley, "Chicago's Surge to See Ol' Satch Collapses Gates," *Chicago Defender*, 28 August 1948, 4, 6; *Sporting News*, 28 August 1948, 8; "Starter Paige Packs 'Em," *Sporting News*, 1 September 1948, 29; *Sporting News*, 8 September 1948, 9; *Sporting News*, 15 September 1948, 10, 13.

17. Ibid.

18. Ibid.

19. See sources in note 15.

20. *Sporting News*, 22 September 1948, 1; *Sporting News*, 28 September 1955, 24.

21. *Sporting News*, 22 September 1948, 1.

22. *Sporting News*, 6 October 1948, 16.

23. Paige, *Maybe I'll Pitch Forever*, 219.

24. Ibid., 220.

25. Ibid., 221.

26. "Satchel Feels Mistreated," *Cleveland News*, 7 October 1948, clippings in Ashland Collection; Paige, *Maybe I'll Pitch Forever*, 221–24.

27. "Cleveland Blows Its Top," *Sporting News*, 12 October 1948, 8. See also "Doby Tips Scale for Tribe," *Chicago Defender*, 16 October 1948, 1; *Sporting News*, 16 November 1949, 15; *Sporting News*, 16 October 1949, 8; *Sporting News*, 12 January 1949, 2; *Sporting News*, 5 January 1949, 11; *Sporting News*, 29 December 1948, 19.

28. "Parade of Conquering Heroes," *Sporting News*, 20 October 1948, 17; Paige, *Maybe I'll Pitch Forever*, 224; exclusive interviews with R. L. Paige.

29. Ibid.

30. "Satchel Feels Mistreated," *Cleveland News*, 7 October 1948, clippings in Ashland Collection; exclusive interviews with R. L. Paige; exclusive interviews with P. P. O'Neal; interviews with Radcliffe. See also sources in note 1.

31. Ibid.

32. "Cleveland Blows Its Top," *Sporting News*, 12 October 1948, 8. See also "Doby Tips Scale for Tribe," *Chicago Defender*, 16 October 1948, 1; *Sporting News*, 16 November 1949, 15; *Sporting News*, 16 October 1949, 8; *Sporting News*, 12 January 1949, 2; *Sporting News*, 5 January 1949, 11; *Sporting News*, 29 December 1948, 19.

33. "Satchel Paige" clipping dated October 1948, Ashland Collection. See also *Sporting News*, 1 September 1948, 4.

34. *Sporting News*, 20 October 1948, 2. For further discussion, see Manley and Hardwick, *Negro Baseball before Integration*, 93–101.

35. "Suggests Help of Majors to Negroes as Gate Cure," *Sporting News*, 27 October 1948, 5.

36. *Sporting News*, 20 October 1948, 15.

37. *Sporting News*, 20 October 1948, 30.

38. *Sporting News*, 27 October 1948, 23.

39. *Sporting News*, 15 December 1948, 17.

40. Mel Watkins, *Stepin Fetchit: The Life and Times of Lincoln Perry*, 250–54; *Sporting News*, 27 April 1949, 43; *Sporting News*, 29 October 1949, 26.

41. Exclusive interviews with R. L. Paige; "Satchel Feels Mistreated," *Cleveland News*, 7 October 1948, clippings in Ashland Collection.

42. Ibid.

43. Ibid.

44. "Hoskins Reveals Three Threats against Life Same Day in 1952; Credits Satchel Paige with Help," *Sporting News*, 4 March 1953, 15. See also *Sporting News*, 20 May 1953, 17; and interviews with O'Neil. Most of the Negro Leagues players who knew Paige say the same thing—that he had a strong sense of self and racial pride.

45. "Satch, Baseball's Drawing Card," *Chicago Defender*, 28 May 1949, 20.

46. Murray Polner, *Branch Rickey: A Biography*, 136–37; Ed McAuley, "Jackie Took the Wrong Tack in Charge against Yanks," *Sporting News*, 17 December 1952, 10; *Sporting News*, 27 May 1953, 15.

Chapter 13. Ninth Inning

1. Exclusive interviews with Robert Leroy Paige, February 2006 and follow-ups, O'Fallon, Mo.; exclusive interviews with Pamela Paige O'Neal, April 2007 and follow-ups, Kansas City, Mo.

2. Paige, *Maybe I'll Pitch Forever*, 227.

3. Ibid., 231–32.

4. This is my conclusion based on careful review of all available written sources. I was unable to corroborate Paige's statement that he actually received a contract. No one else mentions one. If it did exist, it would have, indeed, been for less money than Paige received the previous season.

5. Paige, *Maybe I'll Pitch Forever*, 264.

6. *Sporting News*, 23 May 1951, 35; "Veeck Would Keep Browns in Mound City," *Sporting News*, 13 June 1951, 6; "Boudreau's Battlers Who Went All the Way in 48," *Sporting News*, 14 July 1954, 7; "Satchmo a Big Help," *Sporting News*, 29 September 1954, 11; *Sporting News*, 6 April 1963, 15.

7. "Veeck," *Sporting News*, 27 June 1951, 4, 6.

8. *Sporting News*, 29 August 1951, 7; *Sporting News*, 5 September 1951, 11; "No Dull Moments on Browns after Veeck Purchased Club," *Sporting News*, 2 January 1952, 8; *Sporting News*, 26 September 1951, 6; *Sporting News*, 12 September 1951, 14.

9. "Ned Garver, Aiming at 20 Wins," *Sporting News*, 22 August 1951, 16; Paige, *Maybe I'll Pitch Forever*, 246–48.

10. Paige, *Maybe I'll Pitch Forever*, 243.

11. Ibid., 243–44.

12. Ibid., 245.

13. Ibid.

14. Ibid.

15. Ibid.

16. "Satch Signs 150th Pack, Cuts Another Year from His Age," *Sporting News*, 20 February 1952, 25.

17. Interviews with Theodore Roosevelt "Double Duty" Radcliffe, July 1999 and July 2001, Chicago.

18. *Sporting News*, 11 June 1952, 12.

19. *Sporting News*, 18 June 1952, 10.

20. "Old Satch Keeps Rolling Along; Pitches 10 Scoreless Innings," *Chicago Defender*, 28 June 1952, 1.

21. *Sporting News*, 19 Mars 1952, 13.

22. "Piersall Puts on a Show," *Sporting News*, 18 June 1952, 21; *Sporting News*, 25 June 1952, 3, 8; *Sporting News*, 9 July 1952, 17. See also Jimmy Piersall, *Fear Strikes Out*.

23. "Satchel Paige," *Sporting News*, 9 July 1952, 25; "Fan Gives Satch ERA Trophy," *Sporting News*, 1 October 1952, 31; *Sporting News*, 8 October 1952, 24; *Sporting News*, 29 October 1952, 24; *Sporting News*, 5 November 1952, 13.

24. "The Athletics Welcomes Fans, Players, and Officials to the All-Star Game in Philadelphia," *Sporting News*, 9 July 1952, 24; *Sporting News*, 17 September 1952, 8; *Sporting News*, 16 July 1952, 8.

25. *New York Times*, 7 July 1951, 20; "Fetchit to Do Movie on Paige," *Chicago Defender*, 29 November 1952, 13; *Chicago Defender*, 27 December 1952, 22; Watkins, *Stepin Fetchit*, 250–54. For earlier talk surrounding the possible film "The Satchel Paige Story," see *Chicago Defender*, 29 October 1949, 26; 29 September 1951, 23; and 28 May 1949, 20.

26. *Sporting News*, 3 June 1953, 24; *Sporting News*, 10 June 1953, 9; *Sporting News*, 1 July 1953, 36.

27. See "Satch Makes the Majors," *Collier's*, Ashland Collection. See also *Sporting News*, 20 May 1953, 16; *Sporting News*, 3 June 1953, 14; *Sporting News*, 10 June 1953, 26, 30; *Sporting News*, 24 June 1953, 21; *Sporting News*, 18 November 1953, 16.

28. Ibid.; exclusive interviews with R. L. Paige.

29. "Gibson Best Hitter—Campy," *Sporting News*, 30 July 1958, 38.

30. See "Satch Makes the Majors," *Collier's*, Ashland Collection.

31. Ibid., 56.

32. "Satch Makes the Majors," *Collier's*, 55, Ashland Collection.

33. Ibid., 56.

34. *Sporting News*, 8 July 1953, 8.

35. *Sporting News*, 22 July 1953, 5; "Pitching Choices Bring Criticism for Stengel," *Sporting News*, 15 July 1953, 5.

36. *Sporting News*, 23 July 1953, 21; *Sporting News*, 2 September 1953, 15. See also *Sporting News*, 30 May 1951, 16; *Sporting News*, 20 June 1951, 12; *Sporting News*, 14 January 1953, 2; *Sporting News*, 21 January 1953, 8; *Sporting News*, 25 February 1953, 17; "Satch Comes up with New Pitch," *Sporting News*, 11 March 1953, 18; "Ol' Satch Steals Spotlight," *Sporting News*, 25 March 1953, 23.

37. *Sporting News,* 16 September 1953, 13, 14; *Sporting News,* 30 September 1953, 29; "Where Veeck Goes, Satch Will Follow," *Sporting News,* 30 September 1953, 35; Paige, *Maybe I'll Pitch Forever,* 263.

Chapter 14. Extra Innings

1. "Satch to Hurl 'Paige Day' Kansas City Game October 11," *Sporting News,* 7 October 1953, 27; *Sporting News,* 14 October 1953, 29; "Priddy Beckons to Old Satchmo," *Sporting News,* 27 January 1954, 14; *Sporting News,* 10 February 1954, 29; *Sporting News,* 17 February 1954, 12; "Satchel Paige and Marty Marion Being Continually at Odds," *Sporting News,* 17 February 1954, 14; *Sporting News,* 17 February 1954, 24; *Sporting News,* 28 April 1954, 35; *Sporting News,* 9 January 1957, 15; "Pruitt Curves Satch," *Sporting News,* 19 August 1953, 24; *Sporting News,* 2 September 1953, 14.

2. Interviews with John "Buck" O'Neil, November 2005 and follow-ups, Negro Leagues Museum, Kansas City, Mo.

3. Ibid.

4. "The Fabulous Satchel Paige," *Collier's,* 13 June 1953, 58; "International Cheers, but Miami Yawns over New Club," *Sporting News,* 28 December 1955, 5; "Paige to Pitch Again! He's a Globe Trotter," 5 April 1954, Satchel Paige File, Ashland Collection.

5. Exclusive interviews with Pamela Paige O'Neal, April 2007 and follow-ups, Kansas City, Mo. See related materials in Dr. John O. Brown and Mary Faulkner Brown Papers, the Bob Simms Collection, and the abundant holdings on the cultural life and history of Overtown in the Black Archives.

6. "Old Satch Joins Veeck's Marlins," *Chicago Defender,* 5 May 1956, 19; "International Cheers, but Miami Yawns over New Club," *Sporting News,* 28 December 1955, 5; "Paige to Pitch Again! He's a Globe Trotter," 5 April 1954, Paige File, Ashland Collection; Paige, *Maybe I'll Pitch Forever,* 267; "Satchel Retains Magic, Pitches Marlins to Lead," *Baltimore Afro-American,* 14; "8,000 Watch Miami Open with 10-Three Win," *Fort Pierce News-Tribune,* 19 April 1956; "Satchel Paige Signs as Marlin Pitcher," *Philadelphia Tribune,* 1 May 1956, 10.

7. "The Fabulous Satchel Paige Picked Up Another Victory," *Sporting News,* 1 August 1956, 30; "Satch Miami's Sunday Ace," *Sporting News,* 8 August 1956, 28.

8. *Sporting News,* 8 August 1956, 38.

9. See files pertaining to the "Civil Rights Movement in Miami" in the Black Archives and in the Brown and Brown Papers. See also Chanelle Rose, "Neither Southern nor Northern: Miami, Florida, and the Black Freedom Struggle in America's Tourist Paradise, 1896–1968"; Patricia Stephens Due and Tananarive Due, *Freedom in the Family: A Mother-Daughter Memoir of the Fight for Civil Rights;* Raymond A. Mohl, *South of the South: Jewish Activists and the Civil Rights Movement in Miami, 1945–1960;* Marvin Dunn, *Black Miami in the 20th Century;* Thelma Vernell Anderson Gibson, *The Life Story of a Cocoanut Grove Native.*

10. Interview with Clyde Killans conducted by Professor Gregory Bush in 1997, with Professor Donald Spivey in attendance. Killans was the impresario for the Sir John and Mary Elizabeth hotels. He booked all the major acts throughout the years and was well into his eighties when Professor Bush interviewed him. Mr. Killans later spoke at a history graduate seminar at the University of Miami, sharing more of his unparalleled knowledge of the heyday of the African American cultural scene in Miami's Overtown. Professor Bush videotaped these interviews and has donated them, along with countless others that he has conducted over the years, to the University of Miami Richter Library. This massive oral history collection on Miami and South Florida should be available to researchers in 2012. See also related materials in the Brown and Brown Papers, the Simms Collection,

and the abundant holdings on the cultural life and history of Overtown in the Black Archives, including clippings from the *Miami Times*.

11. Jimmy Burns, "Miami's Quick Kayo Cancels Paula-Paige Bat-Pitch Duel," *Sporting News*, 26 September 1956, 35; Jimmy Burns, "Marlins Counting on Paige, Despite Retirement Talk," *Sporting News*, 30 January 1957, 4.

12. Jimmy Burns, "Satchel Checks on Snake Oil; He's All Set for Spring Drills," *Sporting News*, 13 March 1957, 36.

13. "Miami Marlins All Smiles—Satchel Paige Shows Up," *Sporting News*, 3 April 1957, 31.

14. *Sporting News*, 19 March 1958, 21; *Sporting News*, 30 July 1958, 38; *Sporting News*, 14 July 1958, 34; "Satchel Paige May Be in His 50s, But," *Sporting News*, 16 July 1958, 38; *Sporting News*, 20 August 1958, 29.

15. "Paige Suspended by Miami," *Sporting News*, 13 August 1958, 36.

16. Paige, *Maybe I'll Pitch Forever*, 276; "Marlins Go for Youth," *Sporting News*, 22 April 1959, 28.

17. "Maybe I'll Pitch Forever: Some Say He Was the Greatest Pitcher—Negro or White, of All Time. Even during His Heyday Satch Was a Living Legend," dated 1961 and found in Ashland Collection; exclusive interviews with Robert Leroy Paige, February 2006 and follow-ups, O'Fallon, Mo.; exclusive interviews with P. P. O'Neal.

18. "Marlins and Royals Lead Star Balloting," *Sporting News*, 9 July 1956, 29; "Havana, Cuba—Two of Baseball's Oldest Pitchers, Satchel Paige and Connie Marrero," *Sporting News*, 18 July 1956, 34.

19. "Satch Cited as Argument against Retirement at 55," *Sporting News*, 4 February 1953, 4; "Hirsh Grid's Answer to Satchel Paige," *Sporting News*, 4 February 1953, 4.

20. "Satch Named Relief Hurler on Veeck's All-Star Team," *Baltimore Afro-American*, 9 October 1957, 6; "For Old Men Only," *Baltimore Afro-American*, 17 December 1955, 4; "How Old Is Rookie Olivo? About 42, He Says," *Sporting News*, 23 may 1962, 17.

21. Interview with Hank Aaron; interview with Willie Mays; "Maybe I'll Pitch Forever: Some Say He Was the Greatest Pitcher—Negro or White, of All Time. Even during His Heyday Satch Was a Living Legend," dated 1961 and found in Ashland Collection; interviews with O'Neil.

22. "Satchel Paige" and news clippings "Negro Ballplayers Want Rights in South," "Baseball's Negroes Facing Brighter Spring," and "White Sox Buy Hotel to End Segregation of Players," authored by Wendell Smith and published in 1961 in the *Chicago American*. See the Smith Collection.

23. "Baseball Leads in Reducing Bias, Negro Players Agree," *Sporting News*, 20 April 1968, 8. For further discussion, see Bill Veeck, "Are There Too Many Negroes in Baseball?" *Ebony*, June 1960, 25–31, in Satchel Paige, Vertical File, A. Bartlett Giamatti Research Center. Virtually all the black ballplayers expressed similar sentiments.

24. Interviews with O'Neil; J. O'Neil, *I Was Right on Time*, 100–101, 111. See also episode 5, "Fifth Inning: Shadow Ball," of Ken Burns's series *Baseball*.

25. Ed Plaisted, "Satch Blows Stack—Clowns Aren't Funny," *Sporting News*, dated 1967 and found in Ashland Collection.

26. Ibid. See related document, "Ageless Satchel Paige," *Sporting News*, 25 June 1966; and "Satchel Paige Waived as Player, Will Be a Braves Coach in 1969," press release from the Braves, 18 October 1968, for release on Monday, 21 October, at 6:00 a.m., in Ashland Collection.

27. "Flood Case to Call Satch," Associated Press, 21 May 1970, Ashland Collection; Brad Snyder, *A Well-Paid Slave: Curt Flood's Fight for Free Agency in Professional Sports*,

301 and passim; "Killing of the Reserve Clause Highly Unlikely," *Sporting News*, 14 August 1965, 18.

28. Dick Young, "Satchel Paige Brands Baseball as Prejudiced," from Dick Young's column, 11 June 1969, copy in Ashland Collection.

29. Joe McGuff, "Paige Will Pitch in Finley's Next Novelty Number," *Sporting News*, 25 September 1965, 23; Robert Van Kirk, "Finley's Latest Headline Move Was the Signing of Satchel Paige. There Can Be Only One Purpose for This and That Is to Use Satch's Name as a Drawing Card," *Sporting News*, 2 October 1965, 2.

30. "Satchel Old Self," undated news item in Ashland Collection.

31. Interview with Aaron; "Ageless Satch Ready to Snip More Batters Buttons," *Sporting News*, 7 September 1968, 10; *Sporting News*, 11 September 1968, 12; *Sporting News*, 28 September 1968, 14; "Satch Rests in Richmond," undated report found in Ashland Collection; "Ageless Satchel Paige Pitched a One Inning Exhibition," unnamed newspaper clipping, 12 October 1968, 18; "Koufax for Comeback," undated news item found in Ashland Collection; *Sporting News*, 2 November 1968, 35; Henry Aaron, *I Had a Hammer: The Hank Aaron Story*, 12–13, 268–71.

32. Exclusive interviews with P. P. O'Neal.

33. Exclusive interviews with R. L. Paige; exclusive interviews with P. P. O'Neal.

34. Ibid.

35. Ibid.

36. Ibid.; *Mobile Register*, 6 January 1966.

37. US Census (1880), Beat 1, Choctaw, Ala., Roll T9, 7, Family History Film 1254007, p. 266.1000, Enumeration District 19; US Census (1880), Albemarle, Va., Roll T9, 1352, Family History Film 1255352, p. 134.3000, Enumeration District 6; US Census (1900), Garritys, Mobile, Ala., Roll T623 32, p. B3, Enumeration District 116; US Census (1910), Mobile Ward 10, Mobile, Ala., Roll T624 27, p. B11, Enumeration District 116; US Census (1920), Mobile Ward 9, Mobile, Ala., Roll T625 35, p. B5, Enumeration District 126; US Census (1930), Mobile, Ala., Roll 42, p. B5, Enumeration District 84. See report of death of Mrs. Lula Coleman Paige in *Baltimore Afro-American*, 15 January 1966, 18; *Mobile Register*, 6 January 1966; *Sporting News*, 22 January 1966, 24.

38. Interview of Robert Hieronimus, Negro Leagues Oral History Collection, 5, 23; *Sporting News*, 16 March 1944, 14; *Sporting News*, 7 June 1945, 3; "Lou Contrasts Mathis's of Christopher and Paige," *Sporting News*, 2 March 1949, 9; "Satchel Rides Again," *Sporting News*, 30 March 1949, 24; *Sporting News*, 31 August 1949, 15; *Sporting News*, 21 September 1949, 20; "Paige Role Falls to Flores," *Sporting News*, 22 February 1950, 27; *Sporting News*, 19 April 1950, 13; *Sporting News*, 23 May 1951, 19; *Sporting News*, 5 March 1952, 30; *Sporting News*, 4 February 1953, 14; *Sporting News*, 22 April 1953, 18; "Simple Arithmetic Lesson by Satch," *Sporting News*, 27 May 1953, 16; "Hurler Smart, but the Hitters Seldom Learn," *Sporting News*, 17 August 1955, 12; *Sporting News*, 26 February 1958, 14; *Sporting News*, 7 January 1959, 27; *Sporting News*, 15 September 1962, 37; *Sporting News*, 27 April 1963, 7; "Hats Off," *Sporting News*, 19 August 1967, 26; "Banks Recalls Facing Paige in Batting Drills," *Sporting News*, 31 August 1968, 10; *Sporting News*, 7 June 1969, 54; *Sporting News*, 14 June 1969, 35; "Gomez's Visit to Cuba Includes Chat with Castro," *Sporting News*, 21 February 1970, 32; *Sporting News*, 1 April 1972, 31; "Satch Did It Long before Mike," *Sporting News*, 30 November 1974, 40; *Sporting News*, 10 June 1978, 44; "Eddie Matthews: I Batted against Paige," *Sporting News*, 15 July 1978, 11; "Paige Not Impressed by Marshall's Mark," Ashland Collection; Solomon Otto, "'I Played against Satchel for Three Seasons': Blacks and Whites in the Twilight Leagues," 797–800; "Compares Satchel Paige: The Great Dizzy Dean after

Looking at His Fast One on Coast," *Pittsburgh Courier*, 15 July 1939, 16; "Great Carl Hubbell Lauds Playing of Josh Gibson and Famous 'Satch' Paige," *Pittsburgh Courier*, 22 July 1939, 16; "Jackie Says, by Jackie Robinson," *Pittsburgh Courier*, 8 May 1948, 15; Leslie A. Heaphy, *The Negro Leagues, 1869–1960*, 63, 70, 72, 103–4, 164, 166, 175–78; Lacy with Newsom, *Fighting for Fairness*, 233; Willie Mays, *Say Hey: The Autobiography of Willie Mays*, 16–27; Musick, *Hank Aaron*, 28–33, 36–37, 78–79, 122–23; "Jackson, Mississippi, Names Street for Cool Papa Bell, Fastest Man Ever to Play Baseball," 25; Jerry Polling, *A Summer Up North: Henry Aaron and the Legend of the Eau Claire Baseball*, 3–4; Alan J. Pollock, *Barnstorming to Heaven: Syd Pollock and His Great Black Teams*, 23, 96, 98, 104, 126, 128, 246; Fraser "Slow" Robinson with Paul Bauer, *My Life in the Negro Baseball Leagues*, xxii, 1, 12, 20, 21–43, 65–79, 98, 126, 129–37, 167; Ernest Withers, *Negro Leagues Baseball;* "The Tale of the Satchel Paige Opening-Day Tribute," *Kansas City Star*, 13 April 2006.

39. Interview with Bob Feller, April 2007; undated article from the *Chicago Tribune* on Satchel Paige found in the Ashland Collection, reprinted, in part, in the *Sporting News*, 17 February 1960, 6; Bob Feller, "Hall of Fame Unfair," *Saturday Evening Post*, 27 January 1964.

40. "Hall of Fame for Paige," *Sporting News*, 30 June 1962, 28; "You'll Win Your Fight, Veeck Tells K.C. Fans," *Sporting News*, 1 February 1964, 2; *Sporting News*, 12 October 1964, 34; "Too Bad They Can't Bend Rules for Satchel," *Sporting News*, 19 December 1964, 40; *Sporting News*, 16 January 1965, 16; *Sporting News*, 7 August 1965, 14; *Sporting News*, 5 February 1966, 4; *Sporting News*, 26 March 1966, 27; *Sporting News*, 20 August 1966, 5; "Something Missing," *Sporting News*, 12 November 1966, 4; "Drama at Cooperstown," *Sporting News*, 7 January 1967, 24–25; "Old-Time Negro Stars Get Shrine Boost," *Sporting News*, 9 August 1969, 5; "No Exceptions, Please," *Sporting News*, 6 September 1969, 6.

41. Paul S. Kerr to Leroy Robert Paige, Esquire, 7 July 1971, Ashland Collection.

42. Doc Young, "Satchel Paige," article from the *Los Angeles Times*, in the Ashland Collection; *Sporting News*, 27 February 1971, 17.

43. "Satch Walks and Shrine's Front Door," *Sporting News*, 18 August 1971, 5; "Satchel Paige Happy to Be Voted in Hall," *Amsterdam News*, 13 February 1971, 31; "Proud to Be in It Beams Satchel after Earning Shrine Spot," *Sporting News*, 20 February 1971, 42; "Gibson, Leonard Win Shrine Spots," *Sporting News*, 19 February 1972, 31; "Cool Papa, Black League Speedster, Name to Shrine," *Sporting News*, 23 February 1974, 30; "Junk Negro Shrine Vote, Says Young," *Sporting News*, 15 March 1975, 51; "Dihigo and Lloyd Voted into Shrine," *Sporting News*, 19 February 1977, 42; *Sporting News*, 19 March 1977, 38; *Sporting News*, 24 September 1977, 7; "Tough Test for Vets Committee," *Sporting News*, 4 February 1978, 52; "Satchel Paige, Recently Elected to a Place in Baseball's Hall of Fame by a Special Committee," *Sporting News*, 27 February 1971, 4; "The Hall of Famers: Leroy Robert Paige," National Baseball Hall of Fame and Museum; "Satchel Paige 'Almost' Joins Hall of Fame," *Hartford Courant*, in Ashland Collection; "My Greatest Day in Baseball," Satchel Paige remarks transcribed in Ashland Collection; "Leroy Robert Paige (Satchel)" the official background information and statistics in Ashland Collection; "42nd legislative assembly, state of North Dakota begun and held at the Capitol in the City of Bismarck, on Tuesday, the fifth day of January, 1971, House concurrent resolution number 3032 resolved: That the 42nd legislative assembly, on behalf of all North Dakotans, extends to a former North Dakota resident, Satchel Paige, sincere congratulations for capping a lifetime of baseball achievement with election to the Baseball Hall of Fame, and sends along to him its wishes that each of the next years may be his best in baseball; and be it resolved that, that the Secretary of State sends copies of this resolution to the Baseball Hall of Fame, Baseball Commissioner Bowie Kuhn, the Atlanta Braves, and to Satchel Paige"; Paul S.

Kerr, acknowledgment letters upon receipt of letters to the National Baseball Hall of Fame and Museum after the induction of Satchel Paige, 10 March 1971, in Ashland Collection; "Atonement of Cooperstown," 11 February 1971, in Ashland Collection; "Sports of the Times," regarding Satchel Paige and his induction, in Ashland Collection; "Leroy Paige Is the Greatest Thrower of a Baseball Who Ever Lives," further induction praise, in Ashland Collection; praise and adulation for Satchel Paige, assortment of letters and newspaper clippings, in Ashland Collection; "Satchel Paige: His Lifelong Dream Finally Fulfilled," *Miami Herald,* 10 February 1971; "Why Doesn't Baseball Put Paige in Front of the Hall?" article critical of the earlier decision to place Paige and other eventual Negro Leagues' inductees into a separate wing, in Ashland Collection.

44. Exclusive interviews with R. L. Paige.

45. Bill Ford interview with Satchel Paige, "Looking Back, Paige Relates Good and Bad," *Cincinnati Inquirer,* 24 June 1981, D4, 46, copy also in Ashland Collection.

46. See remarks of Herbert Simmons, Negro Leagues Oral History Collection: "They compared him with Satchel Paige, Leon Day. Compared to satchel there were many times that Leon Day and Satchel would pitch against each other, Leon would win, [and that is why Day] was selected to the Hall of Fame." "Black Latins Rate Hall," *Sporting News,* 25 August 1973; "Jackson, Mississippi, Names Street for Cool Papa Bell," 25.

47. See *This Is Your Life: Leroy 'Satchel' Paige* (Ralph Edwards Productions, YLS 031, taped 22 October 1971, aired in Los Angeles on 26 January 1972), CD 2007. Mark Ribowsky, in his biography of Paige, *Don't Look Back,* states, "*This Is Your Life,* which in 1958 rounded up and brought to Hollywood the now ninety-eight year old Lula Paige and a number of others from the Mobile streets—although Wilbur Hines was about the only one of those whom Satch could clearly remember" (312). The program was taped in 1971, not 1958, and Satchel Paige's mother, Lula Coleman Paige, was not there.

48. Bill Ford interview with Satchel Paige, "Looking Back, Paige Relates Good and Bad," *Cincinnati Inquirer,* 24 June 1981, D4, 46, copy also in Ashland Collection.

49. Ibid.

50. Ibid.

51. Ibid.

52. Ibid.

53. "Obituary of Leroy Robert Satchel Paige," in Ashland Collection; "Satchel Paige, Black Mound Ace, Dies in K.C. at 75 (?)," "Legendary Hall of Fame Hurler Was Rookie at 42," "Satchel Paige Hospitalized," "Death Finally Catches Satchel Paige," "Death Claims Satchel Paige, Pitching Legend," "Pitching Great Paige Dies," "Paige Legend Is Secure," "Satchel Paige Pitcher Became Legend before Color Line Ended," "Paige Remembered in Aftermath of Death," "Paige for Living," "Satchel Paige Legend," "The Satchel Paige Legend," "No Tears, Only Memories, at Satchel Paige's Funeral," all in Ashland Collection; "Mobile Honors Satchel Paige," "Mobile Should Build Monument to Paige," "Mobile's Satchel Paige Dies," and "Sister Shares Memories of Satchel Paige," from *Mobile Register,* 1 April 1990; "Age Is Still Mystery," "Color Line," "Close Friend Monte Irvin Says Thousands of Fans Were Cheated by Not Getting to See Paige Pitch," "Park Named after Paige in Kansas City, Missouri," "Was Mobile Born Satchel Paige the Greatest Pitcher Who Ever Lived?," all in the Paige Vertical File, Mobile, Ala., Public Library; "A Paige in Baseball History," "Satchel—Baseball Giant—Laid to Rest," "A Giant Is Returned to the Earth," "Paige Island Dedicated in Honor of Satchel Paige," and "Respect to Baseball's Legendary Satchel Paige Is Paid by Hundreds Saturday," all in *Kansas City Call;* "We Lost Satchel," "The Life and Times of Satchel Paige," "Loving Hands Restored Paige Stadium" (2001), "Composer Satchel Paige Song," "Old CYC Stadium Named for Kansas City's Own Legend, Satchel Paige," "In Appreciation of Satchel Paige" (2003), "Love Satchel Paige Because He's Ours,"

all in Paige Vertical File, Kansas City, Mo., Public Library. See also John Buck O'Neil, "The Unforgettable Satchel Paige." The death of Satchel Paige, not surprisingly, was carried in virtually every major American newspaper. Perhaps of greater significance was that his death was carried in virtually all small-town newspapers. See, for example, *Marysville (Ohio) Journal-Tribune*, 9 June 1982; *Santa Fe New Mexican*, 9 June 1982; *Elyria (Ohio) Chronicle Telegram*, 9 June 1982; *Waterloo (Iowa) Courier*, 13 June 1982; *Gettysburg (Pa.) Times*, 9 June 1982; *Alton (Ill.) Telegraph*, 9 June 1982; *Huntington (Pa.) Daily News*, 10 June 1982; *Annapolis Capital*, 9 June 1982; *Paris (Tex.) News*, 9 June 1982; *Logansport (Ind.) Pharos-Tribune*, 9 June 1982; *Atchison (Kans.) Globe*, 26 September 1982; and *Daily Sitka (Alaska) Sentinel*, 16 June 1982.

Bibliography

Archival Sources

Annual Report of the Alabama Reform School for Juvenile Negro Law Breakers. Alabama State Archives, Montgomery.

Annual Reports, State of Alabama, Department of Youth Services. Alabama State Archives, Montgomery.

Armstrong Family Papers. Williams College, Williamstown, MA.

Ashland Collection. A. Bartlett Giamatti Research Center, National Baseball Hall of Fame and Museum, Cooperstown, NY.

Biblioteca José M. Lázaro. Universidad de Puerto Rico, San Juan.

Black Archives. Miami, FL.

Brown, Dr. John O., and Mary Faulkner Brown. Papers. Special Collections Department, University of Miami Richter Library.

Central Files. National Archives and Records Administration, College Park, MD.

Colored Alabamian. Alabama State Archives, Montgomery.

Davis, Jackson. Collection. Albert and Shirley Small Special Collections, University of Virginia Library, Charlottesville.

Kendrick-Brooks Family Papers. Library of Congress, Washington, DC.

National Association of Colored Women's Papers. Library of Congress, Washington, DC.

Negro Leagues Oral History Collection. Special Collections Department, University of Baltimore Lansdale Library.

Newark Eagles. Papers. Newark, NJ, Public Library.

Paige, Satchel. FBI File. Federal Bureau of Investigation, Washington, DC.
——. Vertical File. A. Bartlett Giamatti Research Center, National Baseball Hall of Fame and Museum, Cooperstown, NY.
——. Vertical File. Kansas City, MO, Public Library.
——. Vertical File. Mobile, AL, Public Library.
Pan-American Airlines Collection. Special Collections Department, University of Miami Richter Library.
Peabody Collection. Media Archive, University of Georgia, Athens.
Pratt, Richard H. Papers. Library of Congress, Washington, DC.
Simms, Bob. Collection. Special Collections Department, University of Miami Richter Library.
Smith, Wendell. Collection. A. Bartlett Giamatti Research Center, National Baseball Hall of Fame and Museum, Cooperstown, NY.
United States Census Reports.
University of Georgia Special Collections, Athens.
University of Kansas Special Collections, Kansas City.
Veeck, Bill. Papers. Chicago History Museum.
Washington, Booker T. Papers. Library of Congress, Washington, DC.

Newspapers

Amsterdam News
Baltimore Afro-American
Birmingham Reporter
Bismarck Times
Bismarck Tribune
Chicago Defender
Cincinnati Inquirer
Cleveland News
Cleveland Plain Dealer
Daily Worker
Denver Post
Detroit News
Fort Pierce News-Tribune
Kansas City Call
Kansas City Star
Listin Diario
Los Angeles Times
Miami Herald
Mobile Register
Modesto Bee

New York Times
Oakland Tribune
Philadelphia Tribune
Pittsburgh Courier
Sporting News
Winnipeg Free Press

Other Sources

Aaron, Hank. *I Had a Hammer: The Hank Aaron Story.* New York: Harper Perennial, 1991.

Adelson, Bruce. *Brushing Back Jim Crow: The Integration of Minor-League Baseball in the American South.* Charlottesville: University Press of Virginia, 1999.

Alamillo, Jose M. "Peloterros in Paradise: Mexican American Baseball and Oppositional Politics in Southern California, 1930–1950." *Western Historical Quarterly* 34, no. 2 (2004).

Alsobrook, David E. "The Mobile Streetcar Boycott of 1902: African American Protest or Capitulation." *Alabama Review* (April 2003).

Ames, Ethel. *The Story of Coal and Iron in Alabama.* Birmingham: Chamber of Commerce, 1910.

Angell, Roger. *The Summer Game.* Lincoln: University of Nebraska Press, 1962.

Arbena, Joseph L., ed. *Sport and Society in Latin America: Diffusion, Dependency, and the Rise of Mass Culture.* Westport, CT: Greenwood Press, 1988.

Ashe, Arthur, with Arnold Rampersad. *Days of Grace: A Memoir.* New York: Ballantine Books, 1993.

Bachin, Robin F. *Building the South Side: Urban Space and Civic Culture in Chicago, 1890–1919.* Chicago: University of Chicago Press, 2004.

Bak, Richard. *Turkey Stearnes and the Detroit Stars: The Negro Leagues in Detroit, 1919–1933.* Detroit: Wayne State University Press, 1995.

Bankes, Jim. *The Pittsburgh Crawfords.* Jefferson, NC: McFarland, 2001.

Bauer, Paul. *My Life in the Negro Baseball Leagues.* Syracuse: Syracuse University Press, 1999.

Berlage, Gai Ingham. *Women in Baseball: The Forgotten History.* Westport, CT: Praeger, 1994.

Bjarkman, Peter C. *A History of Cuban Baseball, 1864–2006.* Jefferson, NC: McFarland, 2007.

Bloomfield, Gary L. *Duty, Honor, Victory: America's Athletes in World War II.* Guilford, CT: Lyons Press, 2003.

Bodley, Johnny. *These Eyes.* Selma, AL: Publish America, 2002.

Braden, Susan. *The Florida Resort Hotels of Henry Flagler and Henry Plant.* Gainesville: University Press of Florida, 2002.

Brawley, Benjamin. *Women of Achievement: Written for the Fireside Schools under the Auspices of the Women's American Baptist Home Mission Society.* Chapel Hill: University of North Carolina Special Collections, 1919.

Bready, James H. *Baseball in Baltimore.* Baltimore: Johns Hopkins University Press, 1998.

Briody, Dan. *The Halliburton Agenda: The Politics of Oil and Money.* Hoboken, NJ: John Wiley and Sons, 2004.

Brock, Lisa, and Digna Castaneda Fuertes, eds. *Between Race and Empire: African Americans and Cubans before the Cuban Revolution.* Philadelphia: Temple University Press, 1998.

Bruce, Janet. *The Kansas City Monarchs: Champions of Black Baseball.* Lawrence: University Press of Kansas, 1985.

Buerkle, Jack V., and Danny Baker. *Bourbon Street Black: The New Orleans Black Jazzman.* New York: Oxford University Press, 1974.

Bullock, Steven R. *Playing for Their Nation: Baseball and the American Military during World War II.* Lincoln: University of Nebraska Press, 2004.

Burgos, Adrian, Jr. *Playing America's Game: Baseball, Latinos, and the Color Line.* Berkley and Los Angeles: University of California Press, 2007.

Bynum, Mike, ed. *Pop Warner, Football's Greatest Teacher: The Epic Autobiography of Major College Football's Winningest Coach, Glenn S. (Pop) Warner.* Philadelphia: Gridiron Football Properties, 1993.

Campanella, Roy. *It's Good to Be Alive.* Lincoln: University of Nebraska Press, 1995.

Carol, John M. *Fritz Pollard: Pioneer in Racial Advancement.* Urbana: University of Illinois Press, 1992.

Carroll, Brian. *When to Stop the Cheering? The Black Press, the Black Community, and the Integration of Professional Baseball.* New York: Routledge, 2007.

Cash, Floris Barnett. "Kinship and Quilting: An Examination of an African-American Tradition." *Journal of Negro History* 80, no. 1 (1995).

Castner, Charles B. *A Brief History of the Louisville and Nashville Railroad.* Louisville, KY: Louisville and Nashville Railroad Historical Society, 2006.

Chandler, David. *Henry Flagler: The Astonishing Life and Times of the Visionary Robber Baron Who Founded Florida.* New York: Macmillan, 1986.

Chandler, Happy. *Heroes, Plain False, and Skunks: The Life and Times of Happy Chandler.* Chicago: Bonus Books, 1999.

Chattanooga African American Museum. *Black America Series: Chattanooga.* Charleston, SC: Arcadia, 2005.

Clark, Dick, and Larry Lester, eds. *The Negro Leagues Book*. Cleveland, OH: Society for American Baseball Research, 1994.

Clark, Willis G. *History of Education in Alabama, 1702–1889*. Circular of Information no. 3. Washington, DC: Government Printing Office, 1889.

Cochran, Jerome, MD. *History of the Small-Pox Epidemic in the City of Mobile, 1874–5, with Mortuary and Meteorological Tables, Also Notes and Reflections upon Diphtheria and Typho-Malarial Fever; Together with an Ordinance to Secure the Public Health*. Montgomery: Barrett and Brown, Steam Printers and Book Binders, 1875, Mobile Public Library.

Cooper, Michael L. *Indian School: Teaching the White Man's Way*. New York: Clarion Books, 1999.

Cottrell, Robert Charles. *The Best Pitcher in Baseball: The Life of Rube Foster, Negro League Giant*. New York: New York University Press, 2001.

Coulter, Charles E. *Take Up the Black Man's Burden: Kansas City's African-American Communities, 1865–1939*. Columbia: University of Missouri Press, 2006.

Cuhaj, Joe, and Tamra Carraway-Hinckle. *Baseball in Mobile*. Charleston, SC: Arcadia, 2003.

Daniels, Douglas Henry. *Lester Leaps In: The Life and Times of Lester "Pres" Young*. Boston: Beacon Press, 2002.

Dietz, Andrew. *The Last Folk Hero: A True Story of Race and Art, Power and Profit*. Atlanta: Ellis Lane Press, 1993.

Diggs, Frank, and Chuck Haddix. *Kansas City Jazz from Ragtime to Bebop: A History*. New York: Oxford University Press, 2005.

Dittmer, Richard. "An Exploration of the Motivating Forces behind Brig. General R. H. Pratt's Creation of the Indian Industrial School at Carlisle, Pennsylvania." Master's thesis, University of Nebraska, 1993.

Dixon, James L. *Pictorial History of Mobile Civil Rights: Civil Rights Movement to the 1960's Black Revolution*. Mobile: Mobile Public Library History and Genealogy Services, 1996.

Dixon, Phil. *The Negro Baseball Leagues: A Photographic History*. Mattituck, NY: Ameron, 1992.

Due, Patricia Stephens, and Tananarive Due. *Freedom in the Family: A Mother-Daughter Memoir of the Fight for Civil Rights*. New York: One World Press, 2003.

Duke, Eric D. "A Life in the Struggle: John L. LeFlore and the Civil Rights Movements in Mobile, Alabama, 1925–1975." Master's thesis, Florida State University, 1998.

Dunn, Marvin. *Black Miami in the 20th Century*. Gainesville: University Press of Florida, 1997.

Early, Gerald. *The Culture of Bruising: Essays on Prize Fighting, Literature, and Modern American Culture*. Hopewell, NJ: Ecco Press, 1994.

——. *Tuxedo Junction: Essays on American Culture*. New York: Ecco Press, 1989.

Feldmann, Doug. *Dizzy and the Gas House Gang*. Jefferson, NC: McFarland, 2000.

Fox, William Price. *Satchel Paige's America*. Tuscaloosa: University of Alabama Press, 2005.

Fullerton, Christopher. *The Story of the Birmingham Black Barons*. Birmingham: Boozer Press, 1999.

Gates, Henry Louis, Jr. *Signifying Monkey: A Theory of African-American Literary Criticism*. New York: Oxford University Press, 1988.

Gibson, Thelma Vernell Anderson. *The Life Story of a Cocoanut Grove Native*. Homestead, FL: Helena Enterprises, 2000.

Gillis, Delia C. *Kansas City*. Charleston, SC: Arcadia, 2007.

Gilmore, Al-Tony. *Bad Nigger: The National Impact of Jack Johnson*. Port Washington, NY: Kennikat, 1975.

Gitersonke, Don. *Baseball's Bearded Boys: A Historical Look at the Israelite House of David Baseball Club of Benton Harbor, Michigan*. Las Vegas: Gitersonke, 1996.

Glasco, Lawrence A. *The WPA History of the Negro in Pittsburgh*. Pittsburgh: University of Pittsburgh Press, 2004.

Govan, Gilbert E., and James Livingood. *The Chattanooga Country, 1540–1976*. Knoxville: University of Tennessee Press, 1977.

Gray, Jerome A., et al. *History of the Alabama State Teachers Association*. Washington, DC: National Education Association, 1987.

Greenberg, Hank. *Hank Greenberg: The Story of My Life*. Chicago: Triumph Books, 1989.

Gregory, Robert. *Diz: Dizzy Dean and Baseball during the Great Depression*. New York: Viking, 1992.

Guevara, Arturo J. Marcano, and David P. Fidler. *Stealing Lives: The Globalization of Baseball and the Tragic Story of Alex Quizoz*. Bloomington: Indiana University Press, 2002.

Guttmann, Allen. *Sports Spectators*. New York: Columbia University Press, 1986.

Haddock, John, and Steven Ross. *Black Diamonds Blues City: Stories of the Memphis Red Sox*. Film documentary. Memphis: University of Memphis, 1977.

Hagenbuch, Mark O. "Richard Henry Pratt, the Carlisle Indian Industrial School, and U.S. Policies Related to American Indian Education, 1879 to 1904." PhD diss., Pennsylvania State University, 1998.

Handy, W. C. *Father of the Blues: An Autobiography.* New York: Collier Books, 1970.

Harris, Neil. *Humbug: The Art of P. T. Barnum.* Chicago: University of Chicago Press, 1973.

Harthyn, Jonathan. *The Struggle for Democratic Politics in the Dominican Republic.* Chapel Hill: University of North Carolina Press, 1998.

Haskins, Don. *Glory Road: The Story of the 1966 NCAA Basketball Championship and How One Team Triumphed against the Odds and Changed America Forever.* New York: Hyperion, 2006.

Haskins, Jim, and N. R. Mitgang. *Mister Bojangles: The Biography of Bill Robinson.* New York: William Morrow, 1988.

Hawkins, Joel, and Terry Bertolino. *The House of David Baseball Team.* Charleston, SC: Arcadia, 2000.

Haynes, George Edmund. "Conditions among Negroes in the Cities." *Annals of the American Academy of Political and Social Science* 49 (September 1913).

Heaphy, Leslie A., ed. *Black Baseball and Chicago.* Jefferson, NC: McFarland, 2006.

——, ed. *The Negro Leagues, 1869–1960.* Jefferson, NC: McFarland, 2003.

——, ed. *Satchel Paige and Company: Essays on the Kansas City Monarchs, Their Greatest Star, and the Negro Leagues.* Jefferson, NC: McFarland, 2007.

Hoffbeck, Stephen R., ed. *Swinging for the Fences: Black Baseball in Minnesota.* St. Paul: Minnesota Historical Society Press, 2005.

Hogan, Lawrence. *Shades of Glory: The Negro Leagues and the Story of African-American Baseball.* Washington, DC: National Geographic, 2006.

Holloway, Bessie Mae. "A History of Public School Education in Mobile, Alabama, for the Child under Six Years of Age, 1833–1928." PhD diss., Auburn University, 1983.

Holway, John B. *Josh and Satch: The Life and Times of Josh Gibson and Satchel Paige.* New York: Carroll and Graf, 1991.

——. *Voices from the Great Black Baseball Leagues.* New York: Da Capo Press, 1992.

"Jackson, Mississippi, Names Street for Cool Papa Bell, Fastest Man Ever to Play Baseball." *Jet,* July 1994.

Jaimes, M. Annette, ed. *The State of Native America: Genocide, Colonization, and Resistance.* Cambridge, MA: South End Press, 1992.

Jamail, Milton H. *Full Count: Inside Cuban Baseball.* Carbondale: Southern Illinois University Press, 2000.

Kaiser, David. *Epic Season: The 1948 American League Pennant Race.* Amherst: University of Massachusetts Press, 1998.

Kelley, Robin D. G. *Yo' Mama's Disfunktional: Fighting the Culture Wars in Urban America.* Boston: Beacon Press, 1997.

Kirsch, George B. *The Creation of American Team Sports: Baseball and Cricket, 1838–72.* Urbana: University of Illinois Press, 1989.

Kirwin, Bill. *Out of the Shadows: African American Baseball from the Cuban Giants to Jackie Robinson.* Lincoln: University of Nebraska Press, 2005.

Klein, Alan M. *Baseball on the Border: A Tale of Two Laredos.* New Haven: Yale University Press, 1997.

——. *Growing the Game: The Globalization of Major League Baseball.* New Haven: Yale University Press, 2006.

——. *Sugar Ball: The American Game, the Dominican Dream.* New Haven: Yale University Press, 1991.

Kuska, Bob. *Hot Potato: How Washington and New York Gave Birth to Black Basketball and Changed America's Game Forever.* Charlottesville: University Press of Virginia, 2004.

Kyle, Donald G., and Robert B. Fairbanks, eds. *Baseball in America and America in Baseball.* College Station: Texas A&M Press, 2008.

Lacy, Sam, with Moses J. Newson. *Fighting for Fairness: The Life Story of Hall of Fame Sportswriter Sam Lacy.* Centreville, MD: Tidewater, 1998.

Lanctot, Neil. *Negro League Baseball: The Rise and Ruin of a Black Institution.* Philadelphia: University of Pennsylvania Press, 2004.

Lester, Larry. *Black Baseball's National Showcase: The East-West All-Star Game, 1933–1953.* Lincoln: University of Nebraska Press, 2001.

Lester, Larry, and Sammy J. Miller. *Black Baseball in Kansas City.* Charleston, SC: Arcadia, 2000.

——. *Black Baseball in Pittsburgh.* Charleston, SC: Arcadia, 2001.

Livingood, James. *Chattanooga: An Illustrated History.* Woodland Hills, CA: Windsor, 1980.

Lomax, Alan. *Mister Jelly Roll.* Berkeley and Los Angeles: University of California Press, 1973.

Lomax, Michael E. *Black Baseball Entrepreneurs, 1860–1901.* Syracuse: Syracuse University Press, 2003.

Loverro, Tom. *The Encyclopedia of Negro League Baseball.* New York: Checkmark Books, 2003.

Luke, Bob. *Willie Wells: El Diablo of the Negro Leagues.* Austin: University of Texas Press, 2007.

Malloy, Jerry. *Sol White's History of Colored Baseball, with Other Documents on the Early Black Game, 1886–1936.* Lincoln: University of Nebraska Press, 1995.

Manis, Andrew M. *A Fire You Can't Put Out: The Civil Rights Life of Birming-*

ham's Reverend Fred Shuttlesworth. Tuscaloosa: University of Alabama Press, 1999.

Manley, Effa, and Leon Hardwick. *Negro Baseball before Integration.* Hayworth, NJ: St. Johann Press, 1976.

Mannhard, Marilyn. "The Free People of Color in Antebellum Mobile County, Alabama." Master's thesis, University of South Alabama, 1982.

Maraniss, David. *Clemente: The Passion and Grace of Baseball's Last Hero.* New York: Simon and Schuster, 2006.

Mays, Willie. *Say Hey: The Autobiography of Willie Mays.* New York: Pocket Books, 1988.

McMurry, Charles A. *Chattanooga: Its History and Geography.* Morristown, TN: Globe Book, 1923.

McNamara, Brooks. *Step Right Up.* Jackson: University Press of Mississippi, 1995.

McNary, Kyle. *Black Baseball: A History of African Americans and the National Game.* London: PRC Press, 2003.

———. *Ted "Double Duty" Radcliffe: 36 Years of Pitching and Catching in Baseball's Negro Leagues.* Minneapolis: McNary, 1994.

McNeil, Genna Rae. *Groundwork: Charles Hamilton Houston and the Struggle for Civil Rights.* Philadelphia: University of Pennsylvania Press, 1983.

McNeil, William F. *Baseball's Other All-Stars: The Greatest Players from the Negro Leagues, the Japanese Leagues, the Mexican League, and the Pre-1968 Winter Leagues in Cuba, Puerto Rico, and the Dominican Republic.* Jefferson, NC: McFarland, 2000.

———. *Black Baseball Out of Season.* Jefferson, NC: McFarland, 2007.

———. *The California Winter League.* Jefferson, NC: McFarland, 2002.

Messner, Michael A. *Power at Play: Sport and the Problem of Masculinity.* Boston: Beacon Press, 1992.

Miller, Patrick B., and David K. Wiggins, eds. *Sport and the Color Line.* New York: Routledge, 2003.

Mohl, Raymond A. "Clowning Around: The Miami Ethiopian Clowns and Cultural Conflict in Black Baseball." *Tequesta: The Journal of the Historical Association of Southern Florida* 1, no. 62 (2002).

———. *South of the South: Jewish Activists and the Civil Rights Movement in Miami, 1945–1960.* Gainesville: University Press of Florida, 2004.

Moore, Joseph Thomas. *Pride against Prejudice: The Biography of Larry Doby.* Westport, CT: Praeger, 1988.

Musick, Phil. *Hank Aaron: The Man Who Beat the Babe.* New York: Popular Library, 1974.

Nager, Larry. *Memphis Beat: The Lives and Times of America's Musical Crossroads.* New York: St. Martin's Press, 1998.

Naison, Mark. *Communists in Harlem during the Depression*. Urbana: University of Illinois Press, 1983.

Nanita, Abelardo. *Trujillo*. Ciudad Trujillo: Editoria del Caribe, C. Por A. Ciudad Trujillo, 1954.

The Negro Leagues Players' Reunion Alumni Book. Kansas City, MO: Negro Leagues Baseball Museum, 2000.

Niiya, Brian, ed. *More than a Game: Sport in the Japanese American Community*. Los Angeles: Japanese American National Museum, 2000.

Noriega, Jorge. "American Indian Education in the United States: Indoctrination for Subordination to Colonialism." In *The State of Native America: Genocide, Colonization, and Resistance*, edited by M. Annette Jaimes, 380–95. Cambridge, MA: South End Press, 1992.

Nunnelley, William A. *Bull Connor*. Tuscaloosa: University of Alabama Press, 1991.

Oliver, Paul. *Bessie Smith*. South Brunswick, NJ: A. S. Barnes, 1971.

O'Neil, John "Buck." *I Was Right on Time: My Journey from the Negro Leagues to the Majors*. New York: Simon and Schuster, 1997.

——. "The Unforgettable Satchel Paige." *Reader's Digest*, April 1984, 89–93.

Oriard, Michael. *King Football: Sport and Spectacle in the Golden Age of Radio and News Reels, Movies and Magazines, the Weekly and the Daily Press*. Chapel Hill: University of North Carolina Press, 2001.

Ornes, German E. *Trujillo: Little Caesar of the Caribbean*. New York: Thomas Nelson and Sons, 1958.

Ottley, Roi, and William J. Weatherby. *The Negro in New York: An Informal Social History, 1628–1940*. New York: Praeger, 1967.

Otto, Solomon. "'I Played against Satchel for Three Seasons': Blacks and Whites in the Twilight Leagues." *Journal of Popular Culture* 7 (Spring 1974).

Overmyer, James. *Queen of the Negro Leagues: Effa Manley and the Newark Eagles*. Lanham, MD: Scarecrow Press, 1998.

Paige, Leroy Satchel (as told to Hal Lebovitz). *Pitchin' Man: Satchel Paige's Own Story*. Westport, CT: Meckler, 1948.

Paige, Leroy Satchel (as told to David Lipman). *Maybe I'll Pitch Forever*. Lincoln: University of Nebraska Press, 1993.

Painter, Nell. *Exodusters: Black Migration to Kansas after Reconstruction*. New York: Alfred A. Knopf, 1977.

Palmer, Robert. *Deep Blues: A Musical and Cultural History of the Mississippi Delta*. New York: Penguin, 1982.

Pearson, Nathan W. *Goin' to Kansas City*. Urbana: University of Illinois Press, 1994.

Peterson, Robert. *Only the Ball Was White*. New York: Oxford University Press, 1970.

Piersall, Jimmy. *Fear Strikes Out.* Boston: Little, Brown, 1955.

Polling, Jerry. *A Summer Up North: Henry Aaron and the Legend of the Eau Claire Baseball.* Madison: University of Wisconsin Press, 2002.

Pollock, Alan J. *Barnstorming to Heaven: Syd Pollock and His Great Black Teams.* Tuscaloosa: University of Alabama Press, 2006.

Polner, Murray. *Branch Rickey: A Biography.* Jefferson, NC: McFarland, 2007.

Powers-Beck, Jeffrey. *The American Indian Integration of Baseball.* Lincoln: University of Nebraska Press, 2004.

Pratt, Richard H. *Battlefield and Classroom: Four Decades with the American Indian, 1867–1904.* New Haven: Yale University Press, 1964.

Rampersad, Arnold. *Jackie Robinson: A Biography.* New York: Alfred A. Knopf, 1997.

Reisler, Jim. *Black Writers/Black Baseball: An Anthology of Articles from Black Sportswriters Who Covered the Negro Leagues.* Jefferson, NC: McFarland, 1994.

Rhoden, William C. *Forty Million Dollar Slaves: The Rise, Fall, and Redemption of the Black Athlete.* New York: Crown, 2006.

Ribowsky, Mark. *Don't Look Back: Satchel Paige in the Shadows of Baseball.* New York: Simon and Schuster, 1994.

Riess, Steven A. *City Games: The Evolution of American Urban Society and the Rise of Sport.* Urbana: University of Illinois Press, 1989.

——. "The Profits of Major League Baseball, 1900 to 1956." In *Baseball in America and America in Baseball,* edited by Donald G. Kyle and Robert B. Fairbanks, 88–142. College Station: Texas A&M Press, 2008.

Riley, James A. *The Biographical Encyclopedia of the Negro Baseball Leagues.* New York: Carroll and Graf, 1994.

Roberts, Randy. *Papa Jack: Jack Johnson and the Era of White Hopes.* New York: Free Press, 1983.

Roberts, Randy, and James Olson. *Winning Is the Only Thing: Sports in America since 1945.* Baltimore: Johns Hopkins University Press, 1989.

Robinson, Fraser "Slow," with Paul Bauer. *Catching Dreams: My Life in the Negro Baseball Leagues.* Syracuse: Syracuse University Press, 1999.

Robinson, Jackie. *Baseball Has Done It.* Philadelphia: Lippincott, 1964.

——. *I Never Had It Made: The Autobiography of Jackie Robinson.* Hopewell, NJ: Ecco Press, 1995.

Robinson, Sugar Ray, with Dave Anderson. *Sugar Ray: The Sugar Ray Robinson Story.* New York: Da Capo Press, 1994.

Rogosin, Donn. *Invisible Men: Life in Baseball's Negro Leagues.* New York: Kodansha, 1995.

Roper, Scott. "Uncovering Satchel Paige's 1935 Season: A Summer in North Dakota." *Baseball Research Journal,* no. 23 (November 1994).

Rose, Chanelle. "Neither Southern nor Northern: Miami, Florida, and the Black Freedom Struggle in America's Tourist Paradise, 1896–1968." PhD diss., University of Miami, 2007.

Ruck, Rob. *Sandlot Seasons: Sport in Black Pittsburgh.* Urbana: University of Illinois Press, 1987.

——. *The Tropic of Baseball: Baseball in the Dominican Republic.* Lincoln: University of Nebraska Press, 1998.

Rucker, Mark, and Peter Bjarkman. *Smoke: The Romance and Lore of Cuban Baseball.* New York: Total Sports Illustrated, 1999.

Rust, Art. *Get That Nigger Off the Field: An Oral History of Black Ballplayers from the Negro Leagues to the Present.* New York: Book Mail Services, 1992.

Scott, John B. *Memories of the Mount: The Story of Mt. Meigs, Alabama.* Montgomery: Black Belt Press, 1993.

Seidel, Michael. *Ted Williams: A Baseball Life.* Chicago: Contemporary Books, 1991.

Seymour, Harold. *Baseball: The Early Years.* New York: Oxford University Press, 1960.

——. *Baseball: The Golden Years.* New York: Oxford University Press, 1971.

Shrimer, Sherry Lamb. *A City Divided: The Racial Landscape of Kansas City, 1900–1960.* Columbia: University of Missouri Press, 2002.

Sickels, Johns. *Bob Feller: Ace of the Greatest Generation.* Washington, DC: Brassey's, 2004.

Silber, Irwin. *Press Box Red: The Story of Lester Rodney, the Communist Who Helped Break the Color Line in American Sports.* Philadelphia: Temple University Press, 2003.

Smith, Jessie Carney, ed. *Notable Black American Women.* Detroit: Gale Research, 1992.

Smith, Robert. *Pioneers of Baseball.* Boston: Little, Brown, 1978.

Snyder, Brad. *Beyond the Shadow of the Senators: The Untold Story of the Homestead Grays and the Integration of Baseball.* New York: McGraw-Hill, 2003.

——. *A Well-Paid Slave: Curt Flood's Fight for Free Agency in Professional Sports.* New York: Viking Press, 2006.

Social Betterment among Negro Americans: A Social Study Made by Atlanta University, under the Patronage of the Trustees of the John F. Slater Fund. Atlanta: Atlanta University Press, 1909.

Somers, Dale. *The Rise of Sports in New Orleans, 1850–1900.* Baton Rouge: Louisiana State University Press, 1972.

Sowell, Mike. *The Pitch That Killed.* Chicago: Ivan Dee, 1989.

Spatz, Lyle, and the Society for American Baseball Research. *The SABR Baseball List and Record Book.* New York: Scribner, 2007.

Spivey, Donald. "End Jim Crow in Sports: The Protest at New York University, 1940–1941." *Journal Sport History* 15, no. 1 (1988).

——. *Fire from the Soul: A History of the African-American Struggle.* Durham: Carolina Academic Press, 2003.

——. "Satchel Paige's Struggle for Selfhood in the Era of Jim Crow." In *Out of the Shadows: A Biographical History of African American Athletes,* edited by David K. Wiggins, 93–109. Fayetteville: University of Arkansas Press, 2006.

——. *Schooling for the New Slavery: Black Industrial Education, 1868–1915.* Trenton, NJ: Africa World Press, 2007.

——. "Sport, Protest, and Consciousness: The Black Athlete in Big-Time Intercollegiate Sports, 1941–1968." *Phylon* 44, no. 2 (1983): 116–25.

——, ed. *Sport in America: New Historical Perspectives.* 1978. Reprint, Westport, CT: Greenwood Press, 1985.

——, ed. *Union and the Black Musician: The Narrative of William Everett Samuels and Chicago Local 208.* Lanham, MD: University Press of America, 1984.

Sterry, David. *Satchel Sez: The Wit, Wisdom, and World of Leroy "Satchel" Paige.* New York: Three Rivers Press, 2001.

Stewart, Wayne. *Babe Ruth: A Biography.* Westport, CT: Greenwood Press, 2006.

Storb, Ilse. *Louis Armstrong: The Definitive Biography.* New York: Peter Lang, 1989.

Strode, Woody. *Gold Dust: The Warm and Candid Memoirs of a Pioneer Black Athlete and Actor.* Lanham, MD: Madison Books, 1990.

Summersell, Charles Grayson. *Mobile: History of a Seaport Town.* Birmingham: University of Alabama Press, 1949.

Swanton, Barry. *The Mandak League: Haven for Former Negro League Ballplayers, 1950–1957.* Jefferson, NC: McFarland, 2006.

Toll, Robert. *Blacking Up: The Minstrel Show in 19th-Century America.* New York: Oxford University Press, 1974.

Trotter, Joe William, Jr., and Eric Smith, eds. *African America in Pennsylvania: Signifying Historical Perspectives.* University Park: Pennsylvania State University Press, 1992.

——. *From a Raw Deal to a New Deal? African Americans, 1929–1945.* New York: Oxford University Press, 1996.

Trujillo, Rafael L. *The Basic Policies of a Regime.* Ciudad Trujillo: Editora del Carire, 1960.

Tygiel, Jules. *Baseball's Great Experiment: Jackie Robinson and His Legacy.* New York: Oxford University Press, 1983.

——. *Past Time: Baseball as History.* New York: Oxford University Press, 2000.

Tyson, Tim. *Radio Free Dixie: Robert F. Williams and the Roots of Black Power.* Chapel Hill: University of North Carolina Press, 2001.

Van Hyning, Thomas E. *The Santurce Crabbers: Sixty Seasons of Puerto Rican Winter League Baseball.* Jefferson, NC: McFarland, 1999.

Veeck, Bill. *Veeck as in Wreck: The Autobiography of Bill Veeck.* Chicago: University of Chicago Press, 1962.

Virtue, John. *South of the Border: How Jorge Pasquel and the Mexican League Pushed Baseball toward Racial Integration.* Jefferson, NC: McFarland, 2008.

Voigt, David Q. *America through Baseball.* Chicago: Nelson-Hall, 1976.

Von Eschen, Penny. *Satchmo Blows Up the World: Jazz Ambassadors Play the Cold War.* Cambridge: Harvard University Press, 2004.

Wailoo, Keith. *Dying in the City of the Blues: Sickle Cell Anemia and the Politics of Race and Health.* Chapel Hill: University of North Carolina Press, 2001.

Walker, Moses Fleetwood. *Our Home Colony: A Treatise on the Past, Present, and Future of the Negro Race in America.* 1908. Reprint, Steubenville, OH: Rieger, 1993.

Ward, Godfrey C. *Unforgivable Blackness: The Rise and Fall of Jack Johnson.* New York: Vintage, 2006.

Warner, Glenn S. *Pop Warner's Book for Boys.* New York: American Book\-Stratford Press, 1942.

Washington, Booker T. "Signs of Progress among the Negroes." *Century* 59 (1900): 472–78.

——, ed. *Tuskegee and Its People: Their Ideals and Achievements.* New York: Appleton, 1906.

——. "William Henry Lewis." *American Magazine* 75 (June 1913): 34–37.

Watkins, Mel. *Stepin Fetchit: The Life and Times of Lincoln Perry.* New York: Pantheon Books, 2005.

Wheeler, Lonnie. "Hounded Out of Baseball." *Ohio Magazine* (May 1993).

Wiggins, David K. *Glory Bound: Black Athletes in a White America.* Syracuse: Syracuse University Press, 1997.

——. *Out of the Shadows: A Biographical History of African American Athletes.* Fayetteville: University of Arkansas Press, 2006.

Wiggins, David K., and Patrick B. Miller. *The Unlevel Playing Field: A Documentary History of the African-American Experience in Sport.* Urbana: University of Illinois Press, 2003.

Williams, Henry C. *A History of Mobile County Training School.* Mobile: Williams, 1977.

Williamson, Hugh. "The Role of the Courts in the Status of the Negro." *Journal of Negro History* 40, no. 1 (1955): 61–72.

Williamson, Joel. *A Rage for Order: Black-White Relations in the American South since Emancipation.* New York: Oxford University Press, 1986.

Withers, Ernest. *Negro League Baseball.* New York: Harry Abrams, 2004.

Witmer, Linda F. *The Indian Industrial School, Carlisle, Pennsylvania, 1879–1918.* Carlisle, PA: Cumberland County Historical Society, 1993.

Woodward, C. Vann. *Origins of the New South, 1877–1913.* Baton Rouge: Louisiana State University Press, 1970.

Zang, David W. *Fleet Walker's Divided Heart: The Life of Baseball's First Black Major Leaguer.* Lincoln: University of Nebraska Press, 1995.

Index